BOOK 1 – ETHICAL AND PROFESSIONAL STANDARDS AND QUANTITATIVE METHODS

LEVEL 1 BOOK 1: ETHICAL AND PROFESSIONAL STANDARDS, AND QUANTITATIVE METHODS

©2009 Kaplan, Inc. All rights reserved.

Published in 2009 by Kaplan Schweser.

Printed in the United States of America.

ISBN: 1-4277-9457-X

PPN: 4550-0105

WELCOME TO THE 2010 SCHWESERNOTES

Thank you for trusting Kaplan Schweser to help you reach your goals. We are all very pleased to be able to help you prepare for the Level 1 CFA Exam. In this introduction, I want to explain the resources included with the Study Notes, suggest how you can best use Schweser materials to prepare for the exam, and direct you toward other educational resources you will find helpful as you study for the exam.

Besides the SchweserNotes themselves, there are many educational resources available at Schweser.com. Just log in using the individual username and password that you received when you purchased the SchweserNotes, and go to Online Access. All purchasers of our 2010 Level 1 SchweserNotes Package receive:

SchweserNotes – Five volumes that include complete coverage of all 18 Study Sessions and all Learning Outcome Statements (LOS) with examples, Concept Checkers (multiple-choice questions for every reading), and Comprehensive Problems for many readings to help you master the material and check your progress. At the end of each topic area, we include a Self-test. Self-test questions are created to be exam-like in format and difficulty in order for you to evaluate how well your study of each topic has prepared you for the actual exam.

Practice Exams Volume 1 – Three full (240-question, 6-hour) Level 1 practice exams with answer explanations to help you prepare for the exam itself as well as to better target your final review efforts.

Schweser Library – I have created five videos that are available to all SchweserNotes purchasers. Each Schweser Library volume is approximately 30 to 60 minutes in length. Topics include: "CFA Level 1 Exam Overview," "Calculator Basics," "Code and Standards Overview," "Level 1 GIPS®," and "Time Value of Money." The full Schweser Library is included with our 16-week live and online classes and with our video class series.

Schweser Study Planner – Use your Online Access to tell us when you will start and what days of the week you can study. Study Planner will create a study plan just for you, breaking each study session into daily and weekly tasks to keep you on track and help you monitor your progress through the curriculum.

Frequently Asked Questions – Answers to more than 100 questions that candidates most commonly ask about the curriculum and the exam.

Purchasers of the SchweserNotes Package also receive access to **Instructor-led Office Hours.** Office Hours allow you to get your questions about the curriculum answered in real time and to see others' questions (and faculty answers). Office Hours is a text-based live interactive online chat with a Level 1 expert. Archives of previous Office Hours sessions can be sorted by topic or date and are posted shortly after each session. If you purchased the Premium Solution or PremiumPlus, you have full access to **InstructorLink**, which includes Frequently Asked Questions, the Exam-tips Blog, Office Hours, all volumes in the Schweser Library, and instructor tutorial support.

The Level 1 CFA exam is a formidable challenge (74 Readings and 450+ Learning Outcome Statements), and you must devote considerable time and effort to be properly prepared. There is no shortcut; you must learn the material, know the terminology and techniques, understand the concepts, and be able to answer (70% of) 240 questions quickly and correctly. Fifteen to 20 hours per week for 20 weeks is probably a good estimate of the study time required on average, but some candidates will need more time or less depending on their individual backgrounds and experience.

To help you master this material and be well prepared for the CFA Exam, we offer several other educational resources, including:

Live Weekly Classroom Programs – We offer weekly classroom programs around the world. Please check at Schweser.com for locations, dates, and availability.

16-Week Online Class – We teach two live online classes (16 3-hour sessions) each week, beginning in January (August for the December exam). The approximate schedule for the 16-Week Online Class is:

Class #	Class #
1 Exam Intro and Ethics SS#1	9 Financial Reporting and Analysis SS#10
2 Quantitative Methods SS#2	10 Corporate Finance SS#11
3 Quantitative Methods SS#3	11 Portfolio Management, Securities Markets SS#12, 13
4 Economics SS#4, 5	12 Equity Securities SS#14
5 Economics SS#5, 6	13 Fixed Income Investments SS#15, 16
6 Financial Reporting and Analysis SS#7	14 Fixed Income Investments SS#16
7 Financial Reporting and Analysis SS#8	15 Derivatives SS#17
8 Financial Reporting and Analysis SS#9	16 Alternative Investments SS#18

Candidates have a choice of two different live online classes, one at 6:30–9:30 p.m. New York time and one at 6:00–9:00 p.m. London local time. Archived classes are available for viewing at any time prior to the exam. Candidates enrolled in the 16-Week Online Class also have full access to supplemental on-demand video instruction in the Schweser Library and an e-mail address to use to send questions to the instructor.

Intensive Review – Whether you are a self-study student or use a Schweser instruction alternative, attending an Intensive Review Seminar as part of your final preparation can make all the difference. We have several options for final review of the core curriculum material at each level. We offer live classroom 3-Day Intensive Review Seminars in many cities around the United States, an online on-demand archive of the Chicago Intensive 3-Day Review Seminar, 5-Day review programs in Dallas and many western European cities, and our flagship 7-Day residence program, WindsorWeek®, in Windsor, Ontario, Canada. Please visit us at Schweser.com for details and a complete listing of intensive review options.

Practice Questions – In order to retain what you learn, it is important that you quiz yourself often. We offer CD, download, and online versions of SchweserPro, which contains thousands of Level 1 practice questions and explanations. You can create quizzes by LOS, by Reading, or by Study Session, with the degree of difficulty you select.

Practice Exams – Schweser offers six full 6-hour practice exams. Practice Exams Volume 1 and Volume 2 each contain three full 240-question exams. These are important tools for gaining the speed and skills you will need to pass the exam. Each Practice Exam book contains answers for self-grading and explanations for all answers. By entering your answers at Schweser.com, you can use our Performance Tracker to find out how you have performed compared to other Schweser Level 1 candidates.

Mock Exam and Multimedia Tutorial – On May 22, 2010, the Schweser Mock Exam will be offered live in many cities around the world and as an online exam as well. The supplemental Multimedia Tutorial provides extended explanations and topic tutorials to get you exam-ready in areas where you miss questions on the Mock Exam.

How to Succeed

There are no shortcuts; depend on the fact that CFA Institute will test you in a way that will reveal how well you know the Level 1 curriculum. You should begin early and stick to your study plan. You should first read the SchweserNotes and complete the Concept Checkers and Comprehensive Problems for each reading. You should prepare for and attend a live class, an online class, or a study group each week. You should create and take quizzes often using SchweserPro and go back to review previous readings and Study Sessions as well. At the end of each topic area you should take the Self-test to check your progress. You should finish the overall curriculum at least two weeks (preferably four weeks) before the Level 1 exam so that you have sufficient time for Practice Exams and for further review of those topics that you have not yet mastered.

I would like to thank Craig Prochaska, CFA, Content Specialist; Stephanie Downey, Director of Print Production; and Julie Welscher, Lead Editor, for their contributions to producing the 2010 Level 1 SchweserNotes.

Best regards,

Doug Van Eaton

Dr. Douglas Van Eaton, CFA
SVP of CFA Education and Level 1 Manager
Kaplan Schweser

Readings and Learning Outcome Statements

Readings

The following material is a review of the Ethics and Professional Standards and Quantitative Methods principles designed to address the learning outcome statements set forth by CFA Institute.

STUDY SESSION 1

Reading Assignments

Ethical and Professional Standards and Quantitative Methods, CFA Program Curriculum, Volume 1 (CFA Institute, 2010)

STUDY SESSION 2

Reading Assignments

Ethical and Professional Standards and Quantitative Methods, CFA Program Curriculum, Volume 1 (CFA Institute, 2010)

STUDY SESSION 3

Reading Assignments

Ethical and Professional Standards and Quantitative Methods, CFA Program Curriculum, Volume 1 (CFA Institute, 2010)

Learning Outcome Statements (LOS)

STUDY SESSION 1

The topical coverage corresponds with the following CFA Institute assigned reading:

1. **Code of Ethics and Standards of Professional Conduct**
    The candidate should be able to:
    a. describe the structure of the CFA Institute Professional Conduct Program and the process for the enforcement of the Code and Standards. (page 12)
    b. state the six components of the Code of Ethics and the seven Standards of Professional Conduct. (page 13)
    c. explain the ethical responsibilities required by the Code and Standards, including the multiple subsections of each Standard. (page 14)

2. **Guidance for Standards I–VII**
    The candidate should be able to:
    a. demonstrate a thorough knowledge of the Code of Ethics and Standards of Professional Conduct by applying the Code and Standards to situations involving issues of professional integrity. (page 17)
    b. distinguish between conduct that conforms to the Code and Standards and conduct that violates the Code and Standards. (page 17)
    c. recommend practices and procedures designed to prevent violations of the Code of Ethics and Standards of Professional Conduct. (page 17)

3. **Introduction to the Global Investment Performance Standards (GIPS®)**
    The candidate should be able to:
    a. explain why the GIPS standards were created, what parties the GIPS standards apply to, and who is served by the standards. (page 69)
    b. explain the construction and purpose of composites in performance reporting. (page 70)
    c. explain the requirements for verification of compliance with GIPS standards. (page 70)

4. **Global Investment Performance Standards (GIPS®)**
    The candidate should be able to:
    a. describe the key characteristics of the GIPS standards and the fundamentals of compliance. (page 71)
    b. describe the scope of the GIPS standards with respect to an investment firm's definition and historical performance record. (page 73)
    c. explain how the GIPS standards are implemented in countries with existing standards for performance reporting and describe the appropriate response when the GIPS standards and local regulations conflict. (page 73)
    d. characterize the eight major sections of the GIPS standards. (page 73)

STUDY SESSION 2

5. **The Time Value of Money**
   The candidate should be able to:
   a. interpret interest rates as required rate of return, discount rate, or opportunity cost. (page 97)
   b. explain an interest rate as the sum of a real risk-free rate, expected inflation, and premiums that compensate investors for distinct types of risk. (page 97)
   c. calculate and interpret the effective annual rate, given the stated annual interest rate and the frequency of compounding. (page 98)
   d. solve time value of money problems when compounding periods are other than annual. (page 98)
   e. calculate and interpret the future value (FV) and present value (PV) of a single sum of money, an ordinary annuity, an annuity due, a perpetuity (PV only), and a series of unequal cash flows. (page 100)
   f. draw a time line and solve time value of money applications (for example, mortgages and savings for college tuition or retirement). (page 114)

6. **Discounted Cash Flow Applications**
   The candidate should be able to:
   a. calculate and interpret the net present value (NPV) and the internal rate of return (IRR) of an investment, contrast the NPV rule to the IRR rule, and identify problems associated with the IRR rule. (page 134)
   b. define, calculate, and interpret a holding period return (total return). (page 139)
   c. calculate, interpret, and distinguish between the money-weighted and time-weighted rates of return of a portfolio and appraise the performance of portfolios based on these measures. (page 139)
   d. calculate and interpret the bank discount yield, holding period yield, effective annual yield, and money market yield for a U.S. Treasury bill. (page 143)
   e. convert among holding period yields, money market yields, effective annual yields, and bond equivalent yields. (page 146)

7. **Statistical Concepts and Market Returns**
   The candidate should be able to:
   a. differentiate between descriptive statistics and inferential statistics, between a population and a sample, and among the types of measurement scales. (page 157)
   b. explain a parameter, a sample statistic, and a frequency distribution. (page 158)
   c. calculate and interpret relative frequencies and cumulative relative frequencies, given a frequency distribution. (page 160)
   d. describe the properties of a data set presented as a histogram or a frequency polygon. (page 162)
   e. define, calculate, and interpret measures of central tendency, including the population mean, sample mean, arithmetic mean, weighted average or mean (including a portfolio return viewed as a weighted mean), geometric mean, harmonic mean, median, and mode. (page 163)
   f. describe, calculate, and interpret quartiles, quintiles, deciles, and percentiles. (page 168)
   g. define, calculate, and interpret 1) a range and a mean absolute deviation and 2) the variance and standard deviation of a population and of a sample. (page 170)

h. calculate and interpret the proportion of observations falling within a specified number of standard deviations of the mean using Chebyshev's inequality. (page 173)

i. define, calculate, and interpret the coefficient of variation and the Sharpe ratio. (page 174)

j. define and interpret skewness, explain the meaning of a positively or negatively skewed return distribution, and describe the relative locations of the mean, median, and mode for a nonsymmetrical distribution. (page 175)

k. define and interpret measures of sample skewness and kurtosis. (page 177)

l. discuss the use of arithmetic mean or geometric mean when determining investment returns. (page 179)

8. **Probability Concepts**
The candidate should be able to:

a. define a random variable, an outcome, an event, mutually exclusive events, and exhaustive events. (page 194)

b. explain the two defining properties of probability and distinguish among empirical, subjective, and a priori probabilities. (page 194)

c. state the probability of an event in terms of odds for or against the event. (page 195)

d. distinguish between unconditional and conditional probabilities. (page 196)

e. define and explain the multiplication, addition, and total probability rules. (page 196)

f. calculate and interpret 1) the joint probability of two events, 2) the probability that at least one of two events will occur, given the probability of each and the joint probability of the two events, and 3) a joint probability of any number of independent events. (page 197)

g. distinguish between dependent and independent events. (page 200)

h. calculate and interpret, using the total probability rule, an unconditional probability. (page 201)

i. explain the use of conditional expectation in investment applications. (page 205)

j. diagram an investment problem using a tree diagram. (page 205)

k. calculate and interpret covariance and correlation. (page 206)

l. calculate and interpret the expected value, variance, and standard deviation of a random variable and of returns on a portfolio. (page 210)

m. calculate and interpret covariance given a joint probability function. (page 211)

n. calculate and interpret an updated probability using Bayes' formula. (page 215)

o. identify the most appropriate method to solve a particular counting problem and solve counting problems using the factorial, combination, and permutation notations. (page 217)

STUDY SESSION 3

9. **Common Probability Distributions**
The candidate should be able to:

a. explain a probability distribution and distinguish between discrete and continuous random variables. (page 238)

b. describe the set of possible outcomes of a specified discrete random variable. (page 238)

c. interpret a probability function, a probability density function, and a cumulative distribution function. (page 239)

d. calculate and interpret probabilities for a random variable, given its cumulative distribution function. (page 240)
e. define a discrete uniform random variable and a binomial random variable. (page 241)
f. calculate and interpret probabilities given the discrete uniform and the binomial distribution functions. (page 241)
g. construct a binomial tree to describe stock price movement. (page 244)
h. describe the continuous uniform distribution and calculate and interpret probabilities, given a continuous uniform probability distribution. (page 246)
i. explain the key properties of the normal distribution, distinguish between a univariate and a multivariate distribution, and explain the role of correlation in the multivariate normal distribution. (page 247)
j. determine the probability that a normally distributed random variable lies inside a given confidence interval. (page 249)
k. define the standard normal distribution, explain how to standardize a random variable, and calculate and interpret probabilities using the standard normal distribution. (page 251)
l. define shortfall risk, calculate the safety-first ratio, and select an optimal portfolio using Roy's safety-first criterion. (page 254)
m. explain the relationship between normal and lognormal distributions and why the lognormal distribution is used to model asset prices. (page 256)
n. distinguish between discretely and continuously compounded rates of return and calculate and interpret a continuously compounded rate of return, given a specific holding period return. (page 257)
o. explain Monte Carlo simulation and historical simulation and describe their major applications and limitations. (page 259)

10. **Sampling and Estimation**
The candidate should be able to:
a. define simple random sampling, sampling error, and a sampling distribution, and interpret sampling error. (page 273)
b. distinguish between simple random and stratified random sampling. (page 274)
c. distinguish between time-series and cross-sectional data. (page 275)
d. interpret the central limit theorem and describe its importance. (page 275)
e. calculate and interpret the standard error of the sample mean. (page 276)
f. distinguish between a point estimate and a confidence interval estimate of a population parameter. (page 278)
g. identify and describe the desirable properties of an estimator. (page 278)
h. explain the construction of confidence intervals. (page 278)
i. describe the properties of Student's t-distribution and calculate and interpret its degrees of freedom. (page 279)
j. calculate and interpret a confidence interval for a population mean, given a normal distribution with 1) a known population variance, 2) an unknown population variance, or 3) an unknown variance and a large sample size. (page 281)
k. discuss the issues regarding selection of the appropriate sample size, data-mining bias, sample selection bias, survivorship bias, look-ahead bias, and time-period bias. (page 285)

11. Hypothesis Testing

The candidate should be able to:

a. define a hypothesis, describe the steps of hypothesis testing, interpret and discuss the choice of the null hypothesis and alternative hypothesis, and distinguish between one-tailed and two-tailed tests of hypotheses. (page 296)

b. define and interpret a test statistic, a Type I and a Type II error, and a significance level, and explain how significance levels are used in hypothesis testing. (page 301)

c. define and interpret a decision rule and the power of a test, and explain the relation between confidence intervals and hypothesis tests. (page 303)

d. distinguish between a statistical result and an economically meaningful result. (page 305)

e. explain and interpret the p-value as it relates to hypothesis testing. (page 306)

f. identify the appropriate test statistic and interpret the results for a hypothesis test concerning the population mean of both large and small samples when the population is normally or approximately distributed and the variance is 1) known or 2) unknown. (page 307)

g. identify the appropriate test statistic and interpret the results for a hypothesis test concerning the equality of the population means of two at least approximately normally distributed populations, based on independent random samples with 1) equal or 2) unequal assumed variances. (page 310)

h. identify the appropriate test statistic and interpret the results for a hypothesis test concerning the mean difference of two normally distributed populations (paired comparisons test). (page 314)

i. identify the appropriate test statistic and interpret the results for a hypothesis test concerning 1) the variance of a normally distributed population, and 2) the equality of the variances of two normally distributed populations, based on two independent random samples. (page 318)

j. distinguish between parametric and nonparametric tests and describe the situations in which the use of nonparametric tests may be appropriate. (page 325)

12. Technical Analysis

The candidate should be able to:

a. explain the underlying assumptions of technical analysis. (page 337)

b. discuss the advantages of and challenges to technical analysis. (page 338)

c. list and describe examples of each major category of technical trading rules and indicators. (page 339)

The following is a review of the Ethical and Professional Standards principles designed to address the learning outcome statements set forth by CFA Institute®. This topic is also covered in:

CFA INSTITUTE CODE OF ETHICS AND STANDARDS OF PROFESSIONAL CONDUCT GUIDANCE FOR STANDARDS I–VII

EXAM FOCUS

In addition to reading this review of the ethics material, we strongly recommend that all candidates for the CFA® examination read the *Standards of Practice Handbook 9th Edition* (2005) multiple times. As a registered candidate, it is your responsibility to own a copy of the *Code and Standards* and to comply with the *Code and Standards*. The *Code and Standards* are reprinted in Volume 1 of the CFA Program Curriculum.

CFA INSTITUTE CODE OF ETHICS AND STANDARDS OF PROFESSIONAL CONDUCT

LOS 1.a: Describe the structure of the CFA Institute Professional Conduct Program and the process for the enforcement of the Code and Standards.

The CFA Institute Professional Conduct Program is covered by the CFA Institute Bylaws and the Rules of Procedure for Proceedings Related to Professional Conduct. The Program is based on the principles of fairness of the process to members and candidates and maintaining the confidentiality of the proceedings. The Disciplinary Review Committee of the CFA Institute Board of Governors has overall responsibility for the Professional Conduct Program and enforcement of the Code and Standards.

The CFA Institute Designated Officer, through the Professional Conduct staff, conducts inquiries related to professional conduct. Several circumstances can prompt such an inquiry:

1. Self-disclosure by members or candidates on their annual Professional Conduct Statements of involvement in civil litigation or a criminal investigation, or that the member or candidate is the subject of a written complaint.

2. Written complaints about a member or candidate's professional conduct that are received by the Professional Conduct staff.

3. Evidence of misconduct by a member or candidate that the Professional Conduct staff received through public sources, such as a media article or broadcast.

4. A report by a CFA exam proctor of a possible violation during the examination.

Once an inquiry has begun, the Professional Conduct staff may request (in writing) an explanation from the subject member or candidate and may: (1) interview the subject member or candidate, (2) interview the complainant or other third parties, and/or (3) collect documents and records relevant to the investigation.

The Designated Officer may decide: (1) that no disciplinary sanctions are appropriate, (2) to issue a cautionary letter, or (3) to discipline the member or candidate. In a case where the Designated Officer finds a violation has occurred and proposes a disciplinary sanction, the member or candidate may accept or reject the sanction. If the member or candidate chooses to reject the sanction, the matter will be referred to a panel of CFA Institute members for a hearing. Sanctions imposed may include condemnation by the member's peers or suspension of candidate's continued participation in the CFA Program.

LOS 1.b: State the six components of the Code of Ethics and the seven Standards of Professional Conduct.

CODE OF ETHICS

Members of CFA Institute [including Chartered Financial Analyst® (CFA®) charterholders] and candidates for the CFA designation ("Members and Candidates") must:[1]

- Act with integrity, competence, diligence, respect, and in an ethical manner with the public, clients, prospective clients, employers, employees, colleagues in the investment profession, and other participants in the global capital markets.
- Place the integrity of the investment profession and the interests of clients above their own personal interests.
- Use reasonable care and exercise independent professional judgment when conducting investment analysis, making investment recommendations, taking investment actions, and engaging in other professional activities.
- Practice and encourage others to practice in a professional and ethical manner that will reflect credit on themselves and the profession.
- Promote the integrity of, and uphold the rules governing, capital markets.
- Maintain and improve their professional competence and strive to maintain and improve the competence of other investment professionals.

THE STANDARDS OF PROFESSIONAL CONDUCT

I:	Professionalism
II:	Integrity of Capital Markets
III:	Duties to Clients
IV:	Duties to Employers
V:	Investment Analysis, Recommendations, and Actions
VI:	Conflicts of Interest
VII:	Responsibilities as a CFA Institute Member or CFA Candidate

---

1. Copyright 2005, CFA Institute. Reproduced and republished from "The Code of Ethics," from *Standards of Practice Handbook, 9th Ed.,* 2005, with permission from CFA Institute. All rights reserved.

LOS 1.c: Explain the ethical responsibilities required by the Code and Standards, including the multiple subsections of each Standard.

STANDARDS OF PROFESSIONAL CONDUCT[2]

I. PROFESSIONALISM

A. **Knowledge of the Law.** Members and Candidates must understand and comply with all applicable laws, rules, and regulations (including the CFA Institute *Code of Ethics* and *Standards of Professional Conduct*) of any government, regulatory organization, licensing agency, or professional association governing their professional activities. In the event of conflict, Members and Candidates must comply with the more strict law, rule, or regulation. Members and Candidates must not knowingly participate or assist in any violation of laws, rules, or regulations and must disassociate themselves from any such violation.

B. **Independence and Objectivity.** Members and Candidates must use reasonable care and judgment to achieve and maintain independence and objectivity in their professional activities. Members and Candidates must not offer, solicit, or accept any gift, benefit, compensation, or consideration that reasonably could be expected to compromise their own or another's independence and objectivity.

C. **Misrepresentation.** Members and Candidates must not knowingly make any misrepresentations relating to investment analysis, recommendations, actions, or other professional activities.

D. **Misconduct.** Members and Candidates must not engage in any professional conduct involving dishonesty, fraud, or deceit or commit any act that reflects adversely on their professional reputation, integrity, or competence.

II. INTEGRITY OF CAPITAL MARKETS

A. **Material Nonpublic Information.** Members and Candidates who possess material nonpublic information that could affect the value of an investment must not act or cause others to act on the information.

B. **Market Manipulation.** Members and Candidates must not engage in practices that distort prices or artificially inflate trading volume with the intent to mislead market participants.

III. DUTIES TO CLIENTS

A. **Loyalty, Prudence, and Care.** Members and Candidates have a duty of loyalty to their clients and must act with reasonable care and exercise prudent judgment. Members and Candidates must act for the benefit of their clients and place their clients' interests before their employer's or their own interests. In relationships with clients, Members and Candidates must determine

---

2. Ibid.

applicable fiduciary duty and must comply with such duty to persons and interests to whom it is owed.

B. **Fair Dealing.** Members and Candidates must deal fairly and objectively with all clients when providing investment analysis, making investment recommendations, taking investment action, or engaging in other professional activities.

C. **Suitability.**

1. When Members and Candidates are in an advisory relationship with a client, they must:

   a. Make a reasonable inquiry into a client's or prospective clients' investment experience, risk and return objectives, and financial constraints prior to making any investment recommendation or taking investment action and must reassess and update this information regularly.

   b. Determine that an investment is suitable to the client's financial situation and consistent with the client's written objectives, mandates, and constraints before making an investment recommendation or taking investment action.

   c. Judge the suitability of investments in the context of the client's total portfolio.

2. When Members and Candidates are responsible for managing a portfolio to a specific mandate, strategy, or style, they must make only investment recommendations or take investment actions that are consistent with the stated objectives and constraints of the portfolio.

D. **Performance Presentation.** When communicating investment performance information, Members or Candidates must make reasonable efforts to ensure that it is fair, accurate, and complete.

E. **Preservation of Confidentiality.** Members and Candidates must keep information about current, former, and prospective clients confidential unless:

1. The information concerns illegal activities on the part of the client or prospective client,

2. Disclosure is required by law, or

3. The client or prospective client permits disclosure of the information.

IV. DUTIES TO EMPLOYERS

A. **Loyalty.** In matters related to their employment, Members and Candidates must act for the benefit of their employer and not deprive their employer of the advantage of their skills and abilities, divulge confidential information, or otherwise cause harm to their employer.

B. **Additional Compensation Arrangements.** Members and Candidates must not accept gifts, benefits, compensation, or consideration that competes with, or might reasonably be expected to create a conflict of interest with, their employer's interest unless they obtain written consent from all parties involved.

C. **Responsibilities of Supervisors.** Members and Candidates must make reasonable efforts to detect and prevent violations of applicable laws, rules, regulations, and the Code and Standards by anyone subject to their supervision or authority.

V. **INVESTMENT ANALYSIS, RECOMMENDATIONS, AND ACTIONS**

A. **Diligence and Reasonable Basis.** Members and Candidates must:

1. Exercise diligence, independence, and thoroughness in analyzing investments, making investment recommendations, and taking investment actions.

2. Have a reasonable and adequate basis, supported by appropriate research and investigation, for any investment analysis, recommendation, or action.

B. **Communication with Clients and Prospective Clients.** Members and Candidates must:

1. Disclose to clients and prospective clients the basic format and general principles of the investment processes used to analyze investments, select securities, and construct portfolios and must promptly disclose any changes that might materially affect those processes.

2. Use reasonable judgment in identifying which factors are important to their investment analyses, recommendations, or actions and include those factors in communications with clients and prospective clients.

3. Distinguish between fact and opinion in the presentation of investment analysis and recommendations.

C. **Record Retention.** Members and Candidates must develop and maintain appropriate records to support their investment analysis, recommendations, actions, and other investment-related communications with clients and prospective clients.

VI. **CONFLICTS OF INTEREST**

A. **Disclosure of Conflicts.** Members and Candidates must make full and fair disclosure of all matters that could reasonably be expected to impair their independence and objectivity or interfere with respective duties to their clients, prospective clients, and employer. Members and Candidates must ensure that such disclosures are prominent, are delivered in plain language, and communicate the relevant information effectively.

B. **Priority of Transactions.** Investment transactions for clients and employers must have priority over investment transactions in which a Member or Candidate is the beneficial owner.

C. **Referral Fees.** Members and Candidates must disclose to their employer, clients, and prospective clients, as appropriate, any compensation, consideration, or benefit received by, or paid to, others for the recommendation of products or services.

VII. **RESPONSIBILITIES AS A CFA INSTITUTE MEMBER OR CFA CANDIDATE**

A. **Conduct as Members and Candidates in the CFA Program.** Members and Candidates must not engage in any conduct that compromises the reputation or integrity of CFA Institute or the CFA designation or the integrity, validity, or security of the CFA examinations.

B. **Reference to CFA Institute, the CFA Designation, and the CFA Program.** When referring to CFA Institute, CFA Institute membership, the CFA designation, or candidacy in the CFA Program, Members and Candidates must not misrepresent or exaggerate the meaning or implications of membership in CFA Institute, holding the CFA designation, or candidacy in the CFA Program.

GUIDANCE FOR STANDARDS I–VII

LOS 2.a: Demonstrate a thorough knowledge of the Code of Ethics and Standards of Professional Conduct by applying the Code and Standards to situations involving issues of professional integrity.

LOS 2.b: Distinguish between conduct that conforms to the Code and Standards and conduct that violates the Code and Standards.

LOS 2.c: Recommend practices and procedures designed to prevent violations of the Code of Ethics and Standards of Professional Conduct.

I   **Professionalism**

I(A)   Knowledge of the Law. Members and Candidates must understand and comply with all applicable laws, rules, and regulations (including the CFA Institute Code of Ethics and Standards of Professional Conduct) of any government, regulatory organization, licensing agency, or professional association governing their professional activities. In the event of conflict, Members and Candidates must comply with the more strict law, rule, or regulation. Members and Candidates must not knowingly participate or assist in and must dissociate from any violation of such laws, rules, or regulations.

Professor's Note: While we use the term "members" in the following, note that all of the Standards apply to candidates as well.

Guidance—Code and Standards vs. Local Law

Members must know the laws and regulations relating to their professional activities in all countries in which they conduct business. Members must comply with applicable laws and regulations relating to their professional activity. Do not violate Code or Standards even if the activity is otherwise legal. Always adhere to the most strict rules and requirements (law or CFA Institute Standards) that apply.

Guidance—Participation or Association with Violations by Others

Members should dissociate, or separate themselves, from any ongoing client or employee activity that is illegal or unethical, even if it involves leaving an employer (an extreme case). While a member may confront the involved individual first, he must approach his supervisor or compliance department. Inaction with continued association may be construed as knowing participation.

Recommended Procedures for Compliance—Members

- Members should have procedures to keep up with changes in applicable laws, rules, and regulations.
- Compliance procedures should be reviewed on an ongoing basis to assure that they address current law, CFAI Standards, and regulations.
- Members should maintain current reference materials for employees to access in order to keep up to date on laws, rules, and regulations.
- Members should seek advice of counsel or their compliance department when in doubt.
- Members should document any violations when they disassociate themselves from prohibited activity and encourage their employers to bring an end to such activity.
- There is no requirement under the Standards to report violations to governmental authorities, but this may be advisable in some circumstances and required by law in others.

Recommended Procedures for Compliance—Firms

Members should encourage their firms to:

- Develop and/or adopt a code of ethics.
- Make available to employees information that highlights applicable laws and regulations.
- Establish written procedures for reporting suspected violation of laws, regulations, or company policies.

Application of Standard I(A) Knowledge of the Law[3]

Example 1:

Michael Allen works for a brokerage firm and is responsible for an underwriting of securities. A company official gives Allen information indicating that the financial statements Allen filed with the regulator overstate the issuer's earnings. Allen seeks the advice of the brokerage firm's general counsel, who states that it would be difficult for the regulator to prove that Allen has been involved in any wrongdoing.

Comment:

Although it is recommended that members and candidates seek the advice of legal counsel, the reliance on such advice does not absolve a member or candidate from the requirement to comply with the law or regulation. Allen should report this situation to his supervisor, seek an independent legal opinion, and determine whether the regulator should be notified of the error.

Example 2:

Kamisha Washington's firm advertises its past performance record by showing the 10-year return of a composite of its client accounts. However, Washington discovers that the composite omits the performance of accounts that have left the firm during the 10-year period and that this omission has led to an inflated performance figure. Washington is asked to use promotional material that includes the erroneous performance number when soliciting business for the firm.

Comment:

Misrepresenting performance is a violation of the Code and Standards. Although she did not calculate the performance herself, Washington would be assisting in violating this standard if she were to use the inflated performance number when soliciting clients. She must dissociate herself from the activity. She can bring the misleading number to the attention of the person responsible for calculating performance, her supervisor, or the compliance department at her firm. If her firm is unwilling to recalculate performance, she must refrain from using the misleading promotional material and should notify the firm of her reasons. If the firm insists that she use the material, she should consider whether her obligation to dissociate from the activity would require her to seek other employment.

Example 3:

An employee of an investment bank is working on an underwriting and finds out the issuer has altered their financial statements to hide operating losses in one division. These misstated data are included in a preliminary prospectus that has already been released.

Comment:

The employee should report the problem to his supervisors. If the firm doesn't get the misstatement fixed, the employee should dissociate from the underwriting and, further, seek legal advice about whether he should undertake additional reporting or other actions.

---

3. Ibid.

Example 4:

Laura Jameson, a U.S. citizen, works for an investment advisor based in the U.S. and works in a country where investment managers are prohibited from participating in IPOs for their own accounts.

Comment:

Jameson must comply with the strictest requirements among U.S. law (where her firm is based), the CFA Institute Code and Standards, and the laws of the country where she is doing business. In this case that means she must not participate in any IPOs for her personal account.

> **I(B)   Independence and Objectivity.** Members and Candidates must use reasonable care and judgment to achieve and maintain independence and objectivity in their professional activities. Members and Candidates must not offer, solicit, or accept any gift, benefit, compensation, or consideration that reasonably could be expected to compromise their own or another's independence and objectivity.

Guidance

Do not let the investment process be influenced by any external sources. Modest gifts are permitted. Allocation of shares in oversubscribed IPOs to personal accounts is NOT permitted. Distinguish between gifts from clients and gifts from entities seeking influence to the detriment of the client. Gifts must be disclosed to the member's employer in any case.

Guidance—Investment Banking Relationships

Do not be pressured by sell-side firms to issue favorable research on current or prospective investment-banking clients. It is appropriate to have analysts work with investment bankers in "road shows" only when the conflicts are adequately and effectively managed and disclosed. Be sure there are effective "firewalls" between research/investment management and investment banking activities.

Guidance—Public Companies

Analysts should not be pressured to issue favorable research by the companies they follow. Do not confine research to discussions with company management, but rather use a variety of sources, including suppliers, customers, and competitors.

Guidance—Buy-Side Clients

Buy-side clients may try to pressure sell-side analysts. Portfolio managers may have large positions in a particular security, and a rating downgrade may have an effect on the portfolio performance. As a portfolio manager, there is a responsibility to respect and foster intellectual honesty of sell-side research.

Guidance—Issuer-Paid Research

Remember that this type of research is fraught with potential conflicts. Analysts' compensation for preparing such research should be limited, and the preference is for a flat fee, without regard to conclusions or the report's recommendations.

Recommended Procedures for Compliance

- Protect the integrity of opinions—make sure they are unbiased.
- Create a restricted list and distribute only factual information about companies on the list.
- Restrict special cost arrangements—pay for one's own commercial transportation and hotel; limit use of corporate aircraft to cases in which commercial transportation is not available.
- Limit gifts—token items only. Customary, business-related entertainment is okay as long as its purpose is not to influence a member's professional independence or objectivity.
- Restrict employee investments in equity IPOs and private placements.
- Review procedures—have effective supervisory and review procedures.
- Firms should have formal written policies on independence and objectivity of research.

Application of Standard I(B) Independence and Objectivity

Example 1:

Steven Taylor, a mining analyst with Bronson Brokers, is invited by Precision Metals to join a group of his peers in a tour of mining facilities in several western U.S. states. The company arranges for chartered group flights from site to site and for accommodations in Spartan Motels, the only chain with accommodations near the mines, for three nights. Taylor allows Precision Metals to pick up his tab, as do the other analysts, with one exception—John Adams, an employee of a large trust company who insists on following his company's policy and paying for his hotel room himself.

Comment:

The policy of Adams's company complies closely with Standard I(B) by avoiding even the appearance of a conflict of interest, but Taylor and the other analysts were not necessarily violating Standard I(B). In general, when allowing companies to pay for travel and/or accommodations under these circumstances, members and candidates must use their judgment, keeping in mind that such arrangements must not impinge on a member or candidate's independence and objectivity. In this example, the trip was strictly for business and Taylor was not accepting irrelevant or lavish hospitality. The itinerary required chartered flights, for which analysts were not expected to pay. The accommodations were modest. These arrangements are not unusual and did not violate Standard I(B) so long as Taylor's independence and objectivity were not compromised. In the final analysis, members and candidates should consider both whether they can remain objective and whether their integrity might be perceived by their clients to have been compromised.

Example 2:

Walter Fritz is an equity analyst with Hilton Brokerage who covers the mining industry. He has concluded that the stock of Metals & Mining is overpriced at its current level, but he is concerned that a negative research report will hurt the good relationship between Metals & Mining and the investment-banking division of his firm. In fact, a senior manager of Hilton Brokerage has just sent him a copy of a proposal his firm has made to Metals & Mining to underwrite a debt offering. Fritz needs to produce a report right away and is concerned about issuing a less-than-favorable rating.

Comment:

Fritz's analysis of Metals & Mining must be objective and based solely on consideration of company fundamentals. Any pressure from other divisions of his firm is inappropriate. This conflict could have been eliminated if, in anticipation of the offering, Hilton Brokerage had placed Metals & Mining on a restricted list for its sales force.

Example 3:

Tom Wayne is the investment manager of the Franklin City Employees Pension Plan. He recently completed a successful search for firms to manage the foreign equity allocation of the plan's diversified portfolio. He followed the plan's standard procedure of seeking presentations from a number of qualified firms and recommended that his board select Penguin Advisors because of its experience, well-defined investment strategy, and performance record, which was compiled and verified in accordance with the CFA Institute Global Investment Performance Standards. Following the plan selection of Penguin, a reporter from the Franklin City Record called to ask if there was any connection between the action and the fact that Penguin was one of the sponsors of an "investment fact-finding trip to Asia" that Wayne made earlier in the year. The trip was one of several conducted by the Pension Investment Academy, which had arranged the itinerary of meetings with economic, government, and corporate officials in major cities in several Asian countries. The Pension Investment Academy obtains support for the cost of these trips from a number of investment managers, including Penguin Advisors; the Academy then pays the travel expenses of the various pension plan managers on the trip and provides all meals and accommodations. The president of Penguin Advisors was one of the travelers on the trip.

Comment:

Although Wayne can probably put to good use the knowledge he gained from the trip in selecting portfolio managers and in other areas of managing the pension plan, his recommendation of Penguin Advisors may be tainted by the possible conflict incurred when he participated in a trip paid for partly by Penguin Advisors and when he was in the daily company of the president of Penguin Advisors. To avoid violating Standard I(B), Wayne's basic expenses for travel and accommodations should have been paid by his employer or the pension plan; contact with the president of Penguin Advisors should have been limited to informational or educational events only; and the trip, the organizer, and the sponsor should have been made a matter of public record. Even if his actions were not in violation of Standard I(B), Wayne should have been sensitive to the public perception of the trip when reported in the newspaper and the extent to which the subjective elements of his decision might have been affected by the familiarity that the daily contact of such a trip would encourage. This advantage would probably not be shared by competing firms.

Example 4:

An analyst in the corporate finance department promises a client that her firm will provide full research coverage of the issuing company after the offering.

Comment:

This is not a violation, but she cannot promise favorable research coverage. Research must be objective and independent.

Example 5:

An employee's boss tells him to assume coverage of a stock and maintain a buy rating.

Comment:

Research opinions and recommendations must be objective and independently arrived at. Following the boss's instructions would be a violation if the analyst determined a buy rating is inappropriate.

Example 6:

A money manager receives a gift of significant value from a client as a reward for good performance over the prior period and informs her employer of the gift.

Comment:

No violation here since the gift is from a client and is not based on performance going forward, but the gift must be disclosed to her employer. If the gift were contingent on future performance, the money manager would have to obtain permission from her employer. The reason for both the disclosure and permission requirements is that the employer must ensure that the money manager does not give advantage to the client giving or offering additional compensation, to the detriment of other clients.

Example 7:

An analyst enters into a contract to write a research report on a company, paid for by that company, for a flat fee plus a bonus based on attracting new investors to the security.

Comment:

This is a violation because the compensation structure makes total compensation depend on the conclusions of the report (a favorable report will attract investors and increase compensation). Accepting the job for a flat fee that does not depend on the report's conclusions or its impact on share price is permitted, with proper disclosure of the fact that the report is funded by the subject company.

> **I(C)   Misrepresentation.** Members and Candidates must not knowingly make any misrepresentations relating to investment analysis, recommendations, actions, or other professional activities.

Guidance

Trust is a foundation in the investment profession. Do not make any misrepresentations or give false impressions. This includes oral and electronic communications. Misrepresentations include guaranteeing investment performance and plagiarism. Plagiarism encompasses using someone else's work (reports, forecasts, models, ideas, charts, graphs, and spreadsheet models) without giving them credit.

Recommended Procedures for Compliance

A good way to avoid misrepresentation is for firms to provide employees who deal with clients or prospects a written list of the firm's available services and a description of the firm's qualifications. Employee qualifications should be accurately presented as well. To avoid plagiarism, maintain records of all materials used to generate reports or other firm products and properly cite sources (quotes and summaries) in work products. Information from recognized financial and statistical reporting services need not be cited.

Application of Standard I(C) Misrepresentation

Example 1:

Allison Rogers is a partner in the firm of Rogers and Black, a small firm offering investment advisory services. She assures a prospective client who has just inherited $1 million that "we can perform all the financial and investment services you need." Rogers and Black is well equipped to provide investment advice but, in fact, cannot provide asset allocation assistance or a full array of financial and investment services.

Comment:

Rogers has violated Standard I(C) by orally misrepresenting the services her firm can perform for the prospective client. She must limit herself to describing the range of investment advisory services Rogers and Black can provide and offer to help the client obtain elsewhere the financial and investment services that her firm cannot provide.

Example 2:

Anthony McGuire is an issuer-paid analyst hired by publicly traded companies to electronically promote their stocks. McGuire creates a web site that promotes his research efforts as a seemingly independent analyst. McGuire posts a profile and a strong buy recommendation for each company on the web site, indicating that the stock is expected to increase in value. He does not disclose the contractual relationships with the companies he covers on his web site, in the research reports he issues, or in the statements he makes about the companies on internet chat rooms.

Comment:

McGuire has violated Standard I(C) because the internet site and e-mails are misleading to potential investors. Even if the recommendations are valid and supported with thorough research, his omissions regarding the true relationship between himself and the companies he covers constitute a misrepresentation. McGuire has also violated Standard VI(C) by not disclosing the existence of an arrangement with the companies through which he receives compensation in exchange for his services.

Example 3:

Claude Browning, a quantitative analyst for Double Alpha, Inc., returns in great excitement from a seminar. In that seminar, Jack Jorrely, a well-publicized quantitative analyst at a national brokerage firm, discussed one of his new models in great detail, and Browning is intrigued by the new concepts. He proceeds to test this model, making some minor mechanical changes but retaining the concept, until he produces some very positive results. Browning quickly announces to his supervisors at Double Alpha that he has discovered a new model and that clients and prospective clients alike should be informed of this positive finding as ongoing proof of Double Alpha's continuing innovation and ability to add value.

Comment:

Although Browning tested Jorrely's model on his own and even slightly modified it, he must still acknowledge the original source of the idea. Browning can certainly take credit for the final, practical results; he can also support his conclusions with his own test. The credit for the innovative thinking, however, must be awarded to Jorrely.

Example 4:

Gary Ostrowski runs a small, two-person investment management firm. Ostrowski's firm subscribes to a service from a large investment research firm that provides research reports that can be repackaged as in-house research from smaller firms. Ostrowski's firm distributes these reports to clients as its own work.

Comment:

Ostrowski can rely on third-party research that has a reasonable and adequate basis, but he cannot imply that he is the author of the report. Otherwise, Ostrowski would misrepresent the extent of his work in a way that would mislead the firm's clients or prospective clients.

Example 5:

A member makes an error in preparing marketing materials and misstates the amount of assets his firm has under management.

Comment:

The member must attempt to stop distribution of the erroneous material as soon as the error is known. Simply making the error unintentionally is not a violation, but continuing to distribute material known to contain a significant misstatement of fact would be.

Example 6:

The marketing department states in sales literature that an analyst has received an MBA degree, but he has not. The analyst and other members of the firm have distributed this document for years.

Comment:

The analyst has violated the Standards, as he should have known of this misrepresentation after having distributed and used the materials over a period of years.

Example 7:

A member describes an interest-only collateralized mortgage obligation as guaranteed by the U.S government since it is a claim against the cash flows of a pool of guaranteed mortgages, although the payment stream and the market value of the security are not guaranteed.

Comment:

This is a violation because of the misrepresentation.

Example 8:

A member describes a bank CD as "guaranteed."

Comment:

This is not a violation as long as the limits of the guarantee provided by the Federal Deposit Insurance Corporation are not exceeded and the nature of the guarantee is clearly explained to clients.

Example 9:

A member uses definitions he found online for such terms as variance and coefficient of variation in preparing marketing material.

Comment:

Even though these are standard terms, using the work of others word-for-word is plagiarism.

Example 10:

A candidate reads about a research paper in a financial publication and includes the information in a research report, citing the original research report but not the financial publication.

Comment:

To the extent that the candidate used information and interpretation from the financial publication without citing it, the candidate is in violation of the Standard. The candidate should either obtain the report and reference it directly or, if he relies solely on the financial publication, should cite both sources.

I(D)   Misconduct. Members and Candidates must not engage in any professional conduct involving dishonesty, fraud, or deceit or commit any act that reflects adversely on their professional reputation, integrity, or competence.

Guidance

CFA Institute discourages unethical behavior in all aspects of members' and candidates' lives. Do not abuse CFA Institute's Professional Conduct Program by seeking enforcement of this Standard to settle personal, political, or other disputes that are not related to professional ethics.

Recommended Procedures for Compliance

Firms are encouraged to adopt these policies and procedures:

- Develop and adopt a code of ethics and make clear that unethical behavior will not be tolerated.
- Give employees a list of potential violations and sanctions, including dismissal.
- Check references of potential employees.

Application of Standard I(D) Misconduct

Example 1:

Simon Sasserman is a trust investment officer at a bank in a small affluent town. He enjoys lunching every day with friends at the country club, where his clients have observed him having numerous drinks. Back at work after lunch, he clearly is intoxicated while making investment decisions. His colleagues make a point of handling any business with Sasserman in the morning because they distrust his judgment after lunch.

Comment:

Sasserman's excessive drinking at lunch and subsequent intoxication at work constitute a violation of Standard I(D) because this conduct has raised questions about his professionalism and competence. His behavior thus reflects poorly on him, his employer, and the investment industry.

Example 2:

Carmen Garcia manages a mutual fund dedicated to socially responsible investing. She is also an environmental activist. As the result of her participation at nonviolent protests, Garcia has been arrested on numerous occasions for trespassing on the property of a large petrochemical plant that is accused of damaging the environment.

Comment:

Generally, Standard I(D) is not meant to cover legal transgressions resulting from acts of civil disobedience in support of personal beliefs because such conduct does not reflect poorly on the member or candidate's professional reputation, integrity, or competence.

Example 3:

A member intentionally includes a receipt that is not in his expenses for a company trip.

Comment:

Since this act involves deceit and fraud and reflects on the member's integrity and honesty, it is a violation.

Example 4:

A member tells a client that he can get her a good deal on a car through his father-in-law, but instead gets her a poor deal and accepts part of the commission on the car purchase.

Comment:

The member has been dishonest and misrepresented the facts of the situation and has, therefore, violated the Standard.

II   Integrity of Capital Markets

II(A)   Material Nonpublic Information. Members and Candidates who possess material nonpublic information that could affect the value of an investment must not act or cause others to act on the information.

Guidance

Information is "material" if its disclosure would impact the price of a security or if reasonable investors would want the information before making an investment decision. Ambiguous information, as far as its likely effect on price, may not be considered material. Information is "nonpublic" until it has been made available to the marketplace. An analyst conference call is not public disclosure. Selectively disclosing information by corporations creates the potential for insider-trading violations.

Guidance—Mosaic Theory

There is no violation when a perceptive analyst reaches an investment conclusion about a corporate action or event through an analysis of public information together with items of nonmaterial nonpublic information.

Recommended Procedures for Compliance

Make reasonable efforts to achieve public dissemination of the information. Encourage firms to adopt procedures to prevent misuse of material nonpublic information. Use a "firewall" within the firm, with elements including:

- Substantial control of relevant interdepartmental communications, through a clearance area such as the compliance or legal department.
- Review employee trades—maintain "watch," "restricted," and "rumor" lists.
- Monitor and restrict proprietary trading while a firm is in possession of material nonpublic information.

Prohibition of all proprietary trading while a firm is in possession of material nonpublic information may be inappropriate because it may send a signal to the market. In these cases, firms should take the contra side of only unsolicited customer trades.

Application of Standard II(A) Material Nonpublic Information

Example 1:

Josephine Walsh is riding an elevator up to her office when she overhears the chief financial officer (CFO) for the Swan Furniture Company tell the president of Swan that he has just calculated the company's earnings for the past quarter, and they have unexpectedly and significantly dropped. The CFO adds that this drop will not be released to the public until next week. Walsh immediately calls her broker and tells him to sell her Swan stock.

Comment:

Walsh has sufficient information to determine that the information is both material and nonpublic. By trading on the inside information, she has violated Standard II(A).

Example 2:

Samuel Peter, an analyst with Scotland and Pierce, Inc., is assisting his firm with a secondary offering for Bright Ideas Lamp Company. Peter participates, via telephone conference call, in a meeting with Scotland and Pierce investment-banking employees and Bright Ideas' CEO. Peter is advised that the company's earnings projections for the next year have significantly dropped. Throughout the telephone conference call, several Scotland and Pierce salespeople and portfolio managers walk in and out of Peter's office, where the telephone call is taking place. As a result, they are aware of the drop in projected earnings for Bright Ideas. Before the conference call is concluded, the salespeople trade the stock of the company on behalf of the firm's clients, and other firm personnel trade the stock in a firm proprietary account and in employee personal accounts.

Comment:

Peter violated Standard II(A) because he failed to prevent the transfer and misuse of material nonpublic information to others in his firm. Peter's firm should have adopted information barriers to prevent the communication of nonpublic information between departments of the firm. The salespeople and portfolio managers who traded on the information have also violated Standard II(A) by trading on inside information.

Example 3:

Elizabeth Levenson is based in Taipei and covers the Taiwanese market for her firm, which is based in Singapore. She is invited to meet the finance director of a manufacturing company, along with the other ten largest shareholders of the company. During the meeting, the finance director states that the company expects its workforce to strike next Friday, which will cripple productivity and distribution. Can Levenson use this information as a basis to change her rating on the company from "buy" to "sell"?

Comment:

Levenson must first determine whether the material information is public. If the company has not made this information public (a small-group forum does not qualify as a method of public dissemination), she cannot use the information according to Standard II(A).

Example 4:

Jagdish Teja is a buy-side analyst covering the furniture industry. Looking for an attractive company to recommend as a buy, he analyzed several furniture makers by studying their financial reports and visiting their operations. He also talked to some designers and retailers to find out which furniture styles are trendy and popular. Although none of the companies that he analyzed turned out to be a clear buy, he discovered that one of them, Swan Furniture Company (SFC), might be in trouble. Swan's extravagant new designs were introduced at substantial costs. Even though these designs initially attracted attention, in the long run, the public is buying more conservative furniture from other makers. Based on that and on P&L analysis, Teja believes that Swan's next-quarter earnings will drop substantially. He then issues a sell recommendation for SFC. Immediately after receiving that recommendation, investment managers start reducing the stock in their portfolios.

Comment:

Information on quarterly earnings figures is material and nonpublic. However, Teja arrived at his conclusion about the earnings drop based on public information and on pieces of nonmaterial nonpublic information (such as opinions of designers and retailers). Therefore, trading based on Teja's correct conclusion is not prohibited by Standard II(A).

Example 5:

A member's dentist, who is an active investor, tells the member that based on his research he believes that Acme, Inc., will be bought out in the near future by a larger firm in the industry. The member investigates and purchases shares of Acme.

Comment:

There is no violation here because the dentist had no inside information but has reached the conclusion on his own. The information here is not material because there is no reason to suspect that an investor would wish to know what the member's dentist thought before investing in shares of Acme.

Example 6:

A member received an advance copy of a stock recommendation that will appear in a widely read national newspaper column the next day and purchases the stock.

Comment:

A recommendation in a widely read newspaper column will likely cause the stock price to rise, so this is material nonpublic information. The member has violated the Standard.

Example 7:

A member is having lunch with a portfolio manager from a mutual fund who is known for his stock-picking ability and often influences market prices when his stock purchases and sales are disclosed. The manager tells the member that he is selling all his shares in Able, Inc., the next day. The member shorts the stock.

Comment:

The fact that the fund will sell its shares of Able is material because news of it will likely cause the shares to fall in price. Since this is also not currently public information, the member has violated the Standard by acting on the information.

Example 8:

A broker who is a member receives the sell order for the Able, Inc., shares from the portfolio manager in the previous example. The broker sells his shares of Able prior to entering the sell order for the fund, but since his personal holdings are small compared to the stock's trading volume, his trade does not affect the price.

Comment:

The broker has acted on material nonpublic information (the fund's sale of shares) and has violated the Standard.

> *Professor's Note: The member also violated Standard VI(B) Priority of Transactions by front-running the client trade with a trade in his own account. Had the member sold his shares after executing the fund trade, he still would be violating Standard II(A) by acting on his knowledge of the fund trade, which would still not be public information at that point.*

> **II(B)   Market Manipulation.** Members and Candidates must not engage in practices that distort prices or artificially inflate trading volume with the intent to mislead market participants.

Guidance

This Standard applies to transactions that deceive the market by distorting the price-setting mechanism of financial instruments or by securing a controlling position to manipulate the price of a related derivative and/or the asset itself. Spreading false rumors is also prohibited.

Application of Standard II(B) Market Manipulation

Example 1:

Matthew Murphy is an analyst at Divisadero Securities & Co., which has a significant number of hedge funds among its most important brokerage clients. Two trading days before the publication of the quarter-end report, Murphy alerts his sales force that he is about to issue a research report on Wirewolf Semiconductor, which will include his opinion that:

- Quarterly revenues are likely to fall short of management's guidance.

- Earnings will be as much as 5 cents per share (or more than 10%) below consensus.
- Wirewolf's highly respected chief financial officer may be about to join another company.

Knowing that Wirewolf had already entered its declared quarter-end "quiet period" before reporting earnings (and thus would be reluctant to respond to rumors, etc.), Murphy times the release of his research report specifically to sensationalize the negative aspects of the message to create significant downward pressure on Wirewolf's stock to the distinct advantage of Divisadero's hedge fund clients. The report's conclusions are based on speculation, not on fact. The next day, the research report is broadcast to all of Divisadero's clients and to the usual newswire services.

Before Wirewolf's investor relations department can assess its damage on the final trading day of the quarter and refute Murphy's report, its stock opens trading sharply lower, allowing Divisadero's clients to cover their short positions at substantial gains.

Comment:

Murphy violated Standard II(B) by trying to create artificial price volatility designed to have material impact on the price of an issuer's stock. Moreover, by lacking an adequate basis for the recommendation, Murphy also violated Standard V(A).

Example 2:

Sergei Gonchar is the chairman of the ACME Futures Exchange, which seeks to launch a new bond futures contract. In order to convince investors, traders, arbitragers, hedgers, and so on, to use its contract, the exchange attempts to demonstrate that it has the best liquidity. To do so, it enters into agreements with members so that they commit to a substantial minimum trading volume on the new contract over a specific period in exchange for substantial reductions on their regular commissions.

Comment:

Formal liquidity on a market is determined by the obligations set on market makers, but the actual liquidity of a market is better estimated by the actual trading volume and bid-ask spreads. Attempts to mislead participants on the actual liquidity of the market constitute a violation of Standard II(B). In this example, investors have been intentionally misled to believe they chose the most liquid instrument for some specific purpose and could eventually see the actual liquidity of the contract dry up suddenly after the term of the agreement if the "pump-priming" strategy fails. If ACME fully discloses its agreement with members to boost transactions over some initial launch period, it does not violate Standard II(B). ACME's intent is not to harm investors but on the contrary to give them a better service. For that purpose, it may engage in a liquidity-pumping strategy, but it must be disclosed.

Example 3:

A member is seeking to sell a large position in a fairly illiquid stock from a fund he manages. He buys and sells shares of the stock between that fund and another he also manages to create an appearance of activity and stock price appreciation, so that the sale of the whole position will have less market impact and he will realize a better return for the fund's shareholders.

Comment:

The trading activity is meant to mislead market participants and is, therefore, a violation of the Standard. The fact that his fund shareholders gain by this action does not change the fact that it is a violation.

Example 4:

A member posts false information about a firm on internet bulletin boards and stock chat facilities in an attempt to cause the firm's stock to increase in price.

Comment:

This is a violation of the Standard.

III	Duties to Clients

III(A) Loyalty, Prudence, and Care. Members and Candidates have a duty of loyalty to their clients and must act with reasonable care and exercise prudent judgment. Members and Candidates must act for the benefit of their clients and place their clients' interests before their employer's or their own interests. In relationships with clients, Members and Candidates must determine applicable fiduciary duty and must comply with such duty to persons and interests to whom it is owed.

Guidance

Client interests always come first.

- Exercise the prudence, care, skill, and diligence under the circumstances that a person acting in a like capacity and familiar with such matters would use.
- Manage pools of client assets in accordance with the terms of the governing documents, such as trust documents or investment management agreements.
- Make investment decisions in the context of the total portfolio.
- Vote proxies in an informed and responsible manner. Due to cost benefit considerations, it may not be necessary to vote all proxies.
- Client brokerage, or "soft dollars" or "soft commissions" must be used to benefit the client.

Recommended Procedures of Compliance

Submit to clients, at least quarterly, itemized statements showing all securities in custody and all debits, credits, and transactions.

Encourage firms to address these topics when drafting policies and procedures regarding fiduciary duty:

- Follow applicable rules and laws.
- Establish investment objectives of client. Consider suitability of portfolio relative to client's needs and circumstances, the investment's basic characteristics, or the basic characteristics of the total portfolio.
- Diversify.
- Deal fairly with all clients in regards to investment actions.
- Disclose conflicts.

- Disclose compensation arrangements.
- Vote proxies in the best interest of clients and ultimate beneficiaries.
- Maintain confidentiality.
- Seek best execution.
- Place client interests first.

Application of Standard III(A) Loyalty, Prudence, and Care

Example 1:

First Country Bank serves as trustee for the Miller Company's pension plan. Miller is the target of a hostile takeover attempt by Newton, Inc. In attempting to ward off Newton, Miller's managers persuade Julian Wiley, an investment manager at First Country Bank, to purchase Miller common stock in the open market for the employee pension plan. Miller's officials indicate that such action would be favorably received and would probably result in other accounts being placed with the bank. Although Wiley believes the stock to be overvalued and would not ordinarily buy it, he purchases the stock to support Miller's managers, to maintain the company's good favor, and to realize additional new business. The heavy stock purchases cause Miller's market price to rise to such a level that Newton retracts its takeover bid.

Comment:

Standard III(A) requires that a member or candidate, in evaluating a takeover bid, act prudently and solely in the interests of plan participants and beneficiaries. To meet this requirement, a member or candidate must carefully evaluate the long-term prospects of the company against the short-term prospects presented by the takeover offer and by the ability to invest elsewhere. In this instance, Wiley, acting on behalf of his employer, the trustee, clearly violated Standard III(A) by using the profit-sharing plan to perpetuate existing management, perhaps to the detriment of plan participants and the company's shareholders, and to benefit himself. Wiley's responsibilities to the plan participants and beneficiaries should take precedence over any ties to corporate managers and self-interest. A duty exists to examine such a takeover offer on its own merits and to make an independent decision. The guiding principle is the appropriateness of the investment decision to the pension plan, not whether the decision benefits Wiley or the company that hired him.

Example 2:

Emilie Rome is a trust officer for Paget Trust Company. Rome's supervisor is responsible for reviewing Rome's trust account transactions and her monthly reports of personal stock transactions. Rome has been using Nathan Gray, a broker, almost exclusively for trust account brokerage transactions. Where Gray makes a market in stocks, he has been giving Rome a lower price for personal purchases and a higher price for sales than he gives to Rome's trust accounts and other investors.

Comment:

Rome is violating her duty of loyalty to the bank's trust accounts by using Gray for brokerage transactions simply because Gray trades Rome's personal account on favorable terms.

Example 3:

A member uses a broker for client-account trades that has relatively high prices and average research and execution. In return, the broker pays for the rent and other overhead expenses for the member's firm.

Comment:

This is a violation of the Standard since the member used client brokerage for services that do not benefit clients and failed to get the best price and execution for his clients.

Example 4:

In return for receiving account management business from Broker X, a member directs trades to Broker X on the accounts referred to her by Broker X, as well as on other accounts as an incentive to Broker X to send her more account business.

Comment:

This is a violation if Broker X does not offer the best price and execution or if the practice of directing trades to Broker X is not disclosed to clients. The obligation to seek best price and execution is always required unless clients provide a written statement that the member is not to seek best price and execution and that they are aware of the impact of this decision on their accounts.

Example 5:

A member does more trades in client accounts than are necessary to accomplish client goals because she desires to increase her commission income.

Comment:

The member is using client assets (brokerage fees) to benefit herself and has violated the Standard.

III(B) Fair Dealing. Members and Candidates must deal fairly and objectively with all clients when providing investment analysis, making investment recommendations, taking investment action, or engaging in other professional activities.

Guidance

Do not discriminate against any clients when disseminating recommendations or taking investment action. Fairly does not mean equally. In the normal course of business, there will be differences in the time e-mails, faxes, etc., are received by different clients. Different service levels are okay, but they must not negatively affect or disadvantage any clients. Disclose the different service levels to all clients and prospects, and make premium levels of service available to all who wish to pay for them.

Guidance—Investment Recommendations

Give all clients a fair opportunity to act upon every recommendation. Clients who are unaware of a change in a recommendation should be advised before the order is accepted.

Guidance—Investment Actions

Treat clients fairly in light of their investment objectives and circumstances. Treat both individual and institutional clients in a fair and impartial manner. Members and Candidates should not take advantage of their position in the industry to disadvantage clients (e.g., in the context of IPOs).

Recommended Procedures for Compliance

Encourage firms to establish compliance procedures requiring proper dissemination of investment recommendations and fair treatment of all customers and clients. Consider these points when establishing fair dealing compliance procedures:

- Limit the number of people who are aware that a change in recommendation will be made.
- Shorten the time frame between decision and dissemination.
- Publish personnel guidelines for pre-dissemination—have in place guidelines prohibiting personnel who have prior knowledge of a recommendation from discussing it or taking action on the pending recommendation.
- Simultaneous dissemination of new or changed recommendations to all candidates who have expressed an interest or for whom an investment is suitable.
- Maintain list of clients and holdings—use to ensure that all holders are treated fairly.
- Develop written trade allocation procedures—ensure fairness to clients, timely and efficient order execution, and accuracy of client positions.
- Disclose trade allocation procedures.
- Establish systematic account review—ensure that no client is given preferred treatment and that investment actions are consistent with the account's objectives.
- Disclose available levels of service.

Application of Standard III(B) Fair Dealing

Example 1:

Bradley Ames, a well-known and respected analyst, follows the computer industry. In the course of his research, he finds that a small, relatively unknown company whose shares are traded over the counter has just signed significant contracts with some of the companies he follows. After a considerable amount of investigation, Ames decides to write a research report on the company and recommend purchase. While the report is being reviewed by the company for factual accuracy, Ames schedules a luncheon with several of his best clients to discuss the company. At the luncheon, he mentions the purchase recommendation scheduled to be sent early the following week to all the firm's clients.

Comment:

Ames violated Standard III(B) by disseminating the purchase recommendation to the clients with whom he had lunch a week before the recommendation was sent to all clients.

Example 2:

Spencer Rivers, president of XYZ Corporation, moves his company's growth-oriented pension fund to a particular bank primarily because of the excellent investment performance achieved by the bank's commingled fund for the prior 5-year period. A few years later, Rivers compares the results of his pension fund with those of the bank's commingled fund. He is startled to learn that, even though the two accounts have the same investment objectives and similar portfolios, his company's pension fund has significantly underperformed the bank's commingled fund. Questioning this result at his next meeting with the pension fund's manager, Rivers is told that, as a matter of policy, when a new security is placed on the recommended list, Morgan Jackson, the pension fund manager, first purchases the security for the commingled account and then purchases it on a pro rata basis for all other pension fund accounts. Similarly, when a sale is recommended, the security is sold first from the commingled account and then sold on a pro rata basis from all other accounts. Rivers also learns that if the bank cannot get enough shares (especially the hot issues) to be meaningful to all the accounts, its policy is to place the new issues only in the commingled account.

Seeing that Rivers is neither satisfied nor pleased by the explanation, Jackson quickly adds that nondiscretionary pension accounts and personal trust accounts have a lower priority on purchase and sale recommendations than discretionary pension fund accounts. Furthermore, Jackson states, the company's pension fund had the opportunity to invest up to 5% in the commingled fund.

Comment:

The bank's policy did not treat all customers fairly, and Jackson violated her duty to her clients by giving priority to the growth-oriented commingled fund over all other funds and to discretionary accounts over nondiscretionary accounts. Jackson must execute orders on a systematic basis that is fair to all clients. In addition, trade allocation procedures should be disclosed to all clients from the beginning. Of course, in this case, disclosure of the bank's policy would not change the fact that the policy is unfair.

Example 3:

A member gets options for his part in an IPO from the subject firm. The IPO is oversubscribed and the member fills his own and other individuals' orders but has to reduce allocations to his institutional clients.

Comment:

The member has violated the Standard. He must disclose to his employer and to his clients that he has accepted options for putting together the IPO. He should not take any shares of a hot IPO for himself and should have distributed his allocated shares of the IPO to all clients in proportion to their original order amounts.

Example 4:

A member is delayed in allocating some trades to client accounts. When she allocates the trades, she puts some positions that have appreciated in a preferred client's account and puts trades that have not done as well in other client accounts.

Comment:

This is a violation of the Standard. The member should have allocated the trades to specific accounts prior to the trades or should have allocated the trades proportionally to suitable accounts in a timely fashion.

III(C) Suitability

1. When Members and Candidates are in an advisory relationship with a client, they must:

   a. Make a reasonable inquiry into a client's or prospective clients' investment experience, risk and return objectives, and financial constraints prior to making any investment recommendation or taking investment action and must reassess and update this information regularly.

   b. Determine that an investment is suitable to the client's financial situation and consistent with the client's written objectives, mandates, and constraints before making an investment recommendation or taking investment action.

   c. Judge the suitability of investments in the context of the client's total portfolio.

2. When Members and Candidates are responsible for managing a portfolio to a specific mandate, strategy, or style, they must make only investment recommendations or take investment actions that are consistent with the stated objectives and constraints of the portfolio.

Guidance

In advisory relationships, be sure to gather client information at the beginning of the relationship, in the form of an investment policy statement (IPS). Consider clients' needs and circumstances and thus their risk tolerance. Consider whether or not the use of leverage is suitable for the client.

If a member is responsible for managing a fund to an index or other stated mandate, be sure investments are consistent with the stated mandate.

Recommended Procedures for Compliance

Members should:

- Put the needs and circumstances of each client and the client's investment objectives into a written IPS for each client.
- Consider the type of client and whether there are separate beneficiaries, investor objectives (return and risk), investor constraints (liquidity needs, expected cash flows, time, tax, and regulatory and legal circumstances), and performance measurement benchmarks.
- Review investor's objectives and constraints periodically to reflect any changes in client circumstances.

Application of Standard III(C) Suitability

Example 1:

Ann Walters, an investment advisor, suggests to Brian Crosby, a risk-averse client, that covered call options be used in his equity portfolio. The purpose would be to enhance Crosby's income and partially offset any untimely depreciation in value should the stock market or other circumstances affect his holdings unfavorably. Walters educates Crosby about all possible outcomes, including the risk of incurring an added tax liability if a stock rises in price and is called away and, conversely, the risk of his holdings losing protection on the downside if prices drop sharply.

Comment:

When determining suitability of an investment, the primary focus should be on the characteristics of the client's entire portfolio, not on an issue-by-issue analysis. The basic characteristics of the entire portfolio will largely determine whether the investment recommendations are taking client factors into account. Therefore, the most important aspects of a particular investment will be those that will affect the characteristics of the total portfolio. In this case, Walters properly considered the investment in the context of the entire portfolio and thoroughly explained the investment to the client.

Example 2:

Max Gubler, CIO of a property/casualty insurance subsidiary of a large financial conglomerate, wants to better diversify the company's investment portfolio and increase its returns. The company's investment policy statement (IPS) provides for highly liquid investments, such as large caps, governments, and supra-nationals, as well as corporate bonds with a minimum credit rating of AA- and maturity of no more than five years. In a recent presentation, a venture capital group offered very attractive prospective returns on some of their private equity funds providing seed capital. An exit strategy is already contemplated but investors will first have to observe a minimum three-year lock-up period, with a subsequent laddered exit option for a maximum of one third of shares per year. Gubler does not want to miss this opportunity and after an extensive analysis and optimization of this asset class with the company's current portfolio, he invests 4% in this seed fund, leaving the portfolio's total equity exposure still well below its upper limit.

Comment:

Gubler violates Standards III(A) and III(C). His new investment locks up part of the company's assets for at least three and for up to as many as five years and possibly beyond. Since the IPS requires investments in highly liquid investments and describes accepted asset classes, private equity investments with a lock-up period certainly do not qualify. Even without such lock-up periods an asset class with only an occasional, and thus implicitly illiquid, market may not be suitable. Although an IPS typically describes objectives and constraints in great detail, the manager must make every effort to understand the client's business and circumstances. Doing so should also enable the manager to recognize, understand, and discuss with the client other factors that may be or may become material in the investment management process.

Example 3:

A member gives a client account a significant allocation to non-dividend paying high risk securities even though the client has low risk tolerance and modest return objectives.

Comment:

This is a violation of the Standard.

Example 4:

A member puts a security into a fund she manages that does not fit the mandate of the fund and is not a permitted investment according to the fund's disclosures.

Comment:

This, too, is a violation of the Standard.

> **III(D) Performance Presentation.** When communicating investment performance information, Members or Candidates must make reasonable efforts to ensure that it is fair, accurate, and complete.

Guidance

Members must avoid misstating performance or misleading clients/prospects about investment performance of themselves or their firms, should not misrepresent past performance or reasonably expected performance, and should not state or imply the ability to achieve a rate of return similar to that achieved in the past.

Recommended Procedures for Compliance

Encourage firms to adhere to Global Investment Performance Standards. Obligations under this Standard may also be met by:

- Considering the sophistication of the audience to whom a performance presentation is addressed.
- Presenting performance of weighted composite of similar portfolios rather than a single account.
- Including terminated accounts as part of historical performance.
- Including all appropriate disclosures to fully explain results (e.g., model results included, gross or net of fees, etc.).
- Maintaining data and records used to calculate the performance being presented.

Application of Standard III(D) Performance Presentation

Example 1:

Kyle Taylor of Taylor Trust Company, noting the performance of Taylor's common trust fund for the past two years, states in the brochure sent to his potential clients that "You can expect steady 25% annual compound growth of the value of your investments over the year." Taylor Trust's common trust fund did increase at the rate of 25% per annum for the past year which mirrored the increase of the entire market. The fund, however, never averaged that growth for more than one year, and the average rate of growth of all of its trust accounts for five years was 5% per annum.

Comment:

Taylor's brochure is in violation of Standard III(D). Taylor should have disclosed that the 25% growth occurred in only one year. Additionally, Taylor did not include client accounts other than those in the firm's common trust fund. A general claim of firm performance should take into account the performance of all categories of accounts. Finally, by stating that clients can expect a steady 25% annual compound growth rate, Taylor also violated Standard I(C), which prohibits statements of assurances or guarantees regarding an investment.

Example 2:

Aaron McCoy is vice president and managing partner of the equity investment group of Mastermind Financial Advisors, a new business. Mastermind recruited McCoy because he had a proven six-year track record with G&P Financial. In developing Mastermind's advertising and marketing campaign, McCoy prepared an advertisement that included the equity investment performance he achieved at G&P Financial. The advertisement for Mastermind did not identify the equity performance as being earned while at G&P. The advertisement was distributed to existing clients and prospective clients of Mastermind.

Comment:

McCoy violated Standard III(D) by distributing an advertisement that contained material misrepresentations regarding the historical performance of Mastermind. Standard III(D) requires that members and candidates make every reasonable effort to ensure that performance information is a fair, accurate, and complete representation of an individual or firm's performance. As a general matter, this standard does not prohibit showing past performance of funds managed at a prior firm as part of a performance track record so long as it is accompanied by appropriate disclosures detailing where the performance comes from and the person's specific role in achieving that performance. If McCoy chooses to use his past performance from G&P in Mastermind's advertising, he should make full disclosure as to the source of the historical performance.

Example 3:

A member puts simulated results of an investment strategy in a sales brochure without disclosing that the results are not actual performance numbers.

Comment:

The member has violated the Standard.

Example 4:

In materials for prospective clients, a member uses performance figures for a large-cap growth composite she has created by choosing accounts that have done relatively well and including some accounts with significant mid-cap exposure.

Comment:

This is a violation of the Standard as the member has attempted to mislead clients and has misrepresented her performance.

III(E)   Preservation of Confidentiality. Members and Candidates must keep information about current, former, and prospective clients confidential unless:

1.   The information concerns illegal activities on the part of the client or prospective client,

2.   Disclosure is required by law, or

3.   The client or prospective client permits disclosure of the information.

Guidance

If illegal activities by a client are involved, members may have an obligation to report the activities to authorities. The confidentiality Standard extends to former clients as well.

The requirements of this Standard are not intended to prevent Members and Candidates from cooperating with a CFA Institute Professional Conduct Program (PCP) investigation.

Recommended Procedures for Compliance

Members should avoid disclosing information received from a client except to authorized co-workers who are also working for the client.

Application of Standard III(E) Preservation of Confidentiality

Example 1:

Sarah Connor, a financial analyst employed by Johnson Investment Counselors, Inc., provides investment advice to the trustees of City Medical Center. The trustees have given her a number of internal reports concerning City Medical's needs for physical plant renovation and expansion. They have asked Connor to recommend investments that would generate capital appreciation in endowment funds to meet projected capital expenditures. Connor is approached by a local business man, Thomas Kasey, who is considering a substantial contribution either to City Medical Center or to another local hospital. Kasey wants to find out the building plans of both institutions before making a decision, but he does not want to speak to the trustees.

Comment:

The trustees gave Connor the internal reports so she could advise them on how to manage their endowment funds. Because the information in the reports is clearly both confidential and within the scope of the confidential relationship, Standard III(E) requires that Connor refuse to divulge information to Kasey.

Example 2:

David Bradford manages money for a family-owned real estate development corporation. He also manages the individual portfolios of several of the family members and officers of the corporation, including the chief financial officer (CFO). Based on the financial records from the corporation, as well as some questionable practices of the CFO that he has observed, Bradford believes that the CFO is embezzling money from the corporation and putting it into his personal investment account.

Comment:

Bradford should check with his firm's compliance department as well as outside counsel to determine whether applicable securities regulations require reporting the CFO's financial records.

Example 3:

A member has learned from his client that one of his goals is to give more of his portfolio income to charity. The member tells this to a friend who is on the board of a worthy charity and suggests that he should contact the client about a donation.

Comment:

The member has violated the Standard by disclosing information he has learned from the client in the course of their business relationship.

Example 4:

A member learns that a pension account client is violating the law with respect to charges to the pension fund.

Comment:

The member must bring this to the attention of her supervisor and try to end the illegal activity. Failing this, the member should seek legal advice about any disclosure she should make to legal or regulatory authorities and dissociate herself from any continuing association with the pension account.

IV   Duties to Employers

IV(A)   Loyalty. In matters related to their employment, Members and Candidates must act for the benefit of their employer and not deprive their employer of the advantage of their skills and abilities, divulge confidential information, or otherwise cause harm to their employer.

Guidance

Members must not engage in any activities which would injure the firm, deprive it of profit, or deprive it of the advantage of employees' skills and abilities. Always place client interests above interests of employer. There is no requirement that the employee put employer interests ahead of family and other personal obligations; it is expected that employers and employees will discuss such matters and balance these obligations with work obligations.

Guidance—Independent Practice

Independent practice for compensation is allowed if a notification is provided to the employer fully describing all aspects of the services, including compensation, duration, and the nature of the activities *and* if the employer consents to all terms of the proposed independent practice before it begins.

Guidance—Leaving an Employer

Members must continue to act in their employer's best interests until resignation is effective. Activities which may constitute a violation include:

- Misappropriation of trade secrets.
- Misuse of confidential information.
- Soliciting employer's clients prior to leaving.
- Self-dealing.
- Misappropriation of client lists.

Once an employee has left a firm, simple knowledge of names and existence of former clients is generally not confidential. Also there is no prohibition on the use of experience or knowledge gained while with a former employer.

Guidance—Whistleblowing

There may be isolated cases where a duty to one's employer may be violated in order to protect clients or the integrity of the market, and not for personal gain.

Guidance—Nature of Employment

The applicability of this Standard is based on the nature of the employment—employee versus independent contractor. If Members and Candidates are independent contractors, they still have a duty to abide by the terms of the agreement.

Application of Standard IV(A) Loyalty

Example 1:

James Hightower has been employed by Jason Investment Management Corporation for 15 years. He began as an analyst but assumed increasing responsibilities and is now a senior portfolio manager and a member of the firm's investment policy committee. Hightower has decided to leave Jason Investment and start his own investment management business. He has been careful not to tell any of Jason's clients that he is leaving, because he does not want to be accused of breaching his duty to Jason by soliciting Jason's clients before his departure. Hightower is planning to copy and take with him the following documents and information he developed or worked on while at Jason: (1) the client list, with addresses, telephone numbers, and other pertinent client information; (2) client account statements; (3) sample marketing presentations to prospective clients containing Jason's performance record; (4) Jason's recommended list of securities; (5) computer models to determine asset allocations for accounts with different objectives; (6) computer models for stock selection; and (7) personal computer spreadsheets for Hightower's major corporate recommendations which he developed when he was an analyst.

Comment:

Except with the consent of their employer, departing employees may not take employer property, which includes books, records, reports, and other materials, and may not interfere with their employer's business opportunities. Taking any employer records, even those the member or candidate prepared, violates Standard IV(A).

Example 2:

Dennis Elliot has hired Sam Chisolm who previously worked for a competing firm. Chisolm left his former firm after 18 years of employment. When Chisolm begins working for Elliot, he wants to contact his former clients because he knows them well and is certain that many will follow him to his new employer. Is Chisolm in violation of the Standard IV(A) if he contacts his former clients?

Comment:

Because client records are the property of the firm, contacting former clients for any reason through the use of client lists or other information taken from a former employer without permission would be a violation of Standard IV(A). In addition, the nature and extent of the contact with former clients may be governed by the terms of any non-compete agreement signed by the employee and the former employer that covers contact with former clients after employment.

But, simple knowledge of the name and existence of former clients is not confidential information, just as skills or experience that an employee obtains while employed is not "confidential" or "privileged" information. The Code and Standards do not impose a prohibition on the use of experience or knowledge gained at one employer from being used at another employer. The Code and Standards also do not prohibit former employees from contacting clients of their previous firm, absent a non-compete agreement. Members and candidates are free to use public information about their former firm after departing to contact former clients without violating Standard IV(A).

In the absence of a non-compete agreement, as long as Chisolm maintains his duty of loyalty to his employer before joining Elliot's firm, does not take steps to solicit clients until he has left his former firm, and does not make use of material from his former employer without its permission after he has left, he would not be in violation of the Code and Standards.

Example 3:

Several employees are planning to depart their current employer within a few weeks and have been careful to not engage in any activities that would conflict with their duty to their current employer. They have just learned that one of their employer's clients has undertaken a request for proposal (RFP) to review and possibly hire a new investment consultant. The RFP has been sent to the employer and all of its competitors. The group believes that the new entity to be formed would be qualified to respond to the RFP and eligible for the business. The RFP submission period is likely to conclude before the employees' resignations are effective. Is it permissible for the group of departing employees to respond to the RFP under their anticipated new firm?

Comment:

A group of employees responding to an RFP that their employer is also responding to would lead to direct competition between the employees and the employer. Such conduct would violate Standard IV(A) unless the group of employees received permission from their employer as well as the entity sending out the RFP.

Example 4:

A member solicits clients and prospects of his current employer to open accounts at the new firm he will be joining shortly.

Comment:

It is a violation of the Standard to solicit the firm's clients and prospects while he is still employed by the firm.

Example 5:

Two employees discuss joining with others in an employee-led buyout of their employer's emerging markets investment management business.

Comment:

There is no violation here. Their employer can decide how to respond to any buyout offer. If such a buyout takes place, clients should be informed of the nature of the changes in a timely manner.

Example 6:

A member is writing a research report on a company as a contract worker for Employer A (using Employer A's premises and materials) with the understanding that Employer A does not claim exclusive rights to the outcome of her research. As she is finishing the report, she is offered a full-time job by Employer B and sends Employer B a copy of a draft of her report for publication.

Comment:

She has violated the Standard by not giving Employer A the first rights to act on her research. She must also be careful not to take any materials used in preparing the report from Employer A's premises.

Example 7:

A member helps develop software for a firm while acting as an unpaid intern and takes the software, without permission, with her when she takes a full-time job at another firm.

Comment:

She is considered an employee of the firm and has violated the Standard by taking her employer's property without permission.

Example 8:

A member prepares to leave his employer and open his own firm by registering with the SEC, renting an office, and buying office equipment.

Comment:

As long as these preparations have not interfered with the performance of his current job, there has been no violation. The solicitation of firm clients and prospects prior to leaving his employer would, however, be a violation of the Standard.

Example 9:

A member is a full-time employee of an investment management firm and wants to accept a paid position as town mayor without asking his employer's permission.

Comment:

Since the member serving as mayor does not conflict with his employer's business interests, as long as the time commitment does not preclude performing his expected job functions well, there is no violation.

Example 10:

A member who has left one employer uses public sources to get the phone numbers of previous clients and solicits their business for her new employer.

Comment:

As long as there is no agreement in force between the member and his previous employer that prohibits such solicitation, there is no violation of the Standards.

> **IV(B)   Additional Compensation Arrangements.** Members and Candidates must not accept gifts, benefits, compensation, or consideration that competes with, or might reasonably be expected to create a conflict of interest with, their employer's interest unless they obtain written consent from all parties involved.

Guidance

Compensation includes direct and indirect compensation from a client and other benefits received from third parties. Written consent from a member's employer includes e-mail communication.

Recommended Procedures for Compliance

Make an immediate written report to employer detailing proposed compensation and services, if additional to that provided by employer.

Application of Standard IV(B) Additional Compensation Arrangements

Example 1:

Geoff Whitman, a portfolio analyst for Adams Trust Company, manages the account of Carol Cochran, a client. Whitman is paid a salary by his employer, and Cochran pays the trust company a standard fee based on the market value of assets in her portfolio. Cochran proposes to Whitman that "any year that my portfolio achieves at least a 15% return before taxes, you and your wife can fly to Monaco at my expense and use my condominium during the third week of January." Whitman does not inform his employer of the arrangement and vacations in Monaco the following January as Cochran's guest.

Comment:

Whitman violated Standard IV(B) by failing to inform his employer in writing of this supplemental, contingent compensation arrangement. The nature of the arrangement could have resulted in partiality to Cochran's account, which could have detracted from Whitman's performance with respect to other accounts he handles for Adams Trust. Whitman must obtain the consent of his employer to accept such a supplemental benefit.

Example 2:

A member is on the board of directors of a company whose shares he purchases for client accounts. As a member of the board, he receives the company's product at no charge.

Comment:

Since receiving the company's product constitutes compensation for his service, he is in violation of the Standard if he does not disclose this additional compensation to his employer.

> **IV(C) Responsibilities of Supervisors.** Members and Candidates must make reasonable efforts to detect and prevent violations of applicable laws, rules, regulations, and the Code and Standards by anyone subject to their supervision or authority.

Guidance

Members must take steps to *prevent* employees from violating laws, rules, regulations, or the Code and Standards, as well as make reasonable efforts to *detect* violations.

Guidance—Compliance Procedures

Understand that an adequate compliance system must meet industry standards, regulatory requirements, and the requirements of the Code and Standards. Members with supervisory responsibilities have an obligation to bring an inadequate compliance system to the attention of firm's management and recommend corrective action. While investigating a possible breach of compliance procedures, it is appropriate to limit the suspected employee's activities.

A member or candidate faced with no compliance procedures or with procedures he believes are inadequate must decline supervisory responsibility in writing until adequate procedures are adopted by the firm.

Recommended Procedures for Compliance

A member should recommend that his employer adopt a code of ethics. Employers should not commingle compliance procedures with the firm's code of ethics—this can dilute the goal of reinforcing one's ethical obligations. Members should encourage employers to provide their code of ethics to clients.

Adequate compliance procedures should:

- Be clearly written.
- Be easy to understand.
- Designate a compliance officer with authority clearly defined.
- Have a system of checks and balances.
- Outline the scope of procedures.
- Outline what conduct is permitted.
- Contain procedures for reporting violations and sanctions.

Once the compliance program is instituted, the supervisor should:

- Distribute it to the proper personnel.
- Update it as needed.
- Continually educate staff regarding procedures.
- Issue reminders as necessary.
- Require professional conduct evaluations.
- Review employee actions to monitor compliance and identify violations.
- Enforce procedures once a violation occurs.

If there is a violation, respond promptly and conduct a thorough investigation while placing limitations on the wrongdoer's activities.

Application of Standard IV(C) Responsibilities of Supervisors

Example 1:

Jane Mattock, senior vice president and head of the research department of H&V, Inc., a regional brokerage firm, has decided to change her recommendation for Timber Products from buy to sell. In line with H&V's procedures, she orally advises certain other H&V executives of her proposed actions before the report is prepared for publication. As a result of his conversation with Mattock, Dieter Frampton, one of the executives of H&V accountable to Mattock, immediately sells Timber's stock from his own account and from certain discretionary client accounts. In addition, other personnel inform certain institutional customers of the changed recommendation before it is printed and disseminated to all H&V customers who have received previous Timber reports.

Comment:

Mattock failed to supervise reasonably and adequately the actions of those accountable to her. She did not prevent or establish reasonable procedures designed to prevent dissemination of or trading on the information by those who knew of her changed recommendation. She must ensure that her firm has procedures for reviewing or recording trading in the stock of any corporation that has been the subject of an unpublished change in recommendation. Adequate procedures would have informed the subordinates of their duties and detected sales by Frampton and selected customers.

Example 2:

Deion Miller is the research director for Jamestown Investment Programs. The portfolio managers have become critical of Miller and his staff because the Jamestown portfolios do not include any stock that has been the subject of a merger or tender offer. Georgia Ginn, a member of Miller's staff, tells Miller that she has been studying a local company, Excelsior, Inc., and recommends its purchase. Ginn adds that the company has been widely rumored to be the subject of a merger study by a well-known conglomerate and discussions between them are under way. At Miller's request, Ginn prepares a memo recommending the stock. Miller passes along Ginn's memo to the portfolio managers prior to leaving for vacation, noting that he has not reviewed the memo. As a result of the memo, the portfolio managers buy Excelsior stock immediately. The day Miller returns to the office, Miller learns that Ginn's only sources for the report were her brother, who is an acquisitions analyst with Acme Industries and the "well-known conglomerate" and that the merger discussions were planned but not held.

Comment:

Miller violated Standard IV(C) by not exercising reasonable supervision when he disseminated the memo without checking to ensure that Ginn had a reasonable and adequate basis for her recommendations and that Ginn was not relying on material nonpublic information.

Example 3:

A member responsible for compliance by the firm's trading desk notices a high level of trading activity in a stock that is not on the firm's recommended list. Most of this trading is being done by a trainee, and the member does not investigate this trading.

Comment:

This is a violation of the member's responsibilities as supervisor. She must take steps to monitor the activities of traders in training, as well as investigate the reason for the heavy trading of the security by her firm's trading desk.

V	**Investment Analysis, Recommendations, and Actions**
V(A)	**Diligence and Reasonable Basis.** Members and Candidates must:

1. Exercise diligence, independence, and thoroughness in analyzing investments, making investment recommendations, and taking investment actions.

2. Have a reasonable and adequate basis, supported by appropriate research and investigation, for any investment analysis, recommendation, or action.

Guidance

The application of this Standard depends on the investment philosophy adhered to, members' and candidates' roles in the investment decision-making process, and the resources and support provided by employers. These factors dictate the degree of diligence, thoroughness of research, and the proper level of investigation required.

Guidance—Using Secondary or Third-Party Research

See that the research is sound. Examples of criteria to use:

- Review assumptions used.
- Determine how rigorous the analysis was.
- Identify how timely how the research is.
- Evaluate objectivity and independence of the recommendations.

Guidance—Group Research and Decision Making

Even if a member does not agree with the independent and objective view of the group, he does not necessarily have to decline to be identified with the report, as long as there is a reasonable and adequate basis.

Recommended Procedures for Compliance

Members should encourage their firms to consider these policies and procedures supporting this Standard:

- Have a policy requiring that research reports and recommendations have a basis that can be substantiated as reasonable and adequate.
- Have detailed, written guidance for proper research and due diligence.
- Have measurable criteria for judging the quality of research, and base analyst compensation on such criteria.

Application of Standard V(A) Diligence and Reasonable Basis

Example 1:

Helen Hawke manages the corporate finance department of Sarkozi Securities, Ltd. The firm is anticipating that the government will soon close a tax loophole that currently allows oil and gas exploration companies to pass on drilling expenses to holders of a certain class of shares. Because market demand for this tax-advantaged class of stock is currently high, Sarkozi convinces several companies to undertake new equity financings at once before the loophole closes. Time is of the essence, but Sarkozi lacks sufficient resources to conduct adequate research on all the prospective issuing companies. Hawke decides to estimate the IPO prices based on the relative size of each company and to justify the pricing later when her staff has time.

Comment:

Sarkozi should have taken on only the work that it could adequately handle. By categorizing the issuers as to general size, Hawke has bypassed researching all the other relevant aspects that should be considered when pricing new issues and thus has not performed sufficient due diligence. Such an omission can result in investors purchasing shares at prices that have no actual basis. Hawke has violated Standard V(A).

Example 2:

Evelyn Mastakis is a junior analyst asked by her firm to write a research report predicting the expected interest rate for residential mortgages over the next six months. Mastakis submits her report to the fixed-income investment committee of her firm for review, as required by firm procedures. Although some committee members support Mastakis's conclusion, the majority of the committee disagrees with her conclusion and the report is significantly changed to indicate that interest rates are likely to increase more than originally predicted by Mastakis.

Comment:

The results of research are not always clear, and different people may have different opinions based on the same factual evidence. In this case, the majority of the committee may have valid reasons for issuing a report that differs from the analyst's original research. The firm can issue a report different from the original report of the analyst as long as there is a reasonable or adequate basis for its conclusions. Generally, analysts must write research reports that reflect their own opinion and can ask the firm not to put their name on reports that ultimately differ from that opinion. When the work is a group effort, however, not all members of the team may agree with all aspects of the report. Ultimately, members and candidates can ask to have their names removed from the report, but if they are satisfied that the process has produced results or conclusions that have a reasonable or adequate basis, members or candidates do not have to dissociate from the report even when they do not agree with its contents. The member or candidate should document the difference of opinion and any request to remove his or her name from the report.

Example 3:

A member makes a presentation for an offering his firm is underwriting, using maximum production levels as his estimate in order to justify the price of the shares he is recommending for purchase.

Comment:

Using the maximum possible production without acknowledging that this is not the expected level of production (or without presenting a range of possible outcomes and their relative probabilities) does not provide a reasonable basis for the purchase recommendation and is a violation of the Standard.

Example 4:

A member posts buy recommendations in an internet chat room based on "conventional wisdom" and what the public is currently buying.

Comment:

A recommendation that is not based on independent and diligent research into the subject company is a violation of the Standard.

Example 5:

A member is a principal in a small investment firm that bases its securities recommendations on third-party research that it purchases.

Comment:

This is not a violation as long as the member's firm periodically checks the purchased research to determine that it has met, and still meets, the criteria of objectivity and reasonableness required by the Standard.

V(B) Communication with Clients and Prospective Clients. Members and Candidates must:

1. Disclose to clients and prospective clients the basic format and general principles of the investment processes used to analyze investments, select securities, and construct portfolios and must promptly disclose any changes that might materially affect those processes.

2. Use reasonable judgment in identifying which factors are important to their investment analyses, recommendations, or actions and include those factors in communications with clients and prospective clients.

3. Distinguish between fact and opinion in the presentation of investment analysis and recommendations.

Guidance

Proper communication with clients is critical to provide quality financial services. Members must distinguish between opinions and facts and always include the basic characteristics of the security being analyzed in a research report.

Members must illustrate to clients and prospects the investment decision-making process utilized. The suitability of each investment is important in the context of the entire portfolio.

All means of communication are included here, not just research reports.

Recommended Procedures for Compliance

Selection of relevant factors in a report can be a judgment call, so be sure to maintain records indicating the nature of the research, and be able to supply additional information if it is requested by the client or other users of the report.

Application of Standard V(B) Communication with Clients and Prospective Clients

Example 1:

Sarah Williamson, director of marketing for Country Technicians, Inc., is convinced that she has found the perfect formula for increasing Country Technician's income and diversifying its product base. Williamson plans to build on Country Technician's reputation as a leading money manager by marketing an exclusive and expensive investment advice letter to high-net-worth individuals. One hitch in the plan is the complexity of Country Technician's investment system—a combination of technical trading rules (based on historical price and volume fluctuations) and portfolio-construction rules designed to minimize risk. To simplify the newsletter, she decides to include only each week's top-five buy and sell recommendations and to leave out details of the valuation models and the portfolio-structuring scheme.

Comment:

Williamson's plans for the newsletter violate Standard V(B) because she does not intend to include all the relevant factors behind the investment advice. Williamson need not describe the investment system in detail in order to implement the advice effectively, clients must be informed of Country Technician's basic process and logic. Without understanding the basis for a recommendation, clients cannot possibly understand its limitations or its inherent risks.

Example 2:

Richard Dox is a mining analyst for East Bank Securities. He has just finished his report on Boisy Bay Minerals. Included in his report is his own assessment of the geological extent of mineral reserves likely to be found on the company's land. Dox completed this calculation based on the core samples from the company's latest drilling. According to Dox's calculations, the company has in excess of 500,000 ounces of gold on the property. Dox concludes his research report as follows: "Based on the fact that the company has 500,000 ounces of gold to be mined, I recommend a strong BUY."

Comment:

If Dox issues the report as written, he will violate Standard V(B). His calculation of the total gold reserves for the property is an opinion, not a fact. Opinion must be distinguished from fact in research reports.

Example 3:

May & Associates is an aggressive growth manager that has represented itself since its inception as a specialist at investing in small-capitalization domestic stocks. One of May's selection criteria is a maximum capitalization of $250 million for any given company. After a string of successful years of superior relative performance, May expanded its client base significantly, to the point at which assets under management now exceed $3 billion. For liquidity purposes, May's chief investment officer (CIO) decides to lift the maximum permissible market-cap ceiling to $500 million and change the firm's sales and marketing literature accordingly to inform prospective clients and third-party consultants.

Comment:

Although May's CIO is correct about informing potentially interested parties as to the change in investment process, he must also notify May's existing clients. Among the latter group might be a number of clients who not only retained May as a small-cap manager but also retained mid-cap and large-cap specialists in a multiple-manager approach. Such clients could regard May's change of criteria as a style change that could distort their overall asset allocations.

Example 4:

Rather than lifting the ceiling for its universe from $250 million to $500 million, May & Associates extends its small-cap universe to include a number of non-U.S. companies.

Comment:

Standard V(B) requires that May's CIO advise May's clients of this change because the firm may have been retained by some clients specifically for its prowess at investing in domestic small-cap stocks. Other variations requiring client notification include introducing derivatives to emulate a certain market sector or relaxing various other constraints, such as portfolio beta. In all such cases, members and candidates must disclose changes to all interested parties.

Example 5:

A member sends a report to his investment management firm's clients describing a strategy his firm offers in terms of the high returns it will generate in the event interest rate volatility decreases. The report does not provide details of the strategy because they are deemed proprietary. The report does not consider the possible returns if interest rate volatility actually increases.

Comment:

This is a violation on two counts. The basic nature of the strategy must be disclosed, including the extent to which leverage is used to generate the high returns when volatility falls. Further, the report must include how the strategy will perform if volatility rises, as well as if it falls.

Example 6:

A member's firm changes from its old equity selection model, which is based on price-sales ratios, to a new model based on several factors, including future earnings growth rates, but does not inform clients of this change.

Comment:

This is a violation because members must inform their clients of any significant change in their investment process. Here, the introduction of forecast data on earnings growth can be viewed as a significant change since the old single-variable model was based on reported rather than forecast data.

Example 7:

A member's firm, in response to poor results relative to its stated benchmark, decides to structure portfolios to passively track the benchmark and does not inform clients.

Comment:

This is a significant change in the investment process and must be communicated to clients.

Example 8:

At a firm where individual portfolio managers have been responsible for security selection, a new policy is implemented whereby only stocks on an approved list constructed by the firm's senior managers may be purchased in client accounts. A member who is a portfolio manager does not inform his clients.

Comment:

This is a violation of the Standard because it represents a significant change in the investment process.

 Professor's Note: Remember, the argument that clients "won't care" about a process change can be turned around to "there's no reason not to disclose the change."

V(C) **Record Retention.** Members and Candidates must develop and maintain appropriate records to support their investment analysis, recommendations, actions, and other investment-related communications with clients and prospective clients.

Guidance

Members must maintain research records that support the reasons for the analyst's conclusions and any investment actions taken. Such records are the property of the firm. If no other regulatory standards are in place, CFA Institute recommends at least a 7-year holding period.

Recommended Procedures for Compliance

This record-keeping requirement generally is the firm's responsibility.

Application of Standard V(C) Record Retention

Example 1:

One of Nikolas Lindstrom's clients is upset by the negative investment returns in his equity portfolio. The investment policy statement for the client requires that the portfolio manager follow a benchmark-oriented approach. The benchmark for the client included a 35% investment allocation in the technology sector, which the client acknowledged was appropriate. Over the past three years, the portion put into the segment of technology stocks suffered severe losses. The client complains to the investment manager that so much money was allocated to this sector.

Comment:

For Lindstrom, it is important to have appropriate records to show that over the past three years the percentage of technology stocks in the benchmark index was 35%. Therefore, the amount of money invested in the technology sector was appropriate according to the investment policy statement. Lindstrom should also have the investment policy statement for the client stating that the benchmark was appropriate for the client's investment objectives. He should also have records indicating that the investment had been explained appropriately to the client and that the investment policy statement was updated on a regular basis.

Example 2:

A member bases his research reports on interviews, his own analysis, and industry reports from third parties on his industry and related industries.

Comment:

The member must keep records of all the information that went into the research on which his reports and recommendations are based.

Example 3:

When a member leaves a firm at which he has developed a complex trading model, he takes documentation of the model assumptions and how they were derived over time with him, since he will use the model at his new firm.

Comment:

Taking these materials without permission from his previous employer is a violation of his duties to his (previous) employer. While he may use knowledge of the model at the new firm, the member must recreate the supporting documents. The originals are the property of the firm where he worked on developing the model.

VI   Conflicts of Interest

VI(A)   Disclosure of Conflicts. Members and Candidates must make full and fair disclosure of all matters that could reasonably be expected to impair their independence and objectivity or interfere with respective duties to their clients, prospective clients, and employer. Members and Candidates must ensure that such disclosures are prominent, are delivered in plain language, and communicate the relevant information effectively.

Guidance

Members must fully disclose to clients, prospects, and their employers all actual and potential conflicts of interest in order to protect investors and employers. These disclosures must be clearly stated.

Guidance—Disclosure to Clients

The requirement that all potential areas of conflict be disclosed allows clients and prospects to judge motives and potential biases for themselves. Disclosure of broker/dealer market-making activities would be included here. Board service is another area of potential conflict.

The most common conflict which requires disclosure is actual ownership of stock in companies that the member recommends or that clients hold.

Guidance—Disclosure of Conflicts to Employers

Members must give the employer enough information to judge the impact of the conflict. Take reasonable steps to avoid conflicts, and report them promptly if they occur.

Recommended Procedures of Compliance

Any special compensation arrangements, bonus programs, commissions, and incentives should be disclosed.

Application of Standard VI(A) Disclosure of Conflicts

Example 1:

Hunter Weiss is a research analyst with Farmington Company, a broker and investment banking firm. Farmington's merger and acquisition department has represented Vimco, a conglomerate, in all of its acquisitions for 20 years. From time to time, Farmington officers sit on the boards of directors of various Vimco subsidiaries. Weiss is writing a research report on Vimco.

Comment:

Weiss must disclose in his research report Farmington's special relationship with Vimco. Broker/dealer management of and participation in public offerings must be disclosed in research reports. Because the position of underwriter to a company presents a special past and potential future relationship with a company that is the subject of investment advice, it threatens the independence and objectivity of the report and must be disclosed.

Example 2:

Samantha Dyson, a portfolio manager for Thomas Investment Counsel, Inc., specializes in managing defined-benefit pension plan accounts, all of which are in the accumulative phase and have long-term investment objectives. A year ago, Dyson's employer, in an attempt to motivate and retain key investment professionals, introduced a bonus compensation system that rewards portfolio managers on the basis of quarterly performance relative to their peers and certain benchmark indexes. Dyson changes her investment strategy and purchases several high-beta stocks for client portfolios in an attempt to improve short-term performance. These purchases are seemingly contrary to the client investment policy statement. Now, an officer of Griffin Corporation, one of Dyson's pension fund clients, asks why Griffin Corporation's portfolio seems to be dominated by high-beta stocks of companies that often appear among the most actively traded issues. No change in objective or strategy has been recommended by Dyson during the year.

Comment:

Dyson violated Standard VI(A) by failing to inform her clients of the changes in her compensation arrangement with her employer that created a conflict of interest. Firms may pay employees on the basis of performance, but pressure by Thomas Investment Counsel to achieve short-term performance goals is in basic conflict with the objectives of Dyson's accounts.

Example 3:

Bruce Smith covers East European equities for Marlborough investments, an investment management firm with a strong presence in emerging markets. While on a business trip to Russia, Smith learns that investing in Russian equity directly is difficult but that equity-linked notes that replicate the performance of the underlying Russian equity can be purchased from a New York-based investment bank. Believing that his firm would not be interested in such a security, Smith purchases a note linked to a Russian telecommunications company for his own account without informing Marlborough. A month later, Smith decides that the firm should consider investing in Russian equities using equity-linked notes, and he prepares a write-up on the market that concludes with a recommendation to purchase several of the notes. One note recommended is linked to the same Russian telecom company that Smith holds in his personal account.

Comment:

Smith violated Standard VI(A) by failing to disclose his ownership of the note linked to the Russian telecom company. Smith is required by the standard to disclose the investment opportunity to his employer and look to his company's policies on personal trading to determine whether it was proper for him to purchase the note for his own account. By purchasing the note, Smith may or may not have impaired his ability to make an unbiased and objective assessment of the appropriateness of the derivative instrument for his firm, but Smith's failure to disclose the purchase to his employer impaired his employer's ability to render an opinion regarding whether the ownership of a security constituted a conflict of interest that might have affected future recommendations. Once he recommended the notes to his firm, Smith compounded his problems by not disclosing that he owned the notes in his personal account—a clear conflict of interest.

Example 4:

An investment management partnership sells a significant stake to a firm that is publicly traded. The partnership has added the firm's stock to its recommended list and approved its commercial paper for cash management accounts.

Comment:

Members are required to disclose such a change in firm ownership to all clients. Further, any transactions in client accounts involving the securities of the public firm, and any recommendations concerning the public firm's securities, must include a disclosure of the business relation between it and the partnership.

Example 5:

A member provides clients with research about a company's stock, and his wife inherits a significant amount of stock in the company.

Comment:

The member must disclose this potential conflict to his employer and in any subsequent reports or recommendations he authors. His employer may prudently choose to reassign the stock.

Example 6:

A member's investment banking firm receives a significant number of options as partial compensation for bringing a firm public. The member will profit personally from a portion of these options as well.

Comment:

In any research report on the public firm's securities, the member must disclose the fact that these options exist and include their number and the expiration date(s). Since he will profit personally from these, he must also disclose the extent of his participation in these options.

Example 7:

A member accepts an offer from a stock promoter who will provide additional compensation when the member sells Acme stock to his clients. He does not inform his clients or his employer.

Comment:

The member is in violation of the Standard because he must disclose this additional compensation to those clients to whom he recommends the stock and to his employer. Both have a right to determine for themselves the extent to which this additional compensation might affect the member's objectivity.

Example 8:

A member who is a portfolio manager for a small investment management firm serving individuals accepts a job as a trustee of an endowment fund that has over €1.5 billion in assets and does not disclose this to her employer.

Comment:

This is a significant position that may require a substantial portion of the member's time and may involve decisions on security selection and trading. The member is in violation of the Standard by not disclosing this involvement to her employer and by not discussing it with her employer before accepting the position.

> **VI(B)   Priority of Transactions.** Investment transactions for clients and employers must have priority over investment transactions in which a Member or Candidate is the beneficial owner.

Guidance

Client transactions take priority over personal transactions and over transactions made on behalf of the member's firm. Personal transactions include situations where the member is a "beneficial owner." Personal transactions may be undertaken only after clients and the member's employer have had an adequate opportunity to act on a recommendation. Note that family member accounts that are client accounts should be treated just like any client account; they should not be disadvantaged.

Recommended Procedures for Compliance

All firms should have in place basic procedures that address conflicts created by personal investing. The following areas should be included:

- Limited participation in equity IPOs. Members can avoid these conflicts by not participating in IPOs.
- Restrictions on private placements. Strict limits should be placed on employee acquisition of these securities and proper supervisory procedures should be in place. Participation in these investments raises conflict of interest issues, similar to IPOs.
- Establish blackout/restricted periods. Employees involved in investment decision-making should have blackout periods prior to trading for clients—no "front running" (i.e., purchase or sale of securities in advance of anticipated client or employer purchases and sales). The size of the firm and the type of security should help dictate how severe the blackout requirement should be.
- Reporting requirements. Supervisors should establish reporting procedures, including duplicate trade confirmations, disclosure of personal holdings/beneficial ownership positions, and preclearance procedures.
- Disclosure of policies. When requested, members must fully disclose to investors their firm's personal trading policies.

Application of Standard VI(B) Priority of Transactions

Example 1:

Erin Toffler, a portfolio manager at Esposito Investments, manages the retirement account established with the firm by her parents. Whenever IPOs become available, she first allocates shares to all her other clients for whom the investment is appropriate; only then does she place any remaining portion in her parents' account, if the issue is appropriate for them. She has adopted this procedure so that no one can accuse her of favoring her parents.

Comment:

Toffler has breached her duty to her parents by treating them differently from her other accounts simply because of the family relationship. As fee-paying clients of Esposito Investments, Toffler's parents are entitled to the same treatment as any other client of the firm. If Toffler has beneficial ownership in the account, however, and Esposito Investments has preclearance and reporting requirements for personal transactions, she may have to preclear the trades and report the transactions to Esposito.

Example 2:

A brokerage's insurance analyst, Denise Wilson, makes a closed-circuit report to her firm's branches around the country. During the broadcast, she includes negative comments about a major company within the industry. The following day, Wilson's report is printed and distributed to the sales force and public customers. The report recommends that both short-term traders and intermediate investors take profits by selling that company's stocks. Several minutes after the broadcast, Ellen Riley, head of the firm's trading department, closes out a long call position in the stock. Shortly thereafter, Riley establishes a sizable "put" position in the stock. Riley claims she took this action to facilitate anticipated sales by institutional clients.

Comment:

Riley expected that both the stock and option markets would respond to the "sell" recommendation, but she did not give customers an opportunity to buy or sell in the options market before the firm itself did. By taking action before the report was disseminated, Riley's firm could have depressed the price of the "calls" and increased the price of the "puts." The firm could have avoided a conflict of interest if it had waited to trade for its own account until its clients had an opportunity to receive and assimilate Wilson's recommendations. As it is, Riley's actions violated Standard VI(B).

Example 3:

A member who is a research analyst does not recommend a stock to his employer because he wants to purchase it quickly for his personal account.

Comment:

He has violated the priority of transactions by withholding this information from his employer and seeking to profit personally at his employer's expense. The member has likely violated his duty to his employer under Standard IV(A) Loyalty as well.

Example 4:

A member who manages a fund gets hot IPO shares for her husband's account from syndicate firms, even when the fund is unable to get shares.

Comment:

The member has violated the Standard by this action. She must act in the interest of the shareholders of the fund and place allocated shares there first. She must also inform her employer of her participation in these offerings through her beneficial interest in her husband's account(s).

Example 5:

A member allows an employee to continue his duties without having signed a required report of his personal trading activity over the last three months. The employee, a CFA candidate, has been purchasing securities for his own account just before firm buy recommendations have been released.

Comment:

The employee has violated the Standard. The member has also violated Standard IV(C) Responsibilities of Supervisors by allowing the employee to continue in his regular duties.

Example 6:

A member reveals a sell rating on some securities in a broadcast to all of her firm's brokers. The changed rating is sent to clients the next day. Shortly after revealing the change to her firm's brokers and prior to dissemination to clients, she buys puts on the stock for her firm's account.

Comment:

The member did not give clients adequate opportunity to act on the change in recommendation before buying the puts for her firm's account.

VI(C)   Referral Fees. Members and Candidates must disclose to their employer, clients, and prospective clients, as appropriate, any compensation, consideration, or benefit received by, or paid to, others for the recommendation of products or services.

Guidance

Members must inform employers, clients, and prospects of any benefit received for referrals of customers and clients, allowing them to evaluate the full cost of the service as well as any potential impartiality. All types of consideration must be disclosed.

Application of Standard VI(C) Referral Fees

Example 1:

Brady Securities, Inc., a broker/dealer, has established a referral arrangement with Lewis Brothers, Ltd., an investment counseling firm. Under this arrangement, Brady Securities refers all prospective tax-exempt accounts, including pension, profit-sharing, and endowment accounts, to Lewis Brothers. In return, Lewis Brothers makes available to Brady Securities on a regular basis the security recommendations and reports of its research staff, which registered representatives of Brady Securities use in serving customers. In addition, Lewis Brothers conducts monthly economic and market reviews for Brady Securities personnel and directs all stock commission business generated by referral account to Brady Securities. Willard White, a partner in Lewis Brothers, calculates that the incremental costs involved in functioning as the research department of Brady Securities amount to $20,000 annually. Referrals from Brady Securities last year resulted in fee income of $200,000, and directing all stock trades through Brady Securities resulted in additional costs to Lewis Brothers' clients of $10,000.

Diane Branch, the chief financial officer of Maxwell, Inc., contacts White and says that she is seeking an investment manager for Maxwell's profit-sharing plan. She adds, "My friend Harold Hill at Brady Securities recommended your firm without qualification, and that's good enough for me. Do we have a deal?" White accepts the new account but does not disclose his firm's referral arrangement with Brady Securities.

Comment:

White violated Standard VI(C) by failing to inform the prospective customer of the referral fee payable in services and commissions for an indefinite period to Brady Securities. Such disclosure could have caused Branch to reassess Hill's recommendation and make a more critical evaluation of Lewis Brothers' services.

Example 2:

James Handley works for the Trust Department of Central Trust Bank. He receives compensation for each referral he makes to Central Trust's brokerage and personal financial management department that results in a sale. He refers several of his clients to the personal financial management department but does not disclose the arrangement within Central trust to his clients.

Comment:

Handley has violated Standard VI(C) by not disclosing the referral arrangement at Central Trust Bank to his clients. The Standard does not distinguish between referral fees paid by a third party for referring clients to the third party and internal compensation arrangements paid within the firm to attract new business to a subsidiary. Members and candidates must disclose all such referral fees. Therefore, Handley would be required to disclose, at the time of referral, any referral fee agreement in place between Central Trust Bank's departments. The disclosure should include the nature and the value of the benefit and should be made in writing.

Example 3:

Yeshao Wen is a portfolio manager for a bank. He receives additional monetary compensation from his employer when he is successful in assisting in the sales process and generation of assets under management. The assets in question will be invested in proprietary product offerings such as affiliate company mutual funds.

Comment:

Standard VI(C) is meant to address instances where the investment advice provided by a member or candidate appears to be objective and independent but in fact is influenced by an unseen referral arrangement. It is not meant to cover compensation by employers to employees for generating new business when it would be obvious to potential clients that the employees are "referring" potential clients to the services of their employers.

If Wen is selling the bank's investment management services in general, he does not need to disclose to potential clients that he will receive a bonus for finding new clients and acquiring new assets under management for the bank. Potential clients are likely aware that it would be financially beneficial both to the portfolio manager and the manager's firm for the portfolio manager to sell the services of the firm and attract new clients. Therefore, sales efforts attempting to attract new investment management clients need not disclose this fact.

However, in this example, the assets will be managed in "proprietary product offerings" of the manager's company (for example, an in-house mutual fund) and Wen will receive additional compensation for selling firm products. Some sophisticated investors may realize that it would be financially beneficial to the portfolio manager and the manager's firm if the investor buys the product offerings of the firm. Best practice, however, dictates that the portfolio manager must disclose to clients that he is compensated for referring clients to firm products. Such disclosure will meet the purpose of Standard VI(C), which is to allow investors to determine whether there is any partiality on the part of the portfolio manager when giving investment advice.

VII   Responsibilities as a CFA Institute Member or CFA Candidate

VII(A) Conduct as Members and Candidates in the CFA Program. Members and Candidates must not engage in any conduct that compromises the reputation or integrity of CFA Institute or the CFA designation or the integrity, validity, or security of the CFA examinations.

 Professor's Note: The Standard is intended to cover conduct such as cheating on the CFA exam or otherwise violating rules of CFA Institute or the CFA program. It is not intended to prevent anyone from expressing any opinions or beliefs concerning CFA Institute or the CFA program.

Members must not engage in any activity that undermines the integrity of the CFA charter. This Standard applies to conduct which includes:

- Cheating on the CFA exam or any exam.
- Not following rules and policies of the CFA program.
- Giving confidential information on the CFA program to Candidates or the public.
- Improperly using the designation to further personal and professional goals.
- Misrepresenting information on the Professional Conduct Statement (PCS) or the CFA Institute Professional Development Program.

Members and candidates are not precluded from expressing their opinions regarding the exam program or CFA Institute.

Application of Standard VII(A) Conduct as Members and Candidates in the CFA Program

Example 1:

Ashlie Hocking is writing Level II of the CFA examination in London. After completing the exam, she immediately attempts to contact her friend in Sydney, Australia, to tip him off to specific questions on the exam.

Comment:

Hocking has violated Standard VII(A) by attempting to give her friend an unfair advantage, thereby compromising the integrity of the CFA examination process.

Example 2:

Jose Ramirez is an investment-relations consultant for several small companies that are seeking greater exposure to investors. He is also the program chair for the CFA Institute society in the city where he works. To the exclusion of other companies, Ramirez only schedules companies that are his clients to make presentations to the society.

Comment:

Ramirez, by using his volunteer position at CFA Institute to benefit himself and his clients, compromises the reputation and integrity of CFA Institute and, thus, violates Standard VII(A).

Example 3:

A member who is an exam grader discusses with friends the guideline answer for and relative candidate performance on a specific question he graded on the CFA exam.

Comment:

He has violated his Grader's Agreement and also the Standard by compromising the integrity of the CFA exam.

Example 4:

A candidate does not stop writing when asked to by the proctor at the CFA exam.

Comment:

By taking additional time compared to other candidates, this candidate has violated the Standard, compromising the integrity of the exam process.

Example 5:

A member who is a volunteer on a CFA Institute committee tells her clients that what she learns through her committee work will allow her to better serve their interests.

Comment:

She has violated the Standard by using her CFA committee position to benefit herself personally and to any extent her 'inside' knowledge has benefited her clients.

VII(B) Reference to CFA Institute, the CFA designation, and the CFA Program. When referring to CFA Institute, CFA Institute membership, the CFA designation, or candidacy in the CFA Program, Members and Candidates must not misrepresent or exaggerate the meaning or implications of membership in CFA Institute, holding the CFA designation, or candidacy in the CFA Program.

Guidance

Members must not make promotional promises or guarantees tied to the CFA designation. Do not:

- Over-promise individual competence.
- Over-promise investment results in the future (i.e., higher performance, less risk, etc.).

Guidance—CFA Institute Membership

Members must satisfy these requirements to maintain membership:

- Sign PCS annually.
- Pay CFA Institute membership dues annually.

If they fail to do this, they are no longer active members.

Guidance—Using the CFA Designation

Do not misrepresent or exaggerate the meaning of the designation.

Guidance—Referencing Candidacy in the CFA Program

There is no partial designation. It is acceptable to state that a Candidate successfully completed the program in three years, if in fact they did, but claiming superior ability because of this is not permitted.

Guidance—Proper Usage of the CFA Marks

The Chartered Financial Analyst and CFA marks must always be used either after a charterholder's name or as adjectives, but not as nouns, in written and oral communications.

Recommended Procedures for Compliance

Make sure that members' and candidates' firms are aware of the proper references to a member's CFA designation or candidacy, as this is a common error.

Application of Standard VII(B) Reference to CFA Institute, the CFA Designation, and the CFA Program

Example 1:

An advertisement for AZ Investment Advisors states that all the firm's principals are CFA charterholders and all passed the three examinations on their first attempt. The advertisement prominently links this fact to the notion that AZ's mutual funds have achieved superior performance.

Comment:

AZ may state that all principals passed the three examinations on the first try as long as this statement is true and is not linked to performance or does not imply superior ability. Implying that (1) CFA charterholders achieve better investment results and (2) those who pass the exams on the first try may be more successful than those who do not violates Standard VII(B).

Example 2:

Five years after receiving his CFA charter, Louis Vasseur resigns his position as an investment analyst and spends the next two years traveling abroad. Because he is not actively engaged in the investment profession, he does not file a completed Professional Conduct Statement with CFA Institute and does not pay his CFA Institute membership dues. At the conclusion of his travels, Vasseur becomes a self-employed analyst, accepting assignments as an independent contractor. Without reinstating his CFA Institute membership by filing his Professional Conduct Statement and paying his dues, he prints business cards that display "CFA" after his name.

Comment:

Vasseur has violated Standard VII(B) because Vasseur's right to use the CFA designation was suspended when he failed to file his Professional Conduct Statement and stopped paying dues. Therefore, he no longer is able to state or imply that he is an active CFA charterholder. When Vasseur files his Professional Conduct Statement and resumes paying CFA Institute dues to activate his membership, he will be eligible to use the CFA designation upon satisfactory completion of CFA Institute reinstatement procedures.

Example 3:

A member still uses the initials CFA after his name even though his membership has been suspended for not paying dues and for not submitting a personal conduct statement as required.

Comment:

This is a violation of the Standard.

Example 4:

A member puts the CFA logo on his letterhead, his business cards, and the company letterhead.

Comment:

By putting the logo on the company letterhead (rather than the letterhead or business card of an individual who is a CFA charterholder), the member has violated the Standard.

INTRODUCTION TO THE GLOBAL INVESTMENT PERFORMANCE STANDARDS (GIPS®)

Study Session 1

EXAM FOCUS

The following two topic reviews cover the key features of the Global Investment Performance Standards (GIPS®) as adopted by CFA Institute in 1999 and subsequently updated. Compliance with GIPS is voluntary. For the Level 1 exam you are responsible for only the "Introduction to the Global Investment Performance Standards (GIPS®)" and the Preface, Section I, and Section II (through II.0: Fundamentals of Compliance) of the GIPS document. The GIPS document is included in the book of candidate readings for Level 1 and is also available on the CFA Institute Web site. A helpful glossary of terms is included in the document. Candidates should not underestimate the importance of this material for the exam.

LOS 3.a: Explain why the GIPS standards were created, what parties the GIPS standards apply to, and who is served by the standards.

In the past, a variety of reporting procedures were misleading at best. Some of these misleading practices included:

- *Representative accounts*—showing a top-performing portfolio as representative of firm's results.
- *Survivorship bias*—excluding "weak performance" accounts that have been terminated.
- *Varying time periods*—showing performance for selected time periods with outstanding returns.

GIPS are a set of ethical principles based on a standardized, industry-wide approach. Investment firms can *voluntarily* follow GIPS in their presentation of historical investment results to prospective clients. These standards seek to avoid misrepresentations of performance.

GIPS apply to investment management firms and are intended to serve prospective and existing clients of investment firms. GIPS allow clients to more easily compare investment performance among investment firms and have more confidence in reported performance.

LOS 3.b: Explain the construction and purpose of composites in performance reporting.

A composite is a grouping of individual discretionary portfolios representing a similar investment strategy, objective, or mandate. Examples of possible composites are "Large Capitalization Growth Stocks" and "Investment Grade Domestic Bonds." Reporting on the performance of composites gives clients and prospects information about the firm's success in managing various types of securities or results for various investment styles.

A composite, such as International Equities, must include all portfolios (current and past) that the firm has managed in accordance with this particular strategy. The firm should identify which composite each managed portfolio is to be included in before the portfolio's performance is known. This prevents firms from choosing portfolios to include in a composite in order to create composites with superior returns.

LOS 3.c: Explain the requirements for verification of compliance with GIPS standards.

Verification—requirements:

Verification is performed by a third party, not by the firm itself, on a firm-wide basis. This third party verifier must attest that (1) the firm has complied with all GIPS requirements for composite construction on a firm-wide basis and (2) the firm's processes and procedures are established to present performance in accordance with the calculation methodology required by GIPS, the data requirements of GIPS, and in the format required by GIPS.

Verification—recommendations:

- Firms are encouraged to pursue independent verification. Verification applies to the entire firm's performance measurement practices and methods, not a selected composite.
- Verified firms should include the following disclosure language:

    "[Insert name of firm] has been verified for the periods [insert dates] by [name of verifier]. A copy of the verification report is available upon request."

GLOBAL INVESTMENT PERFORMANCE STANDARDS (GIPS®)

Study Session 1

LOS 4.a: Describe the key characteristics of the GIPS standards and the fundamentals of compliance.

GIPS Objectives

- To obtain global acceptance of calculation and presentation standards in a fair, comparable format with full disclosure.
- To ensure consistent, accurate investment performance data in areas of reporting, records, marketing, and presentations.
- To promote fair competition among investment management firms in all markets without unnecessary entry barriers for new firms.
- To promote global "self regulation."

Key Characteristics of GIPS

- To claim compliance, an investment management firm must define its "firm." This definition should reflect the "distinct business entity" that is held out to clients and prospects as the investment firm.
- GIPS are ethical standards for performance presentation which ensure fair representation of results and full disclosure.
- Include all actual fee-paying, discretionary portfolios in composites for a minimum of five years or since firm or composite inception. After presenting five years of compliant data, the firm must add annual performance each year going forward up to a minimum of ten years.
- Firms are required to use certain calculation and presentation standards and make specific disclosures.
- Input data must be accurate.
- GIPS contain both *required* and *recommended* provisions—firms are *encouraged* to adopt the *recommended* provisions.
- Firms are encouraged to present all pertinent additional and supplemental information.
- There will be no partial compliance and only full compliance can be claimed.
- Follow the local laws for cases in which a local or country-specific law or regulation conflicts with GIPS, but disclose the conflict.
- Certain "recommendations" may become "requirements" in the future.
- Supplemental "private equity" and "real estate" provisions contained in GIPS are to be applied to those asset classes.

Study Session 1
Cross-Reference to CFA Institute Assigned Reading #4 – Global Investment Performance Standards (GIPS®)

Study Session 1

Fundamentals of compliance contain both requirements and recommendations:

Definition of the firm—requirements:

- Apply GIPS on a firm-wide basis.
- Firm must be defined as a distinct business unit.
- Total firm assets includes total market value of discretionary and non-discretionary assets, including fee-paying and non-fee-paying accounts.
- Include asset performance of sub-advisors, as long as the firm has discretion over sub-advisor selection.
- If a firm changes its organization, historical composite results cannot be changed.

Definition of the firm—recommendations:

- Include the broadest definition of the firm, including all geographical offices marketed under the same brand name.

Document policies and procedures—requirements:

- Document, in writing, policies and procedures the firm uses to comply with GIPS.

Claim of compliance—requirements:

- Once GIPS requirements have been met, the following compliance statement must be used:

  "[Insert name of firm] has prepared and presented this report in compliance with the Global Investment Performance Standards (GIPS®)."

- There is no such thing as partial compliance.
- There are to be no statements referring to calculation methodologies used in a composite presentation as being "in accordance with GIPS" or the like.
- Similarly, there should be no such statements referring to the performance of an individual, existing client as being "calculated in accordance with GIPS" or the like, unless a compliant firm is reporting results directly to the client.

Firm fundamental responsibilities—requirements:

- Firms must provide a compliant presentation to *all* prospects (prospect must have received a presentation within the previous 12 months).
- Provide a composite list and composite description to all prospects that make a request. List discontinued composites for at least five years.
- Provide, to clients requesting it, a compliant presentation and a composite description for any composite included on the firm's list.
- When jointly marketing with other firms, if one of the firms claims GIPS compliance, be sure it is clearly defined as separate from noncompliant firms.
- Firms are encouraged to comply with recommendations and must comply with all requirements. Be aware of updates, guidance statements, and the like.

LOS 4.b: Describe the scope of the GIPS standards with respect to an investment firm's definition and historical performance record.

The definition of the firm, for purposes of GIPS compliance, must be the corporation, subsidiary, or division that is held out to clients as a business entity. If a firm has different geographic locations (e.g., all doing business under the name of Bluestone Advisers), then the definition of the firm should include all the various geographic locations and their clients. Firms based in any country may present GIPS compliant performance histories.

A firm must initially present a minimum of five years of compliant performance presentation for the firm and each composite unless the firm or composite has been in existence less than five years. For firms or composites in existence less than five years, compliant performance since inception must be presented in order to claim compliance. After the initial compliant performance presentation, one year of compliant performance must be added each year to a required (minimum) performance history of ten years.

Firms may present periods of noncompliant performance immediately prior to the compliant performance history as long as no noncompliant performance is presented for any periods after January 1, 2000. Firms must specify which performance results are noncompliant and the ways in which such (noncompliant) performance does not comply with GIPS.

LOS 4.c: Explain how the GIPS standards are implemented in countries with existing standards for performance reporting and describe the appropriate response when the GIPS standards and local regulations conflict.

Firms that previously presented performance in compliance with a particular Country Version of GIPS (CVG) may claim GIPS compliance for any CVG-compliant results prior to January 1, 2006. Firms that report such CVG-compliant performance data must continue to include that performance data in subsequent GIPS-compliant presentations until a minimum of ten years of compliant performance is presented.

In any cases where country-specific regulations conflict with GIPS, firms must follow the applicable country-specific regulations but must also disclose the nature of the conflict with GIPS.

LOS 4.d: Characterize the eight major sections of the GIPS standards.

0. *Fundamentals of compliance.* The fundamental issues involved in complying with GIPS are (a) definition of the firm, (b) documentation of firm policies and procedures with respect to GIPS compliance, (c) complying with GIPS updates, (d) claiming compliance in the appropriate manner, and (e) appropriate verification statement when a third-party verifier is employed.

Study Session 1
Cross-Reference to CFA Institute Assigned Reading #4 – Global Investment Performance Standards (GIPS®)

Study Session 1

1. *Input data.* Input data should be consistent in order to establish full, fair, and comparable investment performance presentations.

2. *Calculation methodology.* Certain methodologies are required for portfolio return calculations and certain other methodologies are required for composite return calculations. Uniformity in methods across firms is required so that their results are comparable.

3. *Composite construction.* Creation of meaningful, asset-weighted composites is important to achieve a fair presentation. Composite performance is based on the performance of one or more portfolios that have the same investment strategy or investment objective. Composite returns are the asset-weighted average (not a simple average) of the returns on the portfolios that are included in each composite.

4. *Disclosures.* The firm must disclose information about the presentation and the policies adopted by the firm so that the raw numbers presented in the report are understandable to the user. There are some disclosures that all firms must make, but some disclosures may not apply to all firms. If a disclosure is not applicable to a specific firm, the firm is not required to include any statement regarding it.

5. *Presentation and reporting.* Investment performance must be presented according to GIPS requirements. Other firm-specific information not specifically required by GIPS should be included when appropriate.

6. *Real estate.* Certain provisions apply to all real estate investments (land, buildings, etc.) regardless of the level of control the firm has over management of the investment. These provisions apply regardless of whether the asset is producing revenue or there is leverage involved in the investment.

7. *Private equity.* Private equity investments must be valued according to the GIPS Private Equity Valuation Principles, which are contained in Appendix D, unless the investment is an open-end or evergreen fund (which must follow regular GIPS). Private equity investments include all investment in companies that are not publicly traded, regardless of their stage of business development. This would include venture capital investments, ownership of a previously public company that has been purchased (taken private), and mezzanine financing, as well as limited partnership shares in such investments and fund-of-funds investments.

Once a firm claims GIPS compliance, the firm has an option to hire an independent third party to verify the claim of compliance.

The purpose of verification is to provide assurance that compliance has been adhered to on a firm-wide basis. Verification adds credibility.

50 questions: 1 hour 40 minutes

1. Jamie Hutchins, CFA, is a portfolio manager for CNV Investments Inc. Over the years, Hutchins has made several poor personal investments that have led to financial distress and personal bankruptcy. Hutchins feels that her business partner, John Smith, is mostly to blame for her situation since "he did not invest enough money in her investment opportunities and caused them to fail." Hutchins reports Smith to CFA Institute claiming Smith violated the Code and Standards relating to misconduct. Which of the following statements is *most likely* correct?
   A. By reporting Smith to CFA Institute, Hutchins has misused the Professional Conduct Program, thus violating the Code and Standards, but her poor investing and bankruptcy have not violated the Code and Standards.
   B. Hutchins' bankruptcy reflects poorly on her professional reputation and thus violates the Code and Standards, but her reporting of Smith does not.
   C. Hutchins' poor investing and bankruptcy, as well as her reporting of Smith, are both violations of the Standards.

2. While working on a new underwriting project, Jean Brayman, CFA, has just received information from her client that leads her to believe that the firm's financial statements in the registration statement overstate the firm's financial position. Brayman should:
   A. report her finding to the appropriate governmental regulatory authority.
   B. immediately dissociate herself from the underwriting in writing to the client.
   C. seek advice from her firm's compliance department as to the appropriate action to take.

3. Karen Jones, CFA, is an outside director for Valley Manufacturing. At a director's meeting, Jones finds out that Valley Corp. has made several contributions to foreign politicians that she suspects were illegal. Jones checks with her firm's legal counsel and determines that the contributions were indeed illegal. At the next board meeting Jones urges the board to disclose the contributions. The board, however, votes not to make a disclosure. Jones' *most appropriate* action would be to:
   A. protest the board's actions in writing to the executive officer of Valley.
   B. resign from the board and seek legal counsel as to her legal disclosure requirements.
   C. inform her supervisor of her discovery and cease attending meetings until the matter is resolved.

4. Carrie Carlson, CFA, is a citizen of Emerging Market Country (EMC) with no securities laws governing the use of material nonpublic information. Carlson has clients in Emerging Market Country and in Neighboring Country (NC), which has a few poorly defined laws governing the use of material nonpublic information. If Carlson has material nonpublic information on a publicly traded security, she:
   A. can inform her clients in EMC, but not NC.
   B. can use the information for her NC clients to the extent permitted by the laws of NC.
   C. cannot use the information to trade in either EMC or NC.

5. In order to dispel the myth that emerging market stocks are illiquid investments, Green Brothers, a "long only" emerging market fund manager, has two of its subsidiaries simultaneously buy and sell emerging market stocks. In its marketing literature, Green Brothers cites the overall emerging market volume as evidence of the market's liquidity. As a result of its actions, more investors participate in the emerging markets fund. Which of the following is *most likely* correct? Green Brothers:
   A. did not violate the Code and Standards.
   B. violated the Code and Standards by manipulating the volume in the emerging securities markets.
   C. would not have violated the Code and Standards if the subsidiaries only traded stocks not included in the fund.

6. Over the past two days, Lorraine Quigley, CFA, manager of a hedge fund, has been purchasing large quantities of Craeger Industrial Products' common stock while at the same time shorting put options on the same stock. Quigley did not notify her clients of the trades although they are aware of the fund's general strategy to generate returns. Which of the following statements is *most likely* correct? Quigley:
   A. did not violate the Code and Standards.
   B. violated the Code and Standards by manipulating the prices of publicly traded securities.
   C. violated the Code and Standards by failing to disclose the transactions to clients before they occurred.

7. Which of the following statements is *least likely* correct? A member or candidate:
   A. can participate or assist in a violation simply by having knowledge of the violation and not taking action to stop it.
   B. is held responsible for participating in illegal acts in instances where violation of the law is evident to those who know or should know the law.
   C. must report evidence of legal violations to the appropriate governmental or regulatory organization.

8. Paula Osgood, CFA, is promoting her new money management firm by issuing an advertisement. Which of these items is *least likely* a violation of the professional designation Standard? The advertisement states that:
   A. she passed three exams covering ethics, financial statement analysis, asset valuation, and portfolio management, and that she is a member of the local society. Osgood signs the advertisement followed by the letters CFA in oversized and bold strike letters.
   B. she passed three 6-hour exams on her first attempts over the minimum period of one and a half years. Knowledge tested included ethics, financial statement analysis, asset valuation, and portfolio management. In addition, she is a member of the local society.
   C. because of her extensive CFA training she will be able to achieve better investment results than non-CFA managers since she is one of very few professionals to have been awarded this designation.

9. Melvin Byrne, CFA, manages a portfolio for James Martin, a very wealthy client. Martin's portfolio is well diversified with a slight tilt toward capital appreciation. Martin requires very little income from the portfolio. Recently Martin's brother, Cliff, has become a client of Byrne. Byrne proceeds to invest Cliff's portfolio in a similar manner to James' portfolio based on the fact that both brothers have a similar lifestyle and are only two years apart in age. Which of the following statements is *most likely* correct? Byrne:
   A. violated the Code and Standards by knowingly creating a conflict of interest between James' and Cliff's portfolios.
   B. violated the Code and Standards by failing to determine Cliff's objectives and constraints prior to investing his portfolio.
   C. did not violate the Code and Standards.

10. In which of the following has the analyst *least likely* committed plagiarism?
   A. Julie Long takes performance projections and charts from a company she is researching, combines them with her own analysis, and publishes them under her own name.
   B. Bill Cooper finds a statistical table in the Federal Reserve Bulletin that supports the work he has done in his industry analysis and has his secretary include the table as part of his report without citing the source.
   C. Jan Niedfeldt gets a call from one of her fellow analysts stating that the analyst's research shows that XYZ Company is a buy. Niedfeldt calls up her major clients and tells them that her research shows XYZ is a buy.

11. In a marketing brochure, DNR Asset Managers presents the performance of several composite portfolios managed according to similar investment strategies. In constructing composites, the firm excludes individual portfolios with less than $1 million in assets, excludes terminated portfolios, and includes simulated results. DNR includes the following disclosure in the brochure: "Past performance is no guarantee of future results. Composites exclude portfolios under $1 million in assets and include results from simulated model portfolios with similar strategies." DNR's brochure:
    A. does not violate the Code and Standards.
    B. violates the Code and Standards by failing to include terminated portfolios in the performance presentation.
    C. violates the Code and Standards by excluding portfolios under $1 million from the composite performance presentation.

12. Connie Fletcher, CFA, works for a small money management firm that specializes in pension accounts. Recently, a friend asked her to act as an unpaid volunteer manager for the city's street sweep pension fund. As part of the position, the city would grant Fletcher a free parking space in front of her downtown office. Fletcher is considering the offer. Before she accepts, she should *most appropriately*:
    A. do nothing since this is a volunteer position.
    B. inform her current clients in writing and discuss the offer with her employer.
    C. disclose the details of the volunteer position to her employer and obtain written permission from her employer.

13. Which of the following statements about an investment supervisor's responsibilities is *least likely* correct? A supervisor:
    A. should bring an inadequate compliance system to the attention of management and recommend corrective action.
    B. is responsible for instructing those to whom he has delegated authority about methods to detect and prevent violations of the law and standards.
    C. need only report employee violations of the Code and Standards to upper management and provide a written warning to the employee to cease such activities.

14. Robert Blair, CFA, Director of Research, has had an ongoing battle with management about the adequacy of the firm's compliance system. Recently, it has come to Blair's attention that the firm's compliance procedures are inadequate in that they are not being monitored and not carefully followed. What should Blair *most appropriately* do?
    A. Resign from the firm unless the compliance system is strengthened and followed.
    B. Send his superior a memo outlining the problem.
    C. Decline in writing to continue to accept supervisory responsibility until reasonable compliance procedures are adopted.

15. Jack Schleifer, CFA, is an analyst for Brown Investment Managers (BIM). Schleifer has recently accepted an invitation to visit the facilities of ChemCo, a producer of chemical compounds used in a variety of industries. ChemCo offers to pay for Schleifer's accommodations in a penthouse suite at a luxury hotel and allow Schleifer to use the firm's private jet to travel to its three facilities located in New York, Hong Kong, and London. In addition, ChemCo offers two tickets to a formal high-society dinner in New York and a small desk clock with the ChemCo logo. Schleifer declines to use ChemCo's corporate jet or to allow the firm to pay for his accommodations but accepts the clock and the tickets to the dinner (which he discloses to his employer) since he will be able to market his firm's mutual funds to other guests at the dinner. Has Schleifer violated any CFA Institute Standards of Professional Conduct?
    A. Yes.
    B. No, since he is using the gifts accepted to benefit his employer's interests.
    C. No, since the gifts he accepted were fully disclosed in writing to his employer.

16. Based on the Standards of Professional Conduct, a financial analyst is *least likely* required to:
    A. report to his employer the receipt of gifts and additional compensation from clients.
    B. disclose the value of consideration to be received for referrals.
    C. pay for commercial transportation and lodging while visiting a company's headquarters.

17. Beth Anderson, CFA, is a portfolio manager for several wealthy clients including Reuben Carlyle. Anderson manages Carlyle's personal portfolio of stock and bond investments. Carlyle recently told Anderson that he is under investigation by the IRS for tax evasion related to his business, Carlyle Concrete (CC). After learning about the investigation, Anderson proceeds to inform a friend at a local investment bank so that they may withdraw their proposal to take CC public. Which of the following is *most likely* correct? Anderson:
    A. violated the Code and Standards by failing to maintain the confidentiality of her client's information.
    B. violated the Code and Standards by failing to detect and report the tax evasion to the proper authorities.
    C. did not violate the Code and Standards since the information she conveyed pertained to illegal activities on the part of her client.

18. Gail Stefano, CFA, an analyst for a U.S. brokerage firm that serves U.S. investors, researches public utilities in South American emerging markets. Stefano makes the following statement in a recent report: "Based on the fact that the South American utilities sector has seen rapid growth in new service orders, we expect that most companies in the sector will be able to convert the revenue increases into significant profits. We also believe the trend will continue for the next three to five years." The report goes on to describe the major risks of investing in this market, in particular the political and exchange rate instability associated with South American countries. Stefano's report:
    A. has not violated the Code and Standards.
    B. violated the Code and Standards by failing to properly distinguish factual information from opinions.
    C. violated the Code and Standards by failing to properly identify details related to the operations of South American utilities.

19. Which of the following is *least likely* a violation of Standard III(B), Fair Dealing?
    A. A firm makes investment recommendations and also manages a mutual fund. The firm routinely begins trading for the fund's account ten minutes before announcing recommendation changes to client accounts.
    B. After releasing a general recommendation to all clients, an analyst calls the firm's largest institutional clients to discuss the recommendation in more detail.
    C. A portfolio manager allocates IPO shares to her brother's fee-based retirement account only if some remain after allocating shares to all other client accounts.

20. Which of the following is *least likely* a violation of Standard VI(B), Priority of Transactions? An analyst:
    A. trades for her own account before her firm announces a change in a recommendation.
    B. trades for her son's trust account, which is not a firm account, on the day after her firm changes its buy/sell recommendation.
    C. takes a position for her own outside account in a stock one week after she published a buy recommendation for the stock.

21. Jamie Olson, CFA, has just started work as a trainee with Neuvo Management Corp., a small regional money management firm started six months ago. She has been told to make a few cold calls and round up some new clients. In which of the following statements has Olson *least likely* violated the Standards of Practice?
    A. "Sure, we can perform all the financial and investment services you need. We've consistently outperformed the market indexes and will continue to do so under our current management."
    B. "Sure, we can assist you with all the financial and investment services you need. If we don't provide the service in-house, we have arrangements with other full-service firms that I would be happy to tell you about."
    C. "Our firm has a long history of successful performance for our clients. While we can't guarantee future results, we do believe we will continue to benefit our clients."

22. Mary Herbst, CFA, a pension fund manager at GBH Investments, is reviewing some of FreeTime, Inc.'s pension fund activities over the past years. Which of the following actions related to FreeTime, Inc.'s pension fund is *least likely* to be a breach of her fiduciary duties?
    A. Paying higher-than-average brokerage fees to obtain research materials used in the management of other funds by the investment group.
    B. Trading with selected brokers so that the brokers will recommend GBH's managers to potential clients.
    C. Selectively choosing brokers for the quality of research provided for managing FreeTime's pension.

23. Eugene Nieder, CFA, has just accepted a new job as a quantitative analyst for Paschal Investments, LLP. Nieder developed a complex model while working for his previous employer and plans to recreate the model for Paschal. Nieder did not make copies of the model or any supporting documents since his employer refused to grant him permission to do so. Nieder will recreate the model from memory. Which of the following statements is *most likely* correct?
    A. Nieder can recreate the model without violating the Code and Standards as long as he also generates supporting documentation.
    B. Nieder can recreate the model without violating the Code and Standards without documentation if the model is modified from its original form.
    C. Nieder cannot recreate the model without violating the Code and Standards because it is the property of his former employer.

24. As part of an agreement with Baker Brokerage, Hern Investment Company, a money manager for individual clients, provides monthly emerging market overviews in exchange for prospective client referrals and European equity research from Baker. Clients and prospects of Hern are not made aware of the agreement, but clients unanimously rave about the high quality of the research provided by Baker. As a result of the research, many clients with non-discretionary accounts have earned substantial returns on their portfolios. Managers at Hern have also used the research to earn outstanding returns for the firm's discretionary accounts. Which of the following statements is *most likely* correct? Hern:
    A. has not violated the Code and Standards.
    B. has violated the Code and Standards by using third-party research in discretionary accounts.
    C. has violated the Code and Standards by failing to disclose the referral agreement with Baker.

25. Frist Investments, Inc. has just hired Michael Pulin to manage institutional portfolios, most of which are pension related. Pulin has just taken the Level III CFA exam and is awaiting his results. Pulin has more than 15 years of investment management experience with individual clients but has never managed an institutional portfolio. Pulin joined the CFA Institute as an affiliate member two years ago and is in good standing with the organization. Which of the following statements would be *most appropriate* for Frist to use in advertising Pulin as a new member of the firm? Pulin:
    A. has many years of investment experience which, along with his participation in the CFA program, will allow him to deliver superior investment performance relative to other managers.
    B. is a CFA Level III and passed the first two exams on the first attempt. He is an affiliate member of the CFA Institute. We expect him to become a regular member if he passes the Level III examination.
    C. is a Level III CFA candidate and has many years of excellent performance in the investment management industry. Pulin is an affiliate member of the CFA Institute and will be eligible to become a CFA charterholder and regular member if he passes the Level III CFA Exam.

26. Before joining Mitsui Ltd. as an analyst covering the electrical equipment manufacturing industry, Pam Servais, CFA, worked for Internet Security Systems (ISS) where she had access to nonpublic information. While at ISS, Servais learned of a severe environmental problem at two firms handling boron-based components. It is common knowledge that seven firms in the industry worldwide use the same boron handling technique. The two firms for which Servais has knowledge announced the problem last week and had immediate stock price declines of 11% and 17%, respectively. The other five firms have not made an announcement. Servais issues a report recommending Mitsui clients sell shares of the remaining five firms. Servais' issuance of this recommendation:
    A. is not a violation of CFA Institute Standards.
    B. is a violation of CFA Institute Standards because it fails to distinguish between opinion and fact.
    C. constitutes a violation of the Standard pertaining to the use of material nonpublic information.

27. Zanuatu, an island nation, does not have any regulations precluding the use of nonpublic information. Alfredo Romero has a friend and fellow CFA charterholder there with whom he has shared nonpublic information regarding firms outside of his industry. The information concerns several firms' internal earnings and cash flow projections. The friend may:
    A. trade on the information under the laws of Zanuatu, which govern her behavior.
    B. not trade on the information under CFA Institute Standards, which govern her behavior.
    C. trade on the information under CFA Institute Standards since the firms concerned are outside of Romero's industry.

28. Samantha Donovan, CFA, is an exam proctor for the Level II CFA exam. The day before the exam is to be administered, Donovan faxes a copy of one of the questions to two friends, James Smythe and Lynn Yeats, who are Level II candidates in the CFA program. Donovan, Smythe, and Yeats had planned the distribution of an exam question months in advance. Smythe used the fax to prepare for the exam. Yeats, however, had second thoughts and threw the fax away without looking at its contents. Which of the following statements is *most likely* correct?
    A. Smythe violated the Code and Standards, but Yeats did not.
    B. Donovan violated the Code and Standards, but Smythe did not.
    C. Donovan and Yeats both violated the Code and Standards.

29. Julia Green, CFA, has friends from her previous employer who have suggested that she receive information from them via an Internet chat room. In this way, she receives news about an exciting new product being developed by a firm in Singapore that has the potential to double the firm's revenue. The firm has not revealed any information regarding the product to the public. According to the Code and Standards, this information is:
    A. both material and nonpublic and Green may not trade on it in Singapore, but may trade on it elsewhere.
    B. both material and nonpublic and Green may not trade on it in any jurisdiction.
    C. public by virtue of its release in the chat room and Green may trade on it.

30. Sally Albright, CFA, works full-time for Frank & Company, an investment management firm, as a fixed-income security analyst. Albright has been asked by a business contact at KDG Enterprises to accept some analytical work from KDG on a consulting basis. The work would entail investigating potential distressed debt securities in the small-cap market. Albright should *most appropriately*:
    A. accept the work as long as she obtains consent to all the terms of the engagement from Frank & Company.
    B. not accept the work as it violates the Code and Standards by creating a conflict of interest.
    C. accept the work as long as she obtains written consent from KDG and does it on her own time.

31. Beth Bixby, CFA, uses a quantitative model to actively manage a portfolio of stocks with an objective of earning a greater return than the market. Over the last three years, the returns to a portfolio constructed using the model have been greater than the returns to the S&P index by between 2% and 4%. In promotional materials, Bixby states: "Through our complex quantitative approach, we select a portfolio that has similar risk to the S&P 500 Index but will receive a return between 2% and 4% greater than the index." This statement is:
    A. permissible since prior returns to the firm's model provide a reasonable and adequate basis for the promotional material.
    B. permissible since the statement describes the basic characteristics of the fund's risk and return objectives.
    C. not permissible since Bixby is misrepresenting the investment performance her firm can reasonably expect to achieve.

32. Josef Karloff, CFA, acts as liaison between Pinnacle Financial (an investment management firm) and Summit Inc. (an investment banking boutique specializing in penny stocks). When Summit underwrites an IPO, Karloff routinely has Pinnacle issue vague statements implying that the firm has cash flows, financial resources, and growth prospects that are better than is the case in reality. This action is a violation of the section of the Standards concerning:
    A. fair dealing.
    B. nonpublic information.
    C. misconduct.

33. Shane Matthews, CFA, is a principal at Carlson Brothers, a leading regional investment bank specializing in initial public offerings of small to mid-sized biotech firms. Just before many of the IPOs are offered to the general public, Matthews arranges for 10% of the shares of the firm going public to be distributed to management. This action is a violation of the Standard concerning:
    A. additional compensation.
    B. disclosure of conflicts of interest.
    C. fair dealing.

34. Will Hunter, CFA, is a portfolio manager at NV Asset Managers in Baltimore, which specializes in managing labor union pension fund accounts. A friend of Hunter's who is an investment banker asks Hunter to purchase shares in their new IPOs in order to support the price long enough for insiders to liquidate their holdings. Hunter realizes that the price of the shares will almost certainly fall dramatically after his buying support ceases. NV management "strongly suggests" that Hunter "not rock the boat" and honor the investment banker's request since NV has had a long-standing relationship with the investment bank. Hunter agrees to make the purchases. Hunter has:
    A. not violated the Code and Standards.
    B. violated the Code and Standards by attempting to distort prices.
    C. violated the Code and Standards by failing to place orders in the appropriate transaction priority.

35. Neiman Investment Co. receives brokerage business from Pick Asset Management in exchange for referring prospective clients to Pick. Pick advises clients—in writing at the time the relationship is established—of the nature of its arrangement with Neiman. With regard to this practice, Pick has:
    A. complied with the Code and Standards.
    B. violated the Code and Standards by failing to preserve the confidentiality of the agreement with Neiman.
    C. violated the Code and Standards by inappropriately negotiating an agreement that creates a conflict of interest.

36. Fred Johnson, CFA, a financial analyst and avid windsurfer, has begun an investment survey of the water sports leisure industry. His brother sells windsurfing gear in Tampa and tells him that Swordfish9 is the "hottest windsurfing rig on the market and will be highly profitable for Swordfish Enterprises." Johnson had never heard of Swordfish previously, but after testing the board himself became very excited about the Swordfish9 and issued an investment recommendation of "buy" on Swordfish Enterprises. As a result of issuing the recommendation, Johnson has:
    A. not violated the Code and Standards.
    B. violated the Code and Standards by failing to establish a reasonable and adequate basis.
    C. violated the Code and Standards by failing to consider the suitability of the investment for his clients.

37. Daniel Lyons, CFA, is an analyst for a French firm that sells investment research to European companies. Lyons' aunt owns 30,000 shares of French National Bank (FNB). She informs Lyons that as a part of her estate planning she has created a trust in his name into which she has placed 2,000 shares of FNB. The trust is structured so that Lyons will not receive control of the assets for two years, at which time his aunt will also gift her current home to Lyons and move into a retirement community. Lyons is due to update his research coverage of FNB next week. Lyons should *most appropriately*:
    A. advise his superiors that he is no longer able to issue research recommendations on FNB.
    B. update the report without notification since the shares are held in trust and are beyond his direct control.
    C. disclose the situation to his employer and, if then asked to prepare a report, also disclose the situation in the report.

38. Which of the following is *least likely* one of the recommendations included in the Standards of Practice Handbook with regard to Performance Presentation?
    A. Include terminated accounts in past performance history.
    B. Present the performance of a representative account to show how a composite has performed.
    C. Consider the level of financial knowledge of the audience to whom the performance is presented.

39. Which of the following is *least likely* a recommended procedure of the Standard regarding Fair Dealing?
    A. Develop written procedures for trade allocation.
    B. Disseminate initial recommendations to all clients.
    C. Review accounts systematically to ensure that no client is given preferred treatment.

40. Which of the following actions is a *required*, rather than *recommended*, action under the Standard regarding diligence and a reasonable basis for a firm's research recommendations?
    A. Have a policy requiring that research reports and recommendations have a basis that can be substantiated as reasonable and adequate.
    B. Compensate analysts based on measurable criteria to assess the quality of their research.
    C. Review the assumptions used and evaluate the objectivity of externally generated research reports.

41. Ralph Salley, a Level 1 candidate in the CFA Program, is explaining Standard VI(B) Priority of Transactions, to his supervisor. Salley states, "The Standard recommends, but does not require, that members and candidates should not participate in initial public offerings. The Standard also recommends that trades for accounts of family members be made after those for other clients, but before those for the account of the members and candidates responsible for executing the transactions." Salley's explanation of the Standard is:
    A. correct.
    B. incorrect, because the Standard does not recommend that trades for family members be made after those for other clients.
    C. incorrect, because the Standard requires that members and candidates not participate in initial public offerings.

42. Which of the following statements *most accurately* describes the parties that GIPS are intended to apply to and serve? GIPS apply to:
    A. consultants and serve their existing and prospective clients.
    B. firms that issue securities and serve investment management firms.
    C. investment management firms and serve their existing and prospective clients.

43. At a regional conference for institutional portfolio managers, Jason Morris makes three comments in a presentation centered on explaining the reasons for the creation of GIPS. Which of Morris' comments is *least likely* correct? GIPS were created:
    A. to reduce historical performance inflation caused by excluding results of terminated portfolios.
    B. to encourage investment firms to select representative accounts when presenting investment results.
    C. in response to performance reporting abuses which included only reporting results over periods of exceptional returns.

44. Which of the following statements *most accurately* describes verification under GIPS? Verification:
    A. may be performed on single composites.
    B. is required for a firm to claim GIPS compliance.
    C. requires a verification report to be issued for the entire firm.

45. Benson Asset Management Inc. is seeking to become compliant with GIPS. The firm has hired an independent consultant to assist in ensuring that Benson's policies and procedures conform to the standards. Which of the following recommendations made by the consultant is *least likely* required under GIPS?
    A. Benson must disclose the results of an independent verification process in its composite presentations.
    B. All of Benson's accounts managed by third party advisers selected by Benson must be included in the firm's composites.
    C. Compliant presentations for discontinued composites must be made available to any prospect requesting one up to five years after discontinuation.

46. Vivian Müller, compliance director for ABC Investments, is reviewing GIPS compliance policies put in place by her employees. Which of the following policies is currently *required* to comply with GIPS?
    A. Compliance with GIPS must be verified by an independent third party.
    B. Restructuring of the firm's organization cannot be used as a basis to change the historical performance results of a composite.
    C. The definition of the firm must include the firm's offices in all countries and regions.

47. Which of the following is *least likely* an accurate statement about the major components of GIPS?
    A. GIPS cover the professional qualifications of those responsible for managing assets at a firm claiming compliance.
    B. GIPS cover the way investment firms calculate composite returns as well as the method used to create the composite itself.
    C. GIPS apply to many categories of portfolio assets including stocks, bonds, real estate, and private equity.

48. Mason Smith is trying to decide which of the following composite definitions, submitted by his junior analysts, would be considered a viable composite according to GIPS. Which composite will meet the standards? A composite that includes:
    A. all accounts that are managed directly from the firm's Hong Kong office.
    B. all actively managed portfolios but excludes passively managed portfolios.
    C. all portfolios that are managed to provide a return approximately equal to that of the S&P 500 Index.

49. Mack Stevens has assembled several articles written about GIPS. Each article has listed at least one objective of GIPS. Which of the following statements collected from the articles *least likely* describes objectives of GIPS accurately?
    A. GIPS attempt to gain worldwide acceptance of performance calculation and presentations standards in a fair format with full disclosure.
    B. GIPS try to provide an opportunity for large and small firms to compete on an equal footing by imposing external rules and regulations on performance presentation.
    C. GIPS seek to encourage equitable competition among investment firms in all markets without stifling new market entrants in the process.

50. An investment management firm, Investco, Inc., was recently audited by the United States Securities and Exchange Commission (SEC). Investco included the following statement in its performance presentation report: "This report has been verified as GIPS compliant by Investco's Compliance Department and the United States Securities and Exchange Commission." Does this constitute acceptable verification under GIPS?
    A. No, only one party may perform GIPS verification.
    B. No, neither party involved in the audit constitutes an acceptable GIPS verification.
    C. Yes, because an audit was performed implicitly by the SEC and explicitly by the firm's internal audit team.

SELF-TEST ANSWERS: ETHICAL AND PROFESSIONAL STANDARDS

1. **A**   Hutchins' personal bankruptcy may reflect poorly on her professional reputation if it resulted from fraudulent or deceitful business activities. There is no indication of this, however, and the bankruptcy is thus not a violation. Smith has not violated the Code and Standards by refusing to invest with Hutchins in what turned out to be bad investment opportunities. By reporting Smith to CFA Institute for a violation, Hutchins has misused the Professional Conduct Program to settle a dispute unrelated to professional ethics and has thus violated Standard I(D), Misconduct.

2. **C**   According to Standard I(A), informing her supervisor or firm's compliance department is appropriate. Dissociating herself would be premature. She should report her suspicions to a supervisory person and attempt to remedy the situation.

3. **B**   According to Standard I(A), since she has taken steps to stop the illegal activities and the board has ignored her, Jones must dissociate from the board and seek legal advice as to what other actions would be appropriate in this instance. She may need to inform legal or regulatory authorities of the illegal activities.

4. **C**   According to Standard II(A), members and candidates are under no circumstances allowed to use material nonpublic information to trade securities. Carlson must abide by the Code and Standards, which is the most strict regulation in the scenario.

5. **B**   The intent of Green Brothers' actions is to manipulate market liquidity in order to attract investment to its own funds. The increased trading activity was not based on market fundamentals or an actual trading strategy to benefit investors. It was merely an attempt to mislead market participants in order to increase assets under Green Brothers' management. The action violates Standard II(B), Market Manipulation.

6. **A**   Quigley's trades are most likely an attempt to take advantage of an arbitrage opportunity that exists between Craeger's common stock and its put options. She is not manipulating the prices of securities in an attempt to mislead market participants, which would violate Standard II(B), Market Manipulation. She is pursuing a legitimate investment strategy. Participants in her hedge fund are aware of the fund's investment strategy, and thus Quigley did not violate the Code and Standards by not disclosing this specific set of trades in advance of trading.

7. **C**   According to Standard I(A), in some instances reporting a legal violation to governmental or regulatory officials may be appropriate, but this isn't always necessary, and it isn't required under Standard I(A).

8. **B**   According to Standard VII(B), any explanation of the designation in print form should be a concise description of the requirements or of CFA Institute. The other statements contain violations of Standard VII(B), in particular the presentation of the letters CFA. Also, she may not imply superior performance as a result of being a CFA charterholder.

9. **B**   Standard III(C), Suitability, requires that before taking investment action, members and candidates must make a reasonable inquiry into a client's or prospect's investment objectives and constraints as well as their prior investment experience. Byrne cannot assume that because the brothers have similar lifestyles and are close in age that they should have similarly managed portfolios. Byrne should have interviewed Cliff directly before investing his portfolio.

10. **B** According to Standard I(C), Misrepresentation, factual data from a recognized statistical reporting service need not be cited.

11. **B** By failing to include terminated portfolios in the performance presentation, the performance will have an inherent upward bias, making results appear better than they truly are. By excluding the terminated portfolios, DNR misleads its potential investors and thus violates Standard III(D), Performance Presentation, which prohibits any "practice that would lead to misrepresentation of a member or candidate's performance record."

12. **C** According to Standard IV(A), Loyalty, members and candidates are expected to act for the benefit of the employer and not deprive the employer of their skills. Fletcher is performing work similar to the services that her employer provides for a fee. Although the position is a volunteer position, Fletcher will receive compensation in the form of a free parking space. In light of the circumstances, Fletcher must disclose the details of the position and get written permission before accepting the volunteer position.

13. **C** According to Standard IV(C), Responsibilities of Supervisors, reporting the violation and warning the employee to cease activities that violate the law or the Code and Standards are not enough. The supervisor must take steps (such as limiting employee activity or increasing the level of employee monitoring) to prevent further violations while he conducts an investigation.

14. **C** According to Standard IV(C), because he is aware that the firm's compliance procedures are not being monitored and followed and because he has repeatedly tried to get company management to correct the situation, Blair should decline supervisory responsibility until adequate procedures to detect and prevent violations of laws, regulations, and the Code and Standards are adopted and followed. If he does not do so, he will be in violation of the Code and Standards.

15. **A** Standard I(B), Independence and Objectivity, requires that members and candidates reject offers of gifts or compensation that could compromise their independence or objectivity. Schleifer has appropriately rejected the offer of the hotel accommodations and the use of ChemCo's jet. He may accept the desk clock since this gift is of nominal value and is unlikely to compromise his independence and objectivity. Schleifer cannot accept the tickets to the dinner, however. Since it is a formal high-society dinner, the tickets are most likely expensive or difficult to come by. Even though he has disclosed the gift to his employer and he plans to use the dinner as a marketing opportunity for his firm, the gift itself may influence Schliefer's future research in favor of ChemCo. Allowing such potential influence is a violation of Standard I(B).

16. **C** Standard I(B) recommends, but does not require, that an analyst have his firm pay for ordinary travel expenses to visit companies that are the subject of research. The other choices are required by the Standards.

17. **A** Anderson must maintain the confidentiality of client information according to Standard III(E). Confidentiality may be broken in instances involving illegal activities on the part of the client, but the client's information may only be relayed to proper authorities. Anderson did not have the right to inform the investment bank of her client's investigation.

18. **A**   Historical growth can be cited as a fact since it actually happened. Stefano states that her firm expects further growth and profitability, which is an opinion. She does not claim that these are facts. In addition, Stefano identifies relevant factors and highlights in particular the most significant risks of investing in South American utilities. She has fully complied with Standard V(B), Communication with Clients and Prospective Clients. Under the Standard, it is not necessary to include every detail about a potential investment in a report. Members and candidates are expected to use their judgment and identify the most important factors to include.

19. **B**   This is not necessarily a violation. Firms can offer different levels of service to clients as long as this is disclosed to all clients. The largest institutional clients would likely be paying higher fees for a greater level of service. Also note that the analyst's brother's account in choice C should be treated the same as any other client account.

20. **C**   Members and candidates must give clients adequate opportunity to act on new or changed recommendations before taking investment action in their own non-firm accounts or other non-client accounts in which they have a beneficial interest. One week is likely an acceptable waiting period.

21. **B**   In the other choices, Olson violates Standard I(C) by misrepresenting the services that she or her firm are capable of performing, her qualifications, her academic or professional credentials, or the firm's credentials. The firm is small and most likely cannot perform all investment services the client may require. The firm cannot guarantee future outperformance of the market indexes. The firm doesn't have a long history (only six months).

22. **C**   Standard III(A), Loyalty, Prudence, and Care. Herbst is acting as a fiduciary for the pension plan beneficiaries. Choosing brokers based on quality of services provided is reasonable. She may pay higher-than-average brokerage fees so long as doing so benefits the pension beneficiaries, not other clients. Trading with selected brokers solely to gain referrals is not likely to be in the pension beneficiaries' best interest since it does not take into account other important factors for selecting brokerage firms.

23. **A**   Nieder must not take models or documents from his previous employer without explicit permission to do so, or he would violate Standard IV(A), Loyalty. He is allowed, however, to reproduce the model from memory but must recreate the supporting documentation to maintain compliance with Standard V(C), Record Retention.

24. **C**   According to Standard VI(C), Referral Fees, Hern must disclose the referral arrangement between itself and Baker so that potential clients can judge the true cost of Hern's services and assess whether there is any partiality inherent in the recommendation of services.

25. **C**   Standard VII(B) governs acceptable methods of referencing the CFA Institute, CFA designation, and CFA Program. Candidates may reference their candidacy if they are enrolled for or waiting for the results of, a CFA exam. Pulin may also reference his membership status with the CFA Institute as well as his remaining eligibility requirements to become a CFA charterholder.

26. **A**   There is no indication that Servais has inside information pertaining to the situation at the five firms in question—only the two firms that have already gone public with the information. It is common knowledge that the other five firms follow the same boron handing procedures. She is, therefore, in compliance with Standard II(A) concerning the use of material nonpublic information in the issuance of the investment recommendation.

27. **B**   Even though the laws of Zanuatu would not preclude trading on the information, as a CFA Charterholder the friend is bound by the CFA Institute Code and Standards. Standard II(A) prohibits the use of material nonpublic information, and the friend may not trade the stocks about which she has such information under any circumstances.

28. **C**   In this situation, Donovan, Smythe, and Yeats all violated Standard VII(A), Conduct as Members and Candidates in the CFA Program. The Standard prohibits conduct that compromises the integrity, validity, or security of the CFA exams. Donovan clearly breached the exam security. Smythe and Yeats both compromised the integrity of the exams by planning to use the actual exam question to gain an advantage over other candidates. Even though Yeats did not ultimately use the information to study for the exam, she participated in a scheme to cheat on the CFA exam.

29. **B**   The release of such information to a limited circle via an internet chat room does not cause the information to be public. The information is also clearly material. Therefore, Green is not allowed to trade on the information under Standard II(A).

30. **A**   Albright may accept work for which she receives outside compensation and which may compete with her employer only if she obtains her employer's consent. Under Standard IV(A), Loyalty, such consent must be obtained from her employer prior to beginning the work.

31. **C**   There can be no assurance that a premium of 2% to 4% will consistently be obtained. Bixby is in violation of Standard I(C), Misrepresentation, since she has made an implicit guarantee of the fund's expected performance.

32. **C**   Since the statements are vague, we have no direct evidence that a violation of securities law has occurred. However, under Standard I(D), Misconduct, members and candidates are prohibited from engaging in activities involving deceit. Karloff's action is a clear attempt to mislead the investing public regarding the value of Summit IPOs.

33. **C**   Standard III(B), Fair Dealing, requires that members not use their position to disadvantage clients, specifically in the case of IPOs.

34. **B**   NV management is asking Hunter to violate Standard II(B), Market Manipulation, which prohibits taking actions that are designed to distort prices or artificially increase trading volume. The intent of Hunter's actions is to mislead market participants and allow corporate insiders to take advantage of the artificially high prices.

35. **A**   There is no violation of the CFA Institute Standards regarding this matter. The referral arrangement is fully disclosed to clients before they agree to do business with Pick. Therefore clients can fully assess the effect of the agreement on the referral and how the agreement may affect their accounts before hiring Pick as their asset manager.

36. **B**   Johnson has apparently let his recreational passion cloud his judgment. This is not to say that Swordfish Enterprises is not or will not be an excellent investment. However, if he had never heard of the firm previously, issuing an investment recommendation without conducting a thorough financial investigation indicates a failure to exercise diligence and also indicates that he lacks a reasonable and adequate basis for his recommendation. He is in violation of Standard V(A).

37. **C** Even though the shares are held in trust, this could still be construed as a conflict of interest. Lyons is obligated under Standard VI(A), Disclosure of Conflicts, to inform his employer of the potential conflict. If he is then authorized to issue investment recommendations on the security in question, the existence of a potential conflict must be disclosed in the report.

38. **B** The recommended procedure in Standard III(D), Performance Presentation, is to present the performance of a composite as a weighted average of the performance of similar portfolios rather than using a single representative account.

39. **B** The recommended procedure according to Standard III(B), Fair Dealing, is to disseminate new recommendations to all clients who express an interest or for whom the investment is suitable. Not all clients need to be informed but the selection should be based on suitability of the specific investment. The other two are main headings in the "Recommendations" section of the Standard.

40. **C** It is required under Standard V(A), Diligence and Reasonable Basis, that third-party research assumptions be reviewed and both the independence and objectivity of the research and recommendations be evaluated. The other choices are recommended policies and procedures under the Standard.

41. **B** Standard VI(B), Priority of Transactions, recommends that members and candidates avoid the appearance of conflict of interest by not participating in IPOs. If a family member is a fee-paying client, the member or candidate should treat them like any other client, not giving any advantage or disadvantage to their accounts. The fact that a member or candidate has a beneficial interest in a client account does not preclude treating it like any other fee-paying account.

42. **C** GIPS apply to investment management firms. They are intended to serve prospective and existing clients of investment firms and consultants who advise these clients.

43. **B** GIPS were created to reduce ambiguity of performance reporting among investment firms. Past abuses of performance reporting include representative accounts (showing only top performers), survivorship bias (deleting poor performers), and varying time period (showing only the time period with the best performance).

44. **C** A single verification report is issued with respect to the whole firm: GIPS verification cannot be carried out for a single composite.

45. **A** Verification is not currently required under GIPS. Firms that choose to undergo the verification process are encouraged, but not required, to make a specific verification disclosure in composite presentations and advertisements that reference the firm's GIPS verification. When the firm has discretion over the selection of sub-advisors, the firm must include portfolios managed by sub-advisors in its composites. The firm must provide a list of composites and their descriptions to any prospect who requests it. This list must include any composites that have been discontinued within the past five years. Upon request, the firm must provide a compliant presentation for any composite on the firm's list.

46. **B** Firms cannot alter historical performance records of composites simply because of a reorganization of the firm. This is a current requirement of GIPS. The other answer choices are not currently required.

47. **A** There are no GIPS related directly to the qualifications of employees managing assets at an investment firm whether it claims compliance with GIPS or not. The major sections of GIPS are as follows: fundamentals of compliance, input data, calculation methodology, composite construction, disclosures, presentation and reporting, real estate, and private equity.

48. **C** Composites are groups of portfolios that represent a similar investment strategy, objective, or mandate. Clearly, grouping all portfolios managed to mirror the S&P 500 Index return constitutes a composite according to this definition. Organizing composites by office or by a generic active management category is not acceptable as these categories do not reflect any sort of strategy, objective, or mandate.

49. **B** GIPS seek to promote global self regulation through *voluntary* acceptance and adherence to the standards. The other statements correctly state objectives of GIPS.

50. **B** GIPS verification must be performed by an independent third party. The SEC audit does not constitute a GIPS verification.

THE TIME VALUE OF MONEY

EXAM FOCUS

This topic review covers time value of money concepts and applications. Procedures are presented for calculating the future value and present value of a single cash flow, an annuity, and a series of uneven cash flows. The impact of different compounding periods is examined, along with the procedures for solving for other variables in time value of money problems. Your main objective in this chapter is to master time value of money mechanics (i.e., learn how to crunch the numbers). There will be a lot of time value of money problems and applications on the exam, so be prepared to deal with them. Work all the questions and problems found at the end of this review. Make sure you know how to grind out all the time value of money problems on your calculator. The more rapidly you can do them (correctly), the more time you will have for the less predictable parts of the exam.

TIME VALUE OF MONEY CONCEPTS AND APPLICATIONS

The concept of **compound interest** or **interest on interest** is deeply embedded in time value of money (TVM) procedures. When an investment is subjected to compound interest, the growth in the value of the investment from period to period reflects not only the interest earned on the original principal amount but also on the interest earned on the previous period's interest earnings—the interest on interest.

TVM applications frequently call for determining the **future value** (FV) of an investment's cash flows as a result of the effects of compound interest. Computing FV involves projecting the cash flows forward, on the basis of an appropriate compound interest rate, to the end of the investment's life. The computation of the **present value** (PV) works in the opposite direction—it brings the cash flows from an investment back to the beginning of the investment's life based on an appropriate compound rate of return.

Being able to measure the PV and/or FV of an investment's cash flows becomes useful when comparing investment alternatives because the value of the investment's cash flows must be measured at some common point in time, typically at the end of the investment horizon (FV) or at the beginning of the investment horizon (PV).

Using a Financial Calculator

It is very important that you be able to use a financial calculator when working TVM problems because the exam is constructed under the assumption that candidates have the ability to do so. There is simply no other way that you will have time to solve TVM problems. *CFA Institute allows only two types of calculators to be used for the exam—the*

TI BAII Plus® (including the BAII Plus Professional) and the HP 12C® (including the HP 12C Platinum). This topic review is written primarily with the TI BAII Plus in mind. If you don't already own a calculator, go out and buy a TI BAII Plus! However, if you already own the HP 12C and are comfortable with it, by all means continue to use it.

The TI BAII Plus comes preloaded from the factory with the periods per year function (P/Y) set to 12. This automatically converts the annual interest rate (I/Y) into monthly rates. While appropriate for many loan-type problems, this feature is not suitable for the vast majority of the TVM applications we will be studying. So prior to using our SchweserNotes™, please set your P/Y key to "1" using the following sequence of keystrokes:

[2nd] [P/Y] "1" [ENTER] [2nd] [QUIT]

As long as you do not change the P/Y setting, it will remain set at one period per year until the battery from your calculator is removed (it does not change when you turn the calculator on and off). If you want to check this setting at any time, press [2nd] [P/Y]. The display should read P/Y = 1.0. If it does, press [2nd] [QUIT] to get out of the "programming" mode. If it doesn't, repeat the procedure previously described to set the P/Y key. With P/Y set to equal 1, it is now possible to think of I/Y as the interest rate per compounding period and N as the number of compounding periods under analysis. Thinking of these keys in this way should help you keep things straight as we work through TVM problems.

Before we begin working with financial calculators, you should familiarize yourself with your TI by locating the TVM keys noted below. These are the only keys you need to know to work virtually all TVM problems.

- N = Number of compounding periods.
- I/Y = Interest rate per compounding period.
- PV = Present value.
- FV = Future value.
- PMT = Annuity payments, or constant periodic cash flow.
- CPT = Compute.

Professor's Note: We have provided an online video in the Schweser Library on how to use the TI calculator. You can view it by logging in at www.schweser.com.

Time Lines

It is often a good idea to draw a time line before you start to solve a TVM problem. A **time line** is simply a diagram of the cash flows associated with a TVM problem. A cash flow that occurs in the present (today) is put at time zero. Cash outflows (payments) are given a negative sign, and cash inflows (receipts) are given a positive sign. Once the cash flows are assigned to a time line, they may be moved to the beginning of the investment period to calculate the PV through a process called **discounting** or to the end of the period to calculate the FV using a process called **compounding**.

Figure 1 illustrates a time line for an investment that costs $1,000 today (outflow) and will return a stream of cash payments (inflows) of $300 per year at the end of each of the next five years.

Figure 1: Time Line

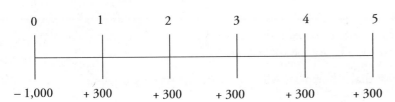

Please recognize that the cash flows occur at the end of the period depicted on the time line. Furthermore, note that the end of one period is the same as the beginning of the next period. For example, the end of the second year (t = 2) is the same as the beginning of the third year, so a cash flow at the beginning of year 3 appears at time t = 2 on the time line. Keeping this convention in mind will help you keep things straight when you are setting up TVM problems.

 Professor's Note: Throughout the problems in this review, rounding differences may occur between the use of different calculators or techniques presented in this document. So don't panic if you are a few cents off in your calculations.

LOS 5.a: Interpret interest rates as required rate of return, discount rate, or opportunity cost.

Interest rates are our measure of the time value of money, although risk differences in financial securities lead to differences in their equilibrium interest rates. Equilibrium interest rates are the **required rate of return** for a particular investment, in the sense that the market rate of return is the return that investors and savers require to get them to willingly lend their funds. Interest rates are also referred to as **discount rates** and, in fact, the terms are often used interchangeably. If an individual can borrow funds at an interest rate of 10%, then that individual should *discount* payments to be made in the future at that rate in order to get their equivalent value in current dollars or other currency. Finally, we can also view interest rates as the **opportunity cost** of current consumption. If the market rate of interest on one-year securities is 5%, earning an additional 5% is the opportunity forgone when current consumption is chosen rather than saving (postponing consumption).

LOS 5.b: Explain an interest rate as the sum of a real risk-free rate, expected inflation, and premiums that compensate investors for distinct types of risk.

The **real risk-free rate** of interest is a theoretical rate on a single period loan that has no expectation of inflation in it. When we speak of a real rate of return, we are referring to an investor's increase in purchasing power (after adjusting for inflation). Since expected inflation in future periods is not zero, the rates we observe on U.S. Treasury bills (T-bills), for example, are risk-free rates but not *real* rates of return. T-bill rates are *nominal risk-free rates* because they contain an *inflation premium*. The approximate relation here is:

nominal risk-free rate = real risk-free rate + expected inflation rate

Securities may have one or more **types of risk**, and each added risk increases the required rate of return on the security. These types of risk are:

- **Default risk**. The risk that a borrower will not make the promised payments in a timely manner.
- **Liquidity risk**. The risk of receiving less than fair value for an investment if it must be sold for cash quickly.
- **Maturity risk**. As we will cover in detail in the section on debt securities, the prices of longer-term bonds are more volatile than those of shorter-term bonds. Longer maturity bonds have more maturity risk than shorter-term bonds and require a maturity risk premium.

Each of these risk factors is associated with a risk premium that we add to the nominal risk-free rate to adjust for greater default risk, less liquidity, and longer maturity relative to a very liquid, short-term, default risk-free rate such as that on T-bills. We can write:

required interest rate on a security = nominal risk-free rate
+ default risk premium
+ liquidity premium
+ maturity risk premium

LOS 5.c: Calculate and interpret the effective annual rate, given the stated annual interest rate and the frequency of compounding.

LOS 5.d: Solve time value of money problems when compounding periods are other than annual.

Financial institutions usually quote rates as stated annual interest rates, along with a compounding frequency, as opposed to quoting rates as periodic rates—the rate of interest earned over a single compounding period. For example, a bank will quote a savings rate as 8%, compounded quarterly, rather than 2% per quarter. The rate of interest that investors actually realize as a result of compounding is known as the **effective annual rate** (EAR). EAR represents the annual rate of return actually being earned *after adjustments have been made for different compounding periods*.

EAR may be determined as follows:

$$EAR = (1 + \text{periodic rate})^m - 1$$

where:
periodic rate = stated annual rate/m
m = the number of compounding periods per year

Obviously, the EAR for a stated rate of 8% *compounded annually* is not the same as the EAR for 8% *compounded semiannually*, or *quarterly*. Indeed, whenever compound interest is being used, the stated rate and the actual (effective) rate of interest are equal only when interest is compounded annually. Otherwise, the greater the compounding frequency, the greater the EAR will be in comparison to the stated rate.

The computation of EAR is necessary when comparing investments that have different compounding periods. It allows for an apples-to-apples rate comparison.

Example: Computing EAR

Compute EAR if the stated annual rate is 12%, compounded quarterly.

Answer:

Here m = 4, so the periodic rate is $\dfrac{12}{4} = 3\%$.

Thus, EAR = $(1 + 0.03)^4 - 1 = 1.1255 - 1 = 0.1255 = 12.55\%$.

This solution uses the $[y^x]$ key on your financial calculator. The exact keystrokes on the TI for the above computation are 1.03 $[y^x]$ 4 [=]. On the HP, the strokes are 1.03 [ENTER] 4 $[y^x]$.

Example: Computing EARs for a range of compounding frequencies

Using a stated rate of 6%, compute EARs for semiannual, quarterly, monthly, and daily compounding.

Answer:

EAR with:

semiannual compounding = $(1 + 0.03)^2 - 1$	= $1.06090 - 1 = 0.06090 = 6.090\%$
quarterly compounding = $(1 + 0.015)^4 - 1$	= $1.06136 - 1 = 0.06136 = 6.136\%$
monthly compounding = $(1 + 0.005)^{12} - 1$	= $1.06168 - 1 = 0.06168 = 6.168\%$
daily compounding = $(1 + 0.00016438)^{365} - 1$	= $1.06183 - 1 = 0.06183 = 6.183\%$

Notice here that the EAR increases as the compounding frequency increases.

The limit of shorter and shorter compounding periods is called continuous compounding. To convert an annual stated rate to the EAR with continuous compounding, we use the formula $e^r - 1 = $ EAR.

For 6%, we have $e^{0.06} - 1 = 6.1837\%$. The keystrokes are 0.06 [2nd] $[e^x]$ [–] 1 [=] 0.061837.

LOS 5.e: Calculate and interpret the future value (FV) and present value (PV) of a single sum of money, an ordinary annuity, an annuity due, a perpetuity (PV only), and a series of unequal cash flows.

Future Value of a Single Sum

Future value is the amount to which a current deposit will grow over time when it is placed in an account paying compound interest. The FV, also called the compound value, is simply an example of compound interest at work.

The formula for the FV of a *single* cash flow is:

$$FV = PV(1 + I/Y)^N$$

where:
PV = amount of money invested today (the present value)
I/Y = rate of return per compounding period
N = total number of compounding periods

In this expression, the investment involves a single cash outflow, PV, which occurs today, at t = 0 on the time line. The single sum FV formula will determine the value of an investment at the end of N compounding periods, given that it can earn a fully compounded rate of return, I/Y, over all of the periods.

The factor $(1 + I/Y)^N$ represents the compounding rate on an investment and is frequently referred to as the **future value factor**, or the **future value interest factor**, for a single cash flow at I/Y over N compounding periods. These are the values that appear in interest factor tables, which we will not be using.

Example: FV of a single sum

Calculate the FV of a $300 investment at the end of ten years if it earns an annually compounded rate of return of 8%.

Answer:

To solve this problem with your calculator, input the relevant data and compute FV.

N = 10; I/Y = 8; PV = –300; CPT → FV = $647.68

 Professor's Note: Note the negative sign on PV. This is not necessary, but it makes the FV come out as a positive number. If you enter PV as a positive number, ignore the negative sign that appears on the FV.

This relatively simple problem could also be solved using the following equation:

$$FV = 300(1 + 0.08)^{10} = \$647.68$$

On the TI calculator, enter 1.08 [y^x] 10 [×] 300 [=].

Present Value of a Single Sum

The PV of a single sum is today's value of a cash flow that is to be received at some point in the future. In other words, it is the amount of money that must be invested today, at a given rate of return over a given period of time, in order to end up with a specified FV. As previously mentioned, the process for finding the PV of a cash flow is known as *discounting* (i.e., future cash flows are "discounted" back to the present). The interest rate used in the discounting process is commonly referred to as the **discount rate** but may also be referred to as the **opportunity cost**, **required rate of return**, and the **cost of capital**. Whatever you want to call it, it represents the annual compound rate of return that can be earned on an investment.

The relationship between PV and FV can be seen by examining the FV expression stated earlier. Rewriting the FV equation in terms of PV, we get:

$$PV = FV \times \left[\frac{1}{(1 + I/Y)^N} \right] = \frac{FV}{(1 + I/Y)^N}$$

Note that for a single future cash flow, PV is always less than the FV whenever the discount rate is positive.

The quantity $1/(1 + I/Y)^N$ in the PV equation is frequently referred to as the **present value factor**, **present value interest factor**, or **discount factor** for a single cash flow at I/Y over N compounding periods.

Example: PV of a single sum

Given a discount rate of 9%, calculate the PV of a $1,000 cash flow that will be received in five years.

Answer:

To solve this problem, input the relevant data and compute PV.

N = 5; I/Y = 9; FV = 1,000; CPT → PV = –$649.93 (ignore the sign)

Professor's Note: With single sum PV problems, you can either enter FV as a positive number and ignore the negative sign on PV or enter FV as a negative number.

This relatively simple problem could also be solved using the following PV equation:

$$PV = \frac{1,000}{(1+0.09)^5} = \$649.93$$

On the TI, enter 1.09 [y^x] 5 [=] [1/x] [×] 1,000 [=].

The PV computed here implies that at a rate of 9%, an investor will be indifferent between $1,000 in five years and $649.93 today. Put another way, $649.93 is the amount that must be invested today at a 9% rate of return in order to generate a cash flow of $1,000 at the end of five years.

Annuities

An **annuity** is a stream of *equal cash flows* that occurs at *equal intervals* over a given period. Receiving $1,000 per year at the end of each of the next eight years is an example of an annuity. There are two types of annuities: **ordinary annuities** and **annuities due**. The *ordinary annuity* is the most common type of annuity. It is characterized by cash flows that occur at the *end* of each compounding period. This is a typical cash flow pattern for many investment and business finance applications. The other type of annuity is called an *annuity due*, where payments or receipts occur at the beginning of each period (i.e., the first payment is today at t = 0).

Computing the FV or PV of an annuity with your calculator is no more difficult than it is for a single cash flow. You will know four of the five relevant variables and solve for the fifth (either PV or FV). The difference between single sum and annuity TVM problems is that instead of solving for the PV or FV of a single cash flow, we solve for the PV or FV of a stream of equal periodic cash flows, where the size of the periodic cash flow is defined by the payment (PMT) variable on your calculator.

Example: FV of an ordinary annuity

What is the future value of an ordinary annuity that pays $150 per year at the end of each of the next 15 years, given the investment is expected to earn a 7% rate of return?

Answer:

This problem can be solved by entering the relevant data and computing FV.

N = 15; I/Y = 7; PMT = –150; CPT → FV = $3,769.35

Implicit here is that PV = 0; clearing the TVM functions sets both PV and FV to zero.

The time line for the cash flows in this problem is depicted in the figure below.

FV of an Ordinary Annuity

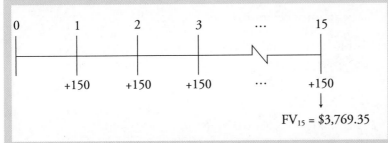

As indicated here, the sum of the compounded values of the individual cash flows in this 15-year ordinary annuity is $3,769.35. Note that the annuity payments themselves amounted to $2,250 = 15 × $150, and the balance is the interest earned at the rate of 7% per year.

To find the PV of an ordinary annuity, we use the future cash flow stream, PMT, that we used with FV annuity problems, but we discount the cash flows back to the present (time = 0) rather than compounding them forward to the terminal date of the annuity.

Here again, the PMT variable is a *single* periodic payment, *not* the total of all the payments (or deposits) in the annuity. The PVA_O measures the collective PV of a stream of equal cash flows received at the end of each compounding period over a stated number of periods, N, given a specified rate of return, I/Y. The following examples illustrate how to determine the PV of an ordinary annuity using a financial calculator.

Example: PV of an ordinary annuity

What is the PV of an annuity that pays $200 per year at the end of each of the next 13 years, given a 6% discount rate?

Answer:

The payments occur at the end of the year, so this annuity is an ordinary annuity. To solve this problem, enter the relevant information and compute PV.

N = 13; I/Y = 6; PMT = –200; FV = 0; CPT → PV = $1,770.54

The $1,770.54 computed here represents the amount of money that an investor would need to invest *today* at a 6% rate of return to generate 13 end-of-year cash flows of $200 each.

Example: PV of an ordinary annuity beginning later than t = 1

What is the present value of four $100 end-of-year payments if the first payment is to be received three years from today and the appropriate rate of return is 9%?

Answer:

The time line for this cash flow stream is shown in the following figure.

PV of an Annuity Beginning at t = 3

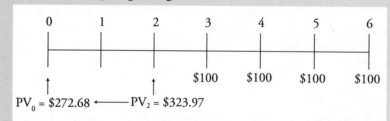

Step 1: Find the present value of the annuity as of the end of year 2 (PV_2).

Input the relevant data and solve for PV_2.

N = 4; I/Y = 9; PMT = –100; FV = 0; CPT → PV = PV_2 = $323.97

Step 2: Find the present value of PV_2.

Input the relevant data and solve for PV_0.

N = 2; I/Y = 9; PMT = 0; FV = –323.97; CPT → PV = PV_0 = $272.68

In this solution, the annuity was treated as an ordinary annuity. The PV was computed one period before the first payment, and we discounted PV_2 = $323.97 over two years. We need to stress this important point. The PV annuity function on your calculator set in "END" mode gives you the value *one period before the annuity begins*. Although the annuity begins at t = 3, we discounted the result for only two periods to get the present (t = 0) value.

Example: PV of a bond's cash flows

A bond will make coupon interest payments of 70 euros (7% of its face value) at the end of each year and will also pay its face value of 1,000 euros at maturity in five years. If the appropriate discount rate is 8%, what is the present value of the bond's promised cash flows?

Answer:

The five annual coupon payments of 70 euros each can be viewed as an ordinary annuity. The maturity value of 1,000 euros is the future value of the bond at the time the last coupon payment is made. On a time line, the promised payment stream is as shown below.

Cash flows for a 5-year, 7%, 1,000 euro bond

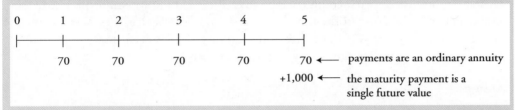

The PV of the bond's cash flows can be broken down into the PV of a 5-payment ordinary annuity, plus the PV of a 1,000 euro lump sum to be received five years from now.

The calculator solution is:

N = 5; PMT = 70; I/Y = 8; FV = 1,000; CPT PV = –960

With a yield to maturity of 8%, the value of the bond is 960 euros.

Note that the PMT and FV must have the same sign, since both are cash flows paid to the investor (paid by the bond issuer). The calculated PV will have the opposite sign from PMT and FV.

Future Value of an Annuity Due

Sometimes it is necessary to find the *FV of an annuity due* (FVA_D), an annuity where the annuity payments (or deposits) occur at the beginning of each compounding period. Fortunately, our financial calculators can be used to do this, but with one slight modification—the calculator must be set to the beginning-of-period (BGN) mode. To switch between the BGN and END modes on the TI, press [2nd] [BGN] [2nd] [SET]. When this is done, "BGN" will appear in the upper right corner of the display window. If the display indicates the desired mode, press [2nd] [QUIT]. You will normally want your calculator to be in the ordinary annuity (END) mode, so remember to switch out of BGN mode after working annuity due problems. Note that nothing appears in the upper right corner of the display window when the TI is set to the END mode. It should be mentioned that while annuity due payments are made or received at the beginning of each period, the FV of an annuity due is calculated as of the end of the last period.

Another way to compute the FV of an annuity due is to calculate the FV of an ordinary annuity, and simply multiply the resulting FV by [1 + periodic compounding rate (I/Y)]. Symbolically, this can be expressed as:

$$FVA_D = FVA_O \times (1 + I/Y)$$

The following examples illustrate how to compute the FV of an annuity due.

Example: FV of an annuity due

What is the future value of an annuity that pays $100 per year at the beginning of each of the next three years, commencing today, if the cash flows can be invested at an annual rate of 10%? Note in the time line in the figure below that the FV is computed as of the end of the last year in the life of the annuity, year 3, even though the final payment occurs at the beginning of year 3 (end of year 2).

Answer:

To solve this problem, put your calculator in the BGN mode ([2nd] [BGN] [2nd] [SET] [2nd] [QUIT] on the TI or [g] [BEG] on the HP), then input the relevant data and compute FV.

N = 3; I/Y = 10; PMT = –100; CPT → FV = $364.10

FV of an Annuity Due

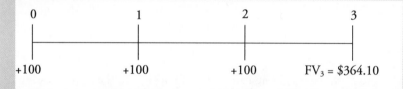

Alternatively, we could calculate the FV for an ordinary annuity and multiply it by (1 + I/Y). Leaving your calculator in the END mode, enter the following inputs:

N = 3; I/Y = 10; PMT = –100; CPT → FVA_O = $331.00

$FVA_D = FVA_O \times (1 + I/Y) = 331.00 \times 1.10 = \$364.10$

Example: FV of an annuity due

If you deposit $1,000 in the bank today and at the beginning of each of the next *three* years, how much will you have six years from today at 6% interest? The time line for this problem is shown in the following figure.

Answer:

FV for an Annuity Due

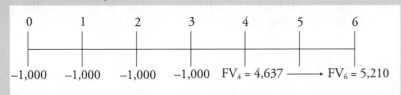

Step 1: Compute the FV of the annuity due at the end of year 4 (FV_4).

Set your calculator to the annuity due (BGN) mode, enter the relevant data, and compute FV_4.

$\quad$ N = 4; I/Y = 6; PMT = –1,000; CPT $\rightarrow$ FV = $4,637.09

Step 2: Find the future value of FV_4 two years from year 4.

Enter the relevant data and compute FV_6.

$\quad$ N = 2; I/Y = 6; PV = –4,637.09; CPT $\rightarrow$ FV = $5,210.23

$\quad$ or

$\quad$ $4,637.09(1.06)^2 = \$5,210.23$

Note that the FV function for an annuity when the calculator is set to BGN is the value one period after the last annuity deposit, at t = 4 in this example.

Present Value of an Annuity Due

While less common than those for ordinary annuities, there may be problems on the exam where you have to find the *PV of an annuity due* (PVA_D). Using a financial calculator, this really shouldn't be much of a problem. With an annuity due, *there is one less discounting period* since the first cash flow occurs at t = 0 and thus is already its PV. This implies that, all else equal, the PV of an annuity due will be greater than the PV of an ordinary annuity.

As you will see in the next example, there are two ways to compute the PV of an annuity due. The first is to put the calculator in the BGN mode and then input all the relevant variables (PMT, I/Y, and N) as you normally would. The second, and far easier way, is to treat the cash flow stream as an ordinary annuity over N compounding periods, and simply multiply the resulting PV by [1 + periodic compounding rate (I/Y)].

Symbolically, this can be stated as:

$$PVA_D = PVA_O \times (1 + I/Y)$$

The advantage of this second method is that you leave your calculator in the END mode and won't run the risk of forgetting to reset it. Regardless of the procedure used, the computed PV is given as of the beginning of the first period, t = 0.

Example: PV of an annuity due

Given a discount rate of 10%, what is the present value of a 3-year annuity that makes a series of $100 payments at the beginning of each of the next three years, starting today? The time line for this problem is shown in the following figure.

Answer:

First, let's solve this problem using the calculator's BGN mode. Set your calculator to the BGN mode ([2nd] [BGN] [2nd] [SET] [2nd] [QUIT] on the TI or [g] [BEG] on the HP), enter the relevant data, and compute PV.

$N = 3; I/Y = 10; PMT = -100; CPT \rightarrow PVA_D = \$273.55$

PV for an Annuity Due

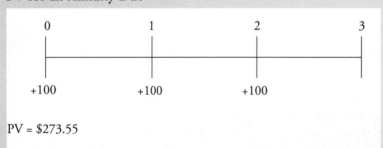

PV = $273.55

Alternatively, this problem can be solved by leaving your calculator in the END mode. First, compute the PV of an ordinary 3-year annuity. Then multiply this PV by (1 + I/Y). To use this approach, enter the relevant inputs and compute PV.

$N = 3; I/Y = 10; PMT = -100; CPT \rightarrow PVA_O = \$248.69$

$PVA_D = PVA_O \times (1 + I/Y) = \$248.69 \times 1.10 = \$273.55$

Present Value of a Perpetuity

A **perpetuity** is a financial instrument that pays a fixed amount of money at set intervals over an *infinite* period of time. In essence, a perpetuity is a perpetual annuity. British consul bonds and most preferred stocks are examples of perpetuities since they promise fixed interest or dividend payments forever. Without going into all the excruciating mathematical details, the discount factor for a perpetuity is just one divided by the appropriate rate of return (i.e., 1/r). Given this, we can compute the PV of a perpetuity.

$$PV_{perpetuity} = \frac{PMT}{I/Y}$$

The PV of a perpetuity is the fixed periodic cash flow divided by the appropriate periodic rate of return.

As with other TVM applications, it is possible to solve for unknown variables in the $PV_{perpetuity}$ equation. In fact, you can solve for any one of the three relevant variables, given the values for the other two.

Example: PV of a perpetuity

Assume the preferred stock of Kodon Corporation pays $4.50 per year in annual dividends and plans to follow this dividend policy forever. Given an 8% rate of return, what is the value of Kodon's preferred stock?

Answer:

Given that the value of the stock is the PV of all future dividends, we have:

$$PV_{perpetuity} = \frac{4.50}{0.08} = \$56.25$$

Thus, if an investor requires an 8% rate of return, the investor should be willing to pay $56.25 for each share of Kodon's preferred stock.

Example: Rate of return for a perpetuity

Using the Kodon preferred stock described in the preceding example, determine the rate of return that an investor would realize if she paid $75 per share for the stock.

Answer:

Rearranging the equation for $PV_{perpetuity}$, we get:

$$I/Y = \frac{PMT}{PV_{perpetuity}} = \frac{4.50}{75.00} = 0.06 = 6.0\%$$

This implies that the return (yield) on a $75 preferred stock that pays a $4.50 annual dividend is 6.0%.

PV and FV of Uneven Cash Flow Series

It is not uncommon to have applications in investments and corporate finance where it is necessary to evaluate a cash flow stream that is not equal from period to period. The time line in Figure 2 depicts such a cash flow stream.

Figure 2: Time Line for Uneven Cash Flows

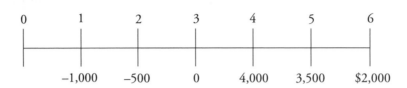

This 6-year cash flow series is not an annuity since the cash flows are different every year. In fact, there is one year with zero cash flow and two others with negative cash flows. In essence, this series of uneven cash flows is nothing more than a stream of annual single sum cash flows. Thus, to find the PV or FV of this cash flow stream, all we need to do is sum the PVs or FVs of the individual cash flows.

Example: Computing the FV of an uneven cash flow series

Using a rate of return of 10%, compute the future value of the 6-year uneven cash flow stream described above at the end of the sixth year.

Answer:

The FV for the cash flow stream is determined by first computing the FV of each individual cash flow, then summing the FVs of the individual cash flows. Note that we need to preserve the signs of the cash flows.

FV_1: PV = –1,000; I/Y = 10; N = 5; CPT → FV = FV_1 = –1,610.51

FV_2: PV = –500; I/Y = 10; N = 4; CPT → FV = FV_2 = –732.05

FV_3: PV = 0; I/Y = 10; N = 3; CPT → FV = FV_3 = 0.00

FV_4: PV = 4,000; I/Y = 10; N = 2; CPT → FV = FV_4 = 4,840.00

FV_5: PV = 3,500; I/Y = 10; N = 1; CPT → FV = FV_5 = 3,850.00

FV_6: PV = 2,000; I/Y = 10; N = 0; CPT → FV = FV_6 = <u>2,000.00</u>

FV of cash flow stream = $\sum FV_{individual}$ = 8,347.44

Example: Computing PV of an uneven cash flow series

Compute the present value of this 6-year uneven cash flow stream described above using a 10% rate of return.

Answer:

This problem is solved by first computing the PV of each individual cash flow, then summing the PVs of the individual cash flows, which yields the PV of the cash flow stream. Again the signs of the cash flows are preserved.

PV_1: FV = –1,000; I/Y = 10; N = 1; CPT → PV = PV_1 = –909.09

PV_2: FV = –500; I/Y = 10; N = 2; CPT → PV = PV_2 = –413.22

PV_3: FV = 0; I/Y = 10; N = 3; CPT → PV = PV_3 = 0

PV_4: FV = 4,000; I/Y = 10; N = 4; CPT → PV = PV_4 = 2,732.05

PV_5: FV = 3,500; I/Y = 10; N = 5; CPT → PV = PV_5 = 2,173.22

PV_6: FV = 2,000; I/Y = 10; N = 6; CPT → PV = PV_6 = <u>1,128.95</u>

PV of cash flow stream = $\sum PV_{individual}$ = **$4,711.91**

It is also possible to compute PV of an uneven cash flow stream by using the cash flow (CF) keys and the *net present value* (NPV) function on your calculator. This procedure is illustrated in the tables in Figures 3 and 4. In Figure 3, we have omitted the F01, F02, etc. values because they are all equal to 1. The Fn variable indicates how many times a particular cash flow amount is repeated.

Figure 3: NPV Calculator Keystrokes—TI BAII Plus®

Key Strokes	Explanation	Display
[CF] [2nd] [CLR WORK]	Clear CF Memory Registers	CF0 = 0.00000
0 [ENTER]	Initial Cash Outlay	CF0 = 0.00000
[↓] 1,000 [+/–] [ENTER]	Period 1 Cash Flow	C01 = –1,000.00000
[↓] [↓] 500 [+/–] [ENTER]	Period 2 Cash Flow	C02 = –500.00000
[↓] [↓] 0 [ENTER]	Period 3 Cash Flow	C03 = 0.00000
[↓] [↓] 4,000 [ENTER]	Period 4 Cash Flow	C04 = 4,000.00000
[↓] [↓] 3,500 [ENTER]	Period 5 Cash Flow	C05 = 3,500.00000
[↓] [↓] 2,000 [ENTER]	Period 6 Cash Flow	C06 = 2,000.00000
[NPV] 10 [ENTER]	10% Discount Rate	I = 10.00000
[↓] [CPT]	Calculate NPV	NPV = 4,711.91226

Note that the BAII Plus Professional will also give the NFV of 8,347.44 if you press the ↓ key.

Figure 4: NPV Calculator Keystrokes—HP12C®

Key Strokes	Explanation	Display
[f] [FIN] [f] [REG]	Clear Memory Registers	0.00000
0 [g] [CF$_0$]	Initial Cash Outlay	0.00000
1,000 [CHS] [g] [CF$_j$]	Period 1 Cash Flow	–1,000.00000
500 [CHS] [g] [CF$_j$]	Period 2 Cash Flow	–500.00000
0 [g] [CF$_j$]	Period 3 Cash Flow	0.00000
4,000 [g] [CF$_j$]	Period 4 Cash Flow	4,000.00000
3,500 [g] [CF$_j$]	Period 5 Cash Flow	3,500.00000
2,000 [g] [CF$_j$]	Period 6 Cash Flow	2,000.00000
10 [i]	10% Discount Rate	10.00000
[f] [NPV]	Calculate NPV	4,711.91226

Solving Time Value of Money Problems When Compounding Periods Are Other Than Annual

While the conceptual foundations of TVM calculations are not affected by the compounding period, more frequent compounding does have an impact on FV and PV computations. Specifically, since an increase in the frequency of compounding increases the effective rate of interest, it also *increases* the FV of a given cash flow and *decreases* the PV of a given cash flow.

Example: The effect of compounding frequency on FV and PV

Compute the FV one year from now of $1,000 today and the PV of $1,000 to be received one year from now using a stated annual interest rate of 6% with a range of compounding periods.

Answer:

Compounding Frequency Effect

Compounding Frequency	Interest Rate per Period	Effective Annual Rate	Future Value	Present Value
Annual (m = 1)	6.000%	6.00%	$1,060.00	$943.396
Semiannual (m = 2)	3.000	6.090	1,060.90	942.596
Quarterly (m = 4)	1.500	6.136	1,061.36	942.184
Monthly (m = 12)	0.500	6.168	1,061.68	941.905
Daily (m = 365)	0.016438	6.183	1,061.83	941.769

There are two ways to use your financial calculator to compute PVs and FVs under different compounding frequencies:

1. Adjust the number of periods per year (P/Y) mode on your calculator to correspond to the compounding frequency (e.g., for quarterly, P/Y = 4). WE DO NOT RECOMMEND THIS APPROACH!

2. Keep the calculator in the annual compounding mode (P/Y = 1) and enter I/Y as the interest rate per compounding period, and N as the number of compounding periods in the investment horizon. Letting m equal the number of compounding periods per year, the basic formulas for the calculator input data are determined as follows:

I/Y = the annual interest rate / m

N   = the number of years × m

The computations for the FV and PV amounts in the previous example are:

PV_A: FV = –1,000; I/Y = 6/1 = 6; N = 1 × 1 = 1:
        CPT → PV = PV_A = 943.396

PV_S: FV = –1,000; I/Y = 6/2 = 3; N = 1 × 2 = 2:
        CPT → PV = PV_S = 942.596

PV_Q: FV = –1,000; I/Y = 6/4 = 1.5; N = 1 × 4 = 4:
        CPT → PV = PV_Q = 942.184

PV_M: FV = –1,000; I/Y = 6/12 = 0.5; N = 1 × 12 = 12:
        CPT → PV = PV_M = 941.905

PV_D: FV = –1,000; I/Y = 6/365 = 0.016438; N = 1 × 365 = 365:
        CPT → PV = PV_D = 941.769

FV_A: PV = –1,000; I/Y = 6/1 = 6; N = 1 × 1 = 1:
        CPT → FV = FV_A = 1,060.00

FV_S: PV = –1,000; I/Y = 6/2 = 3; N = 1 × 2 = 2:
        CPT → FV = FV_S = 1,060.90

FV_Q: PV = –1,000; I/Y = 6/4 = 1.5; N = 1 × 4 = 4:
        CPT → FV = FV_Q =1,061.36

FV_M: PV = –1,000; I/Y = 6/12 = 0.5; N = 1 × 12 = 12:
        CPT → FV = FV_M = 1,061.68

FV_D: PV = –1,000; I/Y = 6/365 = 0.016438; N = 1 × 365 = 365:
        CPT → FV = FV_D = 1,061.83

Example: FV of a single sum using quarterly compounding

Compute the FV of $2,000 today, five years from today using an interest rate of 12%, compounded quarterly.

Answer:

To solve this problem, enter the relevant data and compute FV:

$$N = 5 \times 4 = 20; \ I/Y = 12 / 4 = 3; \ PV = -\$2,000; \ CPT \rightarrow FV = \$3,612.22$$

LOS 5.f: Draw a time line and solve time value of money applications (for example, mortgages and savings for college tuition or retirement).

In most of the PV problems we have discussed, cash flows were discounted back to the current period. In this case, the PV is said to be indexed to t = 0, or the time index is t = 0. For example, the PV of a 3-year ordinary annuity that is indexed to t = 0 is computed at the beginning of year 1 (t = 0). Contrast this situation with another 3-year ordinary annuity that doesn't start until year 4 and extends to year 6. It would not be uncommon to want to know the PV of this annuity at the beginning of year 4, in which case the time index is t = 3. The time line for this annuity is presented in Figure 5.

Figure 5: Indexing Time Line to Other Than t = 0

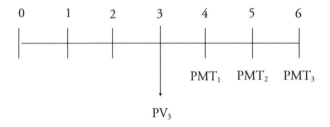

Loan Payments and Amortization

Loan **amortization** is the process of paying off a loan with a series of periodic loan payments, whereby a portion of the outstanding loan amount is paid off, or amortized, with each payment. When a company or individual enters into a long-term loan, the debt is usually paid off over time with a series of equal, periodic loan payments, and each payment includes the repayment of principal and an interest charge. The payments may be made monthly, quarterly, or even annually. Regardless of the payment frequency, the size of the payment remains fixed over the life of the loan. The amount of the principal and interest component of the loan payment, however, does not remain fixed over the term of the loan. Let's look at some examples to more fully develop the concept of amortization.

Example: Loan payment calculation: Annual payments

A company plans to borrow $50,000 for five years. The company's bank will lend the money at a rate of 9% and requires that the loan be paid off in five equal end-of-year payments. Calculate the amount of the payment that the company must make in order to fully amortize this loan in five years.

Answer:

To determine the annual loan payment, input the relevant data and compute PMT.

$$N = 5; I/Y = 9; PV = -50,000; CPT \rightarrow PMT = \$12,854.62$$

Thus, the loan can be paid off in five equal annual payments of $12,854.62. Please note that FV = 0 in this computation; the loan will be fully paid off (amortized) after the five payments have been made.

Example: Loan payment calculation: Quarterly payments

Using the loan described in the preceding example, determine the payment amount if the bank requires the company to make quarterly payments.

Answer:

The quarterly loan payment can be determined by inputting the relevant data and computing the payment (PMT):

$$N = 5 \times 4 = 20; I/Y = 9 / 4 = 2.25; PV = -50,000; CPT \rightarrow PMT = \$3,132.10$$

Example: Constructing an amortization schedule

Construct an amortization schedule to show the interest and principal components of the end-of-year payments for a 10%, 5-year, $10,000 loan.

Answer:

The first step in solving this problem is to compute the amount of the loan payments. This is done by entering the relevant data and computing PMT:

$$N = 5; I/Y = 10\%; PV = -\$10,000; CPT \rightarrow PMT = \$2,637.97$$

Thus, the loan will be repaid via five equal $2,637.97 end-of-year payments. Each payment is made up of an interest component (profit to the lender) plus the partial recovery of loan principal, with principal recovery being scheduled so that the full amount of the loan is paid off by the end of year 5. The exact amount of the principal and interest components of each loan payment are presented and described in the amortization table shown in the following figure.

Amortization Table

Period	Beginning Balance	Payment	Interest Component (1)	Principal Component (2)	Ending Balance (3)
1	$10,000.00	$2,637.97	$1,000.00	$1,637.97	$8,362.03
2	8,362.03	2,637.97	836.20	1,801.77	6,560.26
3	6,560.26	2,637.97	656.03	1,981.94	4,578.32
4	4,578.32	2,637.97	457.83	2,180.14	2,398.18
5	2,398.18	2,638.00*	239.82	2,398.18	0.00

* There is usually a slight amount of rounding error that must be recognized in the final period. The extra $0.03 associated with payment five reflects an adjustment for the rounding error and forces the ending balance to zero.

1. Interest component = beginning balance × periodic interest rate. In period 3, the interest component of the payment is $6,560.26 × 0.10 = $656.03.

2. Principal component = payment – interest. For example, the period 4 principal component is $2,637.97 – $457.83 = 2,180.14.

3. The ending balance in a given period, t, is the period's beginning balance minus the principal component of the payment, where the beginning balance for period t is the ending balance from period t – 1. For example, the period 2 ending balance equals $8,362.03 – $1,801.77 = $6,560.26, which becomes the period 3 beginning balance.

Professor's Note: Once you have solved for the payment, $2,637.97, the remaining principal on any payment date can be calculated by entering N = # of remaining payments and solving for the PV.

Example: Principal and interest component of a specific loan payment

Suppose you borrowed $10,000 at 10% interest to be paid semiannually over ten years. Calculate the amount of the outstanding balance for the loan after the second payment is made.

Answer:

First the amount of the payment must be determined by entering the relevant information and computing the payment.

PV = –$10,000; I/Y = 10 / 2 = 5; N = 10 × 2 = 20; CPT → PMT = $802.43

The principal and interest component of the second payment can be determined using the following process:

Payment 1:   Interest = ($10,000)(0.05) = $500

Principal = $802.43 – $500 = $302.43

Payment 2:   Interest = ($10,000 – $302.43)(0.05) = $484.88

Principal = $802.43 – $484.88 = $317.55

Remaining balance = $10,000 – $302.43 – $317.55 = $9,380.02

The following examples will illustrate how to compute I/Y, N, or PMT in annuity problems.

Example: Computing an annuity payment needed to achieve a given FV

At an expected rate of return of 7%, how much must be deposited at the end of each year for the next 15 years to accumulate $3,000?

Answer:

To solve this problem, enter the three relevant known values and compute PMT.

N = 15; I/Y = 7; FV = +$3,000; CPT → PMT = –$119.38 (ignore sign)

Example: Computing a loan payment

Suppose you are considering applying for a $2,000 loan that will be repaid with equal end-of-year payments over the next 13 years. If the annual interest rate for the loan is 6%, how much will your payments be?

Answer:

The size of the end-of-year loan payment can be determined by inputting values for the three known variables and computing PMT.

N = 13; I/Y = 6; PV = –2,000; CPT → PMT = $225.92

Example: Computing the number of periods in an annuity

How many $100 end-of-year payments are required to accumulate $920 if the discount rate is 9%?

Answer:

The number of payments necessary can be determined by inputting the relevant data and computing N.

I/Y = 9%; FV = $920; PMT = –$100; CPT → N = 7 years

It will take seven annual $100 payments, compounded at 9% annually, to accrue an investment value of $920.

Professor's Note: Remember the sign convention. PMT and FV must have opposite signs or your calculator will issue an error message.

Example: Computing the number of years in an ordinary annuity

Suppose you have a $1,000 ordinary annuity earning an 8% return. How many annual end-of-year $150 withdrawals can be made?

Answer:

The number of years in the annuity can be determined by entering the three relevant variables and computing N.

I/Y = 8; PMT = 150; PV = –1,000; CPT → N = 9.9 years

Example: Computing the rate of return for an annuity

Suppose you have the opportunity to invest $100 at the end of each of the next five years in exchange for $600 at the end of the fifth year. What is the annual rate of return on this investment?

Answer:

The rate of return on this investment can be determined by entering the relevant data and solving for I/Y.

N = 5; FV = $600; PMT = –100; CPT → I/Y = 9.13%

Example: Computing the discount rate for an annuity

What rate of return will you earn on an ordinary annuity that requires a $700 deposit today and promises to pay $100 per year at the end of each of the next ten years?

Answer:

The discount rate on this annuity is determined by entering the three known values and computing I/Y.

N = 10; PV = –700; PMT = 100; CPT → I/Y = 7.07%

Other Applications of TVM Functions

Example: Calculating the rate of compound growth

Sales at Acme, Inc., for the last five years (in millions) have been €4.5, €5.7, €5.3, €6.9, €7.1.

What is the compound annual growth rate of sales over the period?

Answer:

The five years of sales represent four years of growth. Mathematically, the compound annual growth rate of sales is $(7.1/4.5)^{\frac{1}{4}} -1 = 12.1\%$. The interim sales figures do not enter into the 4-year compound growth rate.

The calculator solution using the TVM keys is:

FV = 7.1, PV = –4.5, N = 4, CPT → I/Y = 12.08%

Note that if sales were 4.5 and grew for four years at an annual compound rate of 12.08%, they would grow to $4.5 (1.1208)^4 = 7.1$.

Example: Calculating the number of periods for specific growth

How many years will it take for an investment of $1,000 to grow to $2,000 at an annual compound rate of 14.87%?

Answer:

FV = 2,000, PV = –1,000, I/Y = 14.87, CPT → N = 4.9999

It will take five years for money to double at an annual compound rate of 14.87%.

Funding a Future Obligation

There are many TVM applications where it is necessary to determine the size of the deposit(s) that must be made over a specified period in order to meet a future liability. Two common examples of this type of application are (1) setting up a funding program for future college tuition and (2) the funding of a retirement program. In most of these applications, the objective is to determine the size of the payment(s) or deposit(s) necessary to meet a particular monetary goal.

Example: Computing the required payment to fund an annuity due

Suppose you must make five annual $1,000 payments, the first one starting at the beginning of year 4 (end of year 3). To accumulate the money to make these payments, you want to make three equal payments into an investment account, the first to be made one year from today. Assuming a 10% rate of return, what is the amount of these three payments?

The time line for this annuity problem is shown in the following figure.

Funding an Annuity Due

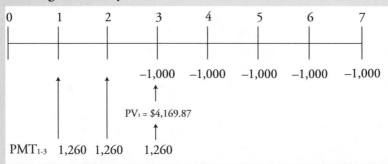

Answer:

The first step in this type of problem is to determine the amount of money that must be available at the beginning of year 4 (t = 3) in order to satisfy the payment requirements. This amount is the PV of a 5-year annuity due at the beginning of year 4 (end of year 3). To determine this amount, set your calculator to the BGN mode, enter the relevant data, and compute PV.

$$N = 5; \ I/Y = 10; \ PMT = -1,000; \ CPT \rightarrow PV = PV_3 = \$4,169.87$$

Alternatively, you can leave your calculator in the END mode, compute the PV of a 5-year ordinary annuity, and multiply by 1.10.

$$N = 5; \ I/Y = 10; \ PMT = -1,000;$$
$$CPT \rightarrow PV = 3,790.79 \times 1.1 = PV_3 = \$4,169.87$$

A third alternative, with the calculator in END mode, is to calculate the t = 3 value of the last four annuity payments and then add $1,000.

$$N = 4; \ I/Y = 10; \ PMT = -1,000;$$
$$CPT \rightarrow PV = 3,169.87 + 1,000 = \$4,169.87 = PV_3$$

PV_3 becomes the FV that you need three years from today from your three equal end-of-year deposits. To determine the amount of the three payments necessary to meet this funding requirement, be sure that your calculator is in the END mode, input the relevant data, and compute PMT.

N = 3; I/Y = 10; FV = –4,169.87; CPT → PMT = $1,259.78

The second part of this problem is an ordinary annuity. If you changed your calculator to BGN mode and failed to put it back in the END mode, you will get a PMT of $1,145, which is incorrect.

Example: Funding a retirement plan

Assume a 35-year-old investor wants to retire in 25 years at the age of 60. She expects to earn 12.5% on her investments prior to her retirement and 10% thereafter. How much must she deposit at the end of each year for the next 25 years in order to be able to withdraw $25,000 per year at the beginning of each year for the 30 years from age 60 to 90?

Answer:

This is a two-step problem. First determine the amount that must be on deposit in the retirement account at the end of year 25 in order to fund the 30-year, $25,000 annuity due. Second, compute the annuity payments that must be made to achieve the required amount.

Step 1: Compute the amount required to meet the desired withdrawals.

The required amount is the present value of the $25,000, 30-year annuity due at the beginning of year 26 (end of year 25). This can be determined by entering the relevant data, with the calculator in the END mode, and computing PV.

N = 29; I/Y = 10; PMT = –$25,000: CPT → PV = $234,240 (for 29 years)

Now add the first annuity payment to get $234,240 + $25,000 = $259,240. The investor will need $259,240 at the end of year 25.

Please note that we could have also performed this computation with our calculator in BGN mode as an annuity due. To do this, put your calculator in BGN mode [2nd] [BGN] [2nd] [SET] [2nd] [QUIT] on the TI or [g] [BEG] on the HP. Then enter:

N = 30; PMT = –25,000; I/Y = 10; CPT → PV = 259,240.14

If you do it this way, make certain you reset your calculator to the END mode.

Step 2: The annuity payment that must be made to accumulate the required amount over 25 years can be determined by entering the relevant data and computing PMT.

N = 25; I/Y = 12.5; FV = –259,240; CPT → PMT = $1,800.02

Thus, the investor must deposit $1,800 per year at the end of each of the next 25 years in order to accumulate $259,240. With this amount she will be able to withdraw $25,000 per year for the following 30 years.

Note that all these calculations assume that the investor will earn 12.5% on the payments prior to retirement and 10% on the funds held in the retirement account thereafter.

The Connection Between Present Values, Future Values, and Series of Cash Flows

As we have explained in the discussion of annuities and series of uneven cash flows, the sum of the present values of the cash flows is the present value of the series. The sum of the future values (at some future time = n) of a series of cash flows is the future value of that series of cash flows.

One interpretation of the present value of a series of cash flows is how much would have to be put in the bank today in order to make these future withdrawals and exhaust the account with the final withdrawal. Let's illustrate this with cash flows of $100 in year 1, $200 in year 2, $300 in year 3, and an assumed interest rate of 10%.

Calculate the present value of these three cash flows as:

$$\frac{100}{1.1} + \frac{200}{1.1^2} + \frac{300}{1.1^3} = \$481.59$$

If we put $481.59 in an account yielding 10%, at the end of the year we would have $481.59 \times 1.1 = \$529.75$. Withdrawing $100 would leave $429.75.

Over the second year, the $429.75 would grow to $429.75 \times 1.1 = \$472.73$. Withdrawing $200 would leave $272.73.

Over the third year, $272.73 would grow to $272.73 \times 1.1 = \$300$, so that the last withdrawal of $300 would empty the account.

The interpretation of the future value of a series of cash flows is straightforward as well. The FV answers the question, "How much would be in an account when the last of a series of deposits is made?" Using the same three cash flows—$100, $200, and $300—and the same interest rate of 10%, we can calculate the future value of the series as:

$$100 (1.1)^2 + 200 (1.1) + 300 = \$641$$

This is simply the sum of the t = 3 value of each of the cash flows. Note that the t = 3 value and the t = 0 (present) value of the series are related by the interest rate, $481.59 (1.1)^3 = 641$.

The $100 cash flow (deposit) comes at t = 1, so it will earn interest of 10% compounded for two periods (until t = 3). The $200 cash flow (deposit) will earn 10% between t = 2 and t = 3, and the final cash flow (deposit) of $300 is made at t = 3, so $300 is the future (t = 3) value of that cash flow.

We can also look at the future value in terms of how the account grows over time. At t = 1 we deposit $100, so at t = 2 it has grown to $110 and the $200 deposit at t = 2 makes the account balance $310. Over the next period, the $310 grows to 310 × 1.1 = $341 at t = 3, and the addition of the final $300 deposit puts the account balance at $641. This is, of course, the future value we calculated initially.

 Professor's Note: This last view of the future value of a series of cash flows suggests a quick way to calculate the future value of an uneven cash flow series. The process described previously for the future value of a series of end-of-period payments can be written mathematically as [(100 × 1.1) + 200] × 1.1 + 300 = 641, and this might be a quick way to do some future value problems.

Note that questions on the future value of an *annuity due* refer to the amount in the account one period after the last deposit is made. If the three deposits considered here were made at the beginning of each period (at t = 0, 1, 2) the amount in the account at the end of three years (t = 3) would be 10% higher (i.e., 641 × 1.1 = $705.10).

The **cash flow additivity principle** refers to the fact that present value of any stream of cash flows equals the sum of the present values of the cash flows. There are different applications of this principle in time value of money problems. If we have two series of cash flows, the sum of the present values of the two series is the same as the present values of the two series taken together, adding cash flows that will be paid at the same point in time. We can also divide up a series of cash flows any way we like, and the present value of the "pieces" will equal the present value of the original series.

Example: Additivity principle

A security will make the following payments at the end of the next four years: $100, $100, $400, and $100. Calculate the present value of these cash flows using the concept of the present value of an annuity when the appropriate discount rate is 10%.

Answer:

We can divide the cash flows so that we have:

t = 1	t = 2	t = 3	t = 4	
100	100	100	100	cash flow series #1
0	0	300	0	cash flow series #2
$100	$100	$400	$100	

The additivity principle tells us that to get the present value of the original series, we can just add the present values of series #1 (a 4-period annuity) and series #2 (a single payment three periods from now).

For the annuity: N = 4, PMT = 100, FV = 0, I/Y = 10, CPT → PV = –$316.99

For the single payment: N = 3, PMT = 0, FV = 300, I/Y = 10, CPT → PV = –$225.39

The sum of these two values is 316.99 + 225.39 = $542.38.

The sum of these two (present) values is identical (except for rounding) to the sum of the present values of the payments of the original series:

$$\frac{100}{1.1} + \frac{100}{1.1^2} + \frac{400}{1.1^3} + \frac{100}{1.1^4} = \$542.38$$

KEY CONCEPTS

LOS 5.a

An interest rate can be interpreted as the rate of return required in equilibrium for a particular investment, the discount rate for calculating the present value of future cash flows, or as the opportunity cost of consuming now, rather than saving and investing.

LOS 5.b

The real risk-free rate is a theoretical rate on a single period loan when there is no expectation of inflation. Nominal risk-free rate = real risk-free rate + expected inflation rate.

Securities may have several risks, and each increases the required rate of return. These include default risk, liquidity risk, and maturity risk.

The required rate of return on a security = real risk-free rate + expected inflation + default risk premium + liquidity premium + maturity risk premium.

LOS 5.c

The effective annual rate when there are m compounding periods =

$$\left(1 + \frac{\text{stated annual rate}}{m}\right)^m - 1 \text{. Each dollar invested will grow to}$$

$$\left(1 + \frac{\text{stated annual rate}}{m}\right)^m \text{ in one year.}$$

LOS 5.d

For non-annual time value of money problems, divide the stated annual interest rate by the number of compounding periods per year, m, and multiply the number of years by the number of compounding periods per year.

LOS 5.e

Future value: $FV = PV(1 + I/Y)^N$

Present value: $PV = FV / (1 + I/Y)^N$

An annuity is a series of equal cash flows that occurs at evenly spaced intervals over time. Ordinary annuity cash flows occur at the end of each time period. Annuity due cash flows occur at the beginning of each time period.

Perpetuities are annuities with infinite lives (perpetual annuities):

$$PV_{\text{perpetuity}} = \frac{PMT}{I/Y}$$

The present (future) value of any series of cash flows is equal to the sum of the present (future) values of the individual cash flows.

LOS 5.f
Constructing a time line showing future cash flows will help in solving many types of TVM problems.

A mortgage is an amortizing loan, repaid in a series of equal payments (an annuity), where each payment consists of the interest for the period (which decreases with each payment) and the amount of principal repaid (which increases with each payment).

CONCEPT CHECKERS

1. The amount an investor will have in 15 years if $1,000 is invested today at an annual interest rate of 9% will be *closest* to:
   A. $1,350.
   B. $3,518.
   C. $3,642.

2. Fifty years ago, an investor bought a share of stock for $10. The stock has paid no dividends during this period, yet it has returned 20%, compounded annually, over the past 50 years. If this is true, the share price is now *closest* to:
   A. $4,550.
   B. $45,502.
   C. $91,004.

3. How much must be invested today at 0% to have $100 in three years?
   A. $77.75.
   B. $100.00.
   C. $126.30.

4. How much must be invested today, at 8% interest, to accumulate enough to retire a $10,000 debt due seven years from today? The amount that must be invested today is *closest* to:
   A. $5,835.
   B. $6,123.
   C. $8,794.

5. An analyst estimates that XYZ's earnings will grow from $3.00 a share to $4.50 per share over the next eight years. The rate of growth in XYZ's earnings is *closest* to:
   A. 4.9%.
   B. 5.2%.
   C. 6.7%.

6. If $5,000 is invested in a fund offering a rate of return of 12% per year, approximately how many years will it take for the investment to reach $10,000?
   A. 4 years.
   B. 5 years.
   C. 6 years.

7. An investment is expected to produce the cash flows of $500, $200, and $800 at the end of the next three years. If the required rate of return is 12%, the present value of this investment is *closest* to:
   A. $835.
   B. $1,175.
   C. $1,235.

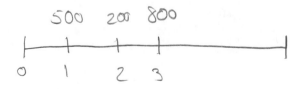

8. Given an 8.5% discount rate, an asset that generates cash flows of $10 in year 1, –$20 in year 2, $10 in year 3, and is then sold for $150 at the end of year 4, has a present value of:
   A. $108.29.
   B. $135.58.
   C. $163.42.

9. An investor has just won the lottery and will receive $50,000 per year at the end of each of the next 20 years. At a 10% interest rate, the present value of the winnings is *closest* to:
   A. $425,678.
   B. $637,241.
   C. $2,863,750.

10. If $10,000 is invested today in an account that earns interest at a rate of 9.5%, what is the value of the equal withdrawals that can be taken out of the account at the end of each of the next five years if the investor plans to deplete the account at the end of the time period?
    A. $2,453.
    B. $2,604.
    C. $2,750.

11. An investor is to receive a 15-year $8,000 annuity, the first payment to be received today. At an 11% discount rate, this annuity's worth today is *closest* to:
    A. $55,855.
    B. $57,527.
    C. $63,855.

12. Given an 11% rate of return, the amount that must be put into an investment account at the end of each of the next ten years in order to accumulate $60,000 to pay for a child's education is *closest* to:
    A. $2,500.
    B. $3,588.
    C. $4,432.

13. An investor will receive an annuity of $4,000 a year for ten years. The first payment is to be received five years from today. At a 9% discount rate, this annuity's worth today is *closest* to:
    A. $16,684.
    B. $18,186.
    C. $25,671.

14. If $1,000 is invested today and $1,000 is invested at the beginning of each of the next three years at 12% interest (compounded annually), the amount an investor will have at the end of the fourth year will be *closest* to:
    A. $4,779.
    B. $5,353.
    C. $6,792.

15. An investor is looking at a $150,000 home. If 20% must be put down and the balance is financed at 9% over the next 30 years, what is the monthly mortgage payment?
    A. $799.33.
    B. $895.21.
    C. $965.55.

16. Given daily compounding, the growth of $5,000 invested for one year at 12% interest will be *closest* to:
    A. $5,600.
    B. $5,628.
    C. $5,637.

17. Terry Corporation preferred stocks are expected to pay a $9 annual dividend forever. If the required rate of return on equivalent investments is 11%, a share of Terry preferred should be worth:
    A. $81.82.
    B. $99.00.
    C. $122.22.

18. A share of George Co. preferred stock is selling for $65. It pays a dividend of $4.50 per year and has a perpetual life. The rate of return it is offering its investors is *closest* to:
    A. 4.5%.
    B. 6.9%.
    C. 14.4%.

19. If $10,000 is borrowed at 10% interest to be paid back over ten years, how much of the second year's payment is interest (assume annual loan payments)?
    A. $937.26.
    B. $954.25.
    C. $1,037.26.

20. What is the effective annual rate for a credit card that charges 18% compounded monthly?
    A. 15.38%.
    B. 18.81%.
    C. 19.56%.

COMPREHENSIVE PROBLEMS

1. The Parks plan to take three cruises, one each year. They will take their first cruise 9 years from today, the second cruise one year after that, and the third cruise 11 years from today. The type of cruise they will take currently costs $5,000, but they expect inflation will increase this cost by 3.5% per year on average. They will contribute to an account to save for these cruises that will earn 8% per year. What equal contributions must they make today and every year until their first cruise (ten contributions) in order to have saved enough at that time for all three cruises? They pay for cruises when taken.

2. A company's dividend in 1995 was $0.88. Over the next eight years, the dividends were $0.91, $0.99, $1.12, $0.95, $1.09, $1.25, $1.42, and $1.26. Calculate the annually compounded growth rate of the dividend over the whole period.

3. An investment (a bond) will pay $1,500 at the end of each year for 25 years and on the date of the last payment will also make a separate payment of $40,000. If your required rate of return on this investment is 4%, how much would you be willing to pay for the bond today?

4. A bank quotes certificate of deposit (CD) yields both as annual percentage rates (APR) without compounding and as annual percentage yields (APY) that include the effects of monthly compounding. A $100,000 CD will pay $110,471.31 at the end of the year. Calculate the APR and APY the bank is quoting.

5. A client has $202,971.39 in an account that earns 8% per year, compounded monthly. The client's 35th birthday was yesterday and she will retire when the account value is $1 million.
   A. At what age can she retire if she puts no more money in the account?
   B. At what age can she retire if she puts $250 per month into the account every month, beginning one month from today?

6. At retirement nine years from now, a client will have the option of receiving a lump sum of £400,000 or 20 annual payments of £40,000, with the first payment made at retirement. What is the annual rate the client would need to earn on a retirement investment to be indifferent between the two choices?

ANSWERS – CONCEPT CHECKERS

1. **C**   N = 15; I/Y = 9; PV = –1,000; PMT = 0; CPT → FV = $3,642.48

2. **C**   N = 50; I/Y = 20; PV = –10; PMT = 0; CPT → FV = $91,004.38

3. **B**   Since no interest is earned, $100 is needed today to have $100 in three years.

4. **A**   N = 7; I/Y = 8; FV = –10,000; PMT = 0; CPT → PV = $5,834.90

5. **B**   N = 8; PV = –3; FV = 4.50; PMT = 0; CPT → I/Y = 5.1989

6. **C**   PV = –5,000; I/Y = 12; FV = 10,000; PMT = 0; CPT → N = 6.12. Rule of 72 → 72/12 = six years.

   Note to HP 12C users: One known problem with the HP 12C is that it does not have the capability to round. In this particular question, you will come up with 7, although the correct answer is 6.1163. CFA Institute is aware of this problem, and hopefully you will not be faced with a situation on exam day where the incorrect solution from the HP is one of the answer choices.

7. **B**   Using your cash flow keys, CF_0 = 0; CF_1 = 500; CF_2 = 200; CF_3 = 800; I/Y = 12; NPV = $1,175.29.

   Or you can add up the present values of each single cash flow.

   PV_1 = N = 1; FV = –500; I/Y = 12; CPT → PV = 446.43
   PV_2 = N = 2; FV = –200; I/Y = 12; CPT → PV = 159.44
   PV_3 = N = 3; FV = –800; I/Y = 12; CPT → PV = 569.42

   Hence, 446.43 + 159.44 + 569.42 = $1,175.29.

8. **A**   Using your cash flow keys, CF_0 = 0; CF_1 = 10; CF_2 = –20; CF_3 = 10; CF_4 = 150; I/Y = 8.5; NPV = $108.29.

9. **A**   N = 20; I/Y = 10; PMT = –50,000; FV = 0; CPT → PV = $425,678.19

10. **B**   PV = –10,000; I/Y = 9.5; N = 5; FV = 0; CPT → PMT = $2,604.36

11. **C**   This is an annuity due. Switch to BGN mode.

    N = 15; PMT = –8,000; I/Y = 11; FV = 0; CPT → PV = 63,854.92. Switch back to END mode.

12. **B**   N = 10; I/Y = 11; FV = –60,000; PV = 0; CPT → PMT = $3,588.08

13. **B**   Two steps: (1) Find the PV of the 10-year annuity: N = 10; I/Y = 9; PMT = –4,000; FV = 0; CPT → PV = 25,670.63. This is the present value as of the end of year 4; (2) Discount PV of the annuity back four years: N = 4; PMT = 0; FV = –25,670.63; I/Y = 9; CPT → PV = 18,185.72.

14. **B**   The key to this problem is to recognize that it is a 4-year annuity due, so switch to BGN mode: N = 4; PMT = –1,000; PV = 0; I/Y = 12; CPT → FV = 5,352.84. Switch back to END mode.

15. **C** $N = 30 \times 12 = 360$; $I/Y = 9 / 12 = 0.75$; $PV = -150,000(1 - 0.2) = -120,000$; $FV = 0$; $CPT \rightarrow PMT = \$965.55$

16. **C** $N = 1 \times 365 = 365$; $I/Y = 12 / 365 = 0.0328767$; $PMT = 0$; $PV = -5,000$; $CPT \rightarrow FV = \$5,637.37$

17. **A** $9 / 0.11 = \$81.82$

18. **B** $4.5 / 65 = 0.0692$ or 6.92%

19. **A** To get the annual payment, enter $PV = -10,000$; $FV = 0$; $I/Y = 10$; $N = 10$; $CPT \rightarrow PMT = 1,627.45$. The first year's interest is $\$1,000 = 10,000 \times 0.10$, so the principal balance going into year 2 is $10,000 - 627.45 = \$9,372.55$. Year 2 interest $= \$9,372.55 \times 0.10 = \$937.26$.

20. **C** $EAR = (1 + 0.18/12)^{12} - 1 = 19.56\%$

ANSWERS – COMPREHENSIVE PROBLEMS

1.   Our suggested solution method is:

$$\text{cost of first cruise} = 5,000 \times 1.035^9$$
$$= 6,814.49$$

$$\text{PV of first cruise cost} = \frac{6,814.49}{(1.08)^9} = \$3,408.94$$

$$\text{PV of second cruise cost} = \frac{(1.035)^{10}}{(1.08)^{10}} \times 5,000 = \$3,266.90$$

$$\text{PV of third cruise cost} = \left(\frac{1.035}{1.08}\right)^{11} \times 5,000 = \$3,130.78$$

PV of all three $= 3,408.94 + 3,266.90 + 3,130.78 = \$9,806.62$. This is the amount needed in the account today, so it's the PV of a 10-payment annuity due. Solve for payment at 8% $= \$1,353.22$.

2.   This problem is simpler than it may appear. The dividend grew from $0.88 to $1.26 in eight years. We know, then, that $0.88(1 + i)^8 = 1.26$, where i is the compound growth rate. Solving for i we get $\left(\frac{1.26}{0.88}\right)^{1/8} - 1 = 4.589\%$. You could also just enter $\frac{1.26}{0.88}$, press

$\left[\sqrt{\ }\right]$ three times, get 1.045890, and see that the answer is 4.589%.

This technique for solving for a compound growth rate is a very useful one, and you will see it often.

Calculator solution: PV = 0.88, N = 8, FV = –1.26, PMT = 0, $CPT \rightarrow I/Y = 4.589$.

3. We can take the present value of the payments (a regular annuity) and the present value of the $40,000 (lump sum) and add them together. N = 25, PMT = –1,500, i = 4,

    CPT → PV = 23,433.12 and $40,000 \times \left(\dfrac{1}{1.04}\right)^{25} = 15,004.67$, for a total value of

    $38,437.79.

    Alternatively, N = 25, PMT = –1,500, i = 4, FV = –40,000, CPT → PV = 38,437.79.

4. For APR, PV = 100,000, FV = –110,471.31, PMT = 0, N = 12, CPT I/Y 0.8333, which is the monthly rate. The APR = 12 × 0.8333, or 10%.

    APY = 110,471.31 / 100,000 – 1 = 0.10471 = 10.471% (equivalent to a compound monthly rate of 0.8333%)

5. A. PV = –202,971.39, I/Y = 8/12 = 0.6667, PMT = 0, FV = 1,000,000,
        CPT → N = 240. 240 months is 20 years; she will be 55 years old.
    B. Don't clear TVM functions. PMT = –250, CPT → N = 220, which is 18.335 years, so she will be 53. (N is actually 220.024, so the HP calculator displays 221.)

6. Setting the retirement date to t = 0 we have the following choices:

t = 0	t = 1	t = 2	...	t = 20
400,000				
40,000	40,000	40,000	...	40,000

    One method: PV = 400,000 – 40,000 = 360,000; PMT = –40,000; N = 19; FV = 0;
    CPT → I/Y = 8.9196%

    Or in *begin mode*: PV = 400,000; N = 20; FV = 0; PMT = –40,000;
    CPT → I/Y = 8.9196%

The following is a review of the Quantitative Methods: Basic Concepts principles designed to address the learning outcome statements set forth by CFA Institute®. This topic is also covered in:

DISCOUNTED CASH FLOW APPLICATIONS

EXAM FOCUS

This topic review has a mix of topics, but all are important because of their usefulness and the certainty that some, if not all, of these topics will be on the exam. You must be able to use the cash flow functions on your calculator to calculate net present value and internal rate of return. We will use both of these in the Corporate Finance section and examine their strengths and weaknesses more closely there; but you must learn how to calculate them here. The time-weighted and money-weighted return calculations are standard tools for analysis. Calculating the various yield measures and the ability to calculate one from another are must-have skills. Don't hurry here, these concepts and techniques are foundation material and will turn up repeatedly at all three levels of the CFA® curriculum.

LOS 6.a: Calculate and interpret the net present value (NPV) and the internal rate of return (IRR) of an investment, contrast the NPV rule to the IRR rule, and identify problems associated with the IRR rule.

The **net present value** (NPV) of an investment project is the present value of expected cash inflows associated with the project less the present value of the project's expected cash outflows, discounted at the appropriate cost of capital. The following procedure may be used to compute NPV:

- Identify all costs (outflows) and benefits (inflows) associated with an investment.
- Determine the appropriate discount rate or opportunity cost for the investment.
- Using the appropriate discount rate, find the PV of each cash flow. Inflows are positive and increase NPV. Outflows are negative and decrease NPV.
- Compute the NPV, the sum of the DCFs.

Mathematically, NPV is expressed as:

$$NPV = \sum_{t=0}^{N} \frac{CF_t}{(1+r)^t}$$

where:
CF_t = the expected net cash flow at time t
N = the estimated life of the investment
r = the discount rate (opportunity cost of capital)

NPV is the PV of the cash flows less the initial (time = 0) outlay.

Example: Computing NPV

Calculate the NPV of an investment project with an initial cost of $5 million and positive cash flows of $1.6 million at the end of year 1, $2.4 million at the end of year 2, and $2.8 million at the end of year 3. Use 12% as the discount rate.

Answer:

The NPV for this project is the sum of the PVs of the project's individual cash flows and is determined as follows:

$$NPV = -\$5.0 + \frac{\$1.6}{1.12} + \frac{\$2.4}{(1.12)^2} + \frac{\$2.8}{(1.12)^3}$$

$$= -\$5.0 + \$1.42857 + \$1.91327 + \$1.99299$$

$$= \$0.3348 \text{ million, or } \$334,800$$

The procedures for calculating NPV with a TI BAII Plus® and an HP 12C® hand-held financial calculator are presented in Figures 1 and 2.

Figure 1: Calculating NPV with the TI Business Analyst II Plus®

Key Strokes	Explanation	Display
[CF] [2nd] [CLR WORK]	Clear CF Memory Registers	CF0 = 0.00000
5 [+/–] [ENTER]	Initial Cash Outlay	CF0 = –5.00000
[↓]1.6 ENTER]	Period 1 Cash Flow	C01 = 1.60000
[↓] [↓] 2.4 [ENTER]	Period 2 Cash Flow	C02 = 2.40000
[↓] [↓] 2.8 [ENTER]	Period 3 Cash Flow	C03 = 2.80000
[NPV] 12 [ENTER]	12% discount rate	I = 12.00000
[↓] [CPT]	Calculate NPV	NPV = 0.33482

Figure 2: Calculating NPV with the HP12C®

Key Strokes	Explanation	Display
[f] [FIN] [f] [REG]	Clear Memory Registers	0.00000
5 [CHS] [g] [CF$_0$]	Initial Cash Outlay	–5.00000
1.6 [g] [CF$_j$]	Period 1 Cash flow	1.60000
2.4 [g] [CF$_j$]	Period 2 Cash flow	2.40000
2.8 [g] [CF$_j$]	Period 3 Cash flow	2.80000
12 [i]	12% discount rate	12.00000
[f] [NPV]	Calculate NPV	0.33482

On the TI BAII Plus calculator, the sequence of [↓][↓] scrolls past the variables F01, F02, et cetera. The F here stands for frequency, and this is set to 1 by default. We did not enter anything because each cash flow amount occurred only once. If the period 2 cash flow, C02, were repeated three times (at t = 2, 3, and 4) we could input F02 = 3 to account for all three of these. The next input, C03, would then refer to the cash flow at t = 5.

On the HP 12C, you can also account for a repeated cash flow amount. Referring to the above example for the TI BAII Plus, the fact that the cash flow at period 2 is repeated for three periods is indicated by the sequence 3 [g] N_j immediately after the CF_j keystroke to input the amount of the period 2 cash flow.

 Professor's Note: The NPV function can also be used to find the present value of any series of cash flows (positive or negative) over future periods. Just set $CF_0 = 0$ and input the cash flows CF_1 through CF_N as outlined above. The NPV is the present value of these cash flows since there is now no initial negative cash flow (initial cost).

The **internal rate of return** (IRR) is defined as the rate of return that equates the PV of an investment's expected benefits (inflows) with the PV of its costs (outflows). Equivalently, the IRR may be defined as the discount rate for which the NPV of an investment is zero.

Calculating IRR requires only that we identify the relevant cash flows for the investment opportunity being evaluated. Market-determined discount rates, or any other external (market-driven) data, are not necessary with the IRR procedure. The general formula for the IRR is:

$$0 = CF_0 + \frac{CF_1}{1+IRR} + \frac{CF_2}{(1+IRR)^2} + \cdots + \frac{CF_N}{(1+IRR)^N}$$

In the majority of IRR applications to capital budgeting, the initial cash flow, CF_0, represents the initial cost of the investment opportunity, and is therefore a negative value. As such, any discount rate less than the IRR will result in a positive NPV, and a discount rate greater than the IRR will result in a negative NPV. This implies that the NPV of an investment is zero when the discount rate used equals the IRR.

Example: Computing IRR

What is the IRR for the investment described in the preceding example?

Answer:

Substituting the investment's cash flows into the previous IRR equation results in the following equation:

$$0 = -5.0 + \frac{1.6}{1+IRR} + \frac{2.4}{(1+IRR)^2} + \frac{2.8}{(1+IRR)^3}$$

Solving this equation yields an IRR = 15.52%.

It is possible to solve IRR problems through a trial and error process. That is, keep guessing IRRs until you get the one that provides an NPV equal to zero. Practically speaking, a financial calculator or an electronic spreadsheet can and should be employed. The procedures for computing IRR with the TI BA II Plus and HP 12C financial calculators are illustrated in the following figures, respectively.

Calculating IRR with the TI Business Analyst II Plus®

Key Strokes	Explanation	Display
[CF] [2nd] [CLR WORK]	Clear Memory Registers	CF0 = 0.00000
5 [+/–] [ENTER]	Initial Cash Outlay	CF0 = –5.00000
[↓] 1.6 [ENTER]	Period 1 Cash Flow	C01 = 1.60000
[↓] [↓] 2.4 [ENTER]	Period 2 Cash Flow	C02 = 2.40000
[↓] [↓] 2.8 [ENTER]	Period 3 Cash Flow	C03 = 2.80000
[IRR] [CPT]	Calculate IRR	IRR = 15.51757

Calculating IRR with the HP12C®

Key Strokes	Explanation	Display
[f] [FIN] [f] [REG]	Clear Memory Registers	0.00000
5 [CHS] [g] [CF$_0$]	Initial Cash Outlay	–5.00000
1.6 [g] [CF$_j$]	Period 1 Cash flow	1.60000
2.4 [g] [CF$_j$]	Period 2 Cash flow	2.40000 ·
2.8 [g] [CF$_j$]	Period 3 Cash flow	2.80000
[f] [IRR]	Calculate IRR	15.51757

The NPV Decision Rule vs. the IRR Rule

NPV decision rule. The basic idea behind NPV analysis is that if a project has a positive NPV, this amount goes to the firm's shareholders. As such, if a firm undertakes a project with a positive NPV, shareholder wealth is increased.

The NPV decision rules are summarized:

- Accept projects with a positive NPV. Positive NPV projects will increase shareholder wealth.
- Reject projects with a negative NPV. Negative NPV projects will decrease shareholder wealth.
- When two projects are mutually exclusive (only one can be accepted), the project with the higher positive NPV should be accepted.

IRR decision rule. Analyzing an investment (project) using the IRR method provides the analyst with a result in terms of a rate of return.

The following are decision rules of IRR analysis:

- Accept projects with an IRR that is greater than the firm's (investor's) required rate of return.

- Reject projects with an IRR that is less than the firm's (investor's) required rate of return.

Note that for a single project, the IRR and NPV rules lead to exactly the same accept/reject decision. If the IRR is greater than the required rate of return, the NPV is positive, and if the IRR is less than the required rate of return, the NPV is negative.

Problems Associated With the IRR Method

When the acceptance or rejection of one project has no effect on the acceptance or rejection of another, the two projects are considered to be independent projects. When only one of two projects may be accepted, the projects are considered to be mutually exclusive. For mutually exclusive projects, the NPV and IRR methods can give conflicting project rankings. This can happen when the projects' initial costs are of different sizes or when the timing of the cash flows is different. Let's look at an example that illustrates how NPV and IRR can yield conflicting results.

Example: Conflicting decisions between NPV and IRR

Assume NPV and IRR analysis of two mutually exclusive projects produced the results shown in the following figure. As indicated, the IRR criteria recommends that Project A should be accepted. On the other hand, the NPV criteria indicates acceptance of Project B. Which project should be selected?

Ranking Reversals With NPV and IRR

Project	Investment at t = 0	Cash Flow at t = 1	IRR	NPV at 10%
A	−$5,000	$8,000	60%	$2,272.72
B	−$30,000	$40,000	33%	$6,363.64

Answer:

Investing in Project A increases shareholder wealth by $2,272.72, while investing in Project B increases shareholder wealth by $6,363.64. Since the overall goal of the firm is to maximize shareholder wealth, Project B should be selected because it adds the most value to the firm.

Mathematically speaking, the NPV method assumes the reinvestment of a project's cash flows at the opportunity cost of capital, while the IRR method assumes that the reinvestment rate is the IRR. The discount rate used with the NPV approach represents the market-based opportunity cost of capital and is the required rate of return for the shareholders of the firm.

Given that shareholder wealth maximization is the ultimate goal of the firm, always *select the project with the greatest NPV when the IRR and NPV rules provide conflicting decisions.*

LOS 6.b: Define, calculate, and interpret a holding period return (total return).

A holding period can be any period of time. The holding period of an investment may be a matter of days or as long as several years. The **holding period return** is simply the percentage change in the value of an investment over the period it is held. If the asset has cash flows, such as dividend or interest payments, we refer to the return, including the value of these interim cash flows, as the **total return**.

As an example, consider a Treasury bill purchased for $980 and sold three months later for $992. The holding period return can be calculated as:

$$\text{HPR} = \frac{\text{ending value} - \text{beginning value}}{\text{beginning value}} = \frac{\text{ending value}}{\text{beginning value}} - 1$$

and we have $\dfrac{992}{980} - 1 = 0.0122$ or 1.22%

We would say that the investor's 3-month holding period return was 1.22%.

As an example of a security that has interim cash payments, consider a stock that is purchased for $30 and is sold for $33 six months later, during which time it paid $0.50 in dividends. The holding period return (total return in this case) can be calculated as:

$$\text{HPR} = \frac{\text{ending value} - \text{beginning value} + \text{cash flow received}}{\text{beginning value}}$$

$$= \frac{\text{ending value} + \text{cash flow received}}{\text{beginning value}} - 1$$

and we have $\dfrac{33 + 0.50}{30} - 1 = 0.1167$ or 11.67%,

which is the investor's total return over the holding period of six months.

LOS 6.c: Calculate, interpret, and distinguish between the money-weighted and time-weighted rates of return of a portfolio and appraise the performance of portfolios based on these measures.

The **money-weighted return** applies the concept of IRR to investment portfolios. The money-weighted rate of return is defined as the internal rate of return on a portfolio, taking into account all cash inflows and outflows. The beginning value of the account is an inflow, as are all deposits into the account. All withdrawals from the account are outflows, as is the ending value.

Example: Money-weighted rate of return

Assume an investor buys a share of stock for $100 at t = 0 and at the end of the next year (t = 1), she buys an additional share for $120. At the end of year 2, the investor sells both shares for $130 each. At the end of each year in the holding period, the stock paid a $2.00 per share dividend. What is the money-weighted rate of return?

Step 1: Determine the timing of each cash flow and whether the cash flow is an inflow (+), into the account, or an outflow (–), available from the account.

t = 0:	purchase of first share	= +$100.00 inflow to account
t = 1:	purchase of second share	= +$120.00
	dividend from first share	= –$2.00
	Subtotal, t = 1	+$118.00 inflow to account
t = 2:	dividend from two shares	= –$4.00
	proceeds from selling shares =	–$260.00
	Subtotal, t = 2	–$264.00 outflow from account

Step 2: Net the cash flows for each time period and set the PV of cash inflows equal to the present value of cash outflows.

$$PV_{inflows} = PV_{outflows}$$

$$\$100 + \frac{\$118}{(1+r)} = \frac{\$264}{(1+r)^2}$$

Step 3: Solve for *r* to find the money-weighted rate of return. This can be done using trial and error or by using the IRR function on a financial calculator or spreadsheet.

The intuition here is that we deposited $100 into the account at t = 0, then added $118 to the account at t = 1 (which, with the $2 dividend, funded the purchase of one more share at $120), and ended with a total value of $264.

To compute this value with a financial calculator, use these net cash flows and follow the procedure(s) described to calculate the IRR.

Net cash flows: CF_0 = +100; CF_1 = +120 – 2 = +118; CF_2 = –260 + –4 = –264

Calculating money-weighted return with the TI Business Analyst II Plus®

Note that the values for F01, F02, etc., are all equal to one.

Key Strokes	Explanation	Display
[CF] [2nd][CLR WORK]	Clear Cash Flow Registers	CF0 = 0.00000
100 [ENTER]	Initial Cash Outlay	CF0 = +100.00000
[↓] 118 [ENTER]	Period 1 Cash Flow	C01 = +118.00000
[↓] [↓] 264 [+/–] [ENTER]	Period 2 Cash Flow	C02 = –264.00000
[IRR] [CPT]	Calculate IRR	IRR = 13.86122

Calculating money-weighted return with the HP12C®

Key Strokes	Explanation	Display
[f] [FIN] [f] [REG]	Clear Memory Registers	0.00000
100 [g] [CF₀]	Initial Cash Outlay	+100.00000
118 [g] [CFⱼ]	Period 1 Cash Flow	+118.00000
264 [CHS] [g] [CFⱼ]	Period 2 Cash Flow	–264.00000
[f] [IRR]	Calculate IRR	13.86122

The money-weighted rate of return for this problem is 13.86%.

Professor's Note: In the preceding example, we entered the flows into the account as positive and the ending value as a negative (the investor could withdraw this amount from the account). Note that there is no difference in the solution if we enter the cash flows into the account as negative values (out of the investor's pocket) and the ending value as a positive value (into the investor's pocket). As long as payments into the account and payments out of the account (including the ending value) are entered with opposite signs, the computed IRR will be correct.

Time-weighted rate of return measures compound growth. It is the rate at which $1 compounds over a specified performance horizon. Time-weighting is the process of averaging a set of values over time. The *annual* time-weighted return for an investment may be computed by performing the following steps:

Step 1: Value the portfolio immediately preceding significant additions or withdrawals. Form subperiods over the evaluation period that correspond to the dates of deposits and withdrawals.

Step 2: Compute the holding period return (HPR) of the portfolio for each subperiod.

Step 3: Compute the product of (1 + HPR) for each subperiod to obtain a total return for the entire measurement period [i.e., $(1 + HPR_1) \times (1 + HPR_2) \ldots (1 + HPR_n)$]. If the total investment period is greater than one year, you must take the geometric mean of the measurement period return to find the annual time-weighted rate of return.

Example: Time-weighted rate of return

A share of stock is purchased at t = 0 for $100, and at the end of the next year, t = 1, another share is purchased for $120. At the end of year 2, both shares are sold for $130 each. At the end of both years 1 and 2, the stock paid a $2 per share dividend. What is the annual time-weighted rate of return for this investment? (This is the same investment as the preceding example.)

Answer:

Step 1: Break the evaluation period into two subperiods based on timing of cash flows.

Holding period 1:	Beginning value	= $100
	Dividends paid	= $2
	Ending value	= $120

Holding period 2:	Beginning value	= $240 (2 shares)
	Dividends paid	= $4 ($2 per share)
	Ending value	= $260 (2 shares)

Step 2: Calculate the HPR for each holding period.

$$HPR_1 = [(\$120 + 2) / \$100] - 1 = 22\%$$

$$HPR_2 = [(\$260 + 4) / \$240] - 1 = 10\%$$

Step 3: Find the compound annual rate that would have produced a total return equal to the return on the account over the 2-year period.

$$(1 + \text{time-weighted rate of return})^2 = (1.22)(1.10)$$

$$\text{time-weighted rate of return} = [(1.22)(1.10)]^{0.5} - 1 = 15.84\%$$

This is the *geometric mean* return, which we examine in more detail later. This allows us to express the time-weighted return as an annual compound rate, even though we have two years of data. In the investment management industry, *the time-weighted rate of return is the preferred method of performance measurement, because it is not affected by the timing of cash inflows and outflows.*

In the preceding examples, the time-weighted rate of return for the portfolio was 15.84%, while the money-weighted rate of return for the same portfolio was 13.86%. The results are different because the money-weighted rate of return gave a larger weight to the year 2 HPR, which was 10%, versus the 22% HPR for year 1. This is because there was more money in the account at the beginning of the second period.

If funds are contributed to an investment portfolio just before a period of relatively poor portfolio performance, the money-weighted rate of return will tend to be lower than the time-weighted rate of return. On the other hand, if funds are contributed to a portfolio at a favorable time (just prior to a period of relatively high returns), the money-weighted rate of return will be higher than the time-weighted rate of return. The use of the time-weighted return removes these distortions and thus provides a better measure of a manager's ability to select investments over the period. If the manager has complete control over money flows into and out of an account, the money-weighted rate of return would be the more appropriate performance measure.

LOS 6.d: Calculate and interpret the bank discount yield, holding period yield, effective annual yield, and money market yield for a U.S. Treasury bill.

Pure discount instruments such as U.S. T-bills are quoted differently from U.S. government bonds. T-bills are quoted on a *bank discount basis*, which is *based on the face value* of the instrument instead of the purchase price. The **bank discount yield** (BDY) is computed using the following formula:

$$r_{BD} = \frac{D}{F} \times \frac{360}{t}$$

where:

r_{BD} = the annualized yield on a bank discount basis

D = the dollar discount, which is equal to the difference between the face value of the bill and the purchase price

F = the face value (par value) of the bill

t = number of days remaining until maturity

360 = bank convention of number of days in a year

The *key distinction* of the bank discount yield is that it expresses the dollar discount from the face (par) value as a fraction of the face value, not the market price of the instrument. Another notable feature of the bank discount yield is that it is annualized by multiplying the discount-to-par by 360/t, where the market convention is to use a 360-day year versus a 365-day year. This type of annualizing method assumes no compounding (i.e., simple interest).

Example: Bank discount yield

Calculate the bank discount yield for a T-bill priced at $98,500, with a face value of $100,000 and 120 days until maturity.

Answer:

Substituting the relevant values into the bank discount yield equation in our example, we get:

$$r_{BD} = \frac{1,500}{100,000} \times \frac{360}{120} = 4.5\%$$

It is important for candidates to realize that a yield quoted on a bank discount basis is not representative of the return earned by an investor for the following reasons:

- Bank discount yield annualizes using simple interest and ignores the effects of compound interest.
- Bank discount yield is based on the face value of the bond, not its purchase price—investment returns should be evaluated relative to the amount invested.

- Bank discount yield is annualized based on a 360-day year rather than a 365-day year.

Holding period yield (HPY), or holding period return, is the total return an investor earns between the purchase date and the sale or maturity date. HPY is calculated using the following formula:

$$HPY = \frac{P_1 - P_0 + D_1}{P_0} = \frac{P_1 + D_1}{P_0} - 1$$

where:
P_0 = initial price of the instrument
P_1 = price received for instrument at maturity
D_1 = interest payment (distribution)

Example: HPY

What is the HPY for a T-bill priced at $98,500 with a face value of $100,000 and 120 days remaining until maturity?

Answer:

Using the HPY equation stated above, we have:

HPY = ($100,000 – $98,500) / $98,500
  = $1,500 / $98,500
  = 1.5228%

$D_1 = 0$ here because T-bills are a pure discount instrument (i.e., they make no interest payments).

The **effective annual yield** (EAY) is an annualized value, based on a 365-day year, that accounts for compound interest. It is calculated using the following equation:

$$EAY = (1 + HPY)^{365/t} - 1$$

Example: EAY

Compute the EAY using the 120-day HPY of 1.5228% from the previous example.

Answer:

The HPY is converted to an EAY as follows:

$$EAY = (1.015228)^{365/120} - 1 = 1.047042 - 1 = 4.7042\%$$

Note that we can convert from an EAY to HPY by using the reciprocal of the exponent and $(1.047042)^{120/365} - 1 = 1.5228\%$

The **money market yield** (or **CD equivalent yield**) is equal to the annualized holding period yield, *assuming a 360-day year*. Using the money market yield makes the quoted yield on a T-bill comparable to yield quotes for interest-bearing money market instruments that pay interest on a 360-day basis. The money market yield is $\frac{360}{\#\,days} \times \text{HPY}$.

$$r_{MM} = \text{HPY} \times (360/t)$$

Given the bank discount yield, r_{BD}, the money market yield, r_{MM}, may be calculated using the equation:

$$r_{MM} = \frac{360 \times r_{BD}}{360 - (t \times r_{BD})}$$

Professor's Note: I couldn't remember this formula with a gun to my head, but I (and you) can easily convert a BDY to an HPY and the HPY to a money market yield using the previous formulas.

Example: Money market yield, r_{MM}

What is the money market yield for a 120-day T-bill that has a bank discount yield of 4.50%?

Answer:

Given the r_{BD} for the T-bill, the first equation for r_{MM} is applied as follows:

$$r_{MM} = \frac{360 \times 0.045}{360 - (120 \times 0.045)}$$
$$= 16.2 \ / \ 354.6$$
$$= 4.569\%$$

Alternatively, we could first calculate the HPY for the T-bill and then annualize that.

Actual discount is $0.045 \times \dfrac{120}{360} = 0.015$. Based on a \$1,000 face value,

price = 1,000 (1 − 0.015) = 985, so that $\text{HPY} = \dfrac{1,000}{985} - 1$ and

$$r_{MM} = \left(\frac{1,000}{985} - 1\right) \times \frac{360}{120} = 0.04569 = 4.569\%.$$

LOS 6.e: Convert among holding period yields, money market yields, effective annual yields, and bond equivalent yields.

Once we have established HPY, EAY, or r_{MM}, we can use one as a basis for calculating the other two. Remember:

- The HPY is the actual return an investor will receive if the money market instrument is held until maturity.
- The EAY is the annualized HPY on the basis of a 365-day year and incorporates the effects of compounding.
- The r_{MM} is the annualized yield that is based on price and a *360-day year* and does not account for the effects of compounding—it assumes simple interest.

Example: Converting among EAY, HPY, and r_{MM}

Assume you purchased a $100,000 T-bill that matures in 150 days for a price of $98,000. The broker who sold you the T-bill quoted the money market yield at 4.898%. Compute the HPY and the EAY.

Answer:

The T-bill HPY is simply $\dfrac{2,000}{98,000} = 2.041\%$, which we can also derive from the money market yield.

Money market to holding period yield—r_{MM} is an annualized yield based on a 360-day year. To change the r_{MM} in this example into its HPY, we need to convert it to a 150-day holding period by multiplying it by (150 / 360). Thus:

$$HPY = r_{MM} \times (150 / 360)$$

$$= 0.04898 \times (150 / 360)$$

$$= 0.02041 = 2.041\%$$

Holding period yield to effective annual yield—the EAY is equal to the annualized HPY based on a 365-day year. Now that we have computed the HPY, simply annualize using a 365-day year to calculate the EAY as follows:

$$EAY = (1 + 0.02041)^{365 / 150} - 1$$

$$= 1.05039 - 1 = 5.039\%$$

Note that to convert the EAY back into the HPY, apply the reciprocal of the exponent to the EAY. This is the same as taking one plus the EAY to the power (t/365). For example, we can convert the EAY we just calculated back to the HPY as follows:

$$HPY = (1.05039)^{150 / 365} - 1 = 2.041\%$$

Professor's Note: On the Level 1 CFA® exam, you may be asked to convert from any one of these three yields into one of the others. You should note that the EAY and r_{MM} are merely annualized versions of the HPY. If you concentrate on converting back and forth between the HPY and the other yield figures, you will be well-prepared to answer these types of questions on the Level 1 exam.

Bond Equivalent Yield

The **bond-equivalent yield** refers to 2 × the semiannual discount rate. This convention stems from the fact that yields on U.S. bonds are quoted as twice the semiannual rate, because the coupon interest is paid in two semiannual payments.

Example: Bond-equivalent yield calculation (1)

A 3-month loan has a holding period yield of 2%. What is the yield on a bond-equivalent basis?

Answer:

The first step is to convert the 3-month yield to an effective semiannual (6-month) yield:

$$1.02^2 - 1 = 4.04\%$$

The second step it to double it (2 × 4.04 = 8.08%) to get the bond-equivalent yield.

Example: Bond-equivalent yield calculation (2)

The effective annual yield on an investment is 8%. What is the yield on a bond-equivalent basis?

Answer:

The first step is to convert the effective annual yield to an effective semiannual yield.

$$1.08^{0.5} - 1 = 3.923\%$$

The second step is to double it: 2 × 3.923 = 7.846%.

 Professor's Note: There is an alternative definition of the bond equivalent yield in the Corporate Finance topic review on Working Capital Management:

$$\left(HPR \times \frac{365}{\text{days to maturity}} \right)$$

KEY CONCEPTS

LOS 6.a

The NPV is the present value of a project's future cash flows, discounted at the firm's cost of capital, less the project's cost. IRR is the discount rate that makes the NPV = 0 (equates the PV of the expected future cash flows to the project's initial cost).

The NPV rule is to accept a project if NPV > 0; the IRR rule is to accept a project if IRR > required rate of return. For an independent (single) project, these rules produce the exact same decision.

For mutually exclusive projects, IRR rankings and NPV rankings may differ due to differences in project size or in the timing of the cash flows. Choose the project with the higher NPV as long as it is positive.

A project may have multiple IRRs or no IRR.

LOS 6.b

The holding period return (or yield) is the total return for holding an investment over a certain period of time and can be calculated as:

$$HPY = \frac{P_1 - P_0 + D_1}{P_0} = \frac{P_1 + D_1}{P_0} - 1$$

LOS 6.c

The money-weighted rate of return is the IRR calculated using periodic cash flows into and out of an account and is the discount rate that makes the PV of cash inflows equal to the PV of cash outflows.

The time-weighted rate of return measures compound growth. It is the rate at which \$1 compounds over a specified performance horizon.

If funds are added to a portfolio just before a period of poor performance, the money-weighted return will be lower than the time-weighted return. If funds are added just prior to a period of high returns, the money-weighted return will be higher than the time-weighted return.

The time-weighted return is the preferred measure of a manager's ability to select investments. If the manager controls the money flows into and out of an account, the money-weighted return is the more appropriate performance measure.

LOS 6.d

Given a $1,000 T-bill with 100 days to maturity and a discount of $10 (price of $990):

- Bank discount yield = $\dfrac{10}{1,000} \times \dfrac{360}{100} = 3.60\%$

- Holding period yield = $\dfrac{1,000 - 990}{990} = 1.01\%$

- Effective annual yield = $1.0101^{365/100} - 1 = 3.74\%$

- Money market yield = $1.01\% \times \dfrac{360}{100} = 3.636\%$

LOS 6.e

Given a money market security with *n* days to maturity:

- Holding period yield = $\dfrac{\text{bank discount yield}\left(\dfrac{n}{360}\right)}{1 - \text{bank discount yield}\left(\dfrac{n}{360}\right)}$

- Money market yield = holding period yield $\times \dfrac{360}{n}$

- Effective annual yield = $(1 + \text{holding period yield})^{365/n} - 1$

- Holding period yield = $(1 + \text{effective annual yield})^{n/365} - 1$

- Bond equivalent yield = $[(1 + \text{effective annual yield})^{1/2} - 1] \times 2$

CONCEPT CHECKERS

1. Which of the following statements *least accurately* describes the IRR and NPV methods?
    A. The discount rate that gives an investment an NPV of zero is the investment's IRR.
    B. If the NPV and IRR methods give conflicting decisions for mutually exclusive projects, the IRR decision should be used to select the project.
    C. The NPV method assumes that a project's cash flows will be reinvested at the cost of capital, while the IRR method assumes they will be reinvested at the IRR.

2. Which of the following statements *least accurately* describes the IRR and NPV methods?
    A. A project's IRR can be positive even if the NPV is negative.
    B. A project with an IRR equal to the cost of capital will have an NPV of zero.
    C. A project's NPV may be positive even if the IRR is less than the cost of capital.

3. Which of the following statements *least accurately* describes the IRR and NPV methods?
    A. The NPV tells how much the value of the firm has increased if you accept the project.
    B. When evaluating independent projects, the IRR and NPV methods always yield the same accept/reject decisions.
    C. When selecting between mutually exclusive projects, the project with the highest NPV should be accepted regardless of the sign of the NPV calculation.

4. A company is considering entering into a joint venture that will require an investment of $10 million. The project is expected to generate cash flows of $4 million, $3 million, and $4 million in each of the next three years, respectively. Assuming a discount rate of 10%, what is the project's NPV?
    A. −$879,000.
    B. −$309,000.
    C. +$243,000.

5. A company is considering entering into a joint venture that will require an investment of $10 million. The project is expected to generate cash flows of $4 million, $3 million, and $4 million in each of the next three years, respectively. Assuming a discount rate of 10%, what is the project's *approximate* IRR?
    A. 5%.
    B. 10%.
    C. 15%.

6.   What should an analyst recommend based on the following information for two
      independent projects?

Project	Investment at t = 0	Cash Flow at t = 1	IRR	NPV at 12%
A	−$3,000	$5,000	66.67%	$1,464.29
B	−$10,000	$15,000	50.00%	$3,392.86

A. Accept A and reject B.
B. Reject A and accept B.
C. Accept A and accept B.

7.   What should an analyst recommend based on the following information for two
      mutually exclusive projects?

Project	Investment at t = 0	Cash Flow at t = 1	IRR	NPV at 12%
A	−$3,000	$5,000	66.67%	$1,464.29
B	−$10,000	$15,000	50.00%	$3,392.86

A. Accept A and reject B.
B. Reject A and accept B.
C. Accept A and accept B.

8.   Goodeal, Inc., is considering the purchase of a new material handling system
      for a cost of $15 million. This system is expected to generate a positive cash
      flow of $1.8 million per year in perpetuity. What is the NPV of the proposed
      investment if the appropriate discount rate is 10.5%?
      A. $2,142,857.
      B. $13,200,000.
      C. $17,142,857.

9.   Goodeal, Inc., is considering the purchase of a new material handling system for
      a cost of $15 million. This system is expected to generate a positive cash flow of
      $1.8 million per year in perpetuity. What is the IRR of the proposed investment
      if the appropriate hurdle rate is 10.5%?
      A. 8.3%.
      B. 10.5%.
      C. 12.0%.

10.   Should a company accept a project that has an IRR of 14% and an NPV of
      $2.8 million if the cost of capital is 12%?
      A. Yes, based only on the NPV.
      B. Yes, based on the NPV and the IRR.
      C. No, based on both the NPV and IRR.

11. Which of the following statements *least likely* represents a characteristic of the time-weighted rate of return? It is:
   A. not affected by the timing of cash flows.
   B. used to measure the compound rate of growth of $1 over a stated measurement period.
   C. defined as the internal rate of return on an investment portfolio, taking into account all inflows and outflows.

Use the following data to answer Questions 12 and 13.

Assume an investor purchases a share of stock for $50 at time t = 0, and another share at $65 at time t = 1, and at the end of year 1 and year 2, the stock paid a $2 dividend. Also, at the end of year 2, the investor sold both shares for $70 each.

12. The money-weighted rate of return on the investment is:
   A. 15.45%.
   B. 16.73%.
   C. 18.02%.

13. The time-weighted rate of return on the investment is:
   A. 18.27%.
   B. 20.13%.
   C. 21.83%.

14. What is the bank discount yield for a T-bill that is selling for $99,000, with a face value of $100,000 and 95 days remaining until maturity?
   A. 1.51%.
   B. 3.79%.
   C. 6.00%.

15. What is the holding period yield for a T-bill that is selling for $99,000 if it has a face value of $100,000 and 95 days remaining until maturity?
   A. 1.01%.
   B. 2.03%.
   C. 3.79%.

16. What is the effective annual yield for a T-bill that is selling for $99,000 if it has a face value of $100,000 and 95 days remaining until maturity?
   A. 3.79%.
   B. 3.94%.
   C. 4.50%.

17. What is the money market yield for a T-bill that is selling for $99,000 if it has a face value of $100,000 and 95 days remaining until maturity?
   A. 3.79%.
   B. 3.83%.
   C. 3.90%.

18. Which of the following is *least accurate* regarding a bank discount yield?
   A. It ignores the opportunity to earn compound interest.
   B. It is based on the face value of the bond, not its purchase price.
   C. It reflects the nonannualized return an investor will earn over a security's life.

19.   A 175-day T-bill has an effective annual yield of 3.80%. Its money-market yield
        is *closest* to:
        A. 1.80%.
        B. 3.65%.
        C. 3.71%.

COMPREHENSIVE PROBLEMS

1.   Allison Rogers, CFA, makes the following statement: "The problems with
        bank discount yields quoted for T-bills is that they aren't yields, they ignore
        compounding, and they are based on a short year."
        A. Is she correct in all regards?
        B. Which of these problems is/are remedied by using the holding period yield?
        C. Which of these problems is/are remedied by using a money market yield?
        D. Which of these problems is/are remedied by using effective annual yields?

2.   L. Adams buys 1,000 shares of Morris Tool stock for $35 per share. One year
        later the stock is $38 per share and has paid a dividend of $1.50 per share.
        Adams reinvests the dividends in additional shares at the time. At the end of the
        second year, the shares are trading for $37 and have paid $2 dividends over the
        period.

        L. Burns buys 500 shares of Morris Tool stock for $35 per share. One year later
        the stock is $38 per share and has paid a dividend of $1.50 per share. Burns
        reinvests the dividends in additional shares at that time and also buys 500
        additional shares. At the end of the second year, the shares are trading for $37
        and have paid $2 in dividends over the period.
        A. Compare the annual time-weighted returns for the accounts of the two
            investors (no calculation required).
        B. Compare the annual money-weighted returns for the accounts of the two
            investors (no calculation required).

ANSWERS – CONCEPT CHECKERS

1. **B** If the NPV and IRR methods give conflicting decisions when selecting among mutually exclusive projects, always select the project with the greatest positive NPV.

2. **C** A project will have a negative NPV if its IRR is less than the firm's cost of capital.

3. **C** When selecting between two mutually exclusive projects, neither project should be accepted if they both have a negative NPV.

4. **A** NPV = 4 / 1.10 + 3 / (1.10)^2 + 4 / (1.10)^3 − $10 = −$0.879038 million, or −$879,038

   Calculator approach: CF0 = −10; CF1 = 4; CF2 = 3; CF3 = 4; I = 10 → NPV = −$0.879038 (million)

5. **A** Use your test-taking skills here. You know from the previous question that the NPV is negative at 10%. Thus, the IRR must be less than 10%. This leaves only choice A to be the answer. Calculator solution: IRR = 4.9%.

6. **C** Both projects should be accepted since both projects have positive NPVs and will thus increase shareholder wealth.

7. **B** When the NPV and IRR rankings conflict, always select the project with the highest positive NPV in order to maximize shareholder wealth.

8. **A** NPV = PV(cash inflows) − CF$_0$ = ($1.8 million / 0.105) − $15 million = $2,142,857 Accept the project.

9. **C** As a perpetuity, the following relationship applies: $1.8 million / IRR = $15 million. Thus, IRR = 1.8 / 15 = 12%. Since IRR > cost of capital (hurdle rate), accept the project.

10. **B** The project should be accepted on the basis of its positive NPV and its IRR, which exceeds the cost of capital.

11. **C** The money-weighted rate of return is the IRR of an investment's net cash flows.

12. **C** One way to do this problem is to set up the cash flows so that the PV of inflows = PV of outflows and plug in each of the multiple choices. 50 + 65 / (1 + r) = 2 / (1 + r) + 144 / (1 + r)^2 → r = 18.02%. Or on your financial calculator, solve for IRR:

$$-50 - \frac{65-2}{1+\text{IRR}} + \frac{2(70+2)}{(1+\text{IRR})^2} = 0$$

Calculating Money-Weighted Return With the TI Business Analyst II Plus®

Key Strokes	Explanation	Display
[CF] [2nd] [CLR WORK]	Clear CF Memory Registers	CF0 = 0.00000
50 [+/−] [ENTER]	Initial cash inflow	CF0 = −50.00000
[↓] 63 [+/−][ENTER]	Period 1 cash inflow	C01 = −63.00000
[↓] [↓] 144 [ENTER]	Period 2 cash outflow	C02 = 144.00000
[IRR] [CPT]	Calculate IRR	IRR = 18.02210

13. **C** $HPR_1 = (65 + 2) / 50 - 1 = 34\%$, $HPR_2 = (140 + 4) / 130 - 1 = 10.77\%$

   Time-weighted return $= [(1.34)(1.1077)]^{0.5} - 1 = 21.83\%$

14. **B** $(1,000 / 100,000) \times (360 / 95) = 3.79\%$

15. **A** $(100,000 - 99,000) / 99,000 = 1.01\%$

16. **B** $(1 + 0.0101)^{365/95} - 1 = 3.94\%$

17. **B** $(360 \times 0.0379) / (360 - (95 \times 0.0379)) = 3.83\%$, or $(1,000 / 99,000)(360 / 95) = 3.83\%$

18. **C**   This is actually the definition of the holding period yield. The other answers are true statements regarding the bank discount yield.

19. **C**   Since the effective yield is 3.8%, we know $\left[\dfrac{1,000}{\text{price}}\right]^{\frac{365}{175}} = 1.038$ and

   $$\text{price} = \left[\dfrac{1,000}{1.038^{\frac{175}{365}}}\right] = \$982.28 \text{ per } \$1,000 \text{ face.}$$

   The money market yield is

   $$\left(\dfrac{360}{175}\right) \times \text{HPY} = \left(\dfrac{360}{175}\right)\left(\dfrac{1,000}{982.28} - 1\right) = \dfrac{360}{175}(0.01804) = 3.711\%.$$

   Alternatively, we can get the HPY from the EAY of 3.8% as $(1.038)^{\frac{175}{365}} - 1 = 1.804\%$.

ANSWERS – COMPREHENSIVE PROBLEMS

1. A. She is correct in all regards. Bank discount yields are not true yields because they are based on a percentage of face (maturity) value instead of on the original amount invested. They are annualized without compounding since the actual discount from face value is simply multiplied by the number of periods in a "year." The "year" used is 360 days, so that is a shortcoming as well.

   B. The holding period yield uses the increase in value divided by the amount invested (purchase price), so it solves the problem that the BDY is not a true yield.

   C. The money market yield is also a true yield (a percentage of the initial investment) but does not solve the other two problems since it does not involve compounding and is based on a 360-day year.

   D. The effective annual yield solves all three shortcomings. It is based on the holding period yield (so it is a true yield), is a compound annual rate, and is based on a 365-day year.

2. A. Both investors have held the same single stock for both periods, so the time-weighted returns must be identical for both accounts.

   B. The performance of the stock (annual total return) was better in the first year than in the second. Since Burns increased his holdings for the second period by more than Adams, the Burns account has a greater weight on the poorer returns in a money-weighted return calculation and will have a lower annual money-weighted rate of return over the two-year period than Burns.

STATISTICAL CONCEPTS AND MARKET RETURNS

Study Session 2

EXAM FOCUS

This quantitative review is about the uses of descriptive statistics to summarize and portray important characteristics of large sets of data. The two key areas that you should concentrate on are (1) measures of central tendency and (2) measures of dispersion. Measures of central tendency include the arithmetic mean, geometric mean, weighted mean, median, and mode. Measures of dispersion include the range, mean absolute deviation, and the most important measure for us, variance. These measures quantify the variability of data around its "center." When describing investments, measures of central tendency provide an indication of an investment's expected return. Measures of dispersion indicate the riskiness of an investment. For the Level 1 exam, you should know the properties of a normal distribution and be able to recognize departures from normality, such as lack of symmetry (skewness) or the extent to which a distribution is peaked (kurtosis).

LOS 7.a: Differentiate between descriptive statistics and inferential statistics, between a population and a sample, and among the types of measurement scales.

The word **statistics** is used to refer to data (e.g., the average return on XYZ stock was 8% over the last ten years) and to the methods we use to analyze data. Statistical methods fall into one of two categories, **descriptive statistics** or **inferential statistics**.

Descriptive statistics are used to summarize the important characteristics of large data sets. The focus of this topic review is on the use of descriptive statistics to consolidate a mass of numerical data into useful information.

Inferential statistics, which will be discussed in subsequent topic reviews, pertain to the procedures used to make forecasts, estimates, or judgments about a large set of data on the basis of the statistical characteristics of a smaller set (a sample).

A **population** is defined as the set of all possible members of a stated group. A cross-section of the returns of all of the stocks traded on the New York Stock Exchange (NYSE) is an example of a population.

It is frequently too costly or time consuming to obtain measurements for every member of a population, if it is even possible. In this case, a sample may be used. A **sample** is defined as a subset of the population of interest. Once a population has been defined, a sample can be drawn from the population, and the sample's characteristics can be used to describe the population as a whole. For example, a sample of 30 stocks may be selected from among all of the stocks listed on the NYSE to represent the population of all NYSE-traded stocks.

Types of Measurement Scales

Different statistical methods use different levels of measurement, or measurement scales. **Measurement scales** may be classified into one of four major categories:

- **Nominal scales.** Nominal scales are the least accurate level of measurement. Observations are classified or counted with no particular order. An example would be assigning the number 1 to a municipal bond fund, the number 2 to a corporate bond fund, and so on for each fund style.

- **Ordinal scales.** Ordinal scales represent a higher level of measurement than nominal scales. When working with an ordinal scale, every observation is assigned to one of several categories. Then these categories are ordered with respect to a specified characteristic. For example, the ranking of 1,000 small cap growth stocks by performance may be done by assigning the number 1 to the 100 best performing stocks, the number 2 to the next 100 best performing stocks, and so on, assigning the number 10 to the 100 worst performing stocks. Based on this type of measurement, it can be concluded that a stock ranked 3 is better than a stock ranked 4, but the scale reveals nothing about performance differences or whether the difference between a 3 and a 4 is the same as the difference between a 4 and a 5.

- **Interval scale.** Interval scale measurements provide relative ranking, like ordinal scales, plus the assurance that differences between scale values are equal. Temperature measurement in degrees is a prime example. Certainly, 49°C is hotter than 32°C, and the temperature difference between 49°C and 32°C is the same as the difference between 67°C and 50°C. The weakness of the interval scale is that a measurement of zero does not necessarily indicate the total absence of what we are measuring. This means that interval-scale-based ratios are meaningless. For example, 30°F is not three times as hot as 10°F.

- **Ratio scales.** Ratio scales represent the most refined level of measurement. Ratio scales provide ranking and equal differences between scale values, and they also have a true zero point as the origin. Order, intervals, and ratios all make sense with a ratio scale. The measurement of money is a good example. If you have zero dollars, you have no purchasing power, but if you have $4.00, you have twice as much purchasing power as a person with $2.00.

 Professor's Note: Candidates sometimes use the French word for black, noir, *to remember the types of scales in order of precision: Nominal, Ordinal, Interval, Ratio.*

LOS 7.b: Explain a parameter, a sample statistic, and a frequency distribution.

A measure used to describe a characteristic of a population is referred to as a **parameter**. While many population parameters exist, investment analysis usually utilizes just a few, particularly the mean return and the standard deviation of returns.

In the same manner that a parameter may be used to describe a characteristic of a population, a **sample statistic** is used to measure a characteristic of a sample.

A **frequency distribution** is a tabular presentation of statistical data that aids the analysis of large data sets. Frequency distributions summarize statistical data by assigning it to specified groups, or intervals. Also, the data employed with a frequency distribution may be measured using any type of measurement scale.

 Professor's Note: Intervals are also known as classes.

The following procedure describes how to construct a frequency distribution.

Step 1: *Define the intervals.* The first step in building a frequency distribution is to define the intervals to which data measurements (observations) will be assigned. An interval, also referred to as a class, is the set of values that an observation may take on. The range of values for each interval must have a lower and upper limit and be all-inclusive and nonoverlapping. Intervals must be *mutually exclusive* in a way that each observation can be placed in only one interval, and the total set of intervals should cover the total range of values for the entire population.

The number of intervals used is an important consideration. If too few intervals are used, the data may be too broadly summarized, and important characteristics may be lost. On the other hand, if too many intervals are used, the data may not be summarized enough.

Step 2: *Tally the observations.* After the intervals have been defined, the observations must be tallied, or assigned to their appropriate interval.

Step 3: *Count the observations.* Having tallied the data set, the number of observations that are assigned to each interval must be counted. The *absolute frequency*, or simply the frequency, is the actual number of observations that fall within a given interval.

Example: Constructing a frequency distribution

Use the data in Table A to construct a frequency distribution for the returns on Intelco's common stock.

Table A: Annual Returns for Intelco, Inc. Common Stock

10.4%	22.5%	11.1%	−12.4%
9.8%	17.0%	2.8%	8.4%
34.6%	−28.6%	0.6%	5.0%
−17.6%	5.6%	8.9%	40.4%
−1.0%	−4.2%	−5.2%	21.0%

Answer:

Step 1: *Defining the interval.* For Intelco's stock, the range of returns is 69.0% (−28.6% → 40.4%). Using a return interval of 1% would result in 69 separate intervals, which in this case is too many. So let's use eight nonoverlapping intervals with a width of 10%. The lowest return intervals will be −30% ≤ R_t < −20%, and the intervals will increase to 40% ≤ R_t ≤ 50%.

Step 2: *Tally the observations and count the observations within each interval.* The tallies and counts of the observations are presented in Table B.

Table B: Tally and Interval Count for Returns Data

Interval	Tallies	Absolute Frequency
−30% ≤ R_t < −20%	/	1
−20% ≤ R_t < −10%	//	2
−10% ≤ R_t < 0%	///	3
0% ≤ R_t < 10%	///// //	7
10% ≤ R_t < 20%	///	3
20% ≤ R_t < 30%	//	2
30% ≤ R_t < 40%	/	1
40% ≤ R_t ≤ 50%	/	1
Total		20

Tallying and counting the observations generates a frequency distribution that summarizes the pattern of annual returns on Intelco common stock. Notice that the interval with the greatest (absolute) frequency is the (0% ≤ R_t < 10%) interval, which includes seven return observations. For any frequency distribution, the interval with the greatest frequency is referred to as the **modal interval**.

LOS 7.c: Calculate and interpret relative frequencies and cumulative relative frequencies, given a frequency distribution.

The **relative frequency** is another useful way to present data. The relative frequency is calculated by dividing the absolute frequency of each return interval by the total number of observations. Simply stated, relative frequency is the percentage of total observations falling within each interval. Continuing with our example, the relative frequencies are presented in Figure 1.

Figure 1: Absolute and Relative Frequencies of Intelco Returns

Interval	Absolute Frequency	Relative Frequency
$-30\% \leq R_t < -20\%$	1	1/20 = 0.05, or 5%
$-20\% \leq R_t < -10\%$	2	2/20 = 0.10, or 10%
$-10\% \leq R_t < 0\%$	3	3/20 = 0.15, or 15%
$0\% \leq R_t < 10\%$	7	7/20 = 0.35, or 35%
$10\% \leq R_t < 20\%$	3	3/20 = 0.15, or 15%
$20\% \leq R_t < 30\%$	2	2/20 = 0.10, or 10%
$30\% \leq R_t < 40\%$	1	1/20 = 0.05, or 5%
$40\% \leq R_t \leq 50\%$	1	1/20 = 0.05, or 5%
Total	20	100%

It is also possible to compute the **cumulative absolute frequency** and **cumulative relative frequency** by summing the absolute or relative frequencies starting at the lowest interval and progressing through the highest. The cumulative absolute frequencies and cumulative relative frequencies for the Intelco stock returns example are presented in Figure 2.

Figure 2: Absolute, Relative, and Cumulative Frequencies of Intelco Returns

Interval	Absolute Frequency	Relative Frequency	Cumulative Absolute Frequency	Cumulative Relative Frequency
$-30\% \leq R_t < -20\%$	1	5%	1	5%
$-20\% \leq R_t < -10\%$	2	10%	3	15%
$-10\% \leq R_t < 0\%$	3	15%	6	30%
$0\% \leq R_t < 10\%$	7	35%	13	65%
$10\% \leq R_t < 20\%$	3	15%	16	80%
$20\% \leq R_t < 30\%$	2	10%	18	90%
$30\% \leq R_t < 40\%$	1	5%	19	95%
$40\% \leq R_t \leq 50\%$	1	5%	20	100%
Total	20	100%		

Notice that the cumulative absolute frequency or cumulative relative frequency for any given interval is the sum of the absolute or relative frequencies up to and including the given interval. For example, the cumulative absolute frequency for the ($0\% \leq R_t < 10\%$) interval is 13 = 1 + 2 + 3 + 7 and the cumulative relative frequency for this interval is 5% + 10% + 15% + 35% = 65%.

LOS 7.d: Describe the properties of a data set presented as a histogram or a frequency polygon.

A **histogram** is the graphical presentation of the absolute frequency distribution. A histogram is simply a bar chart of continuous data that has been classified into a frequency distribution. The attractive feature of a histogram is that it allows us to quickly see where most of the observations are concentrated.

To construct a histogram, the intervals are scaled on the horizontal axis and the absolute frequencies are scaled on the vertical axis. The histogram for the Intelco returns data in Table B from the previous example is provided in Figure 3.

Figure 3: Histogram of Intelco Stock Return Data

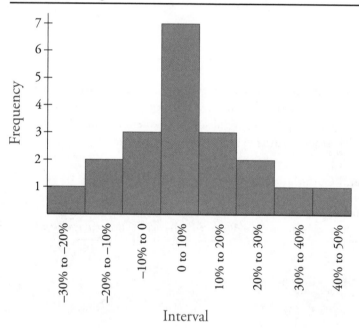

To construct a **frequency polygon**, the midpoint of each interval is plotted on the horizontal axis, and the absolute frequency for that interval is plotted on the vertical axis. Each point is then connected with a straight line. The frequency polygon for the returns data used in our example is illustrated in Figure 4.

©2009 Kaplan, Inc.

Figure 4: Frequency Polygon of Intelco Stock Return Data

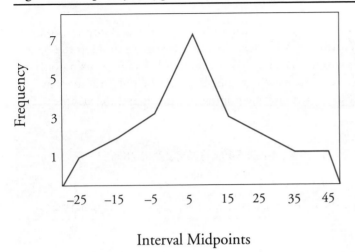

LOS 7.e: Define, calculate, and interpret measures of central tendency, including the population mean, sample mean, arithmetic mean, weighted average or mean (including a portfolio return viewed as a weighted mean), geometric mean, harmonic mean, median, and mode.

Measures of central tendency identify the center, or average, of a data set. This central point can then be used to represent the typical, or expected, value in the data set.

To compute the **population mean**, all the observed values in the population are summed (ΣX) and divided by the number of observations in the population, N. Note that the population mean is unique in that a given population only has one mean. The population mean is expressed as:

$$\mu = \frac{\sum_{i=1}^{N} X_i}{N}$$

The **sample mean** is the sum of all the values in a sample of a population, ΣX, divided by the number of observations in the sample, n. It is used to make *inferences* about the population mean. The sample mean is expressed as:

$$\overline{X} = \frac{\sum_{i=1}^{n} X_i}{n}$$

Note the use of n, the sample size, versus N, the population size.

Example: Population mean and sample mean

Assume you and your research assistant are evaluating the stock of AXZ Corporation. You have calculated the stock returns for AXZ over the last 12 years to develop the data set shown below. Your research assistant has decided to conduct his analysis using only the returns for the five most recent years, which are displayed as the bold numbers in the data set. Given this information, calculate the population mean and the sample mean.

Data set: 12%, **25%**, **34%**, 15%, **19%**, 44%, **54%**, 33%, 22%, 28%, **17%**, 24%

Answer:

$$\mu = \text{population mean} = \frac{12 + 25 + 34 + 15 + 19 + 44 + 54 + 33 + 22 + 28 + 17 + 24}{12}$$

$$= 27.25\%$$

$$\overline{X} = \text{sample mean} = \frac{25 + 34 + 19 + 54 + 17}{5} = 29.8\%$$

The population mean and sample mean are both examples of **arithmetic means**. The arithmetic mean is the sum of the observation values divided by the number of observations. It is the most widely used measure of central tendency and has the following properties:

- All interval and ratio data sets have an arithmetic mean.
- All data values are considered and included in the arithmetic mean computation.
- A data set has only one arithmetic mean (i.e., the arithmetic mean is unique).
- The sum of the deviations of each observation in the data set from the mean is always zero.

The arithmetic mean is the only measure of central tendency for which the sum of the deviations from the mean is zero. Mathematically, this property can be expressed as follows:

$$\text{sum of mean deviations} = \sum_{i=1}^{n}(X_i - \overline{X}) = 0$$

Example: Arithmetic mean and deviations from the mean

Compute the arithmetic mean for a data set described as:

Data set: [5, 9, 4, 10]

Study Session 2

Answer:

The arithmetic mean of these numbers is:

$$\overline{X} = \frac{5+9+4+10}{4} = 7$$

The sum of the deviations from the mean (of 7) is:

$$\sum_{i=1}^{n}(X_i - \overline{X}) = (5-7)+(9-7)+(4-7)+(10-7) = -2+2-3+3 = 0$$

Unusually large or small values can have a disproportionate effect on the computed value for the arithmetic mean. The mean of 1, 2, 3, and 50 is 14 and is not a good indication of what the individual data values really are. On the positive side, the arithmetic mean uses all the information available about the observations. The arithmetic mean of a sample from a population is the best estimate of both the true mean of the sample and the value of the next observation.

The computation of a **weighted mean** recognizes that different observations may have a disproportionate influence on the mean. The weighted mean of a set of numbers is computed with the following equation:

$$\overline{X}_W = \sum_{i=1}^{n} w_i X_i = (w_1 X_1 + w_2 X_2 + \ldots + w_n X_n)$$

where:
$X_1, X_2, \ldots X_n$ = observed values
$w_1, w_2, \ldots w_n$ = corresponding weights associated with each of the observations such that $\Sigma w_i = 1$

Example: Weighted mean as a portfolio return

A portfolio consists of 50% common stocks, 40% bonds, and 10% cash. If the return on common stocks is 12%, the return on bonds is 7%, and the return on cash is 3%, what is the portfolio return?

Answer:

$$\overline{X}_W = w_{stock} R_{stock} + w_{bonds} R_{bonds} + w_{cash} R_{cash}$$

$$\overline{X}_W = (0.50 \times 0.12) + (0.40 \times 0.07) + (0.10 \times 0.03) = 0.091, \text{ or } 9.1\%$$

The example illustrates an extremely important investments concept: *the return for a portfolio is the weighted average of the returns of the individual assets in the portfolio.* Asset weights are market weights, the market value of each asset relative to the market value of the entire portfolio.

The **median** is the midpoint of a data set when the data is arranged in ascending or descending order. Half the observations lie above the median and half are below. To determine the median, arrange the data from the highest to the lowest value, or lowest to highest value, and find the middle observation.

The median is important because the arithmetic mean can be affected by extremely large or small values (outliers). When this occurs, the median is a better measure of central tendency than the mean because it is not affected by extreme values that may actually be the result of errors in the data.

Example: The median using an odd number of observations

What is the median return for five portfolio managers with 10-year annualized total returns record of: 30%, 15%, 25%, 21%, and 23%?

Answer:

First, arrange the returns in descending order.

30%, 25%, 23%, 21%, 15%

Then, select the observation that has an equal number of observations above and below it—the one in the middle. For the given data set, the third observation, 23%, is the median value.

Example: The median using an even number of observations

Suppose we add a sixth manager to the previous example with a return of 28%. What is the median return?

Answer:

Arranging the returns in descending order gives us:

30%, 28%, 25%, 23%, 21%, 15%

With an even number of observations, there is no single middle value. The median value in this case is the arithmetic mean of the two middle observations, 25% and 23%. Thus, the median return for the six managers is 24.0% = 0.5(25 + 23).

Consider that while we calculated the mean of 1, 2, 3, and 50 as 14, the median is 2.5. If the data were 1, 2, 3, and 4 instead, the arithmetic mean and median would both be 2.5.

The **mode** is the value that occurs most frequently in a data set. A data set may have more than one mode or even no mode. When a distribution has one value that appears most frequently, it is said to be **unimodal**. When a set of data has two or three values that occur most frequently, it is said to be **bimodal** or **trimodal**, respectively.

Example: The mode

What is the mode of the following data set?

Data set: [30%, 28%, 25%, 23%, 28%, 15%, 5%]

Answer:

The mode is 28% because it is the value appearing most frequently.

The **geometric mean** is often used when calculating investment returns over multiple periods or when measuring compound growth rates. The general formula for the geometric mean, G, is as follows:

$$G = \sqrt[n]{X_1 \times X_2 \times ... \times X_n} = (X_1 \times X_2 \times ... \times X_n)^{1/n}$$

Note that this equation has a solution only if the product under the radical sign is non-negative.

When calculating the geometric mean for a returns data set, it is necessary to add 1 to each value under the radical and then subtract 1 from the result. The geometric mean return (R_G) can be computed using the following equation:

$$1 + R_G = \sqrt[n]{(1 + R_1) \times (1 + R_2) \times ... \times (1 + R_n)}$$

where:
R_t = the return for period t

Example: Geometric mean return

For the last three years, the returns for Acme Corporation common stock have been −9.34%, 23.45%, and 8.92%. Compute the compound annual rate of return over the 3-year period.

Answer:

$$1 + R_G = \sqrt[3]{(-0.0934 + 1) \times (0.2345 + 1) \times (0.0892 + 1)}$$

$$1 + R_G = \sqrt[3]{0.9066 \times 1.2345 \times 1.0892} = \sqrt[3]{1.21903} = (1.21903)^{1/3} = 1.06825$$

$$R_G = 1.06825 - 1 = 6.825\%$$

Solve this type of problem with your calculator as follows:

- On the TI, enter 1.21903 [y^x] 0.33333 [=], or 1.21903 [y^x] 3 [1/x] [=]
- On the HP, enter 1.21903 [ENTER] 0.33333 [y^x], or 1.21903 [ENTER] 3 [1/x] [y^x]

Note that the 0.33333 represents the one-third power.

Professor's Note: The geometric mean is always less than or equal to the arithmetic mean, and the difference increases as the dispersion of the observations increases. The only time the arithmetic and geometric means are equal is when there is no variability in the observations (i.e., all observations are equal).

A **harmonic mean** is used for certain computations, such as the average cost of shares purchased over time. The harmonic mean is calculated as $\dfrac{N}{\sum\limits_{i=1}^{N} \dfrac{1}{X_i}}$, where there are N values of X_i.

Example: Calculating average cost with the harmonic mean

An investor purchases $1,000 of stock each month, and over the last three months the prices paid per share were $8, $9, and $10. What is the average cost per share for the shares acquired?

Answer:

$$\bar{X}_H = \frac{3}{\frac{1}{8} + \frac{1}{9} + \frac{1}{10}} = \$8.926 \text{ per share}$$

To check this result, calculate the total shares purchased as

$$\frac{1,000}{8} + \frac{1,000}{9} + \frac{1,000}{10} = 336.11 \text{ shares.}$$

The average price is $\dfrac{\$3,000}{336.11} = \$8.926$ per share.

The previous example illustrates the interpretation of the harmonic mean in its most common application. Note that the average price paid per share ($8.93) is less than the arithmetic average of the share prices, $\dfrac{8+9+10}{3} = 9$.

For values that are not all equal: harmonic mean < geometric mean < arithmetic mean. This mathematical fact is the basis for the claimed benefit of purchasing the same dollar amount of mutual fund shares each month or each week. Some refer to this practice as "dollar cost averaging."

LOS 7.f: Describe, calculate, and interpret quartiles, quintiles, deciles, and percentiles.

Quantile is the general term for a value at or below which a stated proportion of the data in a distribution lies. Examples of quantiles include:

- *Quartiles*—the distribution is divided into quarters.
- *Quintile*—the distribution is divided into fifths.
- *Decile*—the distribution is divided into tenths.
- *Percentile*—the distribution is divided into hundredths (percents).

Note that any quantile may be expressed as a percentile. For example, the third quartile partitions the distribution at a value such that three-fourths, or 75%, of the observations fall below that value. Thus, the third quartile is the 75th percentile.

The formula for the position of the observation at a given percentile, y, with n data points sorted in ascending order is:

$$L_y = (n+1)\frac{y}{100}$$

Quantiles and measures of central tendency are known collectively as **measures of location**.

Example: Quartiles

What is the third quartile for the following distribution of returns?

8%, 10%, 12%, 13%, 15%, 17%, 17%, 18%, 19%, 23%, 24%

Answer:

The third quartile is the point below which 75% of the observations lie. Recognizing that there are 11 observations in the data set, the third quartile can be identified as:

$$L_y = (11+1)\times\frac{75}{100} = 9$$

When the data is arranged in ascending order, the third quartile is the ninth data point from the left, or 19%. This means that 75% of all observations lie below 19%.

As you will see in the next example, if L is not a whole number, linear interpolation must be used to find the quantile.

Example: Quartiles

What is the third quartile for the following distribution of returns?

8%, 10%, 12%, 13%, 15%, 17%, 17%, 18%, 19%, 23%, 24%, 26%

Answer:

With 12 observations in this data set, the third quartile can be identified as:

$$L_y = (12+1)\times\frac{75}{100} = 9.75$$

This means that when the data is arranged in ascending order, the third quartile (75th percentile) is the ninth data point from the left, plus 0.75 × (distance between the 9th and 10th data values). Specifically, the third quartile is [19 + 0.75 × (23 − 19)] = 22%, indicating that 75% of all observations lie below 22%.

LOS 7.g: Define, calculate, and interpret 1) a range and a mean absolute deviation and 2) the variance and standard deviation of a population and of a sample.

Dispersion is defined as the *variability around the central tendency*. The common theme in finance and investments is the tradeoff between reward and variability, where the central tendency is the measure of the reward and dispersion is a measure of risk.

The **range** is a relatively simple measure of variability, but when used with other measures it provides extremely useful information. The range is the distance between the largest and the smallest value in the data set, or:

range = maximum value – minimum value

Example: The range

What is the range for the 5-year annualized total returns for five investment managers if the managers' individual returns were 30%, 12%, 25%, 20%, and 23%?

Answer:

range = 30 – 12 = 18%

The **mean absolute deviation** (MAD) is the average of the absolute values of the deviations of individual observations from the arithmetic mean.

$$MAD = \frac{\sum\limits_{i=1}^{n} |X_i - \overline{X}|}{n}$$

The computation of the MAD uses the absolute values of each deviation from the mean because the sum of the actual deviations from the arithmetic mean is zero.

Example: MAD

What is the MAD of the investment returns for the five managers discussed in the preceding example? How is it interpreted?

Answer:

annualized returns: [30%, 12%, 25%, 20%, 23%]

$$\overline{X} = \frac{[30 + 12 + 25 + 20 + 23]}{5} = 22\%$$

$$MAD = \frac{[|30 - 22| + |12 - 22| + |25 - 22| + |20 - 22| + |23 - 22|]}{5}$$

$$MAD = \frac{[8 + 10 + 3 + 2 + 1]}{5} = 4.8\%$$

This result can be interpreted to mean that, on average, an individual return will deviate ±4.8% from the mean return of 22%.

The **population variance** is defined as the average of the squared deviations from the mean. The population variance (σ^2) uses the values for all members of a population and is calculated using the following formula:

$$\sigma^2 = \frac{\sum_{i=1}^{N}(X_i - \mu)^2}{N}$$

Example: Population variance, σ^2

Assume the 5-year annualized total returns for the five investment managers used in the earlier example represent *all* of the managers at a small investment firm. What is the population variance of returns?

Answer:

$$\mu = \frac{[30 + 12 + 25 + 20 + 23]}{5} = 22\%$$

$$\sigma^2 = \frac{\left[(30-22)^2 + (12-22)^2 + (25-22)^2 + (20-22)^2 + (23-22)^2\right]}{5} = 35.60\left(\%^2\right)$$

Interpreting this result, we can say that the average variation from the mean return is 35.60% squared. Had we done the calculation using decimals instead of whole percents, the variance would be 0.00356. What is a percent squared? Yes, this is nonsense, but let's see what we can do so that it makes more sense.

As you have just seen, a major problem with using the variance is the difficulty of interpreting it. The computed variance, unlike the mean, is in terms of squared units of measurement. How does one interpret squared percents, squared dollars, or squared yen? This problem is mitigated through the use of the standard deviation. The **population standard deviation**, σ, is the square root of the population variance and is calculated as follows:

$$\sigma = \sqrt{\frac{\sum_{i=1}^{N}(X - \mu)^2}{N}}$$

Example: Population standard deviation, σ

Using the data from the preceding examples, compute the population standard deviation.

Answer:

$$\sigma = \sqrt{\frac{(30-22)^2 + (12-22)^2 + (25-22)^2 + (20-22)^2 + (23-22)^2}{5}}$$

$$= \sqrt{35.60} = 5.97\%$$

Calculated with decimals instead of whole percents, we would get:

$$\sigma^2 = 0.00356 \text{ and } \sigma = \sqrt{0.00356} = 0.05966 = 5.97\%$$

Since the population standard deviation and population mean are both expressed in the same units (percent), these values are easy to relate. The outcome of this example indicates that the mean return is 22% and the standard deviation about the mean is 5.97%. Note that this is greater than the MAD of 4.8%, a result (σ > MAD) that holds in general.

The **sample variance**, s^2, is the measure of dispersion that applies when we are evaluating a sample of n observations from a population. The sample variance is calculated using the following formula:

$$s^2 = \frac{\sum_{i=1}^{n}(X_i - \overline{X})^2}{n - 1}$$

The most noteworthy difference from the formula for population variance is that the denominator for s^2 is n – 1, one less than the sample size n, where σ^2 uses the entire population size N. Another difference is the use of the sample mean, $\overline{X}$, instead of the population mean, μ. Based on the mathematical theory behind statistical procedures, the use of the entire number of sample observations, n, instead of n – 1 as the divisor in the computation of s^2, will systematically *underestimate* the population parameter, σ^2, particularly for small sample sizes. This systematic underestimation causes the sample variance to be what is referred to as a **biased estimator** of the population variance. Using n – 1 instead of n in the denominator, however, improves the statistical properties of s^2 as an estimator of σ^2. Thus, s^2, as expressed in the equation above, is considered to be an unbiased estimator of σ^2.

Example: Sample variance

Assume that the 5-year annualized total returns for the five investment managers used in the preceding examples represent only a sample of the managers at a large investment firm. What is the sample variance of these returns?

Answer:

$$\overline{X} = \frac{[30 + 12 + 25 + 20 + 23]}{5} = 22\%$$

$$s^2 = \frac{\left[(30-22)^2 + (12-22)^2 + (25-22)^2 + (20-22)^2 + (23-22)^2\right]}{5-1} = 44.5\left(\%^2\right)$$

Thus, the sample variance of 44.5(%²) can be interpreted to be an unbiased estimator of the population variance. Note that 44.5 "percent squared" is 0.00445 and you will get this value if you put the percent returns in decimal form [e.g., $(0.30 - 0.22)^2$, etc.].

As with the population standard deviation, the **sample standard deviation** can be calculated by taking the square root of the sample variance. The sample standard deviation, *s*, is defined as:

$$s = \sqrt{\frac{\sum_{i=1}^{n}(X_i - \overline{X})^2}{n-1}}$$

Example: Sample standard deviation

Compute the sample standard deviation based on the result of the preceding example.

Answer:

Since the sample variance for the preceding example was computed to be $44.5(\%^2)$, the sample standard deviation is:

$$s = [44.5(\%^2)]^{1/2} = 6.67\% \text{ or } \sqrt{0.00445} = 0.0667$$

The results shown here mean that the sample standard deviation, s = 6.67%, can be interpreted as an unbiased estimator of the population standard deviation, σ.

LOS 7.h: Calculate and interpret the proportion of observations falling within a specified number of standard deviations of the mean using Chebyshev's inequality.

Chebyshev's inequality states that for any set of observations, whether sample or population data and regardless of the shape of the distribution, the percentage of the observations that lie within *k* standard deviations of the mean is *at least* $1 - 1/k^2$ for all k > 1.

Example: Chebyshev's inequality

What is the minimum percentage of any distribution that will lie within ±2 standard deviations of the mean?

Answer:

Applying Chebyshev's inequality, we have:

$$1 - 1/k^2 = 1 - 1/2^2 = 1 - 1/4 = 0.75 \text{ or } 75\%$$

According to Chebyshev's inequality, the following relationships hold for any distribution. At least:

- 36% of observations lie within ±1.25 standard deviations of the mean.
- 56% of observations lie within ±1.50 standard deviations of the mean.
- 75% of observations lie within ±2 standard deviations of the mean.

- 89% of observations lie within ±3 standard deviations of the mean.
- 94% of observations lie within ±4 standard deviations of the mean.

The importance of Chebyshev's inequality is that it applies to any distribution. If we actually know the underlying distribution is normal, for example, we can be even more precise about the percentage of observations that will fall within 2 or 3 standard deviations of the mean.

LOS 7.i: Define, calculate, and interpret the coefficient of variation and the Sharpe ratio.

A direct comparison between two or more measures of dispersion may be difficult. For instance, suppose you are comparing the annual returns distribution for retail stocks with a mean of 8% and an annual returns distribution for a real estate portfolio with a mean of 16%. A direct comparison between the dispersion of the two distributions is not meaningful because of the relatively large difference in their means. To make a meaningful comparison, a relative measure of dispersion must be used. **Relative dispersion** is the amount of variability in a distribution relative to a reference point or benchmark. Relative dispersion is commonly measured with the **coefficient of variation** (CV), which is computed as:

$$CV = \frac{s_x}{\overline{X}} = \frac{\text{standard deviation of x}}{\text{average value of x}}$$

CV measures the amount of dispersion in a distribution relative to the distribution's mean. It is useful because it enables us to make a direct comparison of dispersion across different sets of data. In an investments setting, the CV is used to measure the risk (variability) per unit of expected return (mean).

> **Example: Coefficient of variation**
>
> You have just been presented with a report that indicates that the mean monthly return on T-bills is 0.25% with a standard deviation of 0.36%, and the mean monthly return for the S&P 500 is 1.09% with a standard deviation of 7.30%. Your unit manager has asked you to compute the CV for these two investments and to interpret your results.
>
> **Answer:**
>
> $$CV_{\text{T-bills}} = \frac{0.36}{0.25} = 1.44$$
>
> $$CV_{\text{S\&P 500}} = \frac{7.30}{1.09} = 6.70$$
>
> These results indicate that there is less dispersion (risk) per unit of monthly return for T-bills than there is for the S&P 500 (1.44 versus 6.70).

Professor's Note: To remember the formula for CV, remember that the coefficient of variation is a measure of variation, so standard deviation goes in the numerator. CV is variation per unit of return.

The Sharpe Ratio

The **Sharpe measure** (a.k.a., the *Sharpe ratio* or *reward-to-variability ratio*) is widely used for investment performance measurement and measures *excess* return per unit of risk. The Sharpe measure appears over and over throughout the CFA® curriculum. It is defined according to the following formula:

$$\text{Sharpe ratio} = \frac{\bar{r}_p - r_f}{\sigma_p}$$

where:
$\bar{r}_p$ = portfolio return
r_f = risk-free return
σ_p = standard deviation of portfolio returns

Notice that the numerator of the Sharpe ratio uses a measure for a risk-free return. As such, the quantity $(\bar{r}_p - r_f)$, referred to as the **excess return** on Portfolio P, measures the extra reward that investors receive for exposing themselves to risk. Portfolios with large Sharpe ratios are preferred to portfolios with smaller ratios because it is assumed that rational investors prefer return and dislike risk.

Example: The Sharpe ratio

Assume that the mean monthly return on T-bills is 0.25% and that the mean monthly return and standard deviation for the S&P 500 are 1.30% and 7.30%, respectively. Using the T-bill return to represent the risk-free rate, as is common in practice, compute and interpret the Sharpe ratio.

Answer:

$$\text{Sharpe ratio} = \frac{1.30 - 0.25}{7.30} = 0.144$$

The Sharpe ratio of 0.144 indicates that the S&P 500 earned 0.144% of excess return per unit of risk, where risk is measured by standard deviation of portfolio returns.

LOS 7.j: Define and interpret skewness, explain the meaning of a positively or negatively skewed return distribution, and describe the relative locations of the mean, median, and mode for a nonsymmetrical distribution.

A distribution is **symmetrical** if it is shaped identically on both sides of its mean. Distributional symmetry implies that intervals of losses and gains will exhibit the same frequency. For example, a symmetrical distribution with a mean return of zero will have losses in the –6% to –4% interval as frequently as it will have gains in the +4% to +6% interval. The extent to which a returns distribution is symmetrical is important because the degree of symmetry tells analysts if deviations from the mean are more likely to be positive or negative.

Skewness, or skew, refers to the extent to which a distribution is not symmetrical. Nonsymmetrical distributions may be either positively or negatively skewed and result from the occurrence of outliers in the data set. **Outliers** are observations with extraordinarily large values, either positive or negative.

- A *positively skewed* distribution is characterized by many outliers in the upper region, or right tail. A positively skewed distribution is said to be skewed right because of its relatively long upper (right) tail.
- A *negatively skewed* distribution has a disproportionately large amount of outliers that fall within its lower (left) tail. A negatively skewed distribution is said to be skewed left because of its long lower tail.

Mean, Median, and Mode for a Nonsymmetrical Distribution

Skewness affects the **location of the mean, median, and mode** of a distribution.

- For a symmetrical distribution, the mean, median, and mode are equal.
- For a positively skewed distribution, the mode is less than the median, which is less than the mean. The mean is affected by outliers; in a positively skewed distribution, there are large, positive outliers which will tend to "pull" the mean upward, or more positive. An example of a positively skewed distribution is that of housing prices. Suppose that you live in a neighborhood with 100 homes; 99 of them sell for $100,000, and one sells for $1,000,000. The median and the mode will be $100,000, but the mean will be $109,000. Hence, the mean has been "pulled" upward (to the right) by the existence of one home (outlier) in the neighborhood.
- For a negatively skewed distribution, the mean is less than the median, which is less than the mode. In this case, there are large, negative outliers which tend to "pull" the mean downward (to the left).

Professor's Note: The key to remembering how measures of central tendency are affected by skewed data is to recognize that skew affects the mean more than the median and mode, and the mean is "pulled" in the direction of the skew. The relative location of the mean, median, and mode for different distribution shapes is shown in Figure 5. Note the median is between the other two measures for positively or negatively skewed distributions.

Figure 5: Effect of Skewness on Mean, Median, and Mode

Symmetrical
(Mean = Median = Mode)

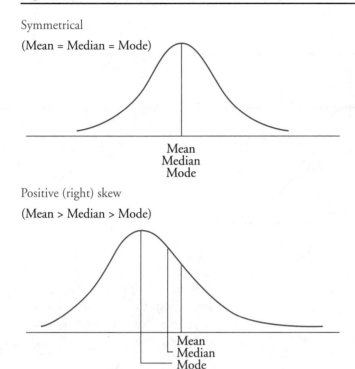

Mean
Median
Mode

Positive (right) skew
(Mean > Median > Mode)

Mean
Median
Mode

Negative (left) skew
(Mean < Median < Mode)

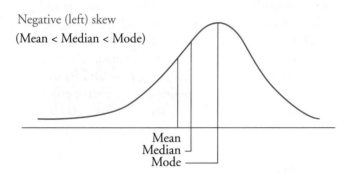

Mean
Median
Mode

LOS 7.k: Define and interpret measures of sample skewness and kurtosis.

Kurtosis is a measure of the degree to which a distribution is more or less "peaked" than a normal distribution. **Leptokurtic** describes a distribution that is more peaked than a normal distribution, whereas **platykurtic** refers to a distribution that is less peaked, or flatter than a normal distribution. A distribution is **mesokurtic** if it has the same kurtosis as a normal distribution.

As indicated in Figure 6, a leptokurtic return distribution will have more returns clustered around the mean and more returns with large deviations from the mean (fatter tails). Relative to a normal distribution, a leptokurtic distribution will have a greater percentage of small deviations from the mean and a greater percentage of extremely large deviations from the mean. This means that there is a relatively greater probability of an observed value being either close to the mean or far from the mean. With regard to an investment returns distribution, a greater likelihood of a large deviation from the mean return is often perceived as an increase in risk.

Figure 6: Kurtosis

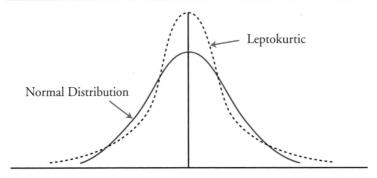

A distribution is said to exhibit **excess kurtosis** if it has either more or less kurtosis than the normal distribution. The computed kurtosis for all normal distributions is three. Statisticians, however, sometimes report excess kurtosis, which is defined as kurtosis minus three. Thus, a normal distribution has excess kurtosis equal to zero, a leptokurtic distribution has excess kurtosis greater than zero, and platykurtic distributions will have excess kurtosis less than zero.

Kurtosis is critical in a risk management setting. Most research about the distribution of securities returns has shown that returns are not normally distributed. Actual securities returns tend to exhibit both skewness and kurtosis. Skewness and kurtosis are critical concepts for risk management because when securities returns are modeled using an assumed normal distribution, the predictions from the models will not take into account the potential for extremely large, negative outcomes. In fact, most risk managers put very little emphasis on the mean and standard deviation of a distribution and focus more on the distribution of returns in the tails of the distribution—that is where the risk is. In general, greater positive kurtosis and more negative skew in returns distributions indicates increased risk.

Measures of Sample Skew and Kurtosis

Sample skewness is equal to the sum of the cubed deviations from the mean divided by the cubed standard deviation and by the number of observations. Sample skewness for large samples is computed as:

$$\text{sample skewness}(S_K) = \frac{1}{n} \frac{\sum_{i=1}^{n}(X_i - \overline{X})^3}{s^3}$$

where:
s = sample standard deviation

Note that the denominator is always positive, but that the numerator can be positive or negative, depending on whether observations above the mean or observations below the mean tend to be further from the mean on average. When a distribution is right skewed, sample skewness is positive because the deviations above the mean are larger on average. A left-skewed distribution has a negative sample skewness.

Dividing by standard deviation cubed standardizes the statistic and allows **interpretation of the skewness measure.** If relative skewness is equal to zero, the data is not skewed. Positive levels of relative skewness imply a positively skewed distribution, whereas negative values of relative skewness imply a negatively skewed distribution. Values of S_K in excess of 0.5 in absolute value indicate significant levels of skewness.

Sample kurtosis is measured using deviations raised to the *fourth power*.

$$\text{sample kurtosis} = \frac{1}{n}\frac{\sum_{i=1}^{n}\left(X_i - \overline{X}\right)^4}{s^4}$$

where:
s = sample standard deviation

To **interpret kurtosis**, note that it is measured relative to the kurtosis of a normal distribution, which is 3. Positive values of excess kurtosis indicate a distribution that is leptokurtic (more peaked, fat tails), whereas negative values indicate a platykurtic distribution (less peaked, thin tails). Excess kurtosis values that exceed 1.0 in absolute value are considered large. We can calculate kurtosis relative to that of a normal distribution as:

excess kurtosis = sample kurtosis – 3

LOS 7.l: Discuss the use of arithmetic mean or geometric mean when determining investment returns.

Since past annual returns are compounded each period, the geometric mean of past annual returns is the appropriate measure of past performance. It gives us the average annual *compound* return. With annual returns of 5%, 12%, and 9% over three years, the geometric mean return of $[(1.05)(1.12)(1.09)]^{1/3} - 1 = 8.63\%$ tells us the single rate that, if compounded over the three periods, would lead to the same increase in wealth as the individual annual rates of return.

The arithmetic mean of (5% + 12% + 9%)/3 = 8.67% is, however, the statistically best estimator of the *next* year's returns given only the three years of return outcomes. To estimate *multi-year* returns (e.g. expected annual return over the next three years), the geometric mean of 8.63% is the appropriate measure.

Consider also a forward-looking model where returns will be either +100% or –50% each year for two years. Note that when returns are +100% in year 1 and –50% in year 2, the annual geometric mean return is $[(1 + 100\%)(1 - 50\%)]^{1/2} - 1 = 0\%$ and the arithmetic mean annual return is (100% – 50%)/2 = 25%.

Consider the following tree model for two years where the outcomes of +100% and −50% are equally likely and beginning wealth is $1,000:

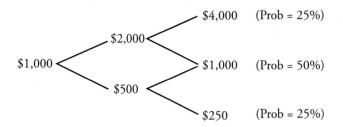

Each of the four possible ending wealth values has a 25% probability, so the expected ending wealth is simply (4,000 + 1,000 + 1,000 + 250)/4 = $1,562.50, or 0.25(4,000) + 0.50(1,000) + 0.25(250) = $1,562.50. This is consistent with earning a compound annual rate of return equal to the arithmetic mean of 25%, $(1.25^2 - 1)$$1,000 = $1,562.50, but not with earning the geometric mean return of 0%. For each single year, the expected rate of return is simply the average of +100% and −50% since those outcomes are equally likely.

KEY CONCEPTS

LOS 7.a

Descriptive statistics summarize the characteristics of a data set; inferential statistics are used to make probabilistic statements about a population based on a sample.

A population includes all members of a specified group, while a sample is a subset of the population used to draw inferences about the population.

Data may be measured using different scales.
- Nominal scale—data is put into categories that have no particular order.
- Ordinal scale—data is put into categories that can be ordered with respect to some characteristic.
- Interval scale—differences in data values are meaningful, but ratios, such as twice as much or twice as large, are not meaningful.
- Ratio scale—ratios of values, such as twice as much or half as large, are meaningful, and zero represents the complete absence of the characteristic being measured.

LOS 7.b

Any measurable characteristic of a population is called a parameter.

A characteristic of a sample is given by a sample statistic.

A frequency distribution groups observations into classes, or intervals. An interval is a range of values.

LOS 7.c

Relative frequency is the percentage of total observations falling within an interval.

Cumulative relative frequency for an interval is the sum of the relative frequencies for all values less than or equal to that interval's maximum value.

LOS 7.d

A histogram is a bar chart of data that has been grouped into a frequency distribution. A frequency polygon plots the midpoint of each interval on the horizontal axis and the absolute frequency for that interval on the vertical axis, and connects the midpoints with straight lines. The advantage of histograms and frequency polygons is that we can quickly see where most of the observations lie.

LOS 7.e

The arithmetic mean is the average. $\bar{X} = \dfrac{\sum\limits_{i=1}^{n} X_i}{n}$.

The geometric mean is used to find a compound growth rate. $G = \sqrt[n]{X_1 \times X_2 \times \ldots \times X_n}$.

The weighted mean weights each value according to its influence. $\bar{X}_W = \sum\limits_{i=1}^{n} w_i X_i$.

The harmonic mean can be used to find an average purchase price, such as dollars per share for equal periodic investments.

$$\bar{X}_H = \dfrac{N}{\sum\limits_{i=1}^{N} \dfrac{1}{x_i}}$$.

The median is the midpoint of a data set when the data is arranged from largest to smallest.

The mode of a data set is the value that occurs most frequently.

LOS 7.f
Quantile is the general term for a value at or below which a stated proportion of the data in a distribution lies. Examples of quantiles include:
- Quartiles—the distribution is divided into quarters.
- Quintile—the distribution is divided into fifths.
- Decile—the distribution is divided into tenths.
- Percentile—the distribution is divided into hundredths (percents).

LOS 7.g
The range is the difference between the largest and smallest values in a data set.

Mean absolute deviation (MAD) is the average of the absolute values of the deviations from the arithmetic mean:

$$MAD = \frac{\sum_{i=1}^{n} |X_i - \bar{X}|}{n}$$

Variance is defined as the mean of the squared deviations from the arithmetic mean or from the expected value of a distribution.

- Population variance = $\sigma^2 = \dfrac{\sum_{i=1}^{N}(X_i - \mu)^2}{N}$, where μ = population mean and N = size.

- Sample variance = $s^2 = \dfrac{\sum_{i=1}^{N}(X_i - \bar{X})^2}{n-1}$, where $\bar{X}$ = sample mean and n = sample size.

Standard deviation is the positive square root of the variance and is frequently used as a quantitative measure of risk.

LOS 7.h
Chebyshev's inequality states that the proportion of the observations within *k* standard deviations of the mean is at least $1 - 1/k^2$ for all k > 1. It states that for any distribution, at least:

36% of observations lie within +/– 1.25 standard deviations of the mean.
56% of observations lie within +/– 1.5 standard deviations of the mean.
75% of observations lie within +/– 2 standard deviations of the mean.
89% of observations lie within +/– 3 standard deviations of the mean.
94% of observations lie within +/– 4 standard deviations of the mean.

LOS 7.i

The coefficient of variation for sample data, $CV = \dfrac{s}{\overline{X}}$, is the ratio of the standard

deviation of the sample to its mean (expected value of the underlying distribution).

The Sharpe ratio measures excess return per unit of risk:

$$\text{Sharpe ratio} \; \frac{\left(\overline{r}_p - r_f\right)}{\sigma_p}$$

LOS 7.j

Skewness describes the degree to which a distribution is not symmetric about its mean.
- A right-skewed distribution has positive sample skewness and has a mean that is greater than its median that is greater than its mode.
- A left-skewed distribution has negative skewness and has a mean that is less than its median that is less than its mode.
- Sample skew with an absolute value greater than 0.5 is considered significantly different from zero.

LOS 7.k

Kurtosis measures the peakedness of a distribution and the probability of extreme outcomes (thickness of tails).
- Excess kurtosis is measured relative to a normal distribution, which has a kurtosis of 3.
- Positive values of excess kurtosis indicate a distribution that is leptokurtic (fat tails, more peaked) so that the probability of extreme outcomes is greater than for a normal distribution.
- Negative values of excess kurtosis indicate a platykurtic distribution (thin tails, less peaked).
- Excess kurtosis with an absolute value greater than 1 is considered significant.

LOS 7.l

The arithmetic mean return is appropriate for forecasting single period returns in future periods, while the geometric mean is appropriate for forecasting future compound returns over multiple periods.

CONCEPT CHECKERS

1. The intervals in a frequency distribution should always have which of the following characteristics? The intervals should always:
    A. be truncated.
    B. be open ended.
    C. be nonoverlapping.

Use the following frequency distribution for Questions 2 through 4.

Return, R	Frequency
–10% up to 0%	3
0% up to 10%	7
10% up to 20%	3
20% up to 30%	2
30% up to 40%	1

2. The number of intervals in this frequency table is:
    A. 1.
    B. 5.
    C. 16.

3. The sample size is:
    A. 1.
    B. 5.
    C. 16.

4. The relative frequency of the second interval is:
    A. 10.0%.
    B. 16.0%.
    C. 43.8%.

Use the following data to answer Questions 5 through 13.

XYZ Corp. Annual Stock Prices

2003	2004	2005	2006	2007	2008
22%	5%	–7%	11%	2%	11%

5. What is the arithmetic mean return for XYZ stock?
    A. 7.3%.
    B. 8.0%.
    C. 11.0%.

6. What is the median return for XYZ stock?
    A. 7.3%.
    B. 8.0%.
    C. 11.0%.

7.   What is the mode of the returns for XYZ stock?
     A. 7.3%.
     B. 8.0%.
     C. 11.0%.

8.   What is the range for XYZ stock returns?
     A. 11.0%.
     B. 22.0%.
     C. 29.0%.

9.   What is the mean absolute deviation for XYZ stock returns?
     A. 5.20%.
     B. 7.33%.
     C. 29.0%.

10. Assuming that the distribution of XYZ stock returns is a population, what is the population variance?
     A. $6.8\%^2$.
     B. $7.7\%^2$.
     C. $80.2\%^2$.

11. Assuming that the distribution of XYZ stock returns is a population, what is the population standard deviation?
     A. 5.02%.
     B. 8.96%.
     C. 46.22%.

12. Assuming that the distribution of XYZ stock returns is a sample, the sample variance is *closest* to:
     A. $5.0\%^2$.
     B. $72.4\%^2$.
     C. $96.3\%^2$.

13. Assuming that the distribution of XYZ stock returns is a sample, what is the sample standard deviation?
     A. 9.8%.
     B. 72.4%.
     C. 96.3%.

14. For a skewed distribution, what is the minimum percentage of the observations that will lie between ±2.5 standard deviations of the mean based on Chebyshev's Inequality?
     A. 56%.
     B. 75%.
     C. 84%.

Use the following data to answer Questions 15 and 16.

The annual returns for FJW's common stock over the years 2003, 2004, 2005, and 2006 were 15%, 19%, –8%, and 14%.

15. What is the arithmetic mean return for FJW's common stock?
    A. 10.00%.
    B. 14.00%.
    C. 15.25%.

16. What is the geometric mean return for FJW's common stock?
    A. 9.45%.
    B. 14.21%.
    C. It cannot be determined because the 2005 return is negative.

17. A distribution of returns that has a greater percentage of small deviations from the mean and a greater percentage of extremely large deviations from the mean compared to a normal distribution:
    A. is positively skewed.
    B. has positive excess kurtosis.
    C. has negative excess kurtosis.

18. Which of the following is *most accurate* regarding a distribution of returns that has a mean greater than its median?
    A. It is positively skewed.
    B. It is a symmetric distribution.
    C. It has positive excess kurtosis.

19. The harmonic mean of 3, 4, and 5 is:
    A. 3.74.
    B. 3.83.
    C. 4.12.

COMPREHENSIVE PROBLEMS

1. Year-end prices and dividends for Nopat Mutual Fund for each of six years are listed below along with the actual yield (return) on a money market fund called Emfund.

Year	Nopat Fund Year-End Price	Nopat Fund Year-End Dividend	Nopat Annual Holding Period Return	Emfund Return for the Year
2004	$28.50	$0.14		3.00%
2005	$26.80	$0.15	?	4.00%
2006	$29.60	$0.17	?	4.30%
2007	$31.40	$0.17	?	5.00%
2008	$34.50	$0.19	?	4.10%
2009	$37.25	$0.22	?	6.00%

Average risk-free rate over the five years 2005 – 2009 is 2.8%. Risk-free rate for 2004 is 2.8%.

A. Calculate the annual holding period returns for a beginning-of-year investment in Nopat fund for each of the five years over the period 2005–2009 (% with two decimal places).

B. What is the arithmetic mean annual total return on an investment in Nopat fund shares (dividends reinvested) over the period 2005–2009?

C. What is the average compound annual rate of return on an investment in Nopat fund made at year end 2004 if it were held (dividends reinvested) until the end of 2009?

D. What is the median annual return on an Emfund investment over the 6-year period 2004–2009?

E. What is the sample standard deviation of the annual returns on money market funds over the 6-year period, using the Emfund returns as a sample?

F. What is the holding period return on a 6-year investment in Emfund made at the beginning of 2004?

G. If an investor bought $10,000 of Nopat Fund shares at the end of the year in each of the three years 2007–2009, what is the average price paid per share? What is the arithmetic mean of the three year-end prices?

H. What would have been the 1-year holding period return on a portfolio that had $60,000 invested in Nopat Fund and $40,000 invested in Emfund as of the beginning of 2009?

I.   What is the coefficient of variation of the Nopat Fund annual total returns 2005–2009 and of the Emfund annual returns for the six years 2004–2009? Which is riskier?

J.   What is the Sharpe ratio for an investment in the Nopat Fund over the five years from 2005–2009? What is the Sharpe ratio for an investment in the Emfund over the six years 2004–2009? Which Sharpe ratio is more preferred?

K.   Calculate the range and mean absolute deviation of returns for an investment in the Emfund over the 6-year period 2004–2009.

L.   What is the annual growth rate of dividends on Nopat Fund over the period from 2004–2009?

2.   Identify the type of scale for each of the following:

A.   Cars ranked as heavy, medium, or light.

B.   Birds divided into categories of songbirds, birds of prey, scavengers, and game birds.

C.   The height of each player on a baseball team.

D.   The average temperature on 20 successive days in January in Chicago.

E.   Interest rates on T-bills each year for 60 years.

3.   Explain the difference between descriptive and inferential statistics.

4.   An analyst has estimated the following parameters for the annual returns distributions for four portfolios:

Portfolio	Mean Return E(R)	Variance of returns	Skewness	Kurtosis
Portfolio A	10%	625	1.8	0
Portfolio B	14%	900	0.0	3
Portfolio C	16%	1250	−0.85	5
Portfolio D	19%	2000	1.4	2

She has been asked to evaluate the portfolios' risk and return characteristics. Assume that a risk-free investment will earn 5%.

A.   Which portfolio would be preferred based on the Sharpe performance measure?

B.   Which portfolio would be the most preferred based on the coefficient of variation?

C.   Which portfolio(s) is/are symmetric?

    D. Which portfolio(s) has/have fatter tails than a normal distribution?

    E. Which portfolio is the riskiest based on its skewness?

    F. Which portfolio is the riskiest based on its kurtosis?

5. Which measure of central tendency is most affected by including rare but very large positive values?

6. A manager is responsible for managing part of an institutional portfolio to mimic the returns on the S&P 500 stock index. He is evaluated based on his ability to exactly match the returns on the index. His portfolio holds 200 stocks but has exactly the same dividend yield as the S&P 500 portfolio. Which of the statistical measures from this review would be an appropriate measure of his performance and how would you use it?

7. Below are the returns on 20 industry groups of stocks over the past year:

12%, –3%, 18%, 9%, –5%, 21%, 2%, 13%, 28%, –14%,

31%, 32%, 5%, 22%, –28%, 7%, 9%, 12%, –17%, 6%

    A. What is the return on the industry group with the lowest rate of return in the top quartile?

    B. What is the 40th percentile of this array of data?

    C. What is the range of the data?

    D. Based on a frequency distribution with 12 intervals, what is the relative frequency and cumulative relative frequency of the 10th interval (ascending order)?

ANSWERS – CONCEPT CHECKERS

1. **C**   Intervals within a frequency distribution should always be nonoverlapping and closed ended so that each data value can be placed into only one interval. Intervals have no set width and should be set at a width so that data is adequately summarized without losing valuable characteristics.

2. **B**   An interval is the set of return values that an observation falls within. Simply count the return intervals on the table—there are five of them.

3. **C**   The sample size is the sum of all of the frequencies in the distribution, or 3 + 7 + 3 + 2 + 1 = 16.

4. **C**   The relative frequency is found by dividing the frequency of the interval by the total number of frequencies.

    $$\frac{7}{16} = 43.8\%$$

5. **A**   [22% + 5% + −7% + 11% + 2% +11%] / 6 = 7.3%

6. **B**   To find the median, rank the returns in order and take the middle value: −7%, 2%, 5%, 11%, 11%, 22%. In this case, because there is an even number of observations, the median is the average of the two middle values, or (5% + 11%) / 2 = 8.0%.

7. **C**   The mode is the value that appears most often, or 11%.

8. **C**   The range is calculated by taking the highest value minus the lowest value.

    22% − (−7%) = 29.0%

9. **B**   The mean absolute deviation is found by taking the mean of the absolute values of the deviations from the mean.

    $(|22 − 7.3| + |5 − 7.3| + |−7 − 7.3| + |11 − 7.3| + |2 − 7.3| + |11 − 7.3|) / 6 = 7.33\%$

10. **C**   The population variance, σ^2, is found by taking the mean of all squared deviations from the mean.

    $\sigma^2 = [(22 − 7.3)^2 + (5 − 7.3)^2 + (−7 − 7.3)^2 + (11 − 7.3)^2 + (2 − 7.3)^2 + (11 − 7.3)^2] / 6 = 80.2\%^2$

11. **B**   The population standard deviation, σ, is found by taking the square root of the population variance.

    $\sigma = \{[(22 − 7.3)^2 + (5 − 7.3)^2 + (−7 − 7.3)^2 + (11 − 7.3)^2 + (2 − 7.3)^2 + (11 − 7.3)^2] / 6\}^{1/2}$
    $= (80.2\%^2)^{0.5}$
    $= 8.96\%$

12. **C**   The sample variance, s^2, uses n − 1 in the denominator.

    $s^2 = [(22 − 7.3)^2 + (5 − 7.3)^2 + (−7 − 7.3)^2 + (11 − 7.3)^2 + (2 − 7.3)^2 + (11 − 7.3)^2] / (6 − 1) = 96.3\%^2$

13. **A**   The sample standard deviation, s, is the square root of the sample variance.

    $s = \{[(22 − 7.3)^2 + (5 − 7.3)^2 + (−7 − 7.3)^2 + (11 − 7.3)^2 + (2 − 7.3)^2 + (11 − 7.3)^2] / (6 − 1)\}^{0.5} = (96.3)^{0.5} = 9.8\%$

14. **C**   Applying Chebyshev's inequality, $1 - [1 / (2.5)^2] = 0.84$, or 84%.

15. **A** $(15\% + 19\% + (-8\%) + 14\%) / 4 = 10\%$

16. **A** $(1.15 \times 1.19 \times 0.92 \times 1.14)^{0.25} - 1 = 9.45\%$

 Professor's Note: This question could have been answered very quickly since the geometric mean must be less than the arithmetic mean computed in the preceding problem.

17. **B**   A distribution that has a greater percentage of small deviations from the mean and a greater percentage of extremely large deviations from the mean will be leptokurtic and will exhibit excess kurtosis (positive). The distribution will be more peaked and have fatter tails than a normal distribution.

18. **A**   A distribution with a mean greater than its median is positively skewed, or skewed to the right. The skew "pulls" the mean. *Note: Kurtosis deals with the overall shape of a distribution and not its skewness.*

19. **B** $\bar{X}_H = \dfrac{3}{\frac{1}{3} + \frac{1}{4} + \frac{1}{5}} = 3.83$

ANSWERS – COMPREHENSIVE PROBLEMS

1.   A.   The annual holding period returns (total returns) are given in the table and are each calculated as (year-end price + year-end dividend)/previous year-end price – 1.

Year	Nopat Fund Year-End Price	Nopat Fund Year-End Dividend	Nopat Annual Holding Period Return	Emfund Return for the Year
2004	$28.50	$0.14		3.00%
2005	$26.80	$0.15	−5.44%	4.00%
2006	$29.60	$0.17	11.08%	4.30%
2007	$31.40	$0.17	6.66%	5.00%
2008	$34.50	$0.19	10.48%	4.10%
2009	$37.25	$0.22	8.61%	6.00%

B.   The arithmetic mean of the holding period returns is 6.28%.

C. $((1 - 0.0544)(1.1108)(1.0666)(1.1048)(1.0861))^{1/5} - 1 = 6.10\%$

D.   Median = (4.3 + 4.1) / 2 = 4.2%.

E.   Sample standard deviation of Emfund returns over the six years is:

$$\{[(3 - 4.4)^2 + (4 - 4.4)^2 + (4.3 - 4.4)^2 + (5 - 4.4)^2 + (4.1 - 4.4)^2 + (6 - 4.4)^2] / 5\}^{1/2}$$

$$= \left(\frac{5.14}{5}\right)^{1/2} = 1.01\%$$

F. $(1.03)(1.04)(1.043)(1.05)(1.041)(1.06) - 1 = 29.45\%$.
    The HPR is the percentage difference between the ending value and the beginning value. Starting with a value of \$1, the ending value is \$1(1.03)(1.04)(1.043)(1.05)(1.041)(1.06) = \$1.2945, or 29.45% greater than the beginning value.

G. The harmonic mean is $3/(1/31.4 + 1/34.5 + 1/37.25) = \$34.22$ average purchase price per share. Arithmetic mean price = $(31.4 + 34.5 + 37.25)/ 3 = \$34.38$.

H. The portfolio return is a weighted average, $0.6 \times 8.61\% + 0.4 \times 6\% = 7.57\%$.

I. CV for Nopat = 6.77/6.28 = 1.08. CV for Emfund = 1.01/4.4 = 0.23. Emfund is less risky by this measure.

J. Sharpe ratio for Nopat is $(6.28 - 2.8)/ 6.77 = 0.51$. Sharpe measure for Emfund is $(4.4 - 2.8) / 1.01 = 1.58$. The Emfund is preferred using this criterion because it has higher excess returns per unit of risk.

K. Range is 6% – 3% = 3%. MAD is 0.73% = [(4.4% – 3%) + (4.4% – 4%) +(4.4% – 4.3%) +(5% – 4.4%) +(4.4% – 4.1%) +(6% – 4.4%)] / 6. Remember to use absolute values; we show all differences as positive to reflect that.

L. Average annual growth rate of dividends is the geometric mean rate of growth: $(0.22/0.14)^{1/5} - 1 = 9.46\%$.

2. A. An ordinal scale.

    B. A nominal scale.

    C. A ratio scale.

    D. An interval scale.

    E. A ratio scale.

3. Descriptive statistics are used to summarize the important characteristics of large data sets to consolidate a mass of numerical data into useful information. Inferential statistics refers to using statistics to make forecasts, estimates, or judgments about a large set of data on the basis of the statistical characteristics of a smaller set (a sample).

4. A. Portfolio D has the highest Sharpe ratio, $\dfrac{19-5}{\sqrt{2000}} = 0.313$ and is therefore the most preferred.

    B. Portfolio B has the lowest coefficient of variation, $\dfrac{\sqrt{900}}{14} = 2.1429$ and is therefore the most preferred.

    C. Portfolio B has no skew and is therefore a symmetric distribution (about its mean of 14%).

    D. The kurtosis of a normal distribution is 3, so only portfolio C has positive excess kurtosis, indicating fatter tails (and more peakedness) relative to a normal distribution.

    E. Negative skew indicates that returns below the mean are more extreme, so we would consider Portfolio C to be the most risky based on skew alone.

    F. Larger kurtosis indicates greater likelihood of extreme outcomes and from a risk-management standpoint this indicates greater risk. Portfolio C has the greatest kurtosis.

5.   The mean is most affected by large outliers in a distribution, compared to the median and mode, which may be unaffected.

6.   Since the goal is to match the index returns, we must focus on the differences between the returns on the manager's portfolio and those on the index he is attempting to mimic. These differences are referred to as "tracking error." The standard deviation or variance of the differences between his portfolio returns and the returns of the index over a number of periods would be a suitable measure of his performance. If you said mean absolute deviation, that is defensible as well as it is certainly one way to measure tracking error. It is, however, not the measure of tracking error we see used in practice.

7. A. With 20 datapoints, the top quartile (¼) is the top 5. Count down from the greatest value to find the 5th from the top is 21%.

    B. The location of the 40th percentile is $(20 + 1)(40/100) = 8.4$. The 8th and 9th lowest returns are 6% and 7%, so the 40th percentile is $6 + 0.4(7 - 6) = 6.4\%$.

    C. The range of the data is $32 - (-28) = 60$.

    D. Divide the range by 12 to get 5. The 10th interval from the bottom is the 3rd from the top. The top three intervals are $27 \leq x \leq 32$, $22 \leq x < 27$, and $17 \leq x < 22$. There are only two observations in the 10th interval, 18% and 21%. The relative frequency is 2/20 = 10%. Since there are four observations $\geq 22\%$, the cumulative relative frequency of the 10th interval is $(20 - 4)/20 = 80\%$.

The following is a review of the Quantitative Methods: Basic Concepts principles designed to address the learning outcome statements set forth by CFA Institute®. This topic is also covered in:

PROBABILITY CONCEPTS

EXAM FOCUS

This topic review covers important terms and concepts associated with probability theory. Random variables, events, outcomes, conditional probability, and joint probability are described. Probability rules such as the addition rule and multiplication rule are introduced. These rules are frequently used by finance practitioners, so your understanding of and ability to apply probability rules is likely to be tested on the exam. Expected value, standard deviation, covariance, and correlation for individual asset and portfolio returns are discussed. A well-prepared candidate will be able to calculate and interpret these widely used measures. This review also discusses counting rules, which lay the foundation for the binomial probability distribution that is covered in the next topic review.

LOS 8.a: Define a random variable, an outcome, an event, mutually exclusive events, and exhaustive events.

- A **random variable** is an uncertain quantity/number.
- An **outcome** is an observed value of a random variable.
- An **event** is a single outcome or a set of outcomes.
- **Mutually exclusive events** are events that cannot both happen at the same time.
- **Exhaustive events** are those that include all possible outcomes.

Consider rolling a 6-sided die. The number that comes up is a *random variable*. If you roll a 4, that is an *outcome*. Rolling a 4 is an *event*, and rolling an even number is an *event*. Rolling a 4 and rolling a 6 are *mutually exclusive events*. Rolling an even number and rolling an odd number is a set of mutually exclusive and *exhaustive events*.

LOS 8.b: Explain the two defining properties of probability and distinguish among empirical, subjective, and a priori probabilities.

There are **two defining properties of probability.**

- The probability of occurrence of any event (E_i) is between 0 and 1 (i.e., $0 \leq P(E_i) \leq 1$).
- If a set of events, E_1, E_2, ... E_n, is mutually exclusive and exhaustive, the probabilities of those events sum to 1 (i.e., $\Sigma P(E_i) = 1$).

The first of the defining properties introduces the term $P(E_i)$, which is shorthand for the "probability of event *i*." If $P(E_i) = 0$, the event will never happen. If $P(E_i) = 1$, the event is certain to occur, and the outcome is not random.

The probability of rolling any one of the numbers 1–6 with a fair die is 1/6 = 0.1667 = 16.7%. The set of events—rolling a number equal to 1, 2, 3, 4, 5, or 6—is exhaustive, and the individual events are mutually exclusive, so the probability of this set of events is equal to 1. We are certain that one of the values in this set of events will occur.

An **empirical probability** is established by analyzing past data. An **a priori probability** is determined using a formal reasoning and inspection process. A **subjective probability** is the least formal method of developing probabilities and involves the use of personal judgment. (Empirical and a priori probabilities, by contrast, are **objective probabilities**.)

The following are examples of statements that use *empirical, a priori,* and *subjective probabilities* for developing probabilities.

- *Empirical probability.* "Historically, the Dow Jones Industrial Average (DJIA) has closed higher than the previous close two out of every three trading days. Therefore, the probability of the Dow going up tomorrow is two-thirds, or 66.7%."
- *A priori probability.* "Yesterday, 24 of the 30 DJIA stocks increased in value. Thus, if 1 of the 30 stocks is selected at random, there is an 80% (= 24 /30) probability that its value increased yesterday."
- *Subjective probability.* "It is my personal feeling that the probability the DJIA will close higher tomorrow is 90%."

LOS 8.c: State the probability of an event in terms of odds for or against the event.

Stating the **odds** that an event will or will not occur is an alternative way of expressing probabilities. Consider an event that has a probability of occurrence of 0.125, which is

one-eighth. The *odds* that the event will occur are $\dfrac{0.125}{(1-0.125)} = \dfrac{1/8}{7/8} = \dfrac{1}{7}$, which we state

as, "the odds for the event occurring are one-to-seven." The *odds against* the event occurring are the reciprocal of 1/7, which is seven-to-one.

We can also get the probability of an event from the odds by reversing these calculations. If we know that the odds for an event are one-to-six, we can compute the probability of

occurrence as $\dfrac{1}{1+6} = \dfrac{1}{7} = 0.1429 = 14.29\%$. Alternatively, the probability that the event

will not occur is $\dfrac{6}{1+6} = \dfrac{6}{7} = 0.8571 = 85.71\%$.

Professor's Note: While I am quite familiar with the use of odds rather than probabilities at the horse track, I can't remember encountering odds for a stock or bond. The use of odds at the horse track lets you know how much you will win per $1 bet on a horse (less the track's percentage). If you bet on a 15-1 long shot and the horse wins, you will receive $15 and your $1 bet will be returned, so the profit is $15. Of course, if the horse loses, you would lose the $1 you bet and the "profit" is –$1.

One last point is that the expected return on the bet is zero, based on the probability of winning expressed in the odds. The probability of the horse winning when the odds are 15-to-1 is $\dfrac{1}{15+1} = \dfrac{1}{16}$ and the probability of the horse losing is 15/16. The expected profit is $\dfrac{1}{16} \times \$15 + \dfrac{15}{16} \times (-\$1) = 0$.

LOS 8.d: Distinguish between unconditional and conditional probabilities.

- **Unconditional probability** (a.k.a. *marginal probability*) refers to the probability of an event regardless of the past or future occurrence of other events. If we are concerned with the probability of an economic recession, regardless of the occurrence of changes in interest rates or inflation, we are concerned with the unconditional probability of a recession.

- A **conditional probability** is one where the occurrence of one event affects the probability of the occurrence of another event. For example, we might be concerned with the probability of a recession *given* that the monetary authority increases interest rates. This is a conditional probability. The key word to watch for here is "given." Using probability notation, "the probability of A *given* the occurrence of B" is expressed as P(A | B), where the vertical bar (|) indicates "given," or "conditional upon." For our interest rate example above, the probability of a recession *given* an increase in interest rates is expressed as P(*recession|increase in interest rates*). A conditional probability of an occurrence is also called its **likelihood**.

LOS 8.e: Define and explain the multiplication, addition, and total probability rules.

The **multiplication rule of probability** is used to determine the joint probability of two events:

P(AB) = P(A|B) × P(B)

The **addition rule of probability** is used to determine the probability that at least one of two events will occur:

P(A or B) = P(A) + P(B) – P(AB)

The **total probability rule** is used to determine the unconditional probability of an event, given conditional probabilities:

$$P(A) = P(A \mid B_1)P(B_1) + P(A \mid B_2)P(B_2) + \dots + P(A \mid B_N)P(B_N)$$

where B_1, B_2,....B_N is a mutually exclusive and exhaustive set of outcomes.

 Professor's Note: Applications of all three probability rules are illustrated in subsequent LOS within this topic review.

LOS 8.f: Calculate and interpret 1) the joint probability of two events, 2) the probability that at least one of two events will occur, given the probability of each and the joint probability of the two events, and 3) a joint probability of any number of independent events.

The **joint probability** of two events is the probability that they will both occur. We can calculate this from the conditional probability that A will occur given B occurs (a conditional probability) and the probability that B will occur (the unconditional probability of B). This calculation is sometimes referred to as the *multiplication rule of probability*. Using the notation for conditional and unconditional probabilities we can express this rule as:

$$P(AB) = P(A \mid B) \times P(B)$$

This expression is read as follows: "The joint probability of A and B, P(AB), is equal to the conditional probability of A *given* B, P(A | B), times the unconditional probability of B, P(B)."

This relationship can be rearranged to define the conditional probability of A given B as follows:

$$P(A \mid B) = \frac{P(AB)}{P(B)}$$

Example: Multiplication rule of probability

Consider the following information:

- P(I) = 0.4, the probability of the monetary authority increasing interest rates (I) is 40%.
- P(R | I) = 0.7, the probability of a recession (R) given an increase in interest rates is 70%.

What is P(RI), the joint probability of a recession *and* an increase in interest rates?

Answer:

Applying the multiplication rule, we get the following result:

$$P(RI) = P(R \mid I) \times P(I)$$

$$P(RI) = 0.7 \times 0.4$$

$$P(RI) = 0.28$$

Don't let the cumbersome notation obscure the simple logic of this result. If an interest rate increase will occur 40% of the time and lead to a recession 70% of the time when it occurs, the joint probability of an interest rate increase and a resulting recession is $(0.4)(0.7) = (0.28) = 28\%$.

Calculating the Probability That at Least One of Two Events Will Occur

The *addition rule* for probabilities is used to determine the probability that at least one of two events will occur. For example, given two events, A and B, the addition rule can be used to determine the probability that either A or B will occur. If the events are *not* mutually exclusive, double counting must be avoided by subtracting the joint probability that *both* A and B will occur from the sum of the unconditional probabilities. This is reflected in the following general expression for the addition rule:

$$P(A \text{ or } B) = P(A) + P(B) - P(AB)$$

For mutually exclusive events, where the joint probability, P(AB), is zero, the probability that either A or B will occur is simply the sum of the unconditional probabilities for each event, $P(A \text{ or } B) = P(A) + P(B)$.

Figure 1 illustrates the addition rule with a Venn Diagram and highlights why the joint probability must be subtracted from the sum of the unconditional probabilities. Note that if the events are *mutually exclusive* the sets do not intersect, P(AB) = 0, and the joint probability is simply P(A) + P(B).

Figure 1: Venn Diagram for Events That Are Not Mutually Exclusive

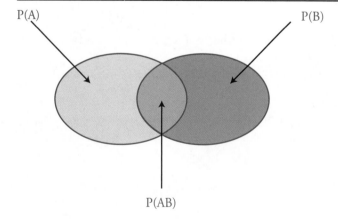

©2009 Kaplan, Inc.

Example: Addition rule of probability

Using the information in our previous interest rate and recession example and the fact that the unconditional probability of a recession, P(R), is 34%, determine the probability that either interest rates will increase *or* a recession will occur.

Answer:

Given that P(R) = 0.34, P(I) = 0.40, and P(RI) = 0.28, we can compute P(R or I) as follows:

$$P(R \text{ or } I) = P(R) + P(I) - P(RI)$$

$$P(R \text{ or } I) = 0.34 + 0.40 - 0.28$$

$$P(R \text{ or } I) = 0.46$$

Calculating a Joint Probability of any Number of Independent Events

On the roll of two dice, the joint probability of getting two 4s is calculated as:

P(4 on first die and 4 on second die) = P(4 on first die) × P(4 on second die)
= 1/6 × 1/6 = 1/36 = 0.0278

On the flip of two coins, the probability of getting two heads is:

P(heads on first coin and heads on second coin) = 1/2 × 1/2 = 1/4 = 0.25

Hint: When dealing with *independent events*, the word *and* indicates multiplication, and the word *or* indicates addition. In probability notation:

$$P(A \textbf{ or } B) = P(A) + P(B) - P(AB), \text{ and } P(A \textbf{ and } B) = P(A) \times P(B)$$

The multiplication rule we used to calculate the joint probability of two independent events may be applied to any number of independent events, as the following examples illustrate.

Example: Joint probability for more than two independent events (1)

What is the probability of rolling three 4s in one simultaneous toss of three dice?

Answer:

Since the probability of rolling a 4 for each die is 1/6, the probability of rolling three 4s is:

$$P(\text{three 4s on the roll of three dice}) = 1/6 \times 1/6 \times 1/6 = 1/216 = 0.00463$$

Similarly:

$$P(\text{four heads on the flip of four coins}) = 1/2 \times 1/2 \times 1/2 \times 1/2 = 1/16 = 0.0625$$

Example: Joint probability for more than two independent events (2)

Using empirical probabilities, suppose we observe that the DJIA has closed higher on two-thirds of all days in the past few decades. Furthermore, it has been determined that up and down days are independent. Based on this information, compute the probability of the DJIA closing higher for five consecutive days.

Answer:

$$P(\text{DJIA up five days in a row}) = 2/3 \times 2/3 \times 2/3 \times 2/3 \times 2/3 = (2/3)^5 = 0.132$$

Similarly:

$$P(\text{DJIA down five days in a row}) = 1/3 \times 1/3 \times 1/3 \times 1/3 \times 1/3 = (1/3)^5 = 0.004$$

LOS 8.g: Distinguish between dependent and independent events.

Independent events refer to events for which the occurrence of one has no influence on the occurrence of the others. The definition of independent events can be expressed in terms of conditional probabilities. Events A and B are independent if and only if:

$$P(A \mid B) = P(A), \text{ or equivalently, } P(B \mid A) = P(B)$$

If this condition is not satisfied, the events are dependent events (i.e., the occurrence of one is dependent on the occurrence of the other).

In our interest rate and recession example, recall that events I and R are not independent; the occurrence of I affects the probability of the occurrence of R. In this example, the independence conditions for I and R are violated because:

$P(R) = 0.34$, but $P(R \mid I) = 0.7$; the probability of a recession is greater when there is an increase in interest rates.

The best examples of independent events are found with the a priori probabilities of dice tosses or coin flips. A die has "no memory." Therefore, the event of rolling a 4 on the second toss is independent of rolling a 4 on the first toss. This idea may be expressed as:

$P(4 \text{ on second toss} \mid 4 \text{ on first toss}) = P(4 \text{ on second toss}) = 1/6 \text{ or } 0.167$

The idea of independent events also applies to flips of a coin:

$P(\text{heads on first coin} \mid \text{heads on second coin}) = P(\text{heads on first coin}) = 1/2 \text{ or } 0.50$

LOS 8.h: Calculate and interpret, using the total probability rule, an unconditional probability.

The *total probability rule* highlights the relationship between unconditional and conditional probabilities of mutually exclusive and exhaustive events. It is used to explain the unconditional probability of an event in terms of probabilities that are conditional upon other events.

In general, the unconditional probability of event R, $P(R) = P(R \mid S_1) \times P(S_1) + P(R \mid S_2) \times P(S_2) + \ldots + P(R \mid S_N) \times P(S_N)$, where the set of events $\{S_1, S_2, \ldots S_N\}$ is mutually exclusive and exhaustive.

Example: An investment application of unconditional probability

Building upon our ongoing example about interest rates and economic recession, we can assume that a recession can only occur with either of the two events—interest rates increase (I) or interest rates do not increase (I^C)—since these events are mutually exclusive and exhaustive. I^C is read "the complement of I," which means "not I." Therefore, the probability of I^C is $1 - P(I)$. It is logical, therefore, that the sum of the two joint probabilities must be the unconditional probability of a recession. This can be expressed as follows:

$P(R) = P(RI) + P(RI^C)$

Applying the multiplication rule, we may restate this expression as:

$$P(R) = P(R \mid I) \times P(I) + P(R \mid I^C) \times P(I^C)$$

Assume that $P(R \mid I) = 0.70$, $P(R \mid I^C)$, the probability of recession if interest rates do not rise, is 10% and that $P(I) = 0.40$ so that $P(I^C) = 0.60$. The unconditional probability of a recession can be calculated as follows:

$$\begin{aligned} P(R) &= P(R \mid I) \times P(I) + P(R \mid I^C) \times P(I^C) \\ &= (0.70)(0.40) + (0.10)(0.60) \\ &= 0.28 + 0.06 = 0.34 \end{aligned}$$

In Figure 2 we illustrate the relation between conditional and unconditional probability.

Figure 2: Unconditional, Conditional, and Joint Probabilities

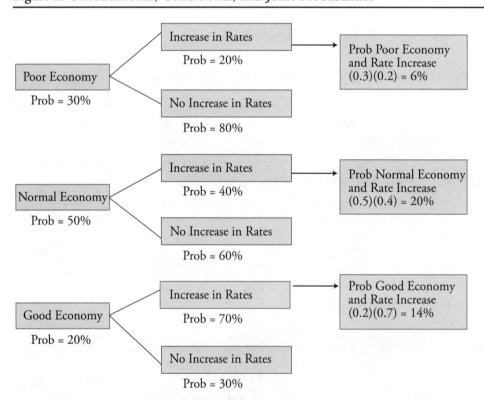

The probabilities for a poor, normal, and good economy are unconditional probabilities. The probabilities of rate increases are conditional probabilities [e.g., Prob (increase in rates | poor economy) = 20%]. The third column has joint probabilities [e.g., Prob (poor economy *and* increase in rates) = 6%]. The unconditional probability of a rate increase is the sum of the joint probabilities, 6% + 20% + 14% = 40% = Prob (increase in rates).

EXPECTED VALUE

Now that we have developed some probability concepts and tools for working with probabilities, we can apply this knowledge to determine the average value for a random variable that results from multiple experiments. This average is called an **expected value**.

In any given experiment, the observed value for a random variable may not equal its expected value, and even if it does, the outcome from one observation to the next will be different. The degree of dispersion of outcomes around the expected value of a random variable is measured using the variance and standard deviation. When pairs of random variables are being observed, the covariance and correlation are used to measure the extent of the relationship between the observed values for the two variables from one observation to the next.

The expected value is the weighted average of the possible outcomes of a random variable, where the weights are the probabilities that the outcomes will occur. The mathematical representation for the expected value of random variable X is:

$$E(X) = \Sigma P(x_i)x_i = P(x_1)x_1 + P(x_2)x_2 + \ldots + P(x_n)x_n$$

Here, E is referred to as the expectations operator and is used to indicate the computation of a probability-weighted average. The symbol x_1 represents the first observed value (observation) for random variable X, x_2 is the second observation, and so on, through the nth observation. The concept of expected value may be demonstrated using the a priori probabilities associated with a coin toss. On the flip of one coin, the occurrence of the event "heads" may be used to assign the value of one to a random variable. Alternatively, the event "tails" means the random variable equals zero. Statistically, we would formally write:

if heads, then X = 1
if tails, then X = 0

For a fair coin, P(heads) = P(X = 1) = 0.5, and P(tails) = P(X = 0) = 0.5. The expected value can be computed as follows:

$$E(X) = \Sigma P(x_i)x_i = P(X = 0)(0) + P(X = 1)(1) = (0.5)(0) + (0.5)(1) = 0.5$$

In any individual flip of a coin, X cannot assume a value of 0.5. Over the long term, however, the average of all the outcomes is expected to be 0.5. Similarly, the expected value of the roll of a fair die, where X = number that faces up on the die, is determined to be:

$$E(X) = \Sigma P(x_i)x_i = (1/6)(1) + (1/6)(2) + (1/6)(3) + (1/6)(4) + (1/6)(5) + (1/6)(6)$$
$$E(X) = 3.5$$

We can never roll a 3.5 on a die, but over the long term, 3.5 should be the average value of all outcomes.

The expected value is, statistically speaking, our "best guess" of the outcome of a random variable. While a 3.5 will never appear when a die is rolled, the average amount by which our guess differs from the actual outcomes is minimized when we use the expected value calculated this way.

Professor's Note: When we had historical data in an earlier topic review, we calculated the mean or simple arithmetic average and used deviations from the mean to calculate the variance and standard deviation. The calculations given here for the expected value (or weighted mean) are based on probability models, whereas our earlier calculations were based on samples or populations of outcomes. Note that when the probabilities are equal, the simple mean is the expected value. For the roll of a die, all six outcomes are equally likely, so

$$\frac{1+2+3+4+5+6}{6} = 3.5 \text{ gives us the same expected value as the probability}$$

model. However, with a probability model, the probabilities of the possible outcomes need not be equal, and the simple mean is not necessarily the expected outcome, as the following example illustrates.

Example: Expected earnings per share

The probability distribution of EPS for Ron's Stores is given in the figure below. Calculate the expected earnings per share.

EPS Probability Distribution

Probability	Earnings Per Share
10%	£1.80
20%	£1.60
40%	£1.20
30%	£1.00
100%	

Answer:

The expected EPS is simply a weighted average of each possible EPS, where the weights are the probabilities of each possible outcome.

$$E[EPS] = 0.10(1.80) + 0.20(1.60) + 0.40(1.20) + 0.30(1.00) = £1.28$$

Once we have expected EPS we can use that to calculate the variance of EPS from the probability model in the previous example. The variance is calculated as the probability-weighted sum of the squared differences between each possible outcome and expected EPS.

Example: Calculating variance from a probability model

Calculate the variance and standard deviation of EPS for Ron's Stores using the probability distribution of EPS from the table in the previous example.

Answer:

Variance of EPS for Ron's Stores is:

$$\sigma^2_{EPS} = 0.10 \, (1.80 - 1.28)^2 + 0.20 \, (1.60 - 1.28)^2 + 0.40 \, (1.20 - 1.28)^2$$
$$+ \, 0.30 \, (1.00 - 1.28)^2 = 0.0736$$

The standard deviation of EPS for Ron's Stores is:

$$\sigma_{EPS} = (0.0736)^{1/2} = 0.27$$

Note that the units of standard deviation are the same as that of EPS, so we would say that the standard deviation of EPS for Ron's Stores is £0.27.

LOS 8.i: Explain the use of conditional expectation in investment applications.

Expected values or returns can be calculated using conditional probabilities. As the name implies, *conditional expected values* are contingent upon the outcome of some other event. An analyst would use a conditional expected value to revise his expectations when new information arrives.

Consider the effect of a tariff on steel imports on the returns of a domestic steel stock. The stock's expected return, given that the government imposes the tariff, will be higher than the expected return if the tariff is not imposed.

Using the total probability rule, we can estimate the (unconditional) expected return on the stock as the sum of the expected return given no tariff times the probability a tariff will not be enacted plus the expected return given a tariff times the probability a tariff will be enacted.

LOS 8.j: Diagram an investment problem using a tree diagram.

You might well wonder where the returns and probabilities used in calculating expected values come from. A general framework called a **tree diagram** is used to show the probabilities of various outcomes. In Figure 3, we have shown estimates of EPS for four different outcomes: (1) a good economy and relatively good results at the company, (2) a good economy and relatively poor results at the company, (3) a poor economy and relatively good results at the company, and (4) a poor economy and relatively poor results at the company. Using the rules of probability, we can calculate the probabilities of each of the four EPS outcomes shown in the boxes on the right-hand side of the "tree."

Figure 3: A Tree Diagram

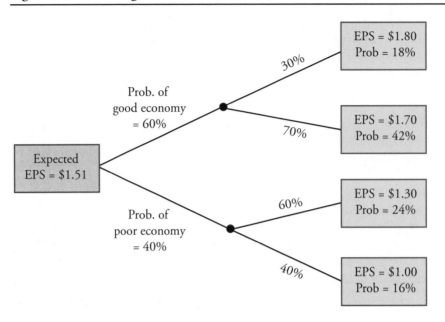

The expected EPS of $1.51 is simply calculated as:

$$0.18 \times 1.80 + 0.42 \times 1.70 + 0.24 \times 1.30 + 0.16 \times 1.00 = \$1.51$$

Note that the probabilities of the four possible outcomes sum to 1.

LOS 8.k: Calculate and interpret covariance and correlation.

The variance and standard deviation measure the dispersion, or volatility, of only one variable. In many finance situations, however, we are interested in how two random variables move in relation to each other. For investment applications, one of the most frequently analyzed pairs of random variables is the returns of two assets. Investors and managers frequently ask questions such as, "what is the relationship between the return for Stock A and Stock B?" or, "what is the relationship between the performance of the S&P 500 and that of the automotive industry?"

Covariance is a measure of how two assets move together. It is the expected value of the product of the deviations of the two random variables from their respective expected values. A common symbol for the covariance between random variables X and Y is $Cov(X,Y)$. Since we will be mostly concerned with the covariance of asset returns, the following formula has been written in terms of the covariance of the return of asset i, R_i, and the return of asset j, R_j:

$$Cov(R_i, R_j) = E\{[R_i - E(R_i)][R_j - E(R_j)]\}$$

The following are *properties of the covariance:*

- The covariance is a general representation of the same concept as the variance. That is, the variance measures how a random variable moves with itself, and the covariance measures how one random variable moves with another random variable.
- The covariance of R_A with itself is equal to the variance of R_A; that is, $Cov(R_A, R_A) = Var(R_A)$.
- The covariance may range from negative infinity to positive infinity.

To aid in the interpretation of covariance, consider the returns of a stock and of a put option on the stock. These two returns will have a negative covariance because they move in opposite directions. The returns of two automotive stocks would likely have a positive covariance, and the returns of a stock and a riskless asset would have a zero covariance because the riskless asset's returns never move, regardless of movements in the stock's return. While the formula for covariance given above is correct, the method of computing the covariance of returns from a joint probability model uses a probability-weighted average of the products of the random variable's deviations from their means for each possible outcome. The following example illustrates this calculation.

Example: Covariance

Assume that the economy can be in three possible states (*S*) next year: boom, normal, or slow economic growth. An expert source has calculated that P(boom) = 0.30, P(normal) = 0.50, and P(slow) = 0.20. The returns for Stock A, R_A, and Stock B, R_B, under each of the economic states are provided in the probability model below. What is the covariance of the returns for Stock A and Stock B?

Probability Distribution of Returns

Event	P(S)	R_A	R_B
Boom	0.3	0.20	0.30
Normal	0.5	0.12	0.10
Slow	0.2	0.05	0.00

Answer:

First, the expected returns for each of the stocks must be determined.

$$E(R_A) = (0.3)(0.20) + (0.5)(0.12) + (0.2)(0.05) = 0.13$$

$$E(R_B) = (0.3)(0.30) + (0.5)(0.10) + (0.2)(0.00) = 0.14$$

The covariance can now be computed using the procedure described in the following table.

Covariance Computation

Event	P(S)	R_A	R_B	$P(S) \times [R_A - E(R_A)] \times [R_B - E(R_B)]$
Boom	0.3	0.20	0.30	$(0.3)(0.2 - 0.13)(0.3 - 0.14) = 0.00336$
Normal	0.5	0.12	0.10	$(0.5)(0.12 - 0.13)(0.1 - 0.14) = 0.00020$
Slow	0.2	0.05	0.00	$(0.2)(0.05 - 0.13)(0 - 0.14) = 0.00224$

$$Cov(R_A, R_B) = \sum P(S) \times [R_A - E(R_A)] \times [R_B - E(R_B)] = 0.00580$$

The preceding example illustrates the use of a joint probability function. A *joint probability function* for two random variables gives the probability of the joint occurrence of specified outcomes. In this case, we only had three joint probabilities:

$$P(R_A = 0.2 \text{ and } R_B = 0.3) = 0.30$$

$$P(R_A = 0.12 \text{ and } R_B = 0.1) = 0.50$$

$$P(R_A = 0.05 \text{ and } R_B = 0.0) = 0.20$$

Joint probabilities are often presented in a table such as the one shown in the following figure. According to the following figure, $P(R_A = 0.12 \text{ and } R_B = 0.10) = 0.50$. This is the probability represented in the cell at the intersection of the column labeled $R_B = 0.10$ and the row labeled $R_A = 0.12$. Similarly, $P(R_A = 0.20 \text{ and } R_B = 0.10) = 0$.

Joint Probability Table

Joint Probabilities	$R_B = 0.30$	$R_B = 0.10$	$R_B = 0.00$
$R_A = 0.20$	0.30	0	0
$R_A = 0.12$	0	0.50	0
$R_A = 0.05$	0	0	0.20

In more complex applications, there would likely be positive values where the zeros appear in the previous table. In any case, the sum of all the probabilities in the cells on the table must equal 1.

In practice, the covariance is difficult to interpret. This is mostly because it can take on extremely large values, ranging from negative to positive infinity, and, like the variance, these values are expressed in terms of square units.

To make the covariance of two random variables easier to interpret, it may be divided by the product of the random variable's standard deviations. The resulting value is called the **correlation coefficient**, or simply, correlation. The relationship between covariances, standard deviations, and correlations can be seen in the following expression for the correlation of the returns for asset i and j:

$$\text{Corr}\left(R_i, R_j\right) = \frac{\text{Cov}\left(R_i, R_j\right)}{\sigma\left(R_i\right)\sigma\left(R_j\right)}, \text{ which implies Cov}\left(R_i, R_j\right) = \text{Corr}\left(R_i, R_j\right)\sigma\left(R_i\right)\sigma\left(R_j\right)$$

The correlation between two random return variables may also be expressed as $\rho(R_i, R_j)$, or $\rho_{i,j}$.

Properties of correlation of two random variables R_i and R_j are summarized here:

- Correlation measures the strength of the linear relationship between two random variables.
- Correlation has no units.
- The correlation ranges from -1 to $+1$. That is, $-1 \leq \text{Corr}(R_i, R_j) \leq +1$.
- If $\text{Corr}(R_i, R_j) = 1.0$, the random variables have perfect positive correlation. This means that a movement in one random variable results in a proportional positive movement in the other relative to its mean.
- If $\text{Corr}(R_i, R_j) = -1.0$, the random variables have perfect negative correlation. This means that a movement in one random variable results in an exact opposite proportional movement in the other relative to its mean.
- If $\text{Corr}(R_i, R_j) = 0$, there is no linear relationship between the variables, indicating that prediction of R_i cannot be made on the basis of R_j using linear methods.

Example: Correlation

Using our previous example, compute and interpret the correlation of the returns for stocks A and B, given that $\sigma^2(R_A) = 0.0028$ and $\sigma^2(R_B) = 0.0124$ and recalling that $\text{Cov}(R_A, R_B) = 0.0058$.

Answer:

First, it is necessary to convert the variances to standard deviations.

$\sigma(R_A) = (0.0028)^{\frac{1}{2}} = 0.0529$

$\sigma(R_B) = (0.0124)^{\frac{1}{2}} = 0.1114$

Now, the correlation between the returns of Stock A and Stock B can be computed as follows:

$$\text{Corr}(R_A, R_B) = \frac{0.0058}{(0.0529)(0.1114)} = 0.9842$$

The fact that this value is close to $+1$ indicates that the linear relationship is not only positive but very strong.

Study Session 2

LOS 8.l: Calculate and interpret the expected value, variance, and standard deviation of a random variable and of returns on a portfolio.

The **expected value and variance for a portfolio of assets** can be determined using the properties of the individual assets in the portfolio. To do this, it is necessary to establish the portfolio weight for each asset. As indicated in the formula, the weight, *w*, of portfolio asset *i* is simply the market value currently invested in the asset divided by the current market value of the entire portfolio.

$$w_i = \frac{\text{market value of investment in asset i}}{\text{market value of the portfolio}}$$

Portfolio expected value. The expected value of a portfolio composed of *n* assets with weights, w_i, and expected values, R_i, can be determined using the following formula:

$$E\left(R_p\right) = \sum_{i=1}^{N} w_i E\left(R_i\right) = w_1 E(R_1) + w_2 E(R_2) + \ldots + w_n E(R_n)$$

More often, we have expected returns (rather than expected prices). When the R_i are returns, the expected return for a portfolio, $E(R_p)$, is calculated using the asset weights and the same formula as above.

Portfolio variance. The variance of the portfolio return uses the portfolio weights also, but in a more complicated way:

$$Var\left(R_p\right) = \sum_{i=1}^{N}\sum_{j=1}^{N} w_i w_j Cov\left(R_i, R_j\right)$$

The way this formula works, particularly in its use of the double summation operator, $\sum\sum$, is best explained using 2-asset and 3-asset portfolio examples.

Example: Variance of a 2-asset portfolio

Symbolically express the variance of a portfolio composed of risky asset A and risky asset B.

Answer:

Application of the variance formula provides the following:

$$Var(R_p) = w_A w_A Cov(R_A, R_A) + w_A w_B Cov(R_A, R_B) + w_B w_A Cov(R_B, R_A) + w_B w_B Cov(R_B, R_B)$$

Now, since $Cov(R_A, R_B) = Cov(R_B, R_A)$, and $Cov(R_A, R_A) = \sigma^2(R_A)$, this expression reduces to the following:

$$Var(R_p) = w_A^2 \sigma^2(R_A) + w_B^2 \sigma^2(R_B) + 2w_A w_B Cov(R_A, R_B)$$

Since $Cov(R_A, R_B) = \sigma(R_B)\sigma(R_A)\rho(R_A, R_B)$, another way to present this formula is:

$$Var(R_p) = w_A^2 \sigma^2(R_A) + w_B^2 \sigma^2(R_B) + 2w_A w_B \sigma(R_A)\sigma(R_B)\rho(R_A, R_B)$$

Example: Variance of a 3-asset portfolio

A portfolio composed of risky assets A, B, and C will have a variance of return determined as:

$$
\begin{aligned}
\text{Var}(R_p) \quad = \quad & w_A w_A \text{Cov}(R_A, R_A) + w_A w_B \text{Cov}(R_A, R_B) + w_A w_C \text{Cov}(R_A, R_C) \\
& + w_B w_A \text{Cov}(R_B, R_A) + w_B w_B \text{Cov}(R_B, R_B) + w_B w_C \text{Cov}(R_B, R_C) \\
& + w_C w_A \text{Cov}(R_C, R_A) + w_C w_B \text{Cov}(R_C, R_B) + w_C w_C \text{Cov}(R_C, R_C)
\end{aligned}
$$

which can be reduced to the following expression:

$$
\begin{aligned}
\text{Var}(R_p) \quad = \quad & w_A^2 \sigma^2(R_A) + w_B^2 \sigma^2(R_B) + w_C^2 \sigma^2(R_C) \\
& + 2w_A w_B \text{Cov}(R_A, R_B) + 2w_A w_C \text{Cov}(R_A, R_C) + 2w_B w_C \text{Cov}(R_B, R_C)
\end{aligned}
$$

A portfolio composed of four assets will have four $w_i^2 \sigma^2(R_i)$ terms and six $2w_i w_j \text{Cov}(R_i, R_j)$ terms. A portfolio with five assets will have five $w_i^2 \sigma^2(R_i)$ terms and ten $2w_i w_j \text{Cov}(R_i, R_j)$ terms. In fact, the expression for the variance of an *n*-asset portfolio will have $n(n-1)/2$ unique $\text{Cov}(R_i, R_j)$ terms since $\text{Cov}(R_i, R_j) = \text{Cov}(R_j, R_i)$.

Professor's Note: I would expect that if there is a problem on the exam that requires the calculation of the variance (standard deviation) of a portfolio of risky assets, it would involve only two risky assets.

The following formula is useful when we want to compute covariances, given correlations and variances:

$$
\text{Cov}(R_i, R_j) = \sigma(R_i)\sigma(R_j)\rho(R_i, R_j)
$$

LOS 8.m: Calculate and interpret covariance given a joint probability function.

Example: Expected value, variance, and covariance

What is the expected value, variance, and covariance(s) for a portfolio that consists of $400 in Asset A and $600 in Asset B? The joint probabilities of the returns of the two assets are in the following figure.

Probability Table

Joint Probabilities	$R_B = 0.40$	$R_B = 0.20$	$R_B = 0.00$
$R_A = 0.20$	0.15	0	0
$R_A = 0.15$	0	0.60	0
$R_A = 0.04$	0	0	0.25

Answer:

The asset weights are:

$$w_A = \$400 \,/\, (\$400 + \$600) = 0.40$$

$$w_B = \$600 \,/\, (\$400 + \$600) = 0.60$$

The expected returns for the individual assets are determined as:

$$E(R_A) = P(R_{A1},R_{B1})R_{A1} + P(R_{A2},R_{B2})R_{A2} + P(R_{A3},R_{B3})R_{A3}$$

$$E(R_A) = (0.15)(0.20) + (0.60)(0.15) + (0.25)(0.04) = 0.13$$

$$E(R_B) = P(R_{B1},R_{A1})R_{B1} + P(R_{B2},R_{A2})R_{B2} + P(R_{B3},R_{A3})R_{B3}$$

$$E(R_B) = (0.15)(0.40) + (0.60)(0.20) + (0.25)(0.00) = 0.18$$

The variances for the individual asset returns are determined as:

$$Var(R_A) = P(R_{A1},R_{B1})[(R_{A1} - E(R_A)]^2 + P(R_{A2},R_{B2})[(R_{A2} - E(R_A)]^2 + P(R_{A3},R_{B3})[(R_{A3} - E(R_A)]^2$$

$$Var(R_A) = (0.15)(0.20 - 0.13)^2 + (0.6)(0.15 - 0.13)^2 + (0.25)(0.04 - 0.13)^2 = 0.0030$$

$$Var(R_B) = P(R_{B1},R_{A1})[(R_{B1} - E(R_B)]^2 + P(R_{A2},R_{B2})[(R_{B2} - E(R_B)]^2 + P(R_{B3},R_{A3})[(R_{B3} - E(R_B)]^2$$

$$Var(R_B) = (0.15)(0.40 - 0.18)^2 + (0.6)(0.20 - 0.18)^2 + (0.25)(0.00 - 0.18)^2 = 0.0156$$

The covariance of the individual asset returns is determined as:

$$
\begin{aligned}
Cov(R_A, R_B) ={}& P(R_{A1},R_{B1})[R_{A1} - E(R_A)][(R_{B1} - E(R_B)] \\
&+ P(R_{A2},R_{B2})[R_{A2} - E(R_A)][(R_{B2} - E(R_B)] \\
&+ P(R_{A3},R_{B3})[R_{A3} - E(R_A)][(R_{B3} - E(R_B)]
\end{aligned}
$$

$$
\begin{aligned}
Cov(R_A, R_B) ={}& 0.15(0.20 - 0.13)(0.40 - 0.18) \\
&+ 0.60(0.15 - 0.13)(0.20 - 0.18) \\
&+ 0.25(0.04 - 0.13)(0.00 - 0.18) \\
&= 0.0066
\end{aligned}
$$

Using the weights $w_A = 0.40$ and $w_B = 0.60$, the expected return and variance of the portfolio are computed as:

$$E(R_p) = w_A E(R_A) + w_B E(R_B) = (0.4)(0.13) + (0.6)(0.18) = 0.16$$

$$\begin{aligned} \text{Var}(R_p) &= (0.40)^2(0.003) + (0.60)^2(0.0156) + 2(0.4)(0.60)(0.0066) \\ &= 0.009264 \end{aligned}$$

Please note that as tedious as this example was, if more of the cells in the joint probability matrix were not zero, it could have been even more tedious.

Example: Correlation and covariance

Consider a portfolio of three assets, X, Y, and Z, where the individual market value of these assets is $600, $900, and $1,500, respectively. The market weight, expected return, and variance for the individual assets are presented below. The correlation matrix for the asset returns are shown in the following figure. Using this information, compute the variance of the portfolio return.

$E(R_X) = 0.10$	$\text{Var}(R_X) = 0.0016$	$w_X = 0.2$
$E(R_Y) = 0.12$	$\text{Var}(R_Y) = 0.0036$	$w_Y = 0.3$
$E(R_Z) = 0.16$	$\text{Var}(R_Z) = 0.0100$	$w_Z = 0.5$

Stock X, Y, and Z Returns Correlation

	Correlation Matrix		
Returns	R_X	R_Y	R_Z
R_X	1.00	0.46	0.22
R_Y	0.46	1.00	0.64
R_Z	0.22	0.64	1.00

Answer:

The expected return for the portfolio may be determined as:

$$E(R_p) = \sum w_i E(R_i) = w_1 E(R_1) + w_2 E(R_2) + w_3 E(R_3)$$

$$E(R_p) = (0.20)(0.10) + (0.30)(0.12) + (0.50)(0.16)$$

$$E(R_p) = 0.136$$

The variance of a 3-asset portfolio return is determined using the formula:

$$Var(R_p) \quad = \quad w_X{}^2\sigma^2(R_X) + w_Y{}^2\sigma^2(R_Y) + w_Z{}^2\sigma^2(R_Z) + 2w_Xw_YCov(R_X,R_Y) + \\ 2w_Xw_ZCov(R_X,R_Z) + 2w_Yw_ZCov(R_Y,R_Z)$$

Here we must make use of the relationship $Cov(R_i,R_j) = \sigma(R_i)\sigma(R_j)\rho(R_i,R_j)$, since we are not provided with the covariances.

Let's solve for the covariances, then substitute the resulting values into the portfolio return variance equation.

$$Cov(R_X,R_Y) = (0.0016)^{\frac{1}{2}}(0.0036)^{\frac{1}{2}}(0.46) = 0.001104$$
$$Cov(R_X,R_Z) = (0.0016)^{\frac{1}{2}}(0.0100)^{\frac{1}{2}}(0.22) = 0.000880$$
$$Cov(R_Y,R_Z) = (0.0036)^{\frac{1}{2}}(0.0100)^{\frac{1}{2}}(0.64) = 0.003840$$

Now we can solve for the variance of the portfolio returns as:

$$Var(R_p) \quad = (0.20)^2(0.0016) + (0.30)^2(0.0036) + (0.50)^2(0.01) + \\ (2)(0.2)(0.3)(0.001104) + (2)(0.2)(0.5)(0.00088) + \\ (2)(0.3)(0.5)(0.00384)$$

$$Var(R_p) \quad = 0.004348$$

The standard deviation of portfolio returns $= (0.004348)^{1/2} = 0.0659 = 6.59\%$

Example: Covariance matrix

Assume you have a portfolio that consists of Stock S and a put option O on Stock S. The corresponding weights of these portfolio assets are $w_S = 0.90$ and $w_O = 0.10$. Using the covariance matrix provided in the following figure, calculate the variance of the return for the portfolio.

Returns Covariance for Stock S and Put O

Returns	Covariance Matrix R_S	R_O
R_S	0.0011	−0.0036
R_O	−0.0036	0.016

Answer:

This is the simplest type of example because the most tedious calculations have already been performed. Simply extract the appropriate values from the covariance matrix and insert them into the variance formula.

Recall that the covariance of an asset with itself is its variance. Thus, the terms along the diagonal in the covariance matrix are return variances.

The portfolio return variance can be computed as:

$$Var(R_p) = (0.90)^2(0.0011) + (0.10)^2(0.016) + 2(0.90)(0.10)(-0.0036)$$
$$= 0.000403$$

LOS 8.n: Calculate and interpret an updated probability using Bayes' formula.

Bayes' formula is used to update a given set of prior probabilities for a given event in response to the arrival of new information. The rule for updating prior probability of an event is:

updated probability =

$$\frac{\text{probability of new information for a given event}}{\text{unconditional probability of new information}} \times \text{prior probability of event}$$

Note in the following example of the application of Bayes' formula that we can essentially reverse a given set of conditional probabilities. This means that given $P(B)$, $P(A \mid B)$, and $P(A \mid B^C)$, it is possible to use Bayes' formula to compute $P(B \mid A)$.

Example: Bayes' formula (1)

Electcomp Corporation manufactures electronic components for computers and other devices. There is speculation that Electcomp is about to announce a major expansion into overseas markets. The expansion will occur, however, only if Electcomp's managers estimate overseas demand to be sufficient to support the necessary sales. Furthermore, if demand is sufficient and overseas expansion occurs, Electcomp is likely to raise its prices.

Using O to represent the event of overseas expansion, I to represent a price increase, and I^C to represent no price increase, an industry analyst has estimated the unconditional and conditional probabilities shown as follows:

$P(I)$	= 0.3
$P(I^C)$	= 0.7
$P(O \mid I)$	= 0.6
$P(O \mid I^C)$	= 0.4

The analyst's estimates for P(I) and $P(I^C)$ are called the *priors* because they reflect what is already known. They do not reflect the current information about the possible overseas expansion.

Application of Bayes' formula allows us to compute P(I | O), the probability that prices will increase given that Electcomp announces that it will expand overseas (the new information). Using the multiplication rule, we can express the joint probability of *I* and *O*:

$$P(O \mid I) = P(IO) / P(I), \text{ and } P(IO) = P(I \mid O) \times P(O)$$

Based on these relationships, Bayes' formula can be expressed using the information from this example, as indicated below [i.e., substitute the second equation into the first [for P(IO)] and solve for P(I | O)]:

$$P(I \mid O) = \frac{P(O \mid I)}{P(O)} \times P(I)$$

In order to solve this equation, P(O) must be determined. This can be done using the total probability rule:

$$P(O) = P(O \mid I) \times P(I) + P(O \mid I^C) \times P(I^C)$$
$$P(O) = (0.6 \times 0.3) + (0.4 \times 0.7)$$
$$P(O) = 0.46$$

Now the updated probability of the increase in prices, given that Electcomp expands overseas, can be computed:

$$P(I \mid O) = \frac{0.60}{0.46} \times 0.30 = 0.3913$$

This means that if the new information of "expand overseas" is announced, the prior probability estimate of P(I) = 0.30 must be increased to 0.3913.

Example: Bayes' formula (2)

Another illustration of the use of Bayes' formula may make it easier to remember and apply. Consider the following possibilities. There is a 60% probability the economy will outperform, and if it does, there is a 70% chance a stock will go up and a 30% chance the stock will go down. There is a 40% chance the economy will underperform, and if it does, there is a 20% chance the stock in question will increase in value (have gains) and an 80% chance it will not. Let's diagram this situation.

A Probability Model

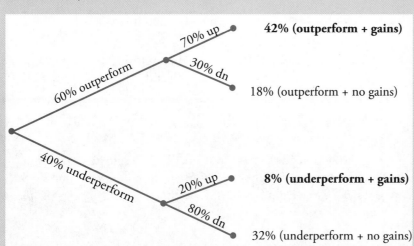

In the figure above, we have multiplied the probabilities to calculate the probabilities of each of the four outcome pairs. Note that these sum to 1. Given that the stock has gains, what is our updated probability of an outperforming economy? We sum the probability of stock gains in both states (outperform and underperform) to get 42% + 8% = 50%. Given that the stock has gains, the probability that the economy has outperformed is $\frac{42\%}{50\%} = 84\%$. In the previous notation the priors are as follows:

probability of economic outperformance = P(O) = 60%, the probability of stock gains given economic outperformance is P(G | O) = 70%, and the (unconditional) probability of a gain in stock price is 50%.

We are seeking P(O | G), the probability of outperformance given gains. Bayes' formula says:

$$P(O|G) = \frac{P(G|O) \times P(O)}{P(G)}, \text{ which is our } \frac{42\%}{50\%} = 84\%$$

LOS 8.o: Identify the most appropriate method to solve a particular counting problem and solve counting problems using the factorial, combination, and permutation notations.

Labeling refers to the situation where there are n items that can each receive one of k different labels. The number of items that receives label 1 is n_1 and the number that receive label 2 is n_2, and so on, such that $n_1 + n_2 + n_3 + \ldots + n_k = n$. The total number of ways that the labels can be assigned is:

$$\frac{n!}{(n_1!) \times (n_2!) \times \ldots \times (n_k!)}$$

where:
the symbol "!" stands for **factorial**. For example, $4! = 4 \times 3 \times 2 \times 1 = 24$, and $2! = 2 \times 1 = 2$.

The general expression for *n* factorial is:

$$n! = n \times (n-1) \times (n-2) \times (n-3) \times \ldots \times 1, \text{ where by definition, } 0! = 1$$

Calculator help: On the TI, factorial is [2nd] [x!] (above the multiplication sign). On the HP, factorial is [g] [n!]. To compute 4! on the TI, enter [4][2nd][x!] = 24. On the HP, press [4][ENTER][g][n!].

Example: Labeling

Consider a portfolio consisting of eight stocks. Your goal is to designate four of the stocks as "long-term holds," three of the stocks as "short-term holds," and one stock as "sell." How many ways can these eight stocks be labeled?

Answer:

There are 8! = 40,320 total possible sequences that can be followed to assign the three labels to the eight stocks. However, the order that each stock is assigned a label does not matter. For example, it does not matter which of the first three stocks labeled "long-term" is the first to be labeled. Thus, there are 4! ways to assign the long-term label. Continuing this reasoning to the other categories, there are 4! × 3! × 1! equivalent sequences for assigning the labels. To eliminate the counting of these redundant sequences, the total number of possible sequences (8!) must be divided by the number of redundant sequences (4! × 3! × 1!).

Thus, the number of *different* ways to label the eight stocks is:

$$\frac{8!}{4! \times 3! \times 1!} = \frac{40,320}{24 \times 6 \times 1} = 280$$

If there are *n* labels (k = n), we have $\frac{n!}{1} = n!$. The number of ways to assign *n* different labels to *n* items is simply *n!*.

A special case of labeling arises when the number of labels equals 2 (k = 2). That is, the *n* items can only be in one of two groups, and $n_1 + n_2 = n$. In this case, we can let $r = n_1$ and $n_2 = n - r$. Since there are only two categories, we usually talk about choosing *r* items. Then (n − r) are not chosen. The general formula for labeling when k = 2 is called the **combination formula** (or *binomial formula*) and is expressed as:

$$_nC_r = \frac{n!}{(n-r)!r!},$$

where $_nC_r$ is the number of possible ways (combinations) of selecting *r* items from a set of *n* items when the order of selection is not important. This is also written $\binom{n}{r}$ and read "n choose r."

Another useful formula is the **permutation formula**. A permutation is a specific ordering of a group of objects. The question of how many different groups of size r in specific order can be chosen from n objects is answered by the permutation formula. The

number of permutations of r objects from n objects $= \dfrac{n!}{(n-r)!}$. We will give an example using this formula shortly.

Professor's Note: The combination formula $_nC_r$ and the permutation formula $_nP_r$ are both available on the TI calculator. To calculate the number of different groups of three stocks from a list of eight stocks (i.e., $_8C_3$), the sequence is 8 [2nd] [$_nC_r$] 3 [=], which yields 56. If we want to know the number of differently ordered groups of three that can be selected from a list of eight, we enter 8 [2nd] [$_nP_r$] 3 [=] to get 336, which is the number of permutations, $\dfrac{8!}{(8-3)!}$. This function is not available on the HP calculator. Remember, current policy permits you to bring both calculators to the exam if you choose.

Example: Number of choices in any order

How many ways can three stocks be sold from an 8-stock portfolio?

Answer:

This is similar to the preceding labeling example. Since order does not matter, we take the total number of possible ways to select three of the eight stocks and divide by the number of possible redundant selections. Thus, the answer is:

$$\frac{8!}{5! \times 3!} = 56$$

In the preceding two examples, ordering did not matter. The order of selection could, however, be important. For example, suppose we want to liquidate only one stock position per week over the next three weeks. Once we choose three particular stocks to sell, the order in which they are sold must be determined. In this case, the concept of permutation comes into play. The *permutation formula* is:

$$_nP_r = \frac{n!}{(n-r)!},$$

where $_nP_r$ is the number of possible ways (permutations) to select r items from a set of n items when the order of selection is important. The permutation formula implies that there are $r!$ *more* ways to choose r items if the order of selection *is important* than if order is not important.

Example: Permutation

How many ways are there to sell three stocks out of eight if the order of the sales is important?

Answer:

$$_n P_r = {}_8 P_3 = \frac{8!}{(8-3)!} = \frac{8!}{5!} = 336$$

This is 3! times the 56 possible combinations computed in the preceding example for selecting the three stocks when the order was not important.

There are five guidelines that may be used to determine which counting method to employ when dealing with counting problems:

- The *multiplication rule of counting* is used when there are *two or more groups*. The key is that only *one* item may be selected from each group. If there are k steps required to complete a task and each step can be done in n ways, the number of different ways to complete the task is $n_1! \times n_2! \times ... \times n_k!$.
- *Factorial* is used by itself when there are *no groups*—we are only arranging a given set of n items. Given n items, there are n! ways of arranging them.
- The *labeling formula* applies to *three or more sub-groups* of predetermined size. Each element of the entire group must be assigned a place, or label, in one of the three or more sub-groups.
- The *combination formula* applies to *only two groups* of predetermined size. Look for the word "choose" or "combination."
- The *permutation formula* applies to *only two groups* of predetermined size. Look for a specific reference to "order" being important.

KEY CONCEPTS

LOS 8.a

A random variable is an uncertain value determined by chance.

An outcome is the realization of a random variable.

An event is a set of one or more outcomes. Two events that cannot both occur are termed "mutually exclusive" and a set of events that includes all possible outcomes is an "exhaustive" set of events.

LOS 8.b

The two properties of probability are:
- The sum of the probabilities of all possible mutually exclusive events is 1.
- The probability of any event cannot be greater than 1 or less than 0.

A priori probability measures predetermined probabilities based on well-defined inputs; empirical probability measures probability from observations or experiments; and subjective probability is an informed guess.

LOS 8.c

Probabilities can be stated as odds that an event will or will not occur. If the probability of an event is A out of B trials (A/B), the "odds for" are A to (B – A) and the "odds against" are (B – A) to A.

LOS 8.d

Unconditional probability (marginal probability) is the probability of an event occurring.

Conditional probability, $P(A \mid B)$, is the probability of an event A occurring given that event B has occurred.

LOS 8.e

The multiplication rule of probability is used to determine the joint probability of two events:

$$P(AB) = P(A \mid B) \times P(B)$$

The addition rule of probability is used to determine the probability that at least one of two events will occur:

$$P(A \text{ or } B) = P(A) + P(B) - P(AB)$$

The total probability rule is used to determine the unconditional probability of an event, given conditional probabilities:

$$P(A) = P(A \mid B_1)P(B_1) + P(A \mid B_2)P(B_2) + \ldots + P(A \mid B_N)P(B_N)$$

where $B_1, B_2, \ldots B_N$ is a mutually exclusive and exhaustive set of outcomes.

LOS 8.f

The joint probability of two events, P(AB), is the probability that they will both occur. P(AB) = P(A | B) × P(B). For independent events, P(A | B) = P(A), so that P(AB) = P(A) × P(B).

The probability that at least one of two events will occur is P(A or B) = P(A) + P(B) – P(AB). For mutually exclusive events, P(A or B) = P(A) + P(B), since P(AB) = 0.

The joint probability of any number of independent events is the product of their individual probabilities.

LOS 8.g

The probability of an independent event is unaffected by the occurrence of other events, but the probability of a dependent event is changed by the occurrence of another event. Events A and B are independent if and only if:

P(A | B) = P(A), or equivalently, P(B | A) = P(B)

LOS 8.h

Using the total probability rule, the unconditional probability of A is the probability weighted sum of the conditional probabilities:

$$P(A) = \sum_{i=1}^{n} \left[P_i \left(B_i \right) \right] \times P \left(A \mid B_i \right),$$

where B_i is a set of mutually exclusive and exhaustive events.

LOS 8.i

Conditional expected values depend on the outcome of some other event.

Forecasts of expected values for a stock's return, earnings, and dividends can be refined, using conditional expected values, when new information arrives that affects the expected outcome.

LOS 8.j

A tree diagram shows the probabilities of two events and the conditional probabilities of two subsequent events.

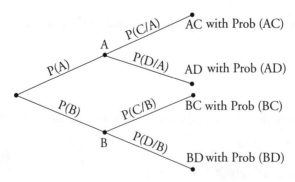

LOS 8.k

Covariance measures the extent to which two random variables tend to be above and below their respective means for each joint realization. It can be calculated as:

$$Cov(A,B) = \sum_{i=1}^{N} P_i \left(A_i - \bar{A} \right)\left(B_i - \bar{B} \right)$$

Correlation is a standardized measure of association between two random variables; it ranges in value from −1 to +1 and is equal to $\dfrac{Cov(A,B)}{\sigma_A \sigma_B}$.

LOS 8.l

The expected value of a random variable, E(X), equals $\sum_{i=1}^{n} P_i(x_i)X_i$.

The variance of a random variable, Var(X), equals $\sum_{i=1}^{n} P(x_i)[X_i - E(X)]^2 = \sigma_X^2$.

Standard deviation: $\sigma_X = \sqrt{\sigma_X^2}$.

The expected returns and variance of a 2-asset portfolio are given by:

$$
\begin{aligned}
E(R_P) &= w_1 E(R_1) + w_2 E(R_2) \\
Var(R_P) &= w_1^2 \sigma_1^2 + w_2^2 \sigma_2^2 + 2w_1 w_2 Cov_{1,2} \\
&= w_1^2 \sigma_1^2 + w_2^2 \sigma_2^2 + 2w_1 w_2 \sigma_1 \sigma_2 \rho_{1,2}
\end{aligned}
$$

LOS 8.m

Given the joint probabilities for X_i and Y_i, i.e., $P(X_i Y_i)$, the covariance is calculated as:

$$\sum_{i=1}^{n} P\left(X_i Y_i\right)\left(X_i - \bar{X}\right)\left(Y_i - \bar{Y}\right)$$

LOS 8.n

Bayes' formula for updating probabilities based on the occurrence of an event O is:

$$P(I \mid O) = \frac{P(O \mid I)}{P(O)} \times P(I)$$

Equivalently, based on the tree diagram below, $P(A \mid C) = \dfrac{P(AC)}{P(AC) + P(BC)}$.

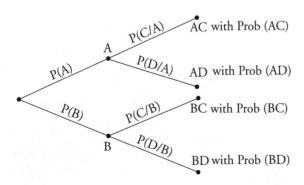

LOS 8.o

The number of ways to order n objects is n factorial, $n! = n \times (n-1) \times (n-2) \times \ldots \times 1$.

There are $\dfrac{N!}{n_1! \times n_2! \times \ldots \times n_k!}$ ways to assign k different labels to N items, where n_i is the number of items with the label i.

The number of ways to choose a subset of size r from a set of size n when order doesn't matter is $\dfrac{n!}{(n-r)!r!}$ combinations; when order matters, there are $\dfrac{n!}{(n-r)!}$ permutations.

CONCEPT CHECKERS

1. Given the conditional probabilities in the table below and the unconditional probabilities $P(Y = 1) = 0.3$ and $P(Y = 2) = 0.7$, what is the expected value of X?

x_i	$P(x_i \mid Y = 1)$	$P(x_i \mid Y = 2)$
0	0.2	0.1
5	0.4	0.8
10	0.4	0.1

A. 5.0.
B. 5.3.
C. 5.7.

Use the following data to answer Questions 2 through 6.

	Joint Probabilities		
Returns	$R_B = 0.5$	$R_B = 0.2$	$R_B = -0.3$
$R_A = -0.1$	0.4	0	0
$R_A = 0.1$	0	0.3	0
$R_A = 0.3$	0	0	0.3

2. Given the joint probability table, the expected return of Stock A is *closest* to:
A. 0.08.
B. 0.12.
C. 0.15.

3. Given the joint probability table, the standard deviation of Stock B is *closest* to:
A. 0.11.
B. 0.22.
C. 0.33.

4. Given the joint probability table, the variance of Stock A is *closest* to:
A. 0.03.
B. 0.12.
C. 0.17.

5. Given the joint probability table, the covariance between A and B is *closest* to:
A. −0.160.
B. −0.055.
C. 0.004.

6. Given the joint probability table, the correlation between R_A and R_B is *closest* to:
A. −0.99.
B. 0.02.
C. 0.86.

7. The probability that the DJIA will increase tomorrow is 2/3. The probability of an increase in the DJIA stated as odds is:
    A. two-to-one.
    B. one-to-three.
    C. two-to-three.

8. A discrete uniform distribution (each event has an equal probability of occurrence) has the following possible outcomes for X: [1, 2, 3, 4]. The variance of this distribution is *closest* to:
    A. 1.00.
    B. 1.25.
    C. 2.00.

9. If events A and B are mutually exclusive, then:
    A. $P(A \mid B) = P(A)$.
    B. $P(AB) = P(A) \times P(B)$.
    C. $P(A \text{ or } B) = P(A) + P(B)$.

10. At a charity ball, 800 names are put into a hat. Four of the names are identical. On a random draw, what is the probability that one of these four names will be drawn?
    A. 0.004.
    B. 0.005.
    C. 0.010.

11. Among 900 taxpayers with incomes below $100,000, 35 were audited by the IRS. The probability that a randomly chosen individual with an income below $100,000 was audited is *closest* to:
    A. 0.039.
    B. 0.125.
    C. 0.350.

12. Which of the following values *cannot* be the probability of an event?
    A. 0.00.
    B. 1.00.
    C. 1.25.

13. Two mutually exclusive events:
    A. always occur together.
    B. cannot occur together.
    C. can sometimes occur together.

14. Two events are said to be independent if the occurrence of one event:
    A. means that the second event cannot occur.
    B. means that the second event is certain to occur.
    C. does not affect the probability of the occurrence of the other event.

Use the following conditional probabilities to answer Questions 15 through 18.

State of the Economy	Probability of the Economic State	Stock Performance	Conditional Probability of Stock Performance
Good	0.30	Good	0.60
		Neutral	0.30
		Poor	0.10
Neutral	0.50	Good	0.30
		Neutral	0.40
		Poor	0.30
Poor	0.20	Good	0.10
		Neutral	0.60
		Poor	0.30

15. What is the conditional probability of having good stock performance in a poor economic environment?
    A. 0.02.
    B. 0.10.
    C. 0.30.

16. What is the joint probability of having a good economy and a neutral stock performance?
    A. 0.09.
    B. 0.20.
    C. 0.30.

17. What is the total probability of having a good performance in the stock?
    A. 0.35.
    B. 0.65.
    C. 1.00.

18. Given that the stock had good performance, the probability the state of the economy was good is *closest* to:
    A. 0.35.
    B. 0.46.
    C. 0.51.

19. Consider a universe of ten bonds from which an investor will ultimately purchase six bonds for his portfolio. If the order in which he buys these bonds is not important, how many potential 6-bond combinations are there?
    A. 7.
    B. 210.
    C. 5,040.

20. The correlation of returns between Stocks A and B is 0.50. The covariance between these two securities is 0.0043, and the standard deviation of the return of Stock B is 26%. The variance of returns for Stock A is:
A. 0.0011.
B. 0.0331.
C. 0.2656.

21. There are ten sprinters in the finals of a race. How many different ways can the gold, silver, and bronze medals be awarded?
A. 120.
B. 720.
C. 1,440.

22. Which of the following is *least likely* a probability distribution?

A. $X = [1,2,3,4]$; Prob $[X_i] = \dfrac{X_i^2}{30}$.

B. $X = [5,10]$; Prob $[X_i] = \dfrac{8 - X_i}{5}$.

C. $X = [5,10]$; Prob $[X_i] = \dfrac{X_i - 3}{9}$.

COMPREHENSIVE PROBLEMS

1. Given the following probability data for the return on the market and the return on Best Oil, calculate the covariance of returns between Best Oil and the market.

Joint Probability Table

	$R_{Best} = 20\%$	$R_{Best} = 10\%$	$R_{Best} = 5\%$
$R_{Mkt} = 15\%$	0.4	0	0
$R_{Mkt} = 10\%$	0	0.2	0
$R_{Mkt} = 0\%$	0	0	0.4

2. The correlation of returns between the returns on Cape Products and Dogger Industries is 0.6. The standard deviation of returns for Cape is 15% and the standard deviation of returns for Dogger is 20%. The expected return for Dogger is 18% and the expected return for Cape is 12%. Calculate the expected returns and standard deviation of returns on a portfolio that has $300,000 invested in Dogger and $200,000 invested in Cape.

3.   M. Atwood, an analyst, has developed a scoring system for bonds and found that if the score from a bond is less than 20, there is an 85% probability that it will default within five years. If a bond's score is greater than or equal to 20, there is only a 40% chance that it will default within five years. Given that a randomly chosen bond currently has a 25% probability of a score less than 20, what is the probability that a bond that defaults within the next five years had a score of 20 or higher?

4.   A bond that matures in one year is priced at $950 today. You estimate that it has a 10% probability of default. If the bond defaults, you expect to recover $600. If it does not default, it will pay $1,080 at maturity. The nominal 1-year risk-free rate is 7.5%.

   A. What are the odds against this bond defaulting?

   B. What is the expected payoff on the bond in one year?

   C. What is the expected return on the bond?

   D. What would be the price of the bond if its expected return were equal to the risk-free rate?

5. You are considering a portfolio of three stocks:
    *   Stock A (55% of the portfolio) has an expected return of 8%, with a standard deviation of 24%.
    *   Stock B (25% of the portfolio) has an expected return of 4%, with a standard deviation of 18%.
    *   Stock C (20% of the portfolio) has an expected return of 3%, with a standard deviation of 15%.

    The correlations between these stocks' returns are:
    *   Stock A with Stock B: 0.85.
    *   Stock A with Stock C: 0.30.
    *   Stock B with Stock C: –0.15.

    A. Based on these data, construct a covariance matrix for the returns on the three stocks.

    B. Calculate the expected return and standard deviation of the portfolio.

    C. Provide a set of three mutually exclusive and exhaustive events with respect to the relation between this portfolio's realized return and its expected return.

    D. If you add three more stocks to the portfolio, how many variances and how many unique covariances will you need to calculate the portfolio variance?

6. You are forecasting the sales of a building materials supplier by assessing the expansion plans of its largest customer, a homebuilder. You estimate the probability that the customer will increase its orders for building materials to 25%. If the customer does increase its orders, you estimate the probability that the homebuilder will start a new development at 70%. If the customer does not increase its orders from this supplier, you estimate only a 20% chance that it will start the new development. Later, you find out that the homebuilder will start the new development. In light of this new information, what is your new (updated) probability that the builder will increase its orders from this supplier?

ANSWERS – CONCEPT CHECKERS

1. **B** $E(X \mid Y = 1) = (0.2)(0) + (0.4)(5) + (0.4)(10) = 6$ and $E(X \mid Y = 2) = (0.1)(0) + (0.8)(5) + (0.1)(10) = 5$

    $E(X) = (0.3)(6) + (0.7)(5) = 5.30$

2. **A** Expected return of Stock A = $(0.4)(-0.1) + (0.3)(0.1) + (0.3)(0.3) = 0.08$

3. **C** Expected return of Stock B = $(0.4)(0.5) + (0.3)(0.2) + (0.3)(-0.3) = 0.17$

    $Var(R_B) = 0.4(0.5 - 0.17)^2 + 0.3(0.2 - 0.17)^2 + 0.3(-0.3 - 0.17)^2 = 0.1101$

    Standard deviation = $\sqrt{0.1101} = 0.3318$

4. **A** $E(R_A) = 0.08$ (from #2 above)

    $Var(R_A) = 0.4(-0.1 - 0.08)^2 + 0.3(0.1 - 0.08)^2 + 0.3(0.3 - 0.08)^2 = 0.0276$

5. **B** $Cov(R_A,R_B) = 0.4(-0.1 - 0.08)(0.5 - 0.17) + 0.3(0.1 - 0.08)(0.2 - 0.17) + 0.3(0.3 - 0.08)(-0.3 - 0.17) = -0.0546$

6. **A** $Corr(R_A,R_B) = Cov(R_A,R_B) / \sigma(R_A)\sigma(R_B)$

    $Cov(R_A,R_B) = -0.0546$ (from #5 above)

    $Var(R_A) = 0.0276$ (from #4 above); $\sigma(R_A) = \sqrt{0.0276} = 0.1661$

    $\sigma(R_B) = 0.3318$ (from #3 above)

    $Corr(R_A,R_B) = -0.0546 / (0.1661)(0.3318) = -0.9907$

7. **A** Odds for $E = P(E) \ / \ [1 - P(E)] = \dfrac{2/3}{1/3} = 2/1 =$ two-to-one

8. **B** Expected value = $(1/4)(1 + 2 + 3 + 4) = 2.5$

    Variance = $(1/4)[(1 - 2.5)^2 + (2 - 2.5)^2 + (3 - 2.5)^2 + (4 - 2.5)^2] = 1.25$

    Note that since each observation is equally likely, each has 25% (1/4) chance of occurrence.

9. **C** There is no intersection of events when events are mutually exclusive. $P(A \mid B) = P(A) \times P(B)$ is only true for independent events. Note that since A and B are mutually exclusive (cannot both happen), $P(A \mid B)$ and $P(AB)$ must both be equal to zero.

10. **B** P(name 1 or name 2 or name 3 or name 4) = 1/800 + 1/800 + 1/800 + 1/800 = 4/800 = 0.005

11. **A** 35 / 900 = 0.0389

12. **C** Probabilities may range from 0 (meaning no chance of occurrence) through 1 (which means a sure thing).

13. **B** One or the other may occur, but not both.

14. **C**   Two events are said to be independent if the occurrence of one event does not affect the probability of the occurrence of the other event.

15. **B**   Go to the poor state and read off the probability of good performance
[i.e., P(poor performance | good economy) = 0.10].

16. **A**   P(good economy and neutral performance) = P(good economy)P(neutral performance | good economy) = (0.3)(0.3) = 0.09.

17. **A**   (0.3)(0.6) + (0.5)(0.3) + (0.2)(0.1) = 0.35. This is the sum of all the joint probabilities for good performance over all states [i.e., $\sum$P(economic state$_i$) P(good performance | economic state$_i$)].

18. **C**   This is an application of Bayes' formula. P(good economy | good performance)
= P(good stock performance | good economy) × P(good economy) / P(good stock performance).

$$= \frac{(0.6)(0.3)}{(0.3)(0.6)+ (0.5)(0.3) + (0.2)(0.1)} = \frac{0.18}{0.35} = 0.5143$$

19. **B** $_nC_r = \dfrac{n!}{(n-r)!r!} = {_{10}C_6} = \dfrac{10!}{(10-6)!6!} = \dfrac{10!}{4!6!} = 210$

20. **A** $\text{Corr}(R_A,R_B) = \dfrac{\text{Cov}(R_A,R_B)}{[\sigma(R_A)][\sigma(R_B)]}$

$$\sigma^2(R_A) = \left[\frac{\text{Cov}(R_A,R_B)}{\sigma(R_B)\text{Corr}(R_A,R_B)}\right]^2 = \left[\frac{0.0043}{(0.26)(0.5)}\right]^2 = 0.0331^2 = 0.0011$$

21. **B**   Since the order of the top three finishers matters, we need to use the permutation formula.

$$_{10}P_3 = \frac{10!}{(10-3)!} = 720$$

22. **B** $\dfrac{8-5}{5} + \dfrac{8-10}{5} = \frac{1}{5}$, and $\dfrac{8-10}{5}$ is negative, so this satisfies neither of the requirements for a probability distribution. The others have P[X$_i$] between zero and one and $\sum$P[X$_i$] = 1, and thus satisfy both requirements for a probability distribution.

ANSWERS – COMPREHENSIVE PROBLEMS

1. $E(R_{Best})$ = 0.4(20%) + 0.2(10%) + 0.4(5%) = 12%

    $E(R_{Mkt})$ = 0.4(15%) + 0.2(10%) + 0.4(0%) = 8%

    $\text{Cov}(R_{Best}, R_{Mkt})$= 0.4(20% – 12%)(15% – 8%)

        +   0.2(10% – 12%)(10% – 8%)

        +   0.4(5% – 12%)(0% – 8%)

        =   0.4(8)(7) + 0.2(–2)(2) + 0.4(–7)(–8) = 44

Remember the units of covariance (like variance) are percent squared here. We used whole number percents in the calculations and got 44; if we had used decimals, we would have gotten 0.0044.

2. The portfolio weight for Dogger (W_D) is $\frac{300}{500} = 60\%$ and for Cape, the portfolio weight is $\frac{200}{500} = 40\%$. The expected return on the portfolio is $0.6(18\%) + 0.4(12\%) = 15.6\%$.

    The variance is $(0.6)^2(0.2)^2 + (0.4)^2(0.15)^2 + 2(0.6)(0.4)(0.6)(0.2)(0.15) = 0.02664$.

    The standard deviation of portfolio returns is $\sqrt{0.02664} = 16.32\%$.

3. Construct the following tree:

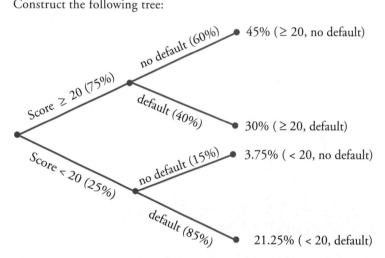

    Total probability of default = 30% + 21.25% = 51.25%. Percent of defaulting bonds with score $\geq 20 = \frac{30\%}{51.25\%} = 58.5\%$. A bond that defaults in the next five years has a 58.5% probability of having a current score greater than or equal to 20. Note that we have employed Bayes' theorem here to update the score expectation, based on the additional information that a bond has defaulted.

4. A. The odds for the bond defaulting are $\frac{0.10}{1-0.10} = \frac{1}{9}$, or 1-to-9. The odds against the bond defaulting are the reciprocal, or 9-to-1.

    B. The expected payoff on the bond at maturity is:

        P(default) × bond value if it defaults + P(no default) × bond value if it does not default = $0.1(600) + 0.9(1,080) = 60 + 972 = \$1,032$

    C. The expected return is $1,032 / 950 - 1 = 0.0863$, or 8.63%.

    D. $\frac{1,032}{\text{price}} - 1 = 0.075$ so price would need to be $\frac{1,032}{1.075} = \$960$.

5.   A.   First, calculate the variances on each of the three stocks:

$Var(A) = (0.24)^2 = 0.0576$

$Var(B) = (0.18)^2 = 0.0324$

$Var(C) = (0.15)^2 = 0.0225$

These will be the diagonal entries in the covariance matrix:

Covariance Matrix of Returns for Stocks A, B, and C

	Stock A	Stock B	Stock C
Stock A	0.0576		
Stock B		0.0324	
Stock C			0.0225

Next, calculate the covariance for each pair of stocks. The correlation $(\rho_{xy}) = Cov(x,y) / \sigma_x \sigma_y$. Rearranging that, we get $Cov(x,y) = \rho_{xy} \sigma_x \sigma_y$. So:

$Cov(A,B) = 0.85 \times 0.24 \times 0.18 = 0.0367$

$Cov(A,C) = 0.30 \times 0.24 \times 0.15 = 0.0108$

$Cov(B,C) = -0.15 \times 0.18 \times 0.15 = -0.0041$

These results complete the covariance matrix:

Covariance Matrix of Returns for Stocks A, B, and C

	Stock A	Stock B	Stock C
Stock A	0.0576	0.0367	0.0108
Stock B	0.0367	0.0324	−0.0041
Stock C	0.0108	−0.0041	0.0225

B.   The expected return on the portfolio is a weighted average of the individual stock returns:

$E[R_p] = 0.55(0.08) + 0.25(0.04) + 0.20(0.03) = 0.06$, or 6%

For a 3-asset portfolio, the portfolio variance is calculated as:

$$Var(R_p) = W_A^2 \sigma^2(R_A) + W_B^2 \sigma^2(R_B) + W_C^2 \sigma^2(R_C) + 2W_A W_B Cov(R_A, R_B) + 2W_A W_C Cov(R_A, R_C) + 2W_B W_C Cov(R_B, R_C)$$

Substituting, we get:

$$\begin{aligned}
\text{Var}(R_p) = \ & 0.55^2\,(0.0576) + 0.25^2\,(0.0324) + 0.20^2\,(0.0225) + 2(0.55)(0.25) \\
& (0.0367) + 2(0.55)(0.20)(0.0108) + 2(0.25)(0.20)(-0.0041)
\end{aligned}$$

$$= 0.0174 + 0.0020 + 0.0009 + 0.0101 + 0.0024 - 0.0004$$

$$= 0.0324$$

The portfolio standard deviation is $\sqrt{0.0324} = 0.1800$, or 18%.

C. You can answer this question any number of different ways, but here is the most obvious:

Event 1: The realized return is greater than the expected return.

Event 2: The realized return is equal to the expected return.

Event 3: The realized return is less than the expected return.

D. With six assets in the portfolio, there will be 6 variance terms and 15 unique covariance terms. The covariance matrix will have $6 \times 6 = 36$ cells. The covariance of a stock return with itself is its variance; those will be the six entries on the diagonal. The other 30 cells are the covariance pairs, but since each pair appears twice in the matrix—Cov(A,B) is the same as Cov(B,A)—the number of unique covariance pairs is half of that, or 15. For any portfolio of n assets, the portfolio variance calculation would involve n variance terms and $n(n-1)/2$ unique covariance terms.

6. The prior probability that the builder will increase its orders is 25%.

P(increase) = 0.25

P(no increase) = 0.75

There are four possible outcomes:
*   Builder increases its orders and starts new development.
*   Builder increases its orders and does not start new development.
*   Builder does not increase its orders and starts new development.
*   Builder does not increase its orders and does not start new development.

The probabilities of each outcome are as follows:
*   P(increase and development) = (0.25)(0.70) = 0.175.
*   P(increase and no development) = (0.25)(0.30) = 0.075.
*   P(no increase and development) = (0.75)(0.20) = 0.15.
*   P(no increase and no development) = (0.75)(0.80) = 0.60.

We want to update the probability of an increase in orders, given the new information that the builder is starting the development. We can apply Bayes' formula:

$$P(\text{increase} \mid \text{development}) = \frac{P\big(\text{development} \mid \text{increase}\big) \times P\big(\text{increase}\big)}{P\big(\text{development}\big)}$$

From our assumptions, P(development | increase) = 0.70, and P(increase) = 0.25, so the numerator is (0.70)(0.25) = 0.175.

P(development) is the sum of P(development and increase) and P(development and no increase).

P(development) = 0.175 + 0.15 = 0.325

Thus, P(increase | development) $= \dfrac{(0.7) \times (0.25)}{0.175 + 0.15} = \dfrac{0.175}{0.325} = 0.5385$, or 53.8

Professor's Note: I can never remember this formula, so I set these problems up like the probability model (tree) in the notes and focus on the probabilities of the new information—development in this case. Total probability of development is 17.5 + 15 = 32.5. Of that probability, 17.5 / 32.5, or 53.85% of the time, development is paired with an increase in sales!

COMMON PROBABILITY DISTRIBUTIONS

EXAM FOCUS

This topic review contains a lot of very testable material. Learn the difference between discrete and continuous probability distributions. The binomial and normal distributions are the most important here. You must learn the properties of both distributions and memorize the formulas for the mean and variance of the binomial distribution and for the probability of a particular value when given a binomial probability distribution. Learn what shortfall risk is and how to calculate and use Roy's safety-first criterion. Know how to standardize a normally distributed random variable, use a z-table, and construct confidence intervals. These skills will be used repeatedly in the topic reviews that follow. Additionally, understand the basic features of the lognormal distribution, Monte Carlo simulation, and historical simulation. Finally, it would be a good idea to know how to get continuously compounded rates of return from holding period returns. Other than that, no problem.

LOS 9.a: Explain a probability distribution and distinguish between discrete and continuous random variables.

LOS 9.b: Describe the set of possible outcomes of a specified discrete random variable.

A **probability distribution** describes the probabilities of all the possible outcomes for a random variable. The probabilities of all possible outcomes must sum to 1. A simple probability distribution is that for the roll of one fair die; there are six possible outcomes and each one has a probability of 1/6, so they sum to 1. The probability distribution of all the possible returns on the S&P 500 Index for the next year is a more complex version of the same idea.

A **discrete random variable** is one for which the number of possible outcomes can be counted, and for each possible outcome, there is a measurable and positive probability. An example of a discrete random variable is the number of days it rains in a given month, because there is a finite number of possible outcomes—the number of days it can rain in a month is defined by the number of days in the month.

A **continuous random variable** is one for which the number of possible outcomes is infinite, even if lower and upper bounds exist. The actual amount of daily rainfall between zero and 100 inches is an example of a continuous random variable because the actual amount of rainfall can take on an infinite number of values. Daily rainfall can be measured in inches, half inches, quarter inches, thousandths of inches, or in even smaller increments. Thus, the number of possible daily rainfall amounts between zero and 100 inches is essentially infinite.

The assignment of probabilities to the possible outcomes for discrete and continuous random variables provides us with discrete probability distributions and continuous probability distributions. The difference between these types of distributions is most apparent for the following properties:

- For a *discrete distribution,* p(x) = 0 when x cannot occur, or p(x) > 0 if it can. Recall that p(x) is read: "the probability that random variable X = x." For example, the probability of it raining on 33 days in June is zero because this cannot occur, but the probability of it raining 25 days in June has some positive value.
- For a *continuous distribution,* p(x) = 0 even though x can occur. We can only consider $P(x_1 \leq X \leq x_2)$ where x_1 and x_2 are actual numbers. For example, the probability of receiving two inches of rain in June is zero because two inches is a single point in an infinite range of possible values. On the other hand, the probability of the amount of rain being between 1.99999999 and 2.00000001 inches has some positive value. In the case of continuous distributions, it is interesting to note that $P(x_1 \leq X \leq x_2)$ = $P(x_1 < X < x_2)$ because $p(x_1) = p(x_2) = 0$.

In finance, some discrete distributions are treated as though they are continuous because the number of possible outcomes is very large. For example, the increase or decrease in the price of a stock traded on an American exchange is recorded in dollars and cents. Yet, the probability of a change of exactly $1.33 or $1.34 or any other specific change is almost zero. It is customary, therefore, to speak in terms of the probability of a range of possible price change, say between $1.00 and $2.00. In other words p(price change = 1.33) is essentially zero, but p($1 < price change < $2) is greater than zero.

LOS 9.c: Interpret a probability function, a probability density function, and a cumulative distribution function.

A **probability function**, denoted p(x), specifies the probability that a random variable is equal to a specific value. More formally, p(x) is the probability that random variable *X* takes on the value x, or p(x) = P(X = x).

The **two key properties of a probability function** are:

- $0 \leq p(x) \leq 1$.
- $\sum p(x) = 1$, the sum of the probabilities for *all* possible outcomes, x, for a random variable, *X*, equals 1.

> **Example: Evaluating a probability function**
>
> Consider the following function: X = {1, 2, 3, 4}, $p(x) = \dfrac{x}{10}$, else p(x) = 0
>
> Determine whether this function satisfies the conditions for a probability function.

Answer:

Note that all of the probabilities are between 0 and 1, and the sum of all probabilities equals 1:

$$\sum p(x) = \frac{1}{10} + \frac{2}{10} + \frac{3}{10} + \frac{4}{10} = 0.1 + 0.2 + 0.3 + 0.4 = 1$$

Both conditions for a probability function are satisfied.

A **probability density function** (pdf) is a function, denoted f(x), that can be used to generate the probability that outcomes of a continuous distribution lie within a particular range of outcomes. For a continuous distribution, it is the equivalent of a *probability function* for a discrete distribution. Remember, for a continuous distribution the probability of any one particular outcome (of the infinite possible outcomes) is zero. A pdf is used to calculate the probability of an outcome between two values (i.e., the probability of the outcome falling within a specified range). How that is actually done (it involves using calculus to take the integral of the function) is, thankfully, beyond the scope of the material required for the exam.

A **cumulative distribution function** (cdf), or simply *distribution function,* defines the probability that a random variable, *X*, takes on a value equal to or less than a specific value, *x*. It represents the sum, or *cumulative value*, of the probabilities for the outcomes up to and including a specified outcome. The cumulative distribution function for random variable, *X*, may be expressed as F(x) = P(X ≤ x).

LOS 9.d: Calculate and interpret probabilities for a random variable, given its cumulative distribution function.

Consider the probability function defined earlier for X = {1, 2, 3, 4}, p(x) = x / 10. For this distribution, F(3) = 0.6 = 0.1 + 0.2 + 0.3 + 0.4. This means that F(3) is the cumulative probability that outcomes 1, 2, or 3 occur, and F(4) is the cumulative probability that one of the possible outcomes occurs.

Figure 1 shows an example of a cumulative distribution function (for a standard normal distribution, described later in this topic). There is a 15.87% probability of a value less than –1. This is the total area to the left of –1 in the pdf in Panel A, and the y-axis value of the cdf for a value of –1 in Panel B.

**Figure 1: Standard Normal Probability Density
and Cumulative Distribution Functions**

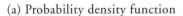

(a) Probability density function

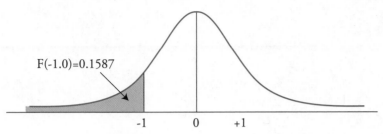

F(-1.0)=0.1587

-1   0   +1

(b) Cumulative distribution function

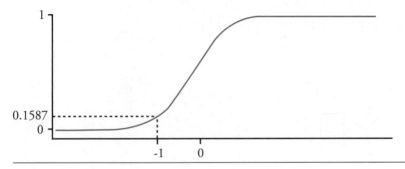

1

0.1587
0

-1   0

LOS 9.e: Define a discrete uniform random variable and a binomial random variable.

LOS 9.f: Calculate and interpret probabilities given the discrete uniform and the binomial distribution functions.

A **discrete uniform random variable** is one for which the probabilities for all possible outcomes for a discrete random variable are equal. For example, consider the *discrete uniform probability distribution* defined as X = {1, 2, 3, 4, 5}, p(x) = 0.2. Here, the probability for each outcome is equal to 0.2 [i.e., p(1) = p(2) = p(3) = p(4) = p(5) = 0.2]. Also, the cumulative distribution function for the *n*th outcome, $F(x_n)$ = np(x), and the probability for a range of outcomes is p(x)k, where *k* is the number of possible outcomes in the range.

Example: Discrete uniform distribution

Determine p(6), F(6), and $P(2 \leq X \leq 8)$ for the discrete uniform distribution function defined as:

X {2, 4, 6, 8, 10}, p(x) = 0.2

Answer:

p(6) = 0.2, since p(x) = 0.2 for all *x*. F(6) = $P(X \leq 6)$ = np(x) = 3(0.2) = 0.6. Note that n = 3 since 6 is the third outcome in the range of possible outcomes.
$P(2 \leq X \leq 8)$ = 4(0.2) = 0.8. Note that k = 4, since there are four outcomes in the range $2 \leq X \leq 8$. The figures below illustrate the concepts of a probability function and cumulative distribution function for this distribution.

Probability and Cumulative Distribution Functions

$X = x$	Probability of x Prob (X = x)	Cumulative Distribution Function Prob (X < x)
2	0.20	0.20
4	0.20	0.40
6	0.20	0.60
8	0.20	0.80

Cumulative Distribution Function for X ~ Uniform {2, 4, 6, 8, 10}

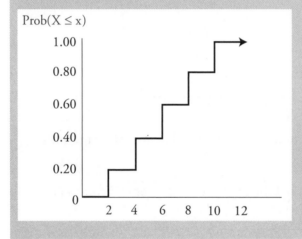

The Binomial Distribution

A **binomial random variable** may be defined as the number of "successes" in a given number of trials, whereby the outcome can be either "success" or "failure." The probability of success, *p*, is constant for each trial, and the trials are independent. (A binomial random variable for which the number of trials is 1 is called a **Bernoulli random variable**.) Think of a trial as a mini-experiment (or "Bernoulli trial"). The final outcome is the number of successes in a series of *n* trials. Under these conditions, the binomial probability function defines the probability of *x* successes in *n* trials. It can be expressed using the following formula:

$$p(x) = P(X = x) = (\text{number of ways to choose } x \text{ from } n)p^x(1 - p)^{n-x}$$

where:

(number of ways to choose *x* from *n*) = $\dfrac{n!}{(n-x)!x!}$ which may also be denoted as $\dbinom{n}{x}$ or stated as "*n* choose *x*"

p = the probability of "success" on each trial [don't confuse it with p(x)]

So the probability of exactly x successes in n trials is:

$$p(x) = \frac{n!}{(n-x)!x!} p^x (1-p)^{n-x}$$

Example: Binomial probability

Assuming a binomial distribution, compute the probability of drawing three black beans from a bowl of black and white beans if the probability of selecting a black bean in any given attempt is 0.6. You will draw five beans from the bowl.

Answer:

$$P(X = 3) = p(3) = \frac{5!}{2!3!}(0.6)^3(0.4)^2 = (120 / 12)(0.216)(0.160) = 0.3456$$

Some intuition about these results may help you remember the calculations. Consider that a (very large) bowl of black and white beans has 60% black beans and that each time you select a bean, you replace it in the bowl before drawing again. We want to know the probability of selecting exactly three black beans in five draws, as in the previous problem.

One way this might happen is BBBWW. Since the draws are independent, the probability of this is easy to calculate. The probability of drawing a black bean is 60% and the probability of drawing a white bean is 1 − 60% = 40%. Therefore, the probability of selecting BBBWW, in order, is 0.6 × 0.6 × 0.6 × 0.4 × 0.4 = 3.456%. This is the $p^3(1 - p)^2$ from the formula and p is 60%, the probability of selecting a black bean on any single draw from the bowl. BBBWW is not, however, the only way to choose exactly three black beans in five trials. Another possibility is BBWWB, and a third is BWWBB. Each of these will have exactly the same probability of occurring as our initial outcome, BBBWW. That's why we need to answer the question of how many ways (different orders) there are for us to choose three black beans in five draws. Using the formula, there are $\frac{5!}{3!(5-3)!} = 10$ ways; 10 × 3.456% = 34.56%, the answer we computed above.

The Expected Value of a Binomial Random Variable

For a given series of n trials, the expected number of successes, or E(X), is given by the following formula:

expected value of X = E(X) = np

The intuition is straightforward; if we perform n trials and the probability of success on each trial is p, we expect np successes.

Example: Expected value of a binomial random variable

Based on empirical data, the probability that the Dow Jones Industrial Average (DJIA) will increase on any given day has been determined to equal 0.67. Assuming that the only other outcome is that it decreases, we can state p(UP) = 0.67 and p(DOWN) = 0.33. Further, assume that movements in the DJIA are independent (i.e., an increase in one day is independent of what happened on another day).

Using the information provided, compute the expected value of the number of up days in a 5-day period.

Answer:

Using binomial terminology, we define success as UP, so p = 0.67. Note that the definition of success is critical to any binomial problem.

$$E(X \mid n = 5, p = 0.67) = (5)(0.67) = 3.35$$

Recall that the "|" symbol means "*given*." Hence, the preceding statement is read as: the expected value of X given that n = 5 and the probability of success = 67% is 3.35.

We should note that since the binomial distribution is a discrete distribution, the result X = 3.35 is not possible. However, if we were to record the results of many 5-day periods, the average number of up days (successes) would converge to 3.35.

LOS 9.g: Construct a binomial tree to describe stock price movement.

A binomial model can be applied to stock price movements. We just need to define the two possible outcomes and the probability that each outcome will occur. Consider a stock with current price S that will, over the next period, either increase in value by 1% or decrease in value by 1% (the only two possible outcomes). The probability of an up-move (the **up transition probability**, u) is *p* and the probability of a down-move (the **down transition probability**, d) is (1 − p). For our example, the up-move factor (U) is 1.01 and the down-move factor (D) is 1/1.01. So there is a probability *p* that the stock price will move to S(1.01) over the next period and a probability (1 − p) that the stock price will move to S / 1.01.

A **binomial tree** is constructed by showing all the possible combinations of up-moves and down-moves over a number of successive periods. For two periods, these combinations are UU, UD, DU, and DD. Importantly, UD and DU result in the same stock price S after two periods since S (1.01)(1/1.01) = S and the order of the moves does not change the result. Each of the possible values along a binomial tree is a **node**. Figure 2 illustrates a binomial tree for three periods.

Figure 2: A Binomial Tree

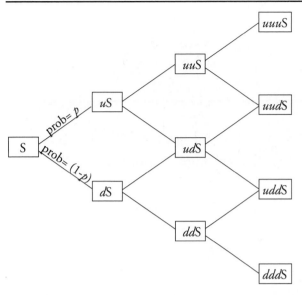

With an initial stock price S = 50, U = 1.01, D = $\frac{1}{1.01}$, and Prob(U) = 0.6, we can

calculate the possible stock prices after two periods as:

$$uuS = 1.01^2 \times 50 = 51.01 \text{ with probability } (0.6)^2 = 0.36$$

$$udS = 1.01\left(\frac{1}{1.01}\right) \times 50 = 50 \text{ with probability } (0.6)(0.4) = 0.24$$

$$duS = \left(\frac{1}{1.01}\right)(1.01) \times 50 = 50 \text{ with probability } (0.4)(0.6) = 0.24$$

$$ddS = \left(\frac{1}{1.01}\right)^2 \times 50 = 49.01 \text{ with probability } (0.4)^2 = 0.16$$

Since a stock price of 50 can result from either *ud* or *du* moves, the probability of a stock price of 50 after two periods (the middle value) is 2 × (0.6)(0.4) = 48%. A binomial tree with S = 50, U = 1.1, and Prob(U) = 0.7 is illustrated in Figure 3. Note that the middle value after two periods (50) is equal to the beginning value. The probability that the stock price is down (<50) after two periods is simply the probability of two down movements, $(1 - 0.7)^2 = 9\%$.

Figure 3: A Two-Period Binomial Tree   S = $50, U = 1.10, Prob(U) = 0.7

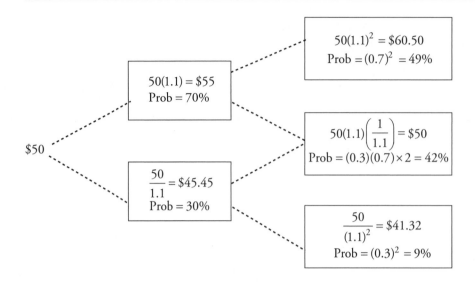

One of the important applications of a binomial stock price model is in pricing options. We can make a binomial tree for asset prices more realistic by shortening the length of the periods and increasing the number of periods and possible outcomes.

LOS 9.h: Describe the continuous uniform distribution and calculate and interpret probabilities, given a continuous uniform probability distribution.

The **continuous uniform distribution** is defined over a range that spans between some lower limit, a, and some upper limit, b, which serve as the parameters of the distribution. Outcomes can only occur between a and b, and since we are dealing with a continuous distribution, even if a < x < b, P(X = x) = 0. Formally, the properties of a continuous uniform distribution may be described as follows:

- For all $a \leq x_1 < x_2 \leq b$ (i.e., for all x_1 and x_2 between the boundaries a and b).
- P(X < a or X > b) = 0 (i.e., the probability of X outside the boundaries is zero).
- $P(x_1 \leq X \leq x_2) = (x_2 - x_1)/(b - a)$. This defines the probability of outcomes between x_1 and x_2.

Don't miss how simple this is just because the notation is so mathematical. For a continuous uniform distribution, the probability of outcomes in a range that is one-half the whole range is 50%. The probability of outcomes in a range that is one-quarter as large as the whole possible range is 25%.

Example: Continuous uniform distribution

X is uniformly distributed between 2 and 12. Calculate the probability that X will be between 4 and 8.

Answer:

$$\frac{8-4}{12-2} = \frac{4}{10} = 40\%$$

The figure below illustrates this continuous uniform distribution. Note that the area bounded by 4 and 8 is 40% of the total probability between 2 and 12 (which is 100%).

Continuous Uniform Distribution

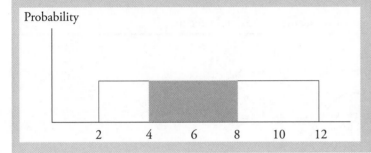

Figure 4: CDF for a Continuous Uniform Variable

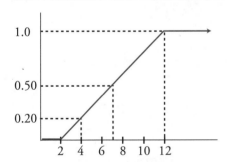

Since outcomes are equal over equal-size possible intervals, the cumulative distribution function (CDF) is linear over the variable's range. The CDF for the distribution in the above example, Prob (X < x), is shown in Figure 4.

LOS 9.i: Explain the key properties of the normal distribution, distinguish between a univariate and a multivariate distribution, and explain the role of correlation in the multivariate normal distribution.

The normal distribution is important for many reasons. Besides the high probability that it will be covered on the exam, many of the random variables that are relevant to finance and other professional disciplines follow a normal distribution. In the area of investment and portfolio management, the normal distribution plays a central role in portfolio theory.

The **normal distribution** has the following key properties:

- It is completely described by its mean, μ, and variance, σ^2, stated as $X \sim N(\mu, \sigma^2)$. In words, this says that "X is normally distributed with mean μ and variance σ^2."
- Skewness = 0, meaning that the normal distribution is symmetric about its mean, so that $P(X \leq \mu) = P(\mu \leq X) = 0.5$, and mean = median = mode.
- Kurtosis = 3; this is a measure of how flat the distribution is. Recall that excess kurtosis is measured relative to 3, the kurtosis of the normal distribution.
- A linear combination of normally distributed random variables is also normally distributed.
- The probabilities of outcomes further above and below the mean get smaller and smaller but do not go to zero (the tails get very thin but extend infinitely).

Many of these properties are evident from examining the graph of a normal distribution's probability density function as illustrated in Figure 5.

Figure 5: Normal Distribution Probability Density Function

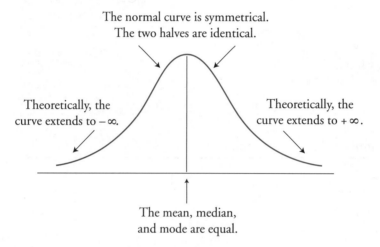

Univariate and Multivariate Distributions

Up to this point, our discussion has been strictly focused on **univariate distributions** (i.e., the distribution of a single random variable). In practice, however, the relationships between two or more random variables are often relevant. For instance, investors and investment managers are frequently interested in the interrelationship among the returns of one or more assets. In fact, as you will see in your study of asset pricing models and modern portfolio theory, the return on a given stock and the return on the S&P 500 or some other market index will have special significance. Regardless of the specific variables, the simultaneous analysis of two or more random variables requires an understanding of multivariate distributions.

A **multivariate distribution** specifies the probabilities associated with a group of random variables and is meaningful only when the behavior of each random variable in the group is in some way dependent upon the behavior of the others. Both discrete and continuous random variables can have multivariate distributions. Multivariate distributions between two discrete random variables are described using joint probability tables. For continuous random variables, a multivariate *normal* distribution may be used to describe them if all of the individual variables follow a normal distribution. As previously mentioned, one of the characteristics of a normal distribution is that a linear combination of normally distributed random variables is normally distributed as well. For example, if the return of each stock in a portfolio is normally distributed, the return on the portfolio will also be normally distributed.

The Role of Correlation in the Multivariate Normal Distribution

Similar to a univariate normal distribution, a multivariate normal distribution can be described by the mean and variance of the individual random variables. Additionally, it is necessary to specify the correlation between the individual pairs of variables when describing a multivariate distribution. Correlation is the feature that distinguishes a multivariate distribution from a univariate normal distribution. *Correlation indicates the strength of the linear relationship between a pair of random variables.*

Using asset returns as our random variables, the multivariate normal distribution for the returns on *n* assets can be completely defined by the following three sets of parameters:

- *n* means of the *n* series of returns (μ_1, μ_2, ..., μ_n).
- *n* variances of the *n* series of returns (σ_1^2, σ_2^2, ..., σ_n^2).
- $0.5n(n-1)$ pair-wise correlations.

For example, if there are two assets, n = 2, then the multivariate returns distribution can be described with two means, two variances, and one correlation [$0.5(2)(2-1) = 1$]. If there are four assets, n = 4, the multivariate distribution can be described with four means, four variances, and six correlations [$0.5(4)(4-1) = 6$]. When building a portfolio of assets, all other things being equal, it is desirable to combine assets having low returns correlation because this will result in a portfolio with a lower variance than one composed of assets with higher correlations.

LOS 9.j: Determine the probability that a normally distributed random variable lies inside a given confidence interval.

A **confidence interval** is a range of values around the expected outcome within which we expect the actual outcome to be some specified percentage of the time. A 95% confidence interval is a range that we expect the random variable to be in 95% of the time. For a normal distribution, this interval is based on the expected value (sometimes called a point estimate) of the random variable and on its variability, which we measure with standard deviation.

Confidence intervals for a normal distribution are illustrated in Figure 6. For any normally distributed random variable, 68% of the outcomes are within one standard deviation of the expected value (mean) and approximately 95% of the outcomes are within two standard deviations of the expected value.

Figure 6: Confidence Intervals for a Normal Distribution

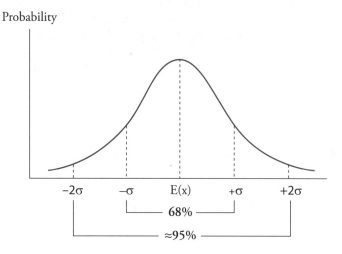

In practice, we will not know the actual values for the mean and standard deviation of the distribution, but will have estimated them as $\overline{X}$ and s. The three confidence intervals of most interest are given by:

- The *90% confidence interval* for X is $\overline{X} - 1.65s$ to $\overline{X} + 1.65s$.
- The *95% confidence interval* for X is $\overline{X} - 1.96s$ to $\overline{X} + 1.96s$.
- The *99% confidence interval* for X is $\overline{X} - 2.58s$ to $\overline{X} + 2.58s$.

Example: Confidence intervals

The average return of a mutual fund is 10.5% per year and the standard deviation of annual returns is 18%. If returns are approximately normal, what is the 95% confidence interval for the mutual fund return next year?

Answer:

Here μ and σ are 10.5% and 18%, respectively. Thus, the 95% confidence interval for the return, R, is:

$$10.5 \pm 1.96(18) = -24.78\% \text{ to } 45.78\%$$

Symbolically, this result can be expressed as:

$$P(-24.78 < R < 45.78) = 0.95 \text{ or } 95\%$$

The interpretation is that the annual return is expected to be within this interval 95% of the time or 95 out of 100 years.

LOS 9.k: Define the standard normal distribution, explain how to standardize a random variable, and calculate and interpret probabilities using the standard normal distribution.

The **standard normal distribution** is a normal distribution that has been standardized so that it has a mean of zero and a standard deviation of 1 [i.e., N~(0,1)]. To standardize an observation from a given normal distribution, the *z-value* of the observation must be calculated. The *z*-value represents the number of standard deviations a given observation is from the population mean. *Standardization* is the process of converting an observed value for a random variable to its *z*-value. The following formula is used to *standardize a random variable*:

$$z = \frac{\text{observation} - \text{population mean}}{\text{standard deviation}} = \frac{x - \mu}{\sigma}$$

 Professor's Note: The term z-value *will be used for a standardized observation in this document. The terms* z-score *and* z-statistic *are also commonly used.*

Example: Standardizing a random variable (calculating *z*-values)

Assume that the annual earnings per share (EPS) for a population of firms are normally distributed with a mean of $6 and a standard deviation of $2.

What are the *z*-values for EPS of $2 and $8?

Answer:

If EPS = x = $8, then z = (x − μ) / σ = ($8 − $6) / $2 = +1

If EPS = x = $2, then z = (x − μ) / σ = ($2 − $6) / $2 = −2

Here, z = +1 indicates that an EPS of $8 is one standard deviation above the mean, and z = −2 means that an EPS of $2 is two standard deviations below the mean.

Calculating Probabilities Using *z*-Values

Now we will show how to use standardized values (*z*-values) and a table of probabilities for Z to determine probabilities. A portion of a table of the cumulative distribution function for a standard normal distribution is shown in Figure 7. We will refer to this table as the *z*-table, as it contains values generated using the cumulative density function for a standard normal distribution, denoted by F(Z). Thus, the values in the *z*-table are the probabilities of observing a *z*-value that is less than a given value, z [i.e., P(Z < z)]. The numbers in the first column are *z*-values that have only one decimal place. The columns to the right supply probabilities for *z*-values with two decimal places.

Note that the *z*-table in Figure 7 only provides probabilities for positive *z*-values. This is not a problem because we know from the symmetry of the standard normal distribution that F(–Z) = 1 – F(Z). The tables in the back of many texts actually provide probabilities for negative z-values, but we will work with only the positive portion of the table because this may be all you get on the exam. In Figure 7 we can find the probability that a standard normal random variable will be less than 1.66, for example. The table value is 95.15%. The probability that the random variable will be less than –1.66 is simply 1 – 0.9515 = 0.0485 = 4.85%, which is also the probability that the variable will be greater than +1.66.

> *Professor's Note: When you use the standard normal probabilities, you have formulated the problem in terms of standard deviations from the mean. Consider a security with returns that are approximately normal, an expected return of 10%, and standard deviation of returns of 12%. The probability of returns greater than 30% is calculated based on the number of standard deviations that 30% is above the expected return of 10%. 30% is 20% above the expected return of 10%, which is 20 / 12 = 1.67 standard deviations above the mean. We look up the probability of returns less than 1.67 standard deviations above the mean (0.9525 or 95.25% from Figure 7) and calculate the probability of returns more than 1.67 standard deviations above the mean as 1 – 0.9525 = 4.75%.*

Figure 7: Cumulative Probabilities for a Standard Normal Distribution

	Cdf Values for the Standard Normal Distribution: The z-table									
z	.00	.01	.02	.03	.04	.05	.06	.07	.08	.09
0.0	.5000	.5040	.5080	.5120	.5160	.5199	.5239	.5279	.5319	.5359
0.1	.5398	.5438	.5478	.5517	.5557	.5596	.5636	.5675	.5714	.5753
0.2	.5793	.5832	.5871	.5910	.5948	.5987	.6026	.6064	.6103	.6141
0.5	.6915	Please note that several of the rows have been deleted to save space.*								
1.2	.8849	.8869	.8888	.8907	.8925	.8944	.8962	.8980	.8997	.9015
1.6	.9452	.9463	.9474	.9484	.9495	.9505	**.9515**	.9525	.9535	.9545
1.8	.9641	.9649	.9656	.9664	.9671	.9678	.9686	.9693	.9699	.9706
1.9	.9713	.9719	.9726	.9732	.9738	.9744	.9750	.9756	.9761	.9767
2.0	.9772	.9778	.9783	.9788	.9793	.9798	.9803	.9808	.9812	.9817
2.5	.9938	.9940	.9941	.9943	.9945	.9946	.9948	.9949	.9951	.9952
3.0	.9987	.9987	.9987	.9988	.9988	.9989	.9989	.9989	.9990	.9990

* A complete cumulative standard normal table is included in Appendix A.

Example: Using the *z*-table (1)

Considering again EPS distributed with μ = $6 and σ = $2, what is the probability that EPS will be $9.70 or more?

Answer:

Here we want to know P(EPS > $9.70), which is the area under the curve to the right of the *z*-value corresponding to EPS = $9.70 (see the figure below).

The *z*-value for EPS = $9.70 is:

$$z = \frac{(x - \mu)}{\sigma} = \frac{(9.70 - 6)}{2} = 1.85$$ that is, $9.70 is 1.85 standard deviations above the mean EPS value of $6.

From the *z*-table we have F(1.85) = 0.9678, but this is P(EPS ≤ 9.70). We want P(EPS > 9.70), which is 1 – P(EPS ≤ 9.70).

P(EPS > 9.70) = 1 – 0.9678 = 0.0322, or 3.2%

P(EPS>$9.70)

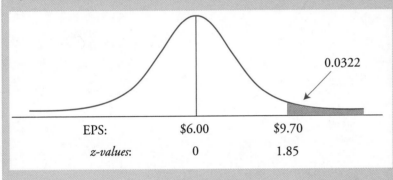

Example: Using the z-table (2)

Using the distribution of EPS with μ = $6 and σ = $2 again, what percent of the observed EPS values are likely to be less than $4.10?

Answer:

As shown graphically in the figure below, we want to know P(EPS < $4.10). This requires a 2-step approach like the one taken in the preceding example.

First, the corresponding z-value must be determined as follows:

$$z = \frac{(\$4.10 - \$6)}{2} = -0.95,$$ so $4.10 is 0.95 standard deviations below the mean of $6.00.

Now, from the z-table for negative values in the back of this book, we find that F(−0.95) = 0.1711, or 17.11%.

Finding a Left-Tail Probability

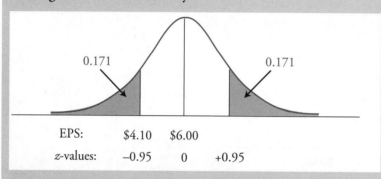

The z-table gave us the probability that the outcome will be more than 0.95 standard deviations below the mean.

LOS 9.l: Define shortfall risk, calculate the safety-first ratio, and select an optimal portfolio using Roy's safety-first criterion.

Shortfall risk is the probability that a portfolio value or return will fall below a particular (target) value or return over a given time period.

Roy's safety-first criterion states that the optimal portfolio minimizes the probability that the return of the portfolio falls below some minimum acceptable level. This minimum acceptable level is called the "threshold" level. Symbolically, Roy's safety-first criterion can be stated as:

minimize P(R$_p$ < R$_L$)

where:
R$_p$ = portfolio return
R$_L$ = threshold level return

If portfolio returns are normally distributed, then Roy's safety-first criterion can be stated as:

maximize the SFRatio where SFRatio = $\dfrac{\left[E\left(R_p\right)-R_L\right]}{\sigma_p}$

Professor's Note: Notice the similarity to the Sharpe ratio:

Sharpe = $\dfrac{\left[E\left(R_p\right)-R_f\right]}{\sigma_p}$. *The only difference is that the SFRatio utilizes the excess return over the threshold return, R_L , where the Sharpe ratio uses the excess return over the risk-free rate, R_f. When the threshold level is the risk-free rate of return, the SFRatio is also the Sharpe ratio.*

The reasoning behind the safety-first criterion is illustrated in Figure 8. Assume an investor is choosing between two portfolios: Portfolio A with expected return of 12% and standard deviation of returns of 18%, and Portfolio B with expected return of 10% and standard deviation of returns of 12%. The investor has stated that he wants to minimize the probability of losing money (negative returns). Assuming that returns are normally distributed, the portfolio with the larger SFR using 0% as the threshold return (R_L) will be the one with the lower probability of negative returns.

Figure 8: The Safety-First Criterion and Shortfall Risk

A. Normally Distributed Returns

Portfolio A: E(R)=12% σ_A=18%   Portfolio B: E(R)=10% σ_B=12%

Probability of returns < 0%
– i.e. short fall risk

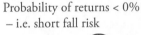

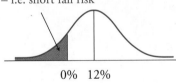

$SFR_A = \dfrac{12-0}{18} = 0.667$ $SFR_B = \dfrac{10-0}{12} = 0.833$

B. Standard Normal

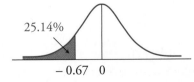

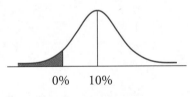

Panel B of Figure 8 relates the SFRatio to the standard normal distribution. Note that the SFR is the number of standard deviations *below* the mean. Thus, the portfolio with the larger SFR has the lower probability of returns below the threshold return, which is a return of 0% in our example. Using a *z*-table for negative values, we can find the probabilities in the left-hand tails as indicated. These probabilities (25% for Portfolio A and 20% for Portfolio B) are also the shortfall risk for a target return of 0%, that is, the probabilty of negative returns. Portfolio B has the higher SFR which means it has the lower probability of negative returns.

In summary, when choosing among portfolios with normally distributed returns using Roy's safety-first criterion, there are two steps:

Step 1: Calculate the SFRatio $= \dfrac{\left[E\left(R_p\right) - R_L \right]}{\sigma_p}$.

Step 2: Choose the portfolio that has the *largest* SFRatio.

Example: Roy's safety-first criterion

For the next year, the managers of a $120 million college endowment plan have set a minimum acceptable end-of-year portfolio value of $123.6 million. Three portfolios are being considered which have the expected returns and standard deviation shown in the first two rows of the table below. Determine which of these portfolios is the most desirable using Roy's safety-first criterion and the probability that the portfolio value will fall short of the target amount.

Answer:

The threshold return is R_L = (123.6 − 120) / 120 = 0.030 = 3%. The SFRs are shown in the table below. As indicated, the best choice is Portfolio A because it has the largest SFR.

Roy's Safety-First Ratios

Portfolio	Portfolio A	Portfolio B	Portfolio C
$E(R_p)$	9%	11%	6.6%
σ_p	12%	20%	8.2%
SFRatio	$0.5 = \dfrac{(9-3)}{12}$	$0.4 = \dfrac{(11-3)}{20}$	$0.44 = \dfrac{(6.6-3)}{8.2}$

The probability of an ending value for Portfolio A less than $123.6 million (a return less than 3%) is simply F(−0.5) which we can find on the *z*-table for negative values. The probability is 0.3085 = 30.85%.

LOS 9.m: Explain the relationship between normal and lognormal distributions and why the lognormal distribution is used to model asset prices.

The **lognormal distribution** is generated by the function e^x, where *x* is normally distributed. Since the natural logarithm, ln, of e^x is *x*, the logarithms of lognormally distributed random variables are normally distributed, thus the name.

Figure 9 illustrates the differences between a normal distribution and a lognormal distribution.

Figure 9: Normal vs. Lognormal Distributions

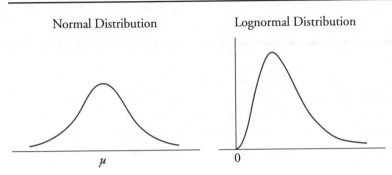

In Figure 9, we can see that:

- The lognormal distribution is skewed to the right.
- The lognormal distribution is bounded from below by zero so that it is useful for modeling asset prices which never take negative values.

If we used a normal distribution of returns to model asset prices over time, we would admit the possibility of returns less than −100%, which would admit the possibility of asset prices less than zero. Using a lognormal distribution to model *price relatives* avoids this problem. A price relative is just the end-of-period price of the asset divided by the beginning price (S_1/S_0) and is equal to (1 + the holding period return). To get the end-of-period asset price, we can simply multiply the price relative times the beginning-of-period asset price. Since a lognormal distribution takes a minimum value of zero, end-of-period asset prices cannot be less than zero. A price relative of zero corresponds to a holding period return of −100% (i.e., the asset price has gone to zero). Recall that we used price relatives as the up-move and down-move (multiplier) terms in constructing a binomial tree for stock price changes over a number of periods.

LOS 9.n: Distinguish between discretely and continuously compounded rates of return and calculate and interpret a continuously compounded rate of return, given a specific holding period return.

Discretely compounded returns are just the compound returns we are familiar with, given some discrete compounding period, such as semiannual or quarterly. Recall that the more frequent the compounding, the greater the effective annual return. For a stated rate of 10%, semiannual compounding results in an effective yield of

$\left(1 + \dfrac{0.10}{2}\right)^2 - 1 = 10.25\%$ and monthly compounding results in an effective yield of

$\left(1 + \dfrac{0.10}{12}\right)^{12} - 1 = 10.47\%$. Daily or even hourly compounding will produce still larger

effective yields. The limit of this exercise, as the compounding periods get shorter and shorter, is called **continuous compounding**. The effective annual rate, based on continuous compounding for a stated annual rate of R_{cc}, can be calculated from the formula:

$$\text{effective annual rate} = e^{R_{cc}} - 1$$

Based on a stated rate of 10%, the effective rate with continuous compounding is $e^{0.10} - 1 = 10.5171\%$. Please verify this by entering 0.1 in your calculator and finding the e^x function.

Since the natural log, ln, of e^x is x, we can get the continuously compounded rate from an effective annual rate by using the ln calculator function. Using our previous example, $\ln(1 + 10.517\%) = \ln 1.105171 = 10\%$. Verify this by entering 1.105171 in your calculator and then entering the ln key. (Using the HP calculator, the keystrokes are 1.105171 [g] [ln].)

We can use this method to find the continuously compounded rate that will generate a particular holding period return. If we are given a holding period return of 12.5% for the year, the equivalent continuously compounded rate is $\ln 1.125 = 11.778\%$. Since the calculation is based on 1 plus the holding period return, we can also do the calculation directly from the *price relative*. The price relative is just the end-of-period value divided by the beginning of period value. The continuously compounded rate of return is:

$$\ln\left(\frac{S_1}{S_0}\right) = \ln(1 + HPR) = R_{cc}$$

Example: Calculating continuously compounded returns

A stock was purchased for $100 and sold one year later for $120. Calculate the investor's annual rate of return on a continuously compounded basis.

Answer:

$$\ln\left(\frac{120}{100}\right) = 18.232\%$$

If we had been given the return (20%) instead, the calculation is:

$$\ln(1 + 0.20) = 18.232\%$$

One property of continuously compounded rates of return is that they are additive for multiple periods. Note that the (effective) holding period return over two years is calculated by doubling the continuously compounded annual rate. If $R_{cc} = 10\%$, the (effective) holding period return over two years is $e^{(0.10)2} - 1 = 22.14\%$. In general, the holding period return after T years, when the annual continuously compounded rate is R_{cc}, is given by:

$$HPR_T = e^{R_{cc} \times T} - 1$$

Given investment results over a 2-year period, we can calculate the 2-year continuously compounded return and divide by two to get the annual rate. Consider an investment that appreciated from $1,000 to $1,221.40 over a 2-year period. The 2-year continuously compounded rate is $\ln(1,221.40 / 1,000) = 20\%$, and the annual continuously compounded rate (R_{cc}) is $20\% / 2 = 10\%$.

LOS 9.o: Explain Monte Carlo simulation and historical simulation and describe their major applications and limitations.

Monte Carlo simulation is a technique based on the repeated generation of one or more risk factors that affect security values, in order to generate a distribution of security values. For each of the risk factors, the analyst must specify the parameters of the probability distribution that the risk factor is assumed to follow. A computer is then used to generate random values for each risk factor based on its assumed probability distributions. Each set of randomly generated risk factors is used with a pricing model to value the security. This procedure is repeated many times (100s, 1,000s, or 10,000s), and the distribution of simulated asset values is used to draw inferences about the expected (mean) value of the security and possibly the variance of security values about the mean as well.

As an example, consider the valuation of stock options that can only be exercised on a particular date. The main risk factor is the value of the stock itself, but interest rates could affect the valuation as well. The simulation procedure would be to:

1. Specify the probability distributions of stock prices and of the relevant interest rate, as well as the parameters (mean, variance, possibly skewness) of the distributions.

2. Randomly generate values for both stock prices and interest rates.

3. Value the options for each pair of risk factor values.

4. After many iterations, calculate the mean option value and use that as your estimate of the option's value.

Monte Carlo simulation is used to:
- Value complex securities.
- Simulate the profits/losses from a trading strategy.
- Calculate estimates of value at risk (VAR) to determine the riskiness of a portfolio of assets and liabilities.
- Simulate pension fund assets and liabilities over time to examine the variability of the difference between the two.
- Value portfolios of assets that have non-normal returns distributions.

The **limitations of Monte Carlo simulation** are that it is fairly complex and will provide answers that are no better than the assumptions about the distributions of the risk factors and the pricing/valuation model that is used. Also, simulation is not an analytic method, but a statistical one, and cannot provide the insights that analytic methods can.

Historical simulation is based on actual changes in value or actual changes in risk factors over some prior period. Rather than model the distribution of risk factors, as in Monte Carlo simulation, the set of all changes in the relevant risk factors over some prior period is used. Each iteration of the simulation involves randomly selecting one of these past changes for each risk factor and calculating the value of the asset or portfolio in question, based on those changes in risk factors.

Historical simulation has the advantage of using the actual distribution of risk factors so that the distribution of changes in the risk factors does not have to be estimated. It suffers from the fact that past changes in risk factors may not be a good indication of future changes. Events that occur infrequently may not be reflected in historical simulation results unless the events occurred during the period from which the values for risk factors are drawn. An additional limitation of historical simulation is that it cannot address the sort of "what if" questions that Monte Carlo simulation can. With Monte Carlo simulation, we can investigate the effect on the distribution of security/portfolio values if we increase the variance of one of the risk factors by 20%; with historical simulation we cannot do this.

KEY CONCEPTS

LOS 9.a
A probability distribution lists all the possible outcomes of an experiment, along with their associated probabilities.

A discrete random variable has positive probabilities associated with a finite number of outcomes.

A continuous random variable has positive probabilities associated with a range of outcome values—the probability of any single value is zero.

LOS 9.b
The set of possible outcomes of a specific discrete random variable is a finite set of values. An example is the number of days last week on which the value of a particular portfolio increased. For a discrete distribution, $p(x) = 0$ when x cannot occur, or $p(x) > 0$ if it can.

LOS 9.c
A probability function specifies the probability that a discrete random variable is equal to a specific value; $P(X = x) = p(x)$.

The two key properties of a probability function are:
- $0 \leq p(x) \leq 1$.
- $\Sigma p(x) = 1$.

A probability density function (pdf) is the term for a function for a continuous random variable used to determine the probability that it will fall in a particular range.

A cumulative distribution function (cdf) gives the probability that a random variable will be less than or equal to specific values.

LOS 9.d
Given the cumulative distribution function for a random variable, the probability that an outcome will be less than or equal to a specific value is represented by the area under the probability distribution to the left of that value.

LOS 9.e
A discrete uniform distribution is one where there are n discrete, equally likely outcomes.

The binomial distribution is a probability distribution for a binomial (discrete) random variable that has two possible outcomes.

LOS 9.f

For a discrete uniform distribution with n possible outcomes, the probability for each outcome equals 1/n.

For a binomial distribution, if the probability of success is p, the probability of x successes in n trials is:

$$p(x) = P(X = x) = \frac{n!}{(n-x)!x!} p^x (1-p)^{n-x} = {}_nC_x \times p^x (1-p)^{n-x}$$

LOS 9.g

A binomial tree illustrates the probabilities of all the possible values that a variable (such as a stock price) can take on, given the probability of an up-move and the magnitude of an up-move (the up-move factor).

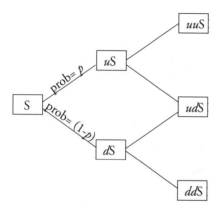

With an initial stock price S = 50, U = 1.01, D = $\frac{1}{1.01}$, and prob(U) = 0.6, the possible stock prices after two periods are:

$$uuS = 1.01^2 \times 50 = 51.01 \text{ with probability } (0.6)^2 = 0.36$$

$$udS = 1.01\left(\frac{1}{1.01}\right) \times 50 = 50 \text{ with probability } (0.6)(0.4) = 0.24$$

$$duS = \left(\frac{1}{1.01}\right)(1.01) \times 50 = 50 \text{ with probability } (0.4)(0.6) = 0.24$$

$$ddS = \left(\frac{1}{1.01}\right)^2 \times 50 = 49.01 \text{ with probability } (0.4)^2 = 0.16$$

LOS 9.h

A continuous uniform distribution is one where the probability of X occurring in a possible range is the length of the range relative to the total of all possible values. Letting a and b be the lower and upper limit of the uniform distribution, respectively, then for:

$$a \leq x_1 \leq x_2 \leq b, \; P(x_1 \leq X \leq x_2) = \frac{(x_2 - x_1)}{(b-a)}$$

LOS 9.i
The normal probability distribution and normal curve have the following characteristics:
- The normal curve is symmetrical and bell-shaped with a single peak at the exact center of the distribution.
- Mean = median = mode, and all are in the exact center of the distribution.
- The normal distribution can be completely defined by its mean and standard deviation because the skew is always zero and kurtosis is always 3.

Multivariate distributions describe the probabilities for more than one random variable, whereas a univariate distribution is for a single random variable.

The correlation(s) of a multivariate distribution describes the relation between the outcomes of its variables relative to their expected values.

LOS 9.j
A confidence interval is a range within which we have a given level of confidence of finding a point estimate (e.g., the 90% confidence interval for X is $\bar{X} - 1.65s$ to $\bar{X} + 1.65s$).

Confidence intervals for any normally distributed random variable are:
- 90%: $\mu \pm 1.65$ standard deviations.
- 95%: $\mu \pm 1.96$ standard deviations.
- 99%: $\mu \pm 2.58$ standard deviations.

The probability that a normally distributed random variable X will be within A standard deviations of its mean, μ, [i.e., $P(\mu - A\sigma \leq X \leq \mu + A\sigma)$], is calculated as two times the cumulative left-hand tail probability, $F(-A)$, or two times the right-hand tail probability, $1 - F(A)$, where $F(A)$ is the cumulative standard normal probability of A.

LOS 9.k
The standard normal probability distribution has a mean of 0 and a standard deviation of 1.

A normally distributed random variable X can be standardized as $Z = \dfrac{x - \mu}{\sigma}$ and Z

will be normally distributed with mean = 0 and standard deviation 1.

The z-table is used to find the probability that X will be less than or equal to a given value.
- $P(X < x) = F(x) = F\left[\dfrac{x - \mu}{\sigma}\right] = F(z)$, which is found in the standard normal probability table.
- $P(X > x) = 1 - P(X < x) = 1 - F(z)$.

LOS 9.l
The safety-first ratio for portfolio P, based on a target return R_T, is:

$$SFRatio = \frac{E(R_P) - R_T}{\sigma_P}$$

Shortfall risk is the probability that a portfolio's value (or return) will fall below a specific value over a given period of time. Greater safety-first ratios are preferred and indicate a smaller shortfall probability. Roy's safety-first criterion states that the optimal portfolio minimizes shortfall risk.

LOS 9.m
If x is normally distributed, e^x follows a lognormal distribution. A lognormal distribution is often used to model asset prices, since a lognormal random variable cannot be negative and can take on any positive value.

LOS 9.n
As we decrease the length of discrete compounding periods (e.g., from quarterly to monthly) the effective annual rate increases. As the length of the compounding period in discrete compounding gets shorter and shorter, the compounding becomes continuous, where the effective annual rate = $e^i - 1$.

For a holding period return (HPR) over any period, the equivalent continuously compounded rate over the period is $\ln(1 + \text{HPR})$.

LOS 9.o
Monte Carlo simulation uses randomly generated values for risk factors, based on their assumed distributions, to produce a distribution of possible security values. Its limitations are that it is fairly complex and will provide answers that are no better than the assumptions used.

Historical simulation uses randomly selected past changes in these risk factors to generate a distribution of possible security values. A limitation is that it cannot consider the effects of significant events that did not occur in the sample period.

CONCEPT CHECKERS

1. Which of the following is *least likely* an example of a discrete random variable?
   A. The number of stocks a person owns.
   B. The time spent by a portfolio manager with a client.
   C. The number of days it rains in a month in Iowa City.

2. For a continuous random variable X, the probability of any single value of X is:
   A. one.
   B. zero.
   C. determined by the cdf.

Use the following table to answer Questions 3 through 7.

			Probability distribution of a discrete random variable X					
X	0	1	2	3	4	5	6	7
P(X)	0.04	0.11	0.18	0.24	0.14	0.17	0.09	0.03

3. The probability that X = 3 is:
   A. 0.18.
   B. 0.24.
   C. 0.43.

4. The cdf of 5, or F(5) is:
   A. 0.17.
   B. 0.71.
   C. 0.88.

5. The probability that X is *greater* than 3 is:
   A. 0.24.
   B. 0.43.
   C. 0.67.

6. What is $P(2 \leq X \leq 5)$?
   A. 0.17.
   B. 0.38.
   C. 0.73.

7. The expected value of the random variable X is:
   A. 3.35.
   B. 3.70.
   C. 5.47.

8. Which of the following is *least likely* a condition of a binomial experiment?
   A. There are only two trials.
   B. The trials are independent.
   C. If p is the probability of success, and q is the probability of failure, then $p + q = 1$.

9. A recent study indicated that 60% of all businesses have a fax machine. From the binomial probability distribution table, the probability that exactly four businesses will have a fax machine in a random selection of six businesses is:
    A. 0.138.
    B. 0.276.
    C. 0.311.

10. Ten percent of all college graduates hired stay with the same company for more than five years. In a random sample of six recently hired college graduates, the probability that exactly two will stay with the same company for more than five years is *closest* to:
    A. 0.098.
    B. 0.114.
    C. 0.185.

11. Assume that 40% of candidates who sit for the CFA® examination pass it the first time. Of a random sample of 15 candidates who are sitting for the exam for the first time, what is the expected number of candidates that will pass?
    A. 0.375.
    B. 4.000.
    C. 6.000.

12. For the standard normal distribution, the *z*-value gives the distance between the mean and a point in terms of the:
    A. variance.
    B. standard deviation.
    C. center of the curve.

13. For a standard normal distribution, F(0) is:
    A. 0.0.
    B. 0.1.
    C. 0.5.

14. For the standard normal distribution, $P(0 \leq Z \leq 1.96)$ is:
    A. 0.4713.
    B. 0.4745.
    C. 0.4750.

Use the following data to answer Questions 15 through 17.

A study of hedge fund investors found that their annual household incomes are normally distributed with a mean of $175,000 and a standard deviation of $25,000.

15. What percent of hedge fund investors have incomes *less* than $100,000?
    A. 0.05%.
    B. 0.10%.
    C. 0.13%.

16. What percent of hedge fund investors have incomes *greater* than $225,000?
    A. 0.50%.
    B. 1.10%.
    C. 2.28%.

17. What percent of hedge fund investors have incomes *greater* than $150,000?
    A. 34.13%.
    B. 68.26%.
    C. 84.13%.

Use the following table to answer Questions 18 and 19.

Portfolio	Portfolio A	Portfolio B	Portfolio C
$E(R_p)$	5%	11%	18%
σ_p	8%	21%	40%

18. Given a threshold level of return of 4%, use Roy's safety-first criterion to choose the optimal portfolio. Portfolio:
    A. A.
    B. B.
    C. C.

19. Given a threshold level of return of 0%, use Roy's safety-first criterion to choose the optimal portfolio. Portfolio:
    A. A.
    B. B.
    C. C.

20. If a stock's initial price is $20 and its year-end price is $23, then its continuously compounded annual rate of return is:
    A. 13.64%.
    B. 13.98%.
    C. 15.00%.

21. For a lognormal distribution, the:
    A. mean equals the median.
    B. probability of a negative outcome is zero.
    C. probability of a positive outcome is 50%.

22. Using hypothesized parameter values and a random number generator to study the behavior of certain asset returns is part of:
    A. historical analysis.
    B. Monte Carlo simulation.
    C. standardizing a random variable.

23. A continuous uniform distribution has the parameters a = 4 and b = 10. The F(20) is:
    A. 0.25.
    B. 0.50.
    C. 1.00.

24. Which of the following statements *least accurately* describes the binomial distribution?
    A. It is a discrete distribution.
    B. The probability of an outcome of zero is zero.
    C. The combination formula is used in computing probabilities.

25. Approximately 95% of all observations for a normally distributed random variable fall in the interval:
    A. $\mu \pm \sigma$.
    B. $\mu \pm 2\sigma$.
    C. $\mu \pm 3\sigma$.

26. The probability that a normally distributed random variable will be more than two standard deviations above its mean is:
    A. 0.0228.
    B. 0.4772.
    C. 0.9772.

27. A stock doubled in value last year. Its continuously compounded return over the period was *closest* to:
    A. 18.2%.
    B. 69.3%.
    C. 100.0%.

28. Portfolio A has a safety-first ratio of 1.3 with a threshold return of 2%. What is the shortfall risk for a target return of 2%?
    A. 9.68%.
    B. 40.30%.
    C. 90.30%.

COMPREHENSIVE PROBLEMS

1. A stock's price is $8.50 today. You decide to model the stock price over time using a binomial model (as a Bernoulli random variable) with a probability of an up-move of 60%. The up-move factor is 1.05.

    A. How many different prices are possible for the stock at the end of two periods?

    B. What are the possible prices after two periods?

    C. What is the probability that the stock price will be $8.50 after three periods?

    D. What is the probability that the stock price will be $8.925 after three periods?

    E. What is the probability that the stock price will be unchanged after six periods?

2. An analyst has developed a model of option prices as a function of a short-term interest rate and the price of the underlying stock. She decides to test the model with a Monte Carlo simulation.

    A. What steps does she need to perform to run the simulation?

    B. What limitations of Monte Carlo simulation does she need to keep in mind when she interprets the results?

    C. What would be the advantages of using historical simulation instead of Monte Carlo simulation? What would be the drawbacks?

3. The monthly returns on an index of investment-grade corporate bonds for the last ten years have averaged 0.7% with a standard deviation of 2.0%.

    A. Assuming the returns are approximately normally distributed, what are the 90%, 95%, and 99% confidence intervals for the monthly return on this index?

    B. You are considering whether to use a lognormal distribution to model the value of one of the bonds in the index. In what ways is the lognormal distribution different from the normal distribution? What property of the lognormal distribution makes it useful for modeling asset prices?

ANSWERS – CONCEPT CHECKERS

1. **B** Time is usually a continuous random variable; the others are discrete.

2. **B** For a continuous distribution p(x) = 0 for all X; only ranges of value of X have positive probabilities.

3. **B** From the table.

4. **C** $(0.04 + 0.11 + 0.18 + 0.24 + 0.14 + 0.17) = 0.88$

5. **B** $(0.14 + 0.17 + 0.09 + 0.03) = 0.43$

6. **C** $(0.18 + 0.24 + 0.14 + 0.17) = 0.73$

7. **A** $0 + 1(0.11) + 2(0.18) + 3(0.24) + 4(0.14) + 5(0.17) + 6(0.09) + 7(0.03) = 3.35$

8. **A** There may be any number of independent trials, each with only two possible outcomes.

9. **C** Success = having a fax machine. $[6! / 4!(6 - 4)!](0.6)^4(0.4)^{6-4} = 15(0.1296)(0.16) = 0.311$.

10. **A** Success = staying for five years. $[6! / 2!(6 - 2)!](0.10)^2(0.90)^{6-2} = 15(0.01)(0.656) = 0.0984$.

11. **C** Success = passing the exam. Then, E(success) = np = $15 \times 0.4 = 6$.

12. **B** This is true by the formula for z.

13. **C** By the symmetry of the z-distribution and F(0) = 0.5. Half the distribution lies on each side of the mean.

14. **C** From the table F(1.96) = 0.9750; thus, the answer is 0.9750 − 0.5 = 0.4750. Knowing that 95% lie between −1.96 and +1.96, and that 0 is the midpoint, we can say that $\dfrac{95\%}{2} = 47.5\%$ lie between 0 and +1.96.

15. **C** $z = (100 - 175) / 25 = -3$, F(−3) = 1 − 0.9987 = 0.0013

16. **C** 1 − F(2), where F(2) equals 0.9772. Hence, 1 − 0.9772 = 0.0228.

17. **C** 1 − F(−1) = F(1) = 0.8413

18. **C** SFR = (18 − 4) / 40 is the largest value.

19. **A** SFR = (5 − 0) / 8 is the largest value.

20. **B** ln(23 / 20) = 0.1398

21. **B** A lognormally distributed variable is never negative.

22. **B** Monte Carlo simulation involves modeling asset prices or returns by generating random values for the risk factors that affect the price of a security.

23. **C** F(x) = 1 for all x > b. Remember F(x) is the cumulative probability, P(x < 20) here.

24. **B** With only two possible outcomes, there must be some positive probability for each. If this were not the case, the variable in question would not be a random variable, and a probability distribution would be meaningless. It does not matter if one of the possible outcomes happens to be zero.

25. **B** $\mu \pm 2\sigma$. Approximately 95% of the outcomes for a normally distributed random variable are within two standard deviations of the mean.

26. **A** $1 - F(2) = 1 - 0.9772 = 0.0228$.

27. **B** $\ln(2) = 0.6931$.

28. **A** Using the tables, the cdf for -1.3 is 9.68%, which is the probability of returns less than 2%.

ANSWERS – COMPREHENSIVE PROBLEMS

1. A. Using u for an up move and d for a down move, there are four possible outcomes (price paths) over two periods: uu, ud, du, and dd. Since ud and du result in the same price at the end of two periods ($8.50), there are three possible prices after two periods.

   B. An up-move factor of 1.05 means the down-move factor is 1 / 1.05. Therefore, the possible prices for each path are as follows:
   - uu: Price = $8.50(1.05)^2 = \$9.37$
   - ud: Price = $8.50(1.05)(1 / 1.05) = \$8.50$
   - du: Price = $8.50(1 / 1.05) (1.05) = \$8.50$
   - dd: Price = $8.50(1 / 1.05)^2 = \$7.71$

   C. For a 3-period model, there is no possible way that the up moves and down moves can exactly offset since the possibilities are: uuu, uud, udu, duu, ddu, dud, udd, ddd. The probability of a price of $8.50 is zero.

   D. $8.925 is the result of a single up move, 8.50(1.05) = 8.925. With three periods, this price could only result from two up moves and one down move (in any order). The probabilities of prices after n periods follow a binomial distribution. Define an up move as a success so that the probability of a success (p) is 0.60, the probability of an up move. The probability of two successes in three trials is $_3C_2 (0.6)^2 (1 - 0.6) = 43.2\%$. This calculation takes account of all three possible price paths that include two up moves and one down move: uud, udu, and duu.

   E. The price will be unchanged after six periods only if the price path includes three up moves and three down moves. The probability of three successes (up moves) in six trials is: $_6C_3 (0.6)^3 (1 - 0.6)^3 = 27.65\%$.

2. A. To construct a Monte Carlo simulation, the analyst would need to:

   1. Identify the distributions that the input variables follow and their means, variances, and any other relevant parameters, such as skewness.

   2. Generate random values from these distributions for both input variables.

   3. Price the option using the randomly generated inputs.

   4. Repeat steps 2 and 3 for many trials. Calculate the mean option price from all the trials. This value is the simulation's estimate of the option value.

B. Whether the results from a Monte Carlo simulation are useful depends on how well the analyst has specified the distributions of the interest rate and the stock price (the old, garbage in—garbage out problem). Also, the simulation results contain no information about whether the valuation model itself is valid.

C. The main advantages of historical simulation are that it uses actual historical values for the model inputs so that the analyst does not need to make assumptions about their probability distributions, and it is a less computer-intensive procedure. A disadvantage of historical simulation is that it assumes the past behavior of the variables is a reliable indicator of their future behavior, which might not be the case. Historical simulation also lacks the Monte Carlo approach's ability to model "what if" questions by changing the assumed probability distributions of the model inputs.

3. A. The 90% confidence interval is the mean ± 1.65 standard deviations.
   0.7 + 1.65(2.0) = 4.0%
   0.7 − 1.65(2.0) = −2.6%

   The 95% confidence interval is the mean ± 1.96 standard deviations.
   0.7 + 1.96(2.0) = 4.62%
   0.7 − 1.96(2.0) = −3.22%

   The 99% confidence interval is the mean ± 2.58 standard deviations.
   0.7 + 2.58(2.0) = 5.86%
   0.7 − 2.58(2.0) = −4.46%

B. The lognormal distribution is skewed to the right, whereas the normal distribution is symmetrical. The lognormal distribution can only have positive values, whereas the normal distribution includes both positive and negative values. This property makes the lognormal distribution useful for modeling asset prices.

The following is a review of the Quantitative Methods: Application principles designed to address the learning outcome statements set forth by CFA Institute®. This topic is also covered in:

SAMPLING AND ESTIMATION

EXAM FOCUS

This topic review covers random samples and inferences about population means from sample data. It is essential that you know the central limit theorem, for it allows us to use sampling statistics to construct confidence intervals for point estimates of population means. Make sure you can calculate confidence intervals for population means given sample parameter estimates and a level of significance, and know when it is appropriate to use the *z*-statistic versus the *t*-statistic. You should also understand the basic procedures for creating random samples, and recognize the warning signs of various sampling biases from nonrandom samples.

APPLIED STATISTICS

In many real-world statistics applications, it is impractical (or impossible) to study an entire population. When this is the case, a subgroup of the population, called a sample, can be evaluated. Based upon this sample, the parameters of the underlying population can be estimated.

For example, rather than attempting to measure the performance of the U.S. stock market by observing the performance of all 10,000 or so stocks trading in the United States at any one time, the performance of the subgroup of 500 stocks in the S&P 500 can be measured. The results of the statistical analysis of this sample can then be used to draw conclusions about the entire population of U.S. stocks.

LOS 10.a: Define simple random sampling, sampling error, and a sampling distribution, and interpret sampling error.

Simple random sampling is a method of selecting a sample in such a way that each item or person in the population being studied has the same likelihood of being included in the sample. As an example of simple random sampling, assume that you want to draw a sample of five items out of a group of 50 items. This can be accomplished by numbering each of the 50 items, placing them in a hat, and shaking the hat. Next, one number can be drawn randomly from the hat. Repeating this process (experiment) four more times results in a set of five numbers. The five drawn numbers (items) comprise a simple random sample from the population. In applications like this one, a random-number table or a computer random-number generator is often used to create the sample. Another way to form an approximately random sample is **systematic sampling**, selecting every *n*th member from a population.

Sampling error is the difference between a sample statistic (the mean, variance, or standard deviation of the sample) and its corresponding population parameter (the true mean, variance, or standard deviation of the population). For example, the sampling error for the mean is as follows:

sampling error of the mean = sample mean – population mean = $\bar{x} - \mu$

A Sampling Distribution

It is important to recognize that the sample statistic itself is a random variable and, therefore, has a probability distribution. The **sampling distribution** of the sample statistic is a probability distribution of all possible sample statistics computed from a set of equal-size samples that were randomly drawn from the same population. Think of it as the probability distribution of a statistic from many samples.

For example, suppose a random sample of 100 bonds is selected from a population of a major municipal bond index consisting of 1,000 bonds, and then the mean return of the 100-bond sample is calculated. Repeating this process many times will result in many different estimates of the population mean return (i.e., one for each sample). The distribution of these estimates of the mean is the *sampling distribution of the mean*.

It is important to note that this sampling distribution is distinct from the distribution of the actual prices of the 1,000 bonds in the underlying population and will have different parameters.

LOS 10.b: Distinguish between simple random and stratified random sampling.

Stratified random sampling uses a classification system to separate the population into smaller groups based on one or more distinguishing characteristics. From each subgroup, or stratum, a random sample is taken and the results are pooled. The size of the samples from each stratum is based on the size of the stratum relative to the population.

Stratified sampling is often used in bond indexing because of the difficulty and cost of completely replicating the entire population of bonds. In this case, bonds in a population are categorized (stratified) according to major bond risk factors such as duration, maturity, coupon rate, and the like. Then samples are drawn from each separate category and combined to form a final sample.

To see how this works, suppose you want to construct a bond portfolio that is indexed to the major municipal bond index using a stratified random sampling approach. First, the entire population of 1,000 municipal bonds in the index can be classified on the basis of maturity and coupon rate. Then, cells (stratum) can be created for different maturity/coupon combinations, and random samples can be drawn from each of the maturity/coupon cells. To sample from a cell containing 50 bonds with 2- to 4-year maturities and coupon rates less than 5%, we would select 5 bonds. The number of bonds drawn from a given cell corresponds to the cell's weight relative to the population (index), or $(50/1000) \times (100) = 5$ bonds. This process is repeated for all of the maturity/coupon cells, and the individual samples are combined to form the portfolio.

©2009 Kaplan, Inc.

By using stratified sampling, we guarantee that we sample five bonds from this cell. If we had used simple random sampling, there would be no guarantee that we would sample any of the bonds in the cell. Or, we may have selected more than five bonds from this cell.

LOS 10.c: Distinguish between time-series and cross-sectional data.

Time-series data consist of observations taken *over a period of time* at specific and equally spaced time intervals. The set of monthly returns on Microsoft stock from January 1994 to January 2004 is an example of a time-series data sample.

Cross-sectional data are a sample of observations taken *at a single point in time*. The sample of reported earnings per share of all NASDAQ companies as of December 31, 2004, is an example of a cross-sectional data sample.

Time-series and cross-sectional data can be pooled in the same data set. **Longitudinal data** are observations over time of multiple characteristics of the same entity, such as unemployment, inflation, and GDP growth rates for a country over 10 years. **Panel data** contain observations over time of the same characteristic for multiple entities, such as debt/equity ratios for 20 companies over the most recent 24 quarters. Panel and longitudinal data are typically presented in table or spreadsheet form.

LOS 10.d: Interpret the central limit theorem and describe its importance.

The **central limit theorem** states that for simple random samples of size n from a *population* with a mean μ and a finite variance σ^2, the sampling distribution of the sample mean $\overline{x}$ approaches a normal probability distribution with mean μ and a variance equal to $\dfrac{\sigma^2}{n}$ as the sample size becomes large.

The central limit theorem is extremely useful because the normal distribution is relatively easy to apply to hypothesis testing and to the construction of confidence intervals. Specific inferences about the population mean can be made from the sample mean, *regardless of the population's distribution*, as long as the sample size is "sufficiently large," which usually means $n \geq 30$.

Important properties of the central limit theorem include the following:

- If the sample size n is sufficiently large ($n \geq 30$), the sampling distribution of the sample means will be approximately normal. Remember what's going on here, random samples of size n are repeatedly being taken from an overall larger population. Each of these random samples has its own mean, which is itself a random variable, and this set of sample means has a distribution that is approximately normal.
- The mean of the population, μ, and the mean of the distribution of all possible sample means are equal.
- The variance of the distribution of sample means is $\dfrac{\sigma^2}{n}$, the population variance divided by the sample size.

LOS 10.e: Calculate and interpret the standard error of the sample mean.

The **standard error of the sample mean** is the standard deviation of the distribution of the sample means.

When the standard deviation of the population, σ, is *known*, the standard error of the sample mean is calculated as:

$$\sigma_{\overline{x}} = \frac{\sigma}{\sqrt{n}}$$

where:

$\sigma_{\overline{x}}$ = standard error of the sample mean

σ = standard deviation of the population

n = size of the sample

Example: Standard error of sample mean (known population variance)

The mean hourly wage for Iowa farm workers is $13.50 with a *population standard deviation* of $2.90. Calculate and interpret the standard error of the sample mean for a sample size of 30.

Answer:

Because the population standard deviation, σ, *is known*, the standard error of the sample mean is expressed as:

$$\sigma_{\overline{x}} = \frac{\sigma}{\sqrt{n}} = \frac{\$2.90}{\sqrt{30}} = \$0.53$$

Professor's Note: On the TI BAII Plus, the use of the square root key is obvious. On the HP 12C, the square root of 30 is computed as: [30] [g] [$\sqrt{x}$].

This means that if we were to take all possible samples of size 30 from the Iowa farm worker population and prepare a sampling distribution of the sample means, we would get a distribution with a mean of $13.50 and standard error of $0.53.

Practically speaking, the *population's standard deviation is almost never known*. Instead, the standard error of the sample mean must be estimated by dividing the standard deviation of *the sample* mean by $\sqrt{n}$:

$$s_{\overline{x}} = \frac{s}{\sqrt{n}}$$

Example: Standard error of sample mean (unknown population variance)

Suppose a sample contains the past 30 monthly returns for McCreary, Inc. The mean return is 2% and the *sample* standard deviation is 20%. Calculate and interpret the standard error of the sample mean.

Answer:

Since σ is unknown, the standard error of the sample mean is:

$$s_{\overline{x}} = \frac{s}{\sqrt{n}} = \frac{20\%}{\sqrt{30}} = 3.6\%$$

This implies that if we took all possible samples of size 30 from McCreary's monthly returns and prepared a sampling distribution of the sample means, the mean would be 2% with a standard error of 3.6%.

Example: Standard error of sample mean (unknown population variance)

Continuing with our example, suppose that instead of a sample size of 30, we take a sample of the past 200 monthly returns for McCreary, Inc. In order to highlight the effect of sample size on the sample standard error, let's assume that the mean return and standard deviation of this larger sample remain at 2% and 20%, respectively. Now, calculate the standard error of the sample mean for the 200-return sample.

Answer:

The standard error of the sample mean is computed as:

$$s_{\overline{x}} = \frac{s}{\sqrt{n}} = \frac{20\%}{\sqrt{200}} = 1.4\%$$

The result of the preceding two examples illustrates an important property of sampling distributions. Notice that the value of the standard error of the sample mean decreased from 3.6% to 1.4% as the sample size increased from 30 to 200. This is because as the sample size increases, the sample mean gets closer, on average, to the true mean of the population. In other words, the distribution of the sample means about the population mean gets smaller and smaller, so the standard error of the sample mean decreases.

Professor's Note: I get a lot of questions about when to use σ and σ/√n . Just remember that the standard deviation of the mean of many observations is less than the standard deviation of a single observation. If the standard deviation of monthly stock returns is 2%, the standard error (deviation) of the average monthly return over the next six months is 2%/√6 = 0.82%. The average of several observations of a random variable will be less widely dispersed (have lower standard deviation) around the expected value than will a single observation of the random variable.

LOS 10.f: Distinguish between a point estimate and a confidence interval estimate of a population parameter.

LOS 10.h: Explain the construction of confidence intervals.

Point estimates are single (sample) values used to estimate population parameters. The formula used to compute the point estimate is called the estimator. For example, the sample mean, $\bar{x}$, is an estimator of the population mean μ and is computed using the familiar formula:

$$\bar{x} = \frac{\sum x}{n}$$

The value generated with this calculation for a given sample is called the *point estimate* of the mean.

Confidence interval estimates result in a range of values within which the actual value of a parameter will lie, given the probability of $1 - \alpha$. Here, alpha, α, is called the *level of significance* for the confidence interval, and the probability $1 - \alpha$ is referred to as the *degree of confidence*. For example, we might estimate that the population mean of random variables will range from 15 to 25 with a 95% degree of confidence, or at the 5% level of significance.

Confidence intervals are usually constructed by adding or subtracting an appropriate value from the point estimate. In general, confidence intervals take on the following form:

point estimate ± (reliability factor × standard error)

where:
point estimate = value of a sample statistic of the population parameter
reliability factor = number that depends on the sampling distribution of the point estimate and the probability that the point estimate falls in the confidence interval, $(1 - \alpha)$
standard error = standard error of the point estimate

LOS 10.g: Identify and describe the desirable properties of an estimator.

Regardless of whether we are concerned with point estimates or confidence intervals, there are certain statistical properties that make some estimates more desirable than others. These **desirable properties of an estimator** are **unbiasedness**, **efficiency**, and **consistency**.

- An *unbiased* estimator is one for which the expected value of the estimator is equal to the parameter you are trying to estimate. For example, because the expected value of the sample mean is equal to the population mean $\left[E(\bar{x}) = \mu \right]$, the sample mean is an unbiased estimator of the population mean.

- An unbiased estimator is also *efficient* if the variance of its sampling distribution is smaller than all the other unbiased estimators of the parameter you are trying to estimate. The sample mean, for example, is an unbiased and efficient estimator of the population mean.

- A *consistent* estimator is one for which the accuracy of the parameter estimate increases as the sample size increases. As the sample size increases, the standard error of the sample mean falls, and the sampling distribution bunches more closely around the population mean. In fact, as the sample size approaches infinity, the standard error approaches zero.

LOS 10.i: Describe the properties of Student's *t*-distribution and calculate and interpret its degrees of freedom.

Student's *t*-distribution, or simply the *t*-distribution, is a bell-shaped probability distribution that is symmetrical about its mean. It is the appropriate distribution to use when constructing confidence intervals based on *small samples* (n < 30) from populations with *unknown variance* and a normal, or approximately normal, distribution. It may also be appropriate to use the *t*-distribution when the population variance is unknown and the sample size is large enough that the central limit theorem will assure that the sampling distribution is approximately normal.

Student's *t*-distribution has the following properties:

- It is symmetrical.
- It is defined by a single parameter, the **degrees of freedom** (df), where the degrees of freedom are equal to the number of sample observations minus 1, n – 1, for sample means.
- It has more probability in the tails ("fatter tails") than the normal distribution.
- As the degrees of freedom (the sample size) gets larger, the shape of the *t*-distribution more closely approaches a standard normal distribution.

When *compared to the normal distribution*, the *t*-distribution is flatter with more area under the tails (i.e., it has fatter tails). As the degrees of freedom for the *t*-distribution increase, however, its shape approaches that of the normal distribution.

The degrees of freedom for tests based on sample means are n – 1 because, given the mean, only n – 1 observations can be unique.

The *t*-distribution is a symmetrical distribution that is centered about zero. The shape of the *t*-distribution is dependent on the number of degrees of freedom, and degrees of freedom are based on the number of sample observations. The *t*-distribution is flatter and has thicker tails than the standard normal distribution. As the number of observations increases (i.e., the degrees of freedom increase), the *t*-distribution becomes more spiked and its tails become thinner. As the number of degrees of freedom increases without bound, the *t*-distribution converges to the standard normal distribution (*z*-distribution). The thickness of the tails relative to those of the *z*-distribution is important in hypothesis testing because thicker tails mean more observations away from the center of the distribution (i.e., more "outliers"). Hence, hypothesis testing using the *t*-distribution makes it more difficult to reject the null relative to hypothesis testing using the *z*-distribution.

The table in Figure 1 contains one-tailed critical values for the t-distribution at the 0.05 and 0.025 levels of significance with various degrees of freedom (df). Note that, unlike the z-table, the t-values are contained within the table, and the probabilities are located at the column headings. Also note that the level of significance of a t-test corresponds to the *one-tailed probabilities*, p, that head the columns in the t-table.

Figure 2 illustrates the different shapes of the t-distribution associated with different degrees of freedom. The tendency is for the t-distribution to become more peaked and to look more and more like the normal distribution as the degrees of freedom increase. Practically speaking, the greater the degrees of freedom, the greater the percentage of observations near the center of the distribution and the lower the percentage of observations in the tails, which are thinner as degrees of freedom increase. This means that confidence intervals for a random variable that follows a t-distribution must be wider (narrower) when the degrees of freedom are less (more) for a given significance level.

Figure 1: Table of Critical t-Values

df	One-Tailed Probabilities, p	
	$p = 0.05$	$p = 0.025$
5	2.015	2.571
10	1.812	2.228
15	1.753	2.131
20	1.725	2.086
25	1.708	2.060
30	1.697	2.042
40	1.684	2.021
50	1.676	2.009
60	1.671	2.000
70	1.667	1.994
80	1.664	1.990
90	1.662	1.987
100	1.660	1.984
120	1.658	1.980
∞	1.645	1.960

Figure 2: t-Distributions for Different Degrees of Freedom (df)

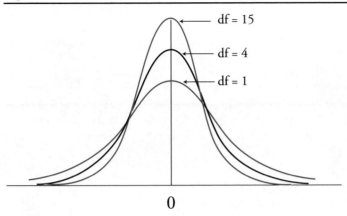

LOS 10.j: Calculate and interpret a confidence interval for a population mean, given a normal distribution with 1) a known population variance, 2) an unknown population variance, or 3) an unknown variance and a large sample size.

If the population has a *normal distribution with a known variance*, a **confidence interval for the population mean** can be calculated as:

$$\bar{x} \pm z_{\alpha/2} \frac{\sigma}{\sqrt{n}}$$

where:

$\bar{x}$ = *point estimate* of the population mean (sample mean).

$z_{\alpha/2}$ = *reliability factor*, a standard normal random variable for which the probability in the right-hand tail of the distribution is $\alpha/2$. In other words, this is the *z*-score that leaves $\alpha/2$ of probability in the upper tail.

$\frac{\sigma}{\sqrt{n}}$ = the *standard error* of the sample mean where σ is the known standard deviation of the population, and *n* is the sample size.

The most commonly used standard normal distribution reliability factors are:

$z_{\alpha/2}$ = 1.645 for 90% confidence intervals (the significance level is 10%, 5% in each tail).

$z_{\alpha/2}$ = 1.960 for 95% confidence intervals (the significance level is 5%, 2.5% in each tail).

$z_{\alpha/2}$ = 2.575 for 99% confidence intervals (the significance level is 1%, 0.5% in each tail).

Do these numbers look familiar? They should! In our review of common probability distributions, we found the probability under the standard normal curve between z = −1.96 and z = +1.96 to be 0.95, or 95%. Owing to symmetry, this leaves a probability of 0.025 under each tail of the curve beyond z = −1.96 of z = +1.96, for a total of 0.05, or 5%—just what we need for a significance level of 0.05, or 5%.

Example: Confidence interval

Consider a practice exam that was administered to 36 Level 1 candidates. The mean score on this practice exam was 80. Assuming a population standard deviation equal to 15, construct and interpret a 99% confidence interval for the mean score on the practice exam for 36 candidates. *Note that in this example the population standard deviation is known, so we don't have to estimate it.*

Answer:

At a confidence level of 99%, $z_{\alpha/2} = z_{0.005} = 2.58$. So, the 99% confidence interval is calculated as follows:

$$\bar{x} \pm z_{\alpha/2} \frac{\sigma}{\sqrt{n}} = 80 \pm 2.58 \frac{15}{\sqrt{36}} = 80 \pm 6.45$$

Thus, the 99% confidence interval ranges from 73.55 to 86.45.

Confidence intervals can be interpreted from a probabilistic perspective or a practical perspective. With regard to the outcome of the CFA® practice exam example, these two perspectives can be described as follows:

- *Probabilistic interpretation.* After repeatedly taking samples of CFA candidates, administering the practice exam, and constructing confidence intervals for each sample's mean, 99% of the resulting confidence intervals will, in the long run, include the population mean.
- *Practical interpretation.* We are 99% confident that the population mean score is between 73.55 and 86.45 for candidates from this population.

Confidence Intervals for the Population Mean: Normal With Unknown Variance

If the distribution of the *population is normal with unknown variance*, we can use the *t*-distribution to construct a confidence interval:

$$\bar{x} \pm t_{\alpha/2} \frac{s}{\sqrt{n}}$$

where:

$\bar{x}$ = the point estimate of the population mean

$t_{\alpha/2}$ = the *t*-reliability factor (a.k.a. *t*-statistic or critical *t*-value) corresponding to a *t*-distributed random variable with n − 1 degrees of freedom, where *n* is the sample size. The area under the tail of the *t*-distribution to the right of $t_{\alpha/2}$ is $\alpha/2$

$\frac{s}{\sqrt{n}}$ = standard error of the sample mean.

s = sample standard deviation.

Unlike the standard normal distribution, the reliability factors for the *t*-distribution depend on the sample size, so we can't rely on a commonly used set of reliability factors. Instead, reliability factors for the *t*-distribution have to be looked up in a table of Student's *t*-distribution, like the one at the back of this book.

Owing to the relatively fatter tails of the *t*-distribution, confidence intervals constructed using *t*-reliability factors ($t_{\alpha/2}$) will be more conservative (wider) than those constructed using *z*-reliability factors ($z_{\alpha/2}$).

Example: Confidence intervals

Let's return to the McCreary, Inc. example. Recall that we took a sample of the past 30 monthly stock returns for McCreary, Inc. and determined that the mean return was 2% and the sample standard deviation was 20%. Since the population variance is unknown, the standard error of the sample was estimated to be:

$$s_{\overline{x}} = \frac{s}{\sqrt{n}} = \frac{20\%}{\sqrt{30}} = 3.6\%$$

Now, let's construct a 95% confidence interval for the mean monthly return.

Answer:

Here we will use the *t*-reliability factor because the population variance is unknown. Since there are 30 observations, the degrees of freedom are 29 = 30 − 1. Remember, because this is a two-tailed test at the 95% confidence level, the probability under each tail must be $\alpha/2 = 2.5\%$, for a total of 5%. So, referencing the one-tailed probabilities for Student's *t*-distribution at the back of this book, we find the critical *t*-value (reliability factor) for $\alpha/2 = 0.025$ and df = 29 to be $t_{29,\ 2.5} = 2.045$. Thus, the 95% confidence interval for the population mean is:

$$2\% \pm 2.045 \left(\frac{20\%}{\sqrt{30}} \right) = 2\% \pm 2.045(3.6\%) = 2\% \pm 7.4\%$$

Thus, the 95% confidence has a lower limit of −5.4% and an upper limit of +9.4%.

We can interpret this confidence interval by saying that we are 95% confident that the population mean monthly return for McCreary stock is between −5.4% and +9.4%.

Professor's Note: You should practice looking up reliability factors (a.k.a. critical t-values or t-statistics) in a t-table. The first step is always to compute the degrees of freedom, which is n − 1. The second step is to find the appropriate level of alpha or significance. This depends on whether the test you're concerned with is one-tailed (use α) or two-tailed (use $\alpha/2$). In this review, our tests will always be two-tailed because confidence intervals are designed to compute an upper and lower limit. Thus, we will use $\alpha/2$. To look up $t_{29,\ 2.5}$, find the 29 df row and match it with the 0.025 column; t = 2.045 is the result. We'll do more of this in our study of hypothesis testing.

Confidence Interval for a Population Mean When the Population Variance Is Unknown Given a Large Sample From Any Type of Distribution

We now know that the *z*-statistic should be used to construct confidence intervals when the population distribution is normal and the variance is known, and the *t*-statistic should be used when the distribution is normal but the variance is unknown. But what do we do when the distribution is *nonnormal*?

As it turns out, the size of the sample influences whether or not we can construct the appropriate confidence interval for the sample mean.

- If the *distribution is nonnormal* but the *population variance is known*, the *z*-statistic can be used as long as the sample size is large ($n \geq 30$). We can do this because the central limit theorem assures us that the distribution of the sample mean is approximately normal when the sample is large.
- If the *distribution is nonnormal* and the *population variance is unknown*, the *t*-statistic can be used as long as the sample size is large ($n \geq 30$). It is also acceptable to use the *z*-statistic, although use of the *t*-statistic is more conservative.

This means that if we are sampling from a nonnormal distribution (which is sometimes the case in finance), *we cannot create a confidence interval if the sample size is less than 30.* So, all else equal, make sure you have a sample of at least 30, and the larger, the better.

Figure 3 summarizes this discussion.

 Professor's Note: You should commit the criteria in this table to memory.

Figure 3: Criteria for Selecting the Appropriate Test Statistic

	Test Statistic	
When sampling from a:	*Small Sample (n < 30)*	*Large Sample (n ≥ 30)*
Normal distribution with *known* variance	*z*-statistic	*z*-statistic
Normal distribution with *unknown* variance	*t*-statistic	*t*-statistic*
Nonnormal distribution with *known* variance	not available	*z*-statistic
Nonnormal distribution with *unknown* variance	not available	*t*-statistic*

* The *z*-statistic is theoretically acceptable here, but use of the *t*-statistic is more conservative.

All of the preceding analysis depends on the sample we draw from the population being random. If the sample isn't random, the central limit theorem doesn't apply, our estimates won't have the desirable properties, and we can't form unbiased confidence intervals. Surprisingly, creating a *random sample* is not as easy as one might believe. There are a number of potential mistakes in sampling methods that can bias the results.

These biases are particularly problematic in financial research, where available historical data are plentiful, but the creation of new sample data by experimentation is restricted.

LOS 10.k: Discuss the issues regarding selection of the appropriate sample size, data-mining bias, sample selection bias, survivorship bias, look-ahead bias, and time-period bias.

We have seen so far that a larger sample reduces the sampling error and the standard deviation of the sample statistic around its true (population) value. Confidence intervals are narrower when samples are larger and the standard errors of the point estimates of population parameters are less.

There are two limitations on this idea of "larger is better" when it comes to selecting an appropriate sample size. One is that larger samples may contain observations from a different population (distribution). If we include observations which come from a different population (one with a different population parameter), we will not necessarily improve, and may even reduce, the precision of our population parameter estimates. The other consideration is cost. The costs of using a larger sample must be weighed against the value of the increase in precision from the increase in sample size. Both of these factors suggest that the largest possible sample size is not always the most appropriate choice.

Data-Mining Bias, Sample Selection Bias, Survivorship Bias, Look-Ahead Bias, and Time-Period Bias

Data mining occurs when analysts repeatedly use the same database to search for patterns or trading rules until one that "works" is discovered. For example, empirical research has provided evidence that value stocks appear to outperform growth stocks. Some researchers argue that this anomaly is actually the product of data mining. Because the data set of historical stock returns is quite limited, it is difficult to know for sure whether the difference between value and growth stock returns is a true economic phenomenon, or simply a chance pattern that was stumbled upon after repeatedly looking for any identifiable pattern in the data.

Data-mining bias refers to results where the statistical significance of the pattern is overestimated because the results were found through data mining.

When reading research findings that suggest a profitable trading strategy, make sure you heed the following warning signs of data mining:

- Evidence that many different variables were tested, most of which are unreported, until significant ones were found.
- The lack of any economic theory that is consistent with the empirical results.

The best way to avoid data mining is to test a potentially profitable trading rule on a data set different from the one you used to develop the rule (i.e., use out-of-sample data).

Sample selection bias occurs when some data is systematically excluded from the analysis, usually because of the lack of availability. This practice renders the observed sample to be nonrandom, and any conclusions drawn from this sample can't be applied to the population because the observed sample and the portion of the population that was not observed are different.

Survivorship bias is the most common form of sample selection bias. A good example of the existence of survivorship bias in investments is the study of mutual fund performance. Most mutual fund databases, like Morningstar®'s, only include funds currently in existence—the "survivors." They do not include funds that have ceased to exist due to closure or merger.

This would not be a problem if the characteristics of the surviving funds and the missing funds were the same; then the sample of survivor funds would still be a random sample drawn from the population of mutual funds. As one would expect, however, and as evidence has shown, the funds that are dropped from the sample have lower returns relative to the surviving funds. Thus, the surviving sample is biased toward the better funds (i.e., it is not random). The analysis of a mutual fund sample with survivorship bias will yield results that overestimate the average mutual fund return because the database only includes the better-performing funds. The solution to survivorship bias is to use a sample of funds that all started at the same time and not drop funds that have been dropped from the sample.

Look-ahead bias occurs when a study tests a relationship using sample data that was not available on the test date. For example, consider the test of a trading rule that is based on the price-to-book ratio at the end of the fiscal year. Stock prices are available for all companies at the same point in time, while end-of-year book values may not be available until 30 to 60 days after the fiscal year ends. In order to account for this bias, a study that uses price-to-book value ratios to test trading strategies might estimate the book value as reported at fiscal year end and the market value two months later.

Time-period bias can result if the time period over which the data is gathered is either too short or too long. If the time period is too short, research results may reflect phenomena specific to that time period, or perhaps even data mining. If the time period is too long, the fundamental economic relationships that underlie the results may have changed.

For example, research findings may indicate that small stocks outperformed large stocks during 1980–1985. This may well be the result of time-period bias—in this case, using too short a time period. It's not clear whether this relationship will continue in the future or if it is just an isolated occurrence.

On the other hand, a study that quantifies the relationship between inflation and unemployment (the Phillips Curve) during the period from 1940–2000 will also result in time-period bias—because this period is too long, and it covers a fundamental change in the relationship between inflation and unemployment that occurred in the 1980s. In this case, the data should be divided into two subsamples that span the period before and after the change.

KEY CONCEPTS

LOS 10.a

Simple random sampling is a method of selecting a sample in such a way that each item or person in the population being studied has the same probability of being included in the sample.

Sampling error is the difference between a sample statistic and its corresponding population parameter (e.g., the sample mean minus the population mean).

A sampling distribution is the distribution of all values that a sample statistic can take on when computed from samples of identical size randomly drawn from the same population.

LOS 10.b

Stratified random sampling involves randomly selecting samples proportionally from subgroups that are formed based on one or more distinguishing characteristics, so that the sample will have the same distribution of these characteristics as the overall population.

LOS 10.c

Time-series data consists of observations taken at specific and equally spaced points in time.

Cross-sectional data consists of observations taken at a single point in time.

LOS 10.d

The central limit theorem states that for a population with a mean μ and a finite variance σ^2, the sampling distribution of the sample mean of all possible samples of size n (for $n \geq 30$) will be approximately normally distributed with a mean equal to μ and a variance equal to σ^2/n.

LOS 10.e

The standard error of the sample mean is the standard deviation of the distribution of the sample means and is calculated as $\sigma_{\bar{X}} = \dfrac{\sigma}{\sqrt{n}}$, where σ, the population standard deviation, is known, and as $s_{\bar{x}} = \dfrac{s}{\sqrt{n}}$, where s, the sample standard deviation, is used because the population standard deviation is unknown.

LOS 10.f

Point estimates are single value estimates of population parameters. An estimator is a formula used to compute a point estimate.

Confidence intervals are ranges of values, within which the actual value of the parameter will lie with a given probability.

LOS 10.g

Desirable statistical properties of an estimator include unbiasedness (sign of estimation error is random), efficiency (lower sampling error than any other unbiased estimator), and consistency (variance of sampling error decreases with sample size).

LOS 10.h

A confidence interval for the true parameter is the point estimate plus or minus a number of standard deviations (of the sampling error), based on the degree of confidence specified.

confidence interval = point estimate ± (reliability factor × standard error)

The reliability factor is a number that depends on the sampling distribution of the point estimate and the probability that the point estimate falls in the confidence interval.

LOS 10.i

The *t*-distribution is similar, but not identical, to the normal distribution in shape—it is defined by the degrees of freedom and has fatter tails compared to the normal distribution.

Degrees of freedom for the *t*-distribution are equal to n − 1. Student's *t*-distribution is closer to the normal distribution when df is greater, and confidence intervals are narrower when df is greater.

LOS 10.j

For a normally distributed population, a confidence interval for its mean can be constructed using a *z*-statistic when variance is known, and a *t*-statistic when the variance is unknown. The *z*-statistic is acceptable in the case of a normal population with an unknown variance if the sample size is large (30+).

In general, we have:

- $\bar{X} \pm Z_{\alpha/2} \dfrac{\sigma}{\sqrt{n}}$ when the variance is known, and
- $\bar{X} \pm t_{\alpha/2} \dfrac{s}{\sqrt{n}}$ when the variance is unknown and the sample standard deviation

  must be used.

LOS 10.k

Increasing the sample size will generally improve parameter estimates and narrow confidence intervals. The cost of more data must be weighed against these benefits, and adding data that is not generated by the same distribution will not necessarily improve accuracy or narrow confidence intervals.

Potential mistakes in the sampling method can bias results. These biases include data mining (significant relationships that have occurred by chance), sample selection bias (selection is non-random), look-ahead bias (basing the test at a point in time on data not available at that time), survivorship bias (using only surviving mutual funds, hedge funds, etc.), and time-period bias (the relation does not hold over other time periods).

CONCEPT CHECKERS

1. A simple random sample is a sample drawn in such a way that each member of the population has:
    A. some chance of being selected in the sample.
    B. an equal chance of being included in the sample.
    C. a 1% chance of being included in the sample.

2. Sampling error is defined as:
    A. an error that occurs when a sample of less than 30 elements is drawn.
    B. an error that occurs during collection, recording, and tabulation of data.
    C. the difference between the value of a sample statistic and the value of the corresponding population parameter.

3. The mean age of all CFA candidates is 28 years. The mean age of a random sample of 100 candidates is found to be 26.5 years. The difference, 28 – 26.5 = 1.5, is called the:
    A. random error.
    B. sampling error.
    C. population error.

4. If n is large and the population standard deviation is unknown, the standard error of the sampling distribution of the sample mean is *equal* to the:
    A. sample standard deviation divided by the sample size.
    B. population standard deviation multiplied by the sample size.
    C. sample standard deviation divided by the square root of the sample size.

5. The standard error of the sampling distribution of the sample mean for a sample size of n drawn from a population with a mean of μ and a standard deviation of σ is:
    A. sample standard deviation divided by the sample size.
    B. sample standard deviation divided by the square root of the sample size.
    C. population standard deviation divided by the square root of the sample size.

6. To apply the central limit theorem to the sampling distribution of the sample mean, the sample is usually considered to be large if n is *greater* than:
    A. 20.
    B. 25.
    C. 30.

7. Assume that a population has a mean of 14 with a standard deviation of 2. If a random sample of 49 observations is drawn from this population, the standard error of the sample mean is *closest* to:
    A. 0.04.
    B. 0.29.
    C. 2.00.

8.   The population's mean is 30 and the mean of a sample of size 100 is 28.5. The variance of the sample is 25. The standard error of the sample mean is *closest* to:
A. 0.05.
B. 0.25.
C. 0.50.

9.   A random sample of 100 computer store customers spent an average of $75 at the store. Assuming the distribution is normal and the population standard deviation is $20, the 95% confidence interval for the population mean is *closest* to:
A. $71.08 to $78.92.
B. $73.89 to $80.11.
C. $74.56 to $79.44.

10.   Best Computers, Inc., sells computers and computer parts by mail. A sample of 25 recent orders showed the mean time taken to ship out these orders was 70 hours with a sample standard deviation of 14 hours. Assuming the population is normally distributed, the 99% confidence interval for the population mean is:
A. 70 ± 2.80 hours.
B. 70 ± 6.98 hours.
C. 70 ± 7.83 hours.

11.   The sampling distribution of a statistic is the probability distribution made up of all possible:
A. observations from the underlying population.
B. sample statistics computed from samples of varying sizes drawn from the same population.
C. sample statistics computed from samples of the same size drawn from the same population.

12.   The sample of debt/equity ratios of 25 publicly traded U.S. banks as of fiscal year-end 2003 is an example of:
A. a point estimate.
B. cross-sectional data.
C. a stratified random sample.

13.   Which of the following is *least likely* a desirable property of an estimate?
A. Reliability.
B. Efficiency.
C. Consistency.

14.   If the variance of the sampling distribution of an estimator is smaller than all other unbiased estimators of the parameter of interest, the estimator is:
A. efficient.
B. unbiased.
C. consistent.

15. Which of the following is *least likely* a property of Student's *t*-distribution?
    A. As the degrees of freedom get larger, the variance approaches zero.
    B. It is defined by a single parameter, the degrees of freedom, which is equal to n − 1.
    C. It has more probability in the tails and less at the peak than a standard normal distribution.

16. An analyst who uses historical data that was not publicly available at the time period being studied will have a sample with:
    A. look-ahead bias.
    B. time-period bias.
    C. sample selection bias.

17. The 95% confidence interval of the sample mean of employee age for a major corporation is 19 years to 44 years based on a *z*-statistic. The population of employees is more than 5,000 and the sample size of this test is 100. Assuming the population is normally distributed, the standard error of mean employee age is *closest* to:
    A. 1.96.
    B. 2.58.
    C. 6.38.

18. Which of the following is *most closely* associated with survivorship bias?
    A. Price-to-book studies.
    B. Stratified bond sampling studies.
    C. Mutual fund performance studies.

19. What is the *most appropriate* test statistic for constructing confidence intervals for the population mean when the population is normally distributed, but the variance is unknown?
    A. The *z*-statistic at α with *n* degrees of freedom.
    B. The *t*-statistic at α/2 with *n* degrees of freedom.
    C. The *t*-statistic at α/2 with n − 1 degrees of freedom.

20. The *acceptable* test statistic for constructing confidence intervals for the population mean of a nonnormal distribution when the population variance is unknown and the sample size is large (n > 30) is the:
    A. *z*-statistic or the *t*-statistic.
    B. *z*-statistic at α with *n* degrees of freedom.
    C. *t*-statistic at α/2 with *n* degrees of freedom.

21. Jenny Fox evaluates managers who have a cross-sectional population standard deviation of returns of 8%. If returns are independent across managers, how large of a sample does Fox need so the standard error of sample means is 1.265%?
    A. 7.
    B. 30.
    C. 40.

22. Annual returns on small stocks have a population mean of 12% and a population standard deviation of 20%. If the returns are normally distributed, a 90% confidence interval on mean returns over a 5-year period is:
    A. 5.40% to 18.60%.
    B. −2.75% to 26.75%.
    C. −5.52% to 29.52%.

COMPREHENSIVE PROBLEMS

1. Using random sampling, a manager wants to construct a portfolio of 50 stocks that will approximate the returns of a broad market index that contains 200 stocks. Explain how he could use simple random sampling and stratified random sampling to select stocks from the index and the possible advantages of stratified random sampling.

2. An analyst has taken a random sample of 50 observations from a population for which she wants to estimate the population mean. She believes this population's distribution is negatively skewed.

   A. Can she use the sample mean to estimate the population mean and construct a confidence interval? Explain.

   B. What are the desirable statistical properties of an estimator?

   C. Which of these properties does the sample mean possess as an estimator of the population mean?

3. A random sample of analyst earnings estimates has a mean of $2.84 and a standard deviation of $0.40. What can we say about the 90% confidence interval for earnings next period if:

   A. the sample size is 20?

   B. the sample size is 40?

   What probabilistic statement could we make at the 90% confidence level:

   C. if the sample size were 15?

   D. if the sample size were 60?

ANSWERS – CONCEPT CHECKERS

1. **B** In a simple random sample, each element of the population has an equal probability of being selected. Choice C allows for an equal chance, but only if there are 100 elements in the population from which the random sample is drawn.

2. **C** An example might be the difference between a particular sample mean and the average value of the overall population.

3. **B** The sampling error is the difference between the population parameter and the sample statistic.

4. **C** The formula for the standard error when the population standard deviation is unknown is $s_{\bar{x}} = \dfrac{s}{\sqrt{n}}$.

5. **C** The formula for the standard error when the population standard deviation is known is $\sigma_{\bar{x}} = \dfrac{\sigma}{\sqrt{n}}$.

6. **C** By definition.

7. **B** $s_{\bar{X}} = \dfrac{s}{\sqrt{n}}$. Given $s = 2$, $s_{\bar{X}} = \dfrac{2}{\sqrt{49}} = \dfrac{2}{7} = 0.2857$.

8. **C** $s_{\bar{X}} = \dfrac{\sigma}{\sqrt{n}}$. Given $\sigma^2 = 25$, $s_{\bar{X}} = \dfrac{5}{\sqrt{100}} = \dfrac{5}{10} = 0.5$.

9. **A** Since the population variance is known and $n \geq 30$, the confidence interval is determined as $\bar{x} \pm z_{\alpha/2} (\sigma/\sqrt{n})$. $z_{\alpha/2} = z_{0.025} = 1.96$. So, the confidence interval is

   $75 \pm 1.96(20/10) = 75 \pm 3.92 = 71.08$ to 78.92.

10. **C** Since the population variance is unknown and $n < 30$, the confidence interval is determined as $\bar{x} \pm t_{\alpha/2} (s/\sqrt{n})$. Look up $t_{\alpha/2}$ and df $= n - 1$ to get critical *t-value*. $t_{0.01/2}$ and df $= 24$ is 2.797. So, the confidence interval is $70 \pm 2.797(14/5) = 70 \pm 7.83$.

11. **C** Suppose you have a population of 10,000 employees. If you take 100 samples of 50 employees each, the distribution of the 100 sample means is the sampling distribution.

12. **B** Cross-sectional data is a set of data that are all collected as of the same point in time.

13. **A** Efficiency, consistency, and unbiasedness are desirable properties of an estimator.

14. **A** By definition. Efficiency is a desirable property of an estimator.

15. **A** As the degrees of freedom get larger, the *t*-distribution approaches the normal distribution. As the degrees of freedom fall, the peak of the *t*-distribution flattens and its tails get fatter (more probability in the tails—that's why, all else the same, the critical *t* increases as the *df* decreases).

16. **A** The primary example of look-ahead bias is using year-end financial information in conjunction with market pricing data to compute ratios like the price/earnings, P/E. The E in the denominator is typically not available for 30-60 days after the end of the period. Hence, data that was available on the test date (P) is mixed with information that was not available (E). That is, the P is "ahead" of the E.

17. **C** At the 95% level of significance, with sample size n = 100 and mean 31.5 years, the appropriate test statistic is $z_{\alpha/2}$ = 1.96. *Note: The mean of 31.5 is calculated as the midpoint of the interval, or (19 + 44) / 2.* Thus, the confidence interval is $31.5 \pm 1.96\, s_{\bar{X}}$, where $s_{\bar{X}}$ is the standard error of the sample mean. If we take the upper bound, we know that $31.5 + 1.96\, s_{\bar{X}}$ = 44, or $1.96\, s_{\bar{X}}$ = 12.5, or $s_{\bar{X}}$ = 6.38 years.

18. **C** Mutual fund performance studies are most closely associated with survivorship bias because only the better-performing funds remain in the sample over time.

19. **C** Use the *t*-statistic at $\alpha/2$ and n – 1 degrees of freedom when the population variance is unknown. While the *z*-statistic is acceptable when the sample size is large, sample size is not given here, and the *t*-statistic is always appropriate under these conditions.

20. **A** When the sample size is large, and the central limit theorem can be relied upon to assure a sampling distribution that is normal, either the *t*-statistic or the *z*-statistic is acceptable for constructing confidence intervals for the population mean. The *t*-statistic, however, will provide a more conservative range (wider) at a given level of significance.

21. **C** $1.265 = \dfrac{8}{\sqrt{N}}, N = \left(\dfrac{8}{1.265}\right)^2 \approx 40$

22. **B** With a known population standard deviation of returns and a normally distributed population, we can use the *z*-distribution. The sample mean for a sample of five years will have a standard deviation of $\dfrac{20}{\sqrt{5}} = 8.94\%$. A 90% confidence interval around the mean return of 12% is $12\% \pm 1.65(8.94\%) = -2.75\%$ to 26.75%.

ANSWERS – COMPREHENSIVE PROBLEMS

1.   In simple random sampling, the analyst would select any 50 stocks using a process that gives each stock in the index an equal chance of being chosen.

      Stratified sampling involves dividing a population into subgroups based on key characteristics, selecting random samples from each subgroup in accordance with the proportion of the population contained in each subgroup, and pooling the results. For example, the analyst could divide the index stocks by capitalization and industry to form the subgroups, and then select stocks randomly from each subgroup. In this context, stratified random sampling has the advantage that the sample will have the same proportion of exposure to each industry and firms of, for example, large, small, and medium size. If these subgroups successfully capture different risk characteristics, tracking error for the portfolio relative to the index can be reduced.

2. **A.** She can use the sample mean to estimate the population mean. The central limit theorem states that for a large enough sample size n (typically more than 30) from a population with a mean μ and variance σ^2, the probability distribution for the sample mean will be approximately normal with mean μ and variance σ^2/n. The theorem allows

us to use the normal distribution to test hypotheses about the population mean, whether the population's distribution is normal or not.

B. An estimator should be:
- Unbiased—the expected value of the estimator should be equal to the population parameter.
- Efficient—the variance of its sampling distribution is smaller than that of all the other unbiased estimators of the parameter.
- Consistent—the standard error of the estimator should decrease as the sample size increases.

C. The sample mean has all of these properties.

3. A,B. This is a bit tricky. We have no direct information about the distribution of possible earnings for the next period. We have information about the distribution of analysts' estimates of next period earnings. Based on the information given, we can make no statement about the 90% confidence interval for earnings next period.

C. Since we cannot assume that the distribution of analyst estimates is normal, we cannot make any inferences about the mean of the population of analyst estimates with a sample size of only 15.

D. With a sample size of 60, we can make a statement about a confidence interval for the mean of the population of analyst estimates. The t-statistic for a 90% confidence interval with 59 degrees of freedom is approximated by using the value for 60 degrees of freedom, which is 1.671.

The confidence interval is $2.84 \pm 1.671\left(\dfrac{0.40}{\sqrt{60}}\right)$, or \$2.75 to \$2.93. We are 90%

confident the true mean of the population of analyst estimates is within this range.

HYPOTHESIS TESTING

EXAM FOCUS

This review addresses common hypothesis testing procedures. These procedures are used to conduct tests of population means, population variances, differences in means, differences in variances, and mean differences. Specific tests reviewed include the z-test, t-test, chi-square test, and F-test. You should know when and how to apply each of these. A standard hypothesis testing procedure is utilized in this review. Know it! You should be able to perform a hypothesis test on the value of the mean without being given any formulas. Confidence intervals, levels of significance, the power of a test, and types of hypothesis testing errors are also discussed. These are concepts you are likely to see on the exam. Don't worry about memorizing the messy formulas on testing for the equalities and differences in means and variances at the end of this review, but be able to interpret these statistics.

HYPOTHESIS TESTING

Hypothesis testing is the statistical assessment of a statement or idea regarding a population. For instance, a statement could be as follows: "The mean return for the U.S. equity market is greater than zero." Given the relevant returns data, hypothesis testing procedures can be employed to test the validity of this statement at a given significance level.

LOS 11.a: Define a hypothesis, describe the steps of hypothesis testing, interpret and discuss the choice of the null hypothesis and alternative hypothesis, and distinguish between one-tailed and two-tailed tests of hypotheses.

A hypothesis is a statement about the value of a population parameter developed for the purpose of testing a theory or belief. Hypotheses are stated in terms of the population parameter to be tested, like the population mean, μ. For example, a researcher may be interested in the mean daily return on stock options. Hence, the hypothesis may be that the mean daily return on a portfolio of stock options is positive.

Hypothesis testing procedures, based on sample statistics and probability theory, are used to determine whether a hypothesis is a reasonable statement and should not be rejected or if it is an unreasonable statement and should be rejected. The process of hypothesis testing consists of a series of steps shown in Figure 1.

Figure 1: Hypothesis Testing Procedure*

State the hypothesis

↓

Select the appropriate test statistic

↓

Specify the level of significance

↓

State the decision rule regarding the hypothesis

↓

Collect the sample and calculate the sample statistics

↓

Make a decision regarding the hypothesis

↓

Make a decision based on the results of the test

* *(Source:* Wayne W. Daniel and James C. Terrell, *Business Statistics, Basic Concepts and Methodology,* Houghton Mifflin, Boston, 1997.)

 Professor's Note: You should know this process!

The Null Hypothesis and Alternative Hypothesis

The **null hypothesis**, designated H_0, is the hypothesis that the researcher wants to reject. It is the hypothesis that is actually tested and is the basis for the selection of the test statistics. The null is generally stated as a simple statement about a population parameter. Typical statements of the null hypothesis for the population mean include $H_0: \mu = \mu_0$, $H_0: \mu \leq \mu_0$, and $H_0: \mu \geq \mu_0$, where μ is the population mean and μ_0 is the hypothesized value of the population mean.

 Professor's Note: The null hypothesis always includes the "equal to" condition.

The **alternative hypothesis**, designated H_a, is what is concluded if there is sufficient evidence to reject the null hypothesis. It is usually the alternative hypothesis that you are really trying to assess. Why? Since you can never really prove anything with statistics, when the null hypothesis is discredited, the implication is that the alternative hypothesis is valid.

One-Tailed and Two-Tailed Tests of Hypotheses

The alternative hypothesis can be one-sided or two-sided. A one-sided test is referred to as a **one-tailed test**, and a two-sided test is referred to as a **two-tailed test**. Whether the test is one- or two-sided depends on the proposition being tested. If a researcher wants to test whether the return on stock options is greater than zero, a one-tailed test should be used. However, a two-tailed test should be used if the research question is whether the return on options is simply different from zero. Two-sided tests allow for deviation on both sides of the hypothesized value (zero). In practice, most hypothesis tests are constructed as two-tailed tests.

A **two-tailed test** for the population mean may be structured as:

$H_0: \mu = \mu_0$ versus $H_a: \mu \neq \mu_0$

Since the alternative hypothesis allows for values above and below the hypothesized parameter, a two-tailed test uses two **critical values** (or **rejection points**).

The *general decision rule for a two-tailed test* is:

Reject H_0 if: test statistic > upper critical value or
test statistic < lower critical value

Let's look at the development of the decision rule for a two-tailed test using a *z*-distributed test statistic (a *z*-test) at a 5% level of significance, $\alpha = 0.05$.

- At $\alpha = 0.05$, the computed test statistic is compared with the critical *z*-values of ± 1.96. The values of ± 1.96 correspond to $\pm z_{\alpha/2} = \pm z_{0.025}$, which is the range of *z*-values within which 95% of the probability lies. These values are obtained from the cumulative probability table for the standard normal distribution (*z*-table), which is included at the back of this book.
- If the computed test statistic falls outside the range of critical *z*-values (i.e., test statistic > 1.96, or test statistic < −1.96), we reject the null and conclude that the sample statistic is sufficiently different from the hypothesized value.
- If the computed test statistic falls within the range ± 1.96, we conclude that the sample statistic is not sufficiently different from the hypothesized value ($\mu = \mu_0$ in this case), and we fail to reject the null hypothesis.

The *decision rule* (rejection rule) *for a two-tailed* z-test at $\alpha = 0.05$ can be stated as:

Reject H_0 if: test statistic < −1.96 or
test statistic > 1.96

Figure 2 shows the standard normal distribution for a two-tailed hypothesis test using the *z*-distribution. Notice that the significance level of 0.05 means that there is 0.05 / 2 = 0.025 probability (area) under each tail of the distribution beyond ±1.96.

Figure 2: Two-Tailed Hypothesis Test Using the Standard Normal (*z*) Distribution

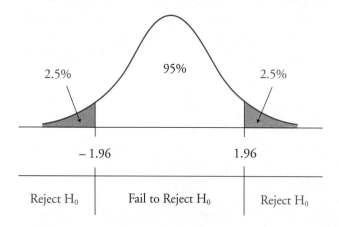

Professor's Note: The next two examples are extremely important. Don't move on until you understand them!

Example: Two-tailed test

A researcher has gathered data on the daily returns on a portfolio of call options over a recent 250-day period. The mean daily return has been 0.1%, and the sample standard deviation of daily portfolio returns is 0.25%. The researcher believes that the mean daily portfolio return is not equal to zero. Construct a hypothesis test of the researcher's belief.

Answer:

First we need to specify the null and alternative hypotheses. The null hypothesis is the one the researcher expects to reject.

$$H_0: \mu_0 = 0 \text{ versus } H_a: \mu_0 \neq 0$$

Since the null hypothesis is an equality, this is a two-tailed test. At a 5% level of significance, the critical z-values for a two-tailed test are ±1.96, so the decision rule can be stated as:

Reject H_0 if +1.96 < test statistic < −1.96

The *standard error* of the sample mean is the adjusted standard deviation of the sample. When the sample statistic is the sample mean, x, the standard error of the sample statistic for sample size n is calculated as:

$$s_{\bar{x}} = \frac{s}{\sqrt{n}}$$

Since our sample statistic here is a sample mean, the standard error of the sample mean for a sample size of 250 is $\frac{0.0025}{\sqrt{250}}$ and our test statistic is:

$$\frac{0.001}{\left(\frac{0.0025}{\sqrt{250}}\right)} = \frac{0.001}{0.000158} = 6.33$$

Since 6.33 > 1.96, we reject the null hypothesis that the mean daily option return is equal to zero. Note that when we reject the null, we conclude that the sample value is significantly different from the hypothesized value. We are saying that the two values are different from one another *after considering the variation in the sample*. That is, the mean daily return of 0.001 is statistically different from zero given the sample's standard deviation and size.

For a **one-tailed hypothesis test** of the population mean, the null and alternative hypotheses are either:

Upper tail: $H_0: \mu \le \mu_0$ versus $H_a: \mu > \mu_0$, or
Lower tail: $H_0: \mu \ge \mu_0$ versus $H_a: \mu < \mu_0$

The appropriate set of hypotheses depends on whether we believe the population mean, μ, to be greater than (upper tail) or less than (lower tail) the hypothesized value, μ_0. Using a z-test at the 5% level of significance, the computed test statistic is compared with the critical values of 1.645 for the upper tail tests (i.e., $H_a: \mu > \mu_0$) or –1.645 for lower tail tests (i.e., $H_a: \mu < \mu_0$). These critical values are obtained from a z-table, where $-z_{0.05} = -1.645$ corresponds to a cumulative probability equal to 5%, and the $z_{0.05} = 1.645$ corresponds to a cumulative probability of 95% (1 – 0.05).

Let's use the upper tail test structure where $H_0: \mu \le \mu_0$ and $H_a: \mu > \mu_0$.

- If the calculated test statistic is greater than 1.645, we conclude that the sample statistic is sufficiently greater than the hypothesized value. In other words, we reject the null hypothesis.
- If the calculated test statistic is less than 1.645, we conclude that the sample statistic is not sufficiently different from the hypothesized value, and we fail to reject the null hypothesis.

Figure 3 shows the standard normal distribution and the rejection region for a one-tailed test (upper tail) at the 5% level of significance.

Figure 3: One-Tailed Hypothesis Test Using the Standard Normal (z) Distribution

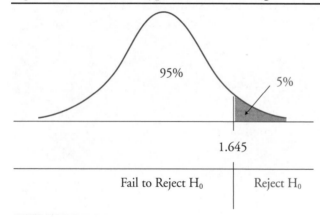

Example: One-tailed test

Perform a *z*-test using the option portfolio data from the previous example to test the belief that option returns are positive.

Answer:

In this case, we use a one-tailed test with the following structure:

H_0: $\mu \leq 0$ versus H_a: $\mu > 0$

The appropriate decision rule for this one-tailed *z*-test at a significance level of 5% is:

Reject H_0 if test statistic > 1.645

The test statistic is computed the same way, regardless of whether we are using a one-tailed or two-tailed test. From the previous example, we know that the test statistic for the option return sample is 6.33. Since 6.33 > 1.645, we reject the null hypothesis and conclude that mean returns are statistically greater than zero at a 5% level of significance.

The Choice of the Null and Alternative Hypotheses

The most common null hypothesis will be an "equal to" hypothesis. Combined with a "not equal to" alternative, this will require a two-tailed test. The alternative is often the hoped-for hypothesis. When the null is that a coefficient is equal to zero, we hope to reject it and show the significance of the relationship.

When the null is less than or equal to, the (mutually exclusive) alternative is framed as greater than, and a one-tail test is appropriate. If we are trying to demonstrate that a return is greater than the risk-free rate, this would be the correct formulation. We will have set up the null and alternative hypothesis so that rejection of the null will lead to acceptance of the alternative, our goal in performing the test.

LOS 11.b: Define and interpret a test statistic, a Type I and a Type II error, and a significance level, and explain how significance levels are used in hypothesis testing.

Hypothesis testing involves two statistics: the test statistic calculated from the sample data and the *critical value* of the test statistic. The value of the computed test statistic relative to the critical value is a key step in assessing the validity of a hypothesis.

A test statistic is calculated by comparing the point estimate of the population parameter with the hypothesized value of the parameter (i.e., the value specified in the null hypothesis). With reference to our option return example, this means we are concerned with the difference between the mean return of the sample (i.e., $\bar{x} = 0.001$) and the hypothesized mean return (i.e., $\mu_0 = 0$). As indicated in the following expression, the **test**

statistic is the difference between the sample statistic and the hypothesized value, scaled by the standard error of the sample statistic.

$$\text{test statistic} = \frac{\text{sample statistic} - \text{hypothesized value}}{\text{standard error of the sample statistic}}$$

The standard error of the sample statistic is the adjusted standard deviation of the sample. When the sample statistic is the sample mean, $\overline{x}$, the standard error of the sample statistic for sample size n, is calculated as:

$$\sigma_{\overline{x}} = \frac{\sigma}{\sqrt{n}}$$

when the population standard deviation, σ, *is known*, or

$$s_{\overline{x}} = \frac{s}{\sqrt{n}}$$

when the population standard deviation, σ, *is not known*. In this case, it is estimated using the standard deviation of the sample, *s*.

Professor's Note: Don't be confused by the notation here. A lot of the literature you will encounter in your studies simply uses the term $\sigma_{\overline{x}}$ for the standard error of the test statistic, regardless of whether the population standard deviation or sample standard deviation was used in its computation.

As you will soon see, a test statistic is a random variable that may follow one of several distributions, depending on the characteristics of the sample and the population. We will look at four distributions for test statistics: the *t*-distribution, the *z*-distribution (standard normal distribution), the chi-square distribution, and the *F*-distribution. The critical value for the appropriate test statistic—the value against which the computed test statistic is compared—depends on its distribution.

Type I and Type II Errors

Keep in mind that hypothesis testing is used to make inferences about the parameters of a given population on the basis of statistics computed for a sample that is drawn from that population. We must be aware that there is some probability that the sample, in some way, does not represent the population, and any conclusion based on the sample about the population may be made in error.

When drawing inferences from a hypothesis test, there are two types of errors:

- **Type I error**: the rejection of the null hypothesis when it is actually true.
- **Type II error**: the failure to reject the null hypothesis when it is actually false.

The **significance level** is the probability of making a Type I error (rejecting the null when it is true) and is designated by the Greek letter alpha (α). For instance, a significance level of 5% ($\alpha = 0.05$) means there is a 5% chance of rejecting a true null hypothesis. When conducting hypothesis tests, a significance level must be specified in order to identify the critical values needed to evaluate the test statistic.

LOS 11.c: Define and interpret a decision rule and the power of a test, and explain the relation between confidence intervals and hypothesis tests.

The decision for a hypothesis test is to either reject the null hypothesis or fail to reject the null hypothesis. Note that it is statistically incorrect to say "accept" the null hypothesis; it can only be supported or rejected. The **decision rule** for rejecting or failing to reject the null hypothesis is based on the distribution of the test statistic. For example, if the test statistic follows a normal distribution, the decision rule is based on critical values determined from the standard normal distribution (z-distribution). Regardless of the appropriate distribution, it must be determined if a one-tailed or two-tailed hypothesis test is appropriate before a decision rule (rejection rule) can be determined.

A decision rule is specific and quantitative. Once we have determined whether a one- or two-tailed test is appropriate, the significance level we require, and the distribution of the test statistic, we can calculate the exact critical value for the test statistic. Then we have a decision rule of the following form: if the test statistic is (greater, less than) the value X, reject the null.

The Power of a Test

While the significance level of a test is the probability of rejecting the null hypothesis when it is true, the **power of a test** is the probability of correctly rejecting the null hypothesis when it is false. The power of a test is actually one minus the probability of making a Type II error, or $1 - P(\text{Type II error})$. In other words, the probability of rejecting the null when it is false (power of the test) equals one minus the probability of *not* rejecting the null when it is false (Type II error). When more than one test statistic may be used, the power of the test for the competing test statistics may be useful in deciding which test statistic to use. Ordinarily, we wish to use the test statistic that provides the most powerful test among all possible tests.

Figure 4 shows the relationship between the level of significance, the power of a test, and the two types of errors.

Figure 4: Type I and Type II Errors in Hypothesis Testing

Decision	True Condition	
	H_0 is true	H_0 is false
Do not reject H_0	Correct decision	Incorrect decision **Type II error**
Reject H_0	Incorrect decision **Type I error** Significance level, α, = P(Type I error)	Correct decision Power of the test = 1 -- P(Type II error)

Sample size and the choice of significance level (Type I error probability) will together determine the probability of a Type II error. The relation is not simple, however, and calculating the probability of a Type II error in practice is quite difficult. Decreasing the significance level (probability of a Type I error) from 5% to 1%, for example, will increase the probability of failing to reject a false null (Type II error) and therefore reduce the power of the test. Conversely, for a given sample size, we can increase the power of a test only with the cost that the probability of rejecting a true null (Type I error) increases. For a given significance level, we can decrease the probability of a Type II error and increase the power of a test, only by increasing the sample size.

The Relation Between Confidence Intervals and Hypothesis Tests

A confidence interval is a range of values within which the researcher believes the true population parameter may lie.

A confidence interval is determined as:

$$\left\{ \left[\begin{matrix} \text{sample} \\ \text{statistic} \end{matrix} - \begin{pmatrix} \text{critical} \\ \text{value} \end{pmatrix} \begin{pmatrix} \text{standard} \\ \text{error} \end{pmatrix} \right] \le \begin{matrix} \text{population} \\ \text{parameter} \end{matrix} \le \left[\begin{matrix} \text{sample} \\ \text{statistic} \end{matrix} + \begin{pmatrix} \text{critical} \\ \text{value} \end{pmatrix} \begin{pmatrix} \text{standard} \\ \text{error} \end{pmatrix} \right] \right\}$$

The interpretation of a confidence interval is that for a level of confidence of 95%, for example, there is a 95% probability that the true population parameter is contained in the interval.

From the previous expression, we see that a confidence interval and a hypothesis test are linked by the critical value. For example, a 95% confidence interval uses a critical value associated with a given distribution at the 5% level of significance. Similarly, a hypothesis test would compare a test statistic to a critical value at the 5% level of significance. To see this relationship more clearly, the expression for the confidence interval can be manipulated and restated as:

–critical value $\le$ test statistic $\le$ +critical value

This is the range within which we fail to reject the null for a two-tailed hypothesis test at a given level of significance.

Example: Confidence interval

Using option portfolio data from the previous examples, construct a 95% confidence interval for the population mean daily return over the 250-day sample period. Use a z-distribution. Decide if the hypothesis $\mu = 0$ should be rejected.

Answer:

Given a sample size of 250 with a standard deviation of 0.25%, the standard error can be computed as $s_{\bar{x}} = \dfrac{s}{\sqrt{n}} = 0.25/\sqrt{250} = 0.0158\%$.

At the 5% level of significance, the critical z-values for the confidence interval are $z_{0.025} = 1.96$ and $-z_{0.025} = -1.96$. Thus, given a sample mean equal to 0.1%, the 95% confidence interval for the population mean is:

$$0.1 - 1.96(0.0158) \leq \mu \leq 0.1 + 1.96(0.0158), \text{ or}$$

$$0.069\% \leq \mu \leq 0.1310\%$$

Since there is a 95% probability that the true mean is within this confidence interval, we can reject the hypothesis $\mu = 0$ because 0 is not within the confidence interval.

Notice the similarity of this analysis with our test of whether $\mu = 0$. We rejected the hypothesis $\mu = 0$ because the sample mean of 0.1% is more than 1.96 standard errors from zero. Based on the 95% confidence interval, we reject $\mu = 0$ because zero is more than 1.96 standard errors from the sample mean of 0.1%.

LOS 11.d: Distinguish between a statistical result and an economically meaningful result.

Statistical significance does not necessarily imply **economic significance**. For example, we may have tested a null hypothesis that a strategy of going long all the stocks that satisfy some criteria and shorting all the stocks that do not satisfy the criteria resulted in returns that were less than or equal to zero over a 20-year period. Assume we have rejected the null in favor of the alternative hypothesis that the returns to the strategy are greater than zero (positive). This does not necessarily mean that investing in that strategy will result in economically meaningful positive returns. Several factors must be considered.

One important consideration is transactions costs. Once we consider the costs of buying and selling the securities, we may find that the mean positive returns to the strategy are not enough to generate positive returns. Taxes are another factor that may make a seemingly attractive strategy a poor one in practice. A third reason that statistically significant results may not be economically significant is risk. In the above strategy, we have additional risk from short sales (they may have to be closed out earlier than in the test strategy). Since the statistically significant results were for a period of 20 years, it may be the case that there is significant variation from year to year in the returns from the strategy, even though the mean strategy return is greater than zero. This variation in returns from period to period is an additional risk to the strategy that is not accounted for in our test of statistical significance.

Any of these factors could make committing funds to a strategy unattractive, even though the statistical evidence of positive returns is highly significant. By the nature of statistical tests, a very large sample size can result in highly (statistically) significant results that are quite small in absolute terms.

LOS 11.e: Explain and interpret the p-value as it relates to hypothesis testing.

The *p*-value is the probability of obtaining a test statistic that would lead to a rejection of the null hypothesis, assuming the null hypothesis is true. It is the smallest level of significance for which the null hypothesis can be rejected. For one-tailed tests, the *p*-value is the probability that lies above the computed test statistic for upper tail tests or below the computed test statistic for lower tail tests. For two-tailed tests, the *p*-value is the probability that lies above the positive value of the computed test statistic *plus* the probability that lies below the negative value of the computed test statistic.

Consider a two-tailed hypothesis test about the mean value of a random variable at the 95% significance level where the test statistic is 2.3, greater than the upper critical value of 1.96. If we consult the *Z*-table, we find the probability of getting a value greater than 2.3 is $(1 - 0.9893) = 1.07\%$. Since it's a two-tailed test, our *p*-value is $2 \times 1.07 = 2.14\%$, as illustrated in Figure 5. At a 3%, 4%, or 5% significance level, we would reject the null hypothesis, but at a 2% or 1% significance level we would not. Many researchers report *p*-values without selecting a significance level and allow the reader to judge how strong the evidence for rejection is.

Figure 5: Two-Tailed Hypothesis Test with *p*-value = 2.14%

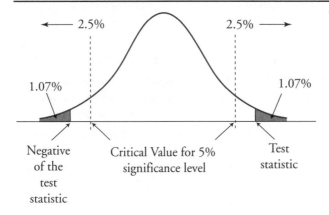

LOS 11.f: Identify the appropriate test statistic and interpret the results for a hypothesis test concerning the population mean of both large and small samples when the population is normally or approximately distributed and the variance is 1) known or 2) unknown.

When hypothesis testing, the choice between using a critical value based on the *t*-distribution or the *z*-distribution depends on sample size, the distribution of the population, and whether or not the variance of the population is known.

The *t*-Test

The *t*-test is a widely used hypothesis test that employs a test statistic that is distributed according to a *t*-distribution. Following are the rules for when it is appropriate to use the *t*-test for hypothesis tests of the population mean.

Use the t*-test if the population variance is unknown* and either of the following conditions exist:

- The sample is large ($n \geq 30$).
- The sample is small (less than 30), but the distribution of the population is normal or approximately normal.

If the sample is small and the distribution is non-normal, we have no reliable statistical test.

The computed value for the test statistic based on the *t*-distribution is referred to as the *t*-statistic. For hypothesis tests of a population mean, a *t*-statistic with $n - 1$ degrees of freedom is computed as:

$$t_{n-1} = \frac{\overline{x} - \mu_0}{s / \sqrt{n}}$$

where:
$\overline{x}$ = sample mean
μ_0 = hypothesized population mean (i.e., the null)
s = standard deviation of the sample
n = sample size

 Professor's Note: This computation is not new. It is the same test statistic computation that we have been performing all along. Note the use of the sample standard deviation, s, *in the standard error term in the denominator.*

To conduct a *t*-test, the *t*-statistic is compared to a critical *t*-value at the desired level of significance with the appropriate degrees of freedom.

In the real world, the underlying variance of the population is rarely known, so the *t*-test enjoys widespread application.

The *z*-Test

The *z*-test is the appropriate hypothesis test of the population mean when the *population is normally distributed with known variance*. The computed test statistic used with the *z*-test is referred to as the *z*-statistic. The *z*-statistic for a hypothesis test for a population mean is computed as follows:

$$\text{z-statistic} = \frac{\bar{x} - \mu_0}{\sigma / \sqrt{n}}$$

where:
$\bar{x}$ = sample mean
μ_0 = hypothesized population mean
σ = standard deviation of the *population*
n = sample size

To test a hypothesis, the *z*-statistic is compared to the critical *z*-value corresponding to the significance of the test. Critical *z*-values for the most common levels of significance are displayed in Figure 6. You should have these memorized by now.

Figure 6: Critical *z*-Values

Level of Significance	Two-Tailed Test	One-Tailed Test
0.10 = 10%	±1.65	+1.28 or −1.28
0.05 = 5%	±1.96	+1.65 or −1.65
0.01 = 1%	±2.58	+2.33 or −2.33

When the *sample size is large* and the *population variance is unknown*, the *z*-statistic is:

$$\text{z-statistic} = \frac{\bar{x} - \mu_0}{s / \sqrt{n}}$$

where:
$\bar{x}$ = sample mean
μ_0 = hypothesized population mean
s = standard deviation of the *sample*
n = sample size

Note the use of the sample standard deviation, *s*, versus the population standard deviation, σ. Remember, this is acceptable if the sample size is large, although the *t*-statistic is the more conservative measure when the population variance is unknown.

Example: *z*-test or *t*-test?

Referring to our previous option portfolio mean return problem once more, determine which test statistic (*z* or *t*) should be used and the difference in the likelihood of rejecting a true null with each distribution.

Answer:

The population variance for our sample of returns is unknown. Hence, the *t*-distribution is appropriate. With 250 observations, however, the sample is considered to be large, so the *z*-distribution would also be acceptable. This is a trick question—either distribution, *t* or *z*, is appropriate. With regard to the difference in the likelihood of rejecting a true null, since our sample is so large, the critical values for the *t* and *z* are almost identical. Hence, there is almost no difference in the likelihood of rejecting a true null.

Example: The *z*-test

When your company's gizmo machine is working properly, the mean length of gizmos is 2.5 inches. However, from time to time the machine gets out of alignment and produces gizmos that are either too long or too short. When this happens, production is stopped and the machine is adjusted. To check the machine, the quality control department takes a gizmo sample each day. Today, a random sample of 49 gizmos showed a mean length of 2.49 inches. The population standard deviation is known to be 0.021 inches. Using a 5% significance level, determine if the machine should be shut down and adjusted.

Answer:

Let μ be the mean length of all gizmos made by this machine, and let $\bar{x}$ be the corresponding mean for the sample.

Let's follow the hypothesis testing procedure presented earlier in Figure 1. Again, you should know this process!

Statement of hypothesis. For the information provided, the null and alternative hypotheses are appropriately structured as:

H_0: $\mu = 2.5$ (The machine does not need an adjustment.)

H_a: $\mu \neq 2.5$ (The machine needs an adjustment.)

Note that since this is a two-tailed test, H_a allows for values above and below 2.5.

Select the appropriate test statistic. Since the population variance is known and the sample size is > 30, the z-statistic is the appropriate test statistic. The z-statistic is computed as:

$$z = \frac{\bar{x} - \mu_0}{\sigma / \sqrt{n}}$$

Specify the level of significance. The level of significance is given at 5%, implying that we are willing to accept a 5% probability of rejecting a true null hypothesis.

State the decision rule regarding the hypothesis. The $\neq$ sign in the alternative hypothesis indicates that the test is two-tailed with two rejection regions, one in each tail of the standard normal distribution curve. Because the total area of both rejection regions combined is 0.05 (the significance level), the area of the rejection region in each tail is 0.025. You should know that the critical z-values for $\pm z_{0.025}$ are ± 1.96. This means that the null hypothesis should not be rejected if the computed z-statistic lies between -1.96 and $+1.96$ and should be rejected if it lies outside of these critical values. The decision rule can be stated as:

Reject H_0 if $-z_{0.025}$ > z-statistic > $z_{0.025}$, or equivalently,

Reject H_0 if: -1.96 > z-statistic > $+1.96$

Collect the sample and calculate the test statistic. The value of $\bar{x}$ from the sample is 2.49. Since σ is given as 0.021, we calculate the z-statistic using σ as follows:

$$z = \frac{\bar{x} - \mu_0}{\sigma / \sqrt{n}} = \frac{2.49 - 2.5}{0.021 / \sqrt{49}} = \frac{-0.01}{0.003} = -3.33$$

Make a decision regarding the hypothesis. The calculated value of the z-statistic is -3.33. Since this value is less than the critical value, $-z_{0.025} = -1.96$, it falls in the rejection region in the left tail of the z-distribution. Hence, there is sufficient evidence to reject H_0.

Make a decision based on the results of the test. Based on the sample information and the results of the test, it is concluded that the machine is out of adjustment and should be shut down for repair.

LOS 11.g: Identify the appropriate test statistic and interpret the results for a hypothesis test concerning the equality of the population means of two at least approximately normally distributed populations, based on independent random samples with 1) equal or 2) unequal assumed variances.

Up to this point, we have been concerned with tests of a single population mean. In practice, we frequently want to know if there is a difference between the means of two populations. There are two t-tests that are used to test differences between the means of two populations. Application of either of these tests requires that we are reasonably certain that our samples are independent and that they are taken from two populations that are approximately normally distributed. Both of these t-tests are used when the population variance is unknown. In one case, the population variances are assumed to be equal, and the sample observations are pooled. In the other case, however, no assumption is made regarding the equality between the two population variances, and the t-test uses an approximated value for the degrees of freedom.

When testing differences between the mean of Population 1, μ_1, and mean of Population 2, μ_2, we may be interested in knowing if the two means are equal (i.e., $\mu_1 = \mu_2$), if the mean of Population 1 is greater than that of Population 2 (i.e., $\mu_1 > \mu_2$), or if the mean of Population 2 exceeds that of Population 1 (i.e., $\mu_2 > \mu_1$). These three sets of hypotheses are structured as:

H_0: $\mu_1 - \mu_2 = 0$ versus H_a: $\mu_1 - \mu_2 \neq 0$ (a two-tail test)
H_0: $\mu_1 - \mu_2 \leq 0$ versus H_a: $\mu_1 - \mu_2 > 0$ (a one-tail test)
H_0: $\mu_1 - \mu_2 \geq 0$ versus H_a: $\mu_1 - \mu_2 < 0$ (a one-tail test)

Note that it is also possible to structure other hypotheses, such as H_0: $\mu_1 - \mu_2 = 50$ versus Ha: $\mu_1 - \mu_2 \neq 50$. Regardless of the specific structure, the hypothesis testing procedure is the same.

A pooled variance is used with the t-test for testing differences between the means of normally distributed populations with **unknown variances that are assumed to be equal**.

Assuming independent samples, the t-statistic in this case is computed as:

$$t = \frac{(\overline{x}_1 - \overline{x}_2) - (\mu_1 - \mu_2)}{\left(\dfrac{s_p^2}{n_1} + \dfrac{s_p^2}{n_2}\right)^{1/2}}$$

where:

$$s_p^2 = \frac{(n_1 - 1)s_1^2 + (n_2 - 1)s_2^2}{n_1 + n_2 - 2}$$

s_1^2 = variance of the first sample
s_2^2 = variance of the second sample
n_1 = number of observations in the first sample
n_2 = number of observations in the second sample

Note: The degrees of freedom, df, is $(n_1 + n_2 - 2)$, and for a test of equality of means, $\mu_1 - \mu_2 = 0$.

When testing the hypothesis of equality, $\mu_1 - \mu_2 = 0$, so that the numerator is just the difference between the sample means, $\overline{x}_1 - \overline{x}_2$. Since we assume that the variances are equal, we just add the variances of the two sample means in order to calculate the standard error in the denominator.

The *t*-test for differences between population means when the populations are normally distributed having **variances that are unknown and assumed to be unequal** uses the sample variances for both populations. Assuming independent samples, the *t*-statistic in this case is computed as follows:

$$t = \frac{(\bar{x}_1 - \bar{x}_2) - (\mu_1 - \mu_2)}{\left(\dfrac{s_1^2}{n_1} + \dfrac{s_2^2}{n_2}\right)^{1/2}}$$

where:

$$\text{degrees of freedom} = \frac{\left(\dfrac{s_1^2}{n_1} + \dfrac{s_2^2}{n_2}\right)^2}{\dfrac{\left(s_1^2/n_1\right)^2}{n_1} + \dfrac{\left(s_2^2/n_2\right)^2}{n_2}}$$

and where:

s_1^2 = variance of the first sample
s_2^2 = variance of the second sample
n_1 = number of observations in the first sample
n_2 = number of observations in the second sample

Again, a test of equality of means will have only the difference in sample means in the numerator. However, with no assumption of equal variances, the denominator (standard error) is based on the individual sample variances of the means for each sample. You do not need to memorize these two formulas, but should understand the numerator, the fact that these are *t*-statistics, and that the variance of the pooled sample is used when the sample variances are assumed to be equal.

Example: Difference between means – equal variances

Sue Smith is investigating whether the abnormal returns that occur in acquiring firms during merger announcement periods differ for horizontal and vertical mergers. She estimated the abnormal returns for a sample of acquiring firms associated with horizontal mergers and a sample of acquiring firms involved in vertical mergers. Her sample findings are reported in the following figure.

Abnormal Returns During Merger Announcement Periods

	Abnormal Returns Horizontal Mergers	Abnormal Returns Vertical Mergers
Mean	1.0%	2.5%
Standard deviation	1.0%	2.0%
Sample size (*n*)	64	81

Assuming the samples are independent, the population means are normally distributed, and the population variances are equal, determine if there is a statistically significant difference in the announcement period abnormal returns for these two types of mergers.

Answer:

State the hypothesis. Since this is a two-sided test, the structure of the hypotheses takes the following form:

$$H_0: \mu_1 - \mu_2 = 0 \text{ versus } H_a: \mu_1 - \mu_2 \neq 0$$

where:
μ_1 = the mean of the abnormal returns for the horizontal mergers
μ_2 = the mean of the abnormal returns for the vertical mergers

Select the appropriate test statistic. Since we are assuming equal variances, the test statistic is computed using the following formula:

$$t = \frac{(\overline{x}_1 - \overline{x}_2) - (\mu_1 - \mu_2)}{\left(\dfrac{s_p^2}{n_1} + \dfrac{s_p^2}{n_2}\right)^{1/2}}$$

where:

$$s_p^2 = \frac{(n_1 - 1)s_1^2 + (n_2 - 1)s_2^2}{n_1 + n_2 - 2}$$

Specify the level of significance. We will use the common significance level of 5% ($\alpha = 0.05$). In order to look up the critical t-value, we also need the degrees of freedom, which in this case is $n_1 + n_2 - 2$, or df = 64 + 81 − 2 = 143.

State the decision rule regarding the hypothesis. We must identify the critical t-value for a 5% level of significance and the *closest* degrees of freedom specified in a t-table. As you should verify with the partial t-table contained in the following figure, the closest entry for df = 143 is df = 120. At $\alpha / 2 = p = 0.025$ with df = 120, the critical t-value = 1.980.

Partial *t*-Table

df	One-Tailed Probabilities (p)		
	p = 0.10	*p = 0.05*	*p = 0.025*
110	1.289	1.659	1.982
120	1.289	1.658	1.980
200	1.286	1.653	1.972

Thus, the decision rule can be stated as:

Reject H_0 if t-statistic < -1.980 or t-statistic > 1.980

The rejection region for this test is illustrated in the following figure.

Decision Rule for Two-Tailed t-Test

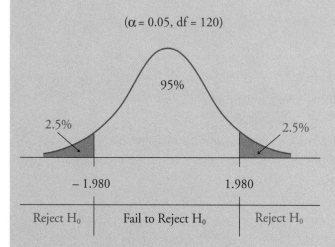

Collect the sample and calculate the sample statistics. Using the information provided, the t-statistic can be computed as follows (note that the -0.015 in the numerator equals $0.01 - 0.025$, which represents the difference in means) since the hypothesized difference in means $(\mu_1 - \mu_2)$ is zero.

$$t = \frac{(\overline{x}_1 - \overline{x}_2) - (\mu_1 - \mu_2)}{\left(s_p^2/n_1 + s_p^2/n_2\right)^{1/2}} = \frac{-0.015}{0.00274} = -5.474$$

where:

$$s_p^2 = \frac{(n_1 - 1)s_1^2 + (n_2 - 1)s_2^2}{n_1 + n_2 - 2} = \frac{(63)(0.0001) + (80)(0.0004)}{143} = 0.000268$$

Make a decision regarding the hypothesis. Since the calculated test statistic falls to the left of the lowest critical t-value, we reject the null hypothesis and conclude that the announcement period abnormal returns are different for horizontal and vertical mergers.

LOS 11.h: Identify the appropriate test statistic and interpret the results for a hypothesis test concerning the mean difference of two normally distributed populations (paired comparisons test).

While the tests considered in the previous section were of the difference between the means of two independent samples, sometimes our samples may be dependent. If the observations in the two samples both depend on some other factor, we can construct a "paired comparisons" test of whether the means of the differences between observations for the two samples are different. Dependence may result from an event that affects both sets of observations for a number of companies or because observations for two firms over time are both influenced by market returns or economic conditions.

For an example of a paired comparisons test, consider a test of whether the returns on two steel firms were equal over a 5-year period. We can't use the difference in means test because we have reason to believe that the samples are not independent. To some extent, both will depend on the returns on the overall market (market risk) and the conditions in the steel industry (industry specific risk). In this case, our pairs will be the returns on each firm over the same time periods, so we use the differences in monthly returns for the two companies. The paired comparisons test is just a test of whether the average difference between monthly returns is significantly different from zero, based on the standard error of the average difference estimated from the sample data.

Remember, the paired comparisons test also requires that the sample data be normally distributed. Although we frequently just want to test the hypothesis that the mean of the differences in the pairs is zero ($\mu_{dz} = 0$), the general form of the test for any hypothesized mean difference, μ_{dz}, is as follows:

$H_0: \mu_d = \mu_{dz}$ versus $H_a: \mu_d \neq \mu_{dz}$

where:

μ_d = mean of the population of paired differences

μ_{dz} = hypothesized mean of paired differences, which is commonly zero

For one-sided tests, the hypotheses are structured as either:

$H_0: \mu_d \leq \mu_{dz}$ versus $H_a: \mu_d > \mu_{dz}$, or $H_0: \mu_d \geq \mu_{dz}$ versus $H_a: \mu_d < \mu_{dz}$

For the paired comparisons test, the *t*-statistic with n − 1 degrees of freedom is computed as:

$$t = \frac{\bar{d} - \mu_{dz}}{s_{\bar{d}}}$$

where:

$\bar{d}$ = sample mean difference = $\dfrac{1}{n}\displaystyle\sum_{i=1}^{n} d_i$

d_i = difference between the *i*th pair of observations

$s_{\bar{d}}$ = standard error of the mean difference = $\dfrac{s_d}{\sqrt{n}}$

s_d = sample standard deviation = $\left(\dfrac{\displaystyle\sum_{i=1}^{n}\left(d_i - \bar{d}\right)^2}{n-1} \right)^{1/2}$

n = the number of paired observations

Example: Paired comparisons test

Joe Andrews is examining changes in estimated betas for the common stock of companies in the telecommunications industry before and after deregulation. Andrews believes that the betas may decline because of deregulation since companies are no longer subject to the uncertainties of rate regulation or that they may increase because there is more uncertainty regarding competition in the industry. The sample information he gathered is reported in the following figure. Determine whether there is a change in betas.

Beta Differences After Deregulation

Mean of differences in betas (before minus after)	0.23
Sample standard deviation of differences	0.14
Sample size	39

Answer:

Once again, we follow our hypothesis testing procedure.

State the hypothesis. There is reason to believe that the mean differences may be positive or negative, so a two-sided alternative hypothesis is in order here. Thus, the hypotheses are structured as:

$$H_0: \mu_d = 0 \text{ versus } H_a: \mu_d \neq 0$$

Select the appropriate test statistic. As described above, the test statistic for a paired comparisons test is:

$$t = \frac{\overline{d} - \mu_{dz}}{s_{\overline{d}}}$$

Specify the level of significance. Let's use a 5% level of significance.

State the decision rule regarding the hypothesis. There are $39 - 1 = 38$ degrees of freedom. Using the t-distribution, the two-tailed critical t-values for a 5% level of significance with df = 38 is ±2.024. As indicated in the following table, the critical t-value of 2.024 is located at the intersection of the p = 0.025 column and the df = 38 row. The one-tailed probability of 0.025 is used because we need 2.5% in each tail for 5% significance with a two-tailed test.

Partial *t*-Table

df	One-Tailed Probabilities (p)		
	p = 0.10	P = 0.05	p = 0.025
38	1.304	1.686	**2.024**
39	1.304	1.685	2.023
40	1.303	1.684	2.021

Thus, the decision rule becomes:

Reject H_0 if *t*-statistic < −2.024, or *t*-statistic > 2.024

This decision rule is illustrated in the following figure.

Decision Rule for a Two-Tailed Paired Comparisons Test

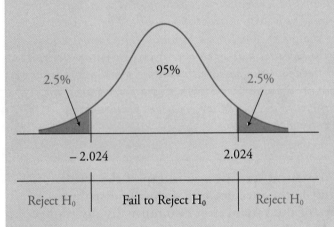

(α = 0.05, df = 38)

2.5%   95%   2.5%

− 2.024   2.024

Reject H_0 Fail to Reject H_0 Reject H_0

Collect the sample and calculate the sample statistics. Using the sample data provided, the test statistic is computed as follows:

$$t = \frac{\overline{d} - \mu_{dz}}{s_{\overline{d}}} = \frac{0.23}{0.14/\sqrt{39}} = \frac{0.23}{0.022418} = 10.2596$$

Make a decision regarding the hypotheses. The computed test statistic, 10.2596, is greater than the critical *t*-value, 2.024—it falls in the rejection region to the right of 2.024 in the previous figure. Thus, we reject the null hypothesis of no difference, concluding that there *is* a statistically significant difference in betas from before to after deregulation.

Make a decision based on the results of the test. We have support for the hypothesis that betas are lower as a result of deregulation, providing support for the proposition that deregulation resulted in decreased risk.

Keep in mind that we have been describing two distinct hypothesis tests, one about the significance of the difference between the means of two populations and one about the significance of the mean of the differences between pairs of observations. Here are rules for when these tests may be applied:

- The test of the differences in means is used when there are two *independent samples*.
- A test of the significance of the mean of the differences between paired observations is used when the samples are *not independent*.

 Professor's Note: The LOS here say "Identify the appropriate test statistic and interpret the results..." I can't believe candidates are expected to memorize these formulas (or that you would be a better analyst if you did). The CFA exam is not known for requiring the use of complicated formulas from memory. You should instead focus on the fact that both of these tests involve t-statistics and depend on the degrees of freedom. Also note that when samples are independent, you can use the difference in means test, and when they are dependent, the statistic is the average difference in (paired) observations divided by the standard error of the average difference.

LOS 11.i: Identify the appropriate test statistic and interpret the results for a hypothesis test concerning 1) the variance of a normally distributed population, and 2) the equality of the variances of two normally distributed populations, based on two independent random samples.

The *chi-square test* is used for hypothesis tests concerning the variance of a normally distributed population. Letting σ^2 represent the true population variance and σ_0^2 represent the hypothesized variance, the hypotheses for a two-tailed test of a single population variance are structured as:

$$H_0: \sigma^2 = \sigma_0^2 \text{ versus } H_a: \sigma^2 \neq \sigma_0^2$$

The hypotheses for one-tailed tests are structured as:

$$H_0: \sigma^2 \leq \sigma_0^2 \text{ versus } H_a: \sigma^2 > \sigma_0^2 \text{, or}$$
$$H_0: \sigma^2 \geq \sigma_0^2 \text{ versus } H_a: \sigma^2 < \sigma_0^2$$

Hypothesis testing of the population variance requires the use of a chi-square distributed test statistic, denoted χ^2. The chi-square distribution is asymmetrical and approaches the normal distribution in shape as the degrees of freedom increase.

To illustrate the chi-square distribution, consider a two-tailed test with a 5% level of significance and 30 degrees of freedom. As displayed in Figure 7, the critical chi-square values are 16.791 and 46.979 for the lower and upper bounds, respectively. These values are obtained from a chi-square table, which is used in the same manner as a *t*-table. A portion of a chi-square table is presented in Figure 8.

Note that the chi-square values in Figure 8 correspond to the probabilities in the right tail of the distribution. As such, the 16.791 in Figure 7 is from the column headed *0.975* because 95% + 2.5% of the probability is to the right of it. The 46.979 is from the column headed *0.025* because only 2.5% probability is to the right of it. Similarly, at a 5% level of significance with 10 degrees of freedom, Figure 8 shows that the critical chi-square values for a two-tailed test are 3.247 and 20.483.

Figure 7: Decision Rule for a Two-Tailed Chi-Square Test

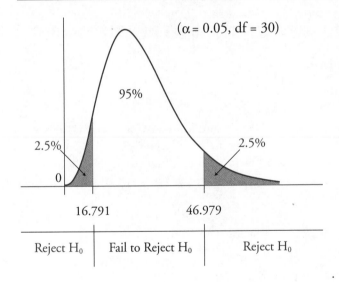

Figure 8: Chi-Square Table

Degrees of Freedom	Probability in Right Tail					
	0.975	0.95	0.90	0.1	0.05	0.025
9	2.700	3.325	4.168	14.684	16.919	19.023
10	3.247	3.940	4.865	15.987	18.307	20.483
11	3.816	4.575	5.578	17.275	19.675	21.920
30	**16.791**	18.493	20.599	40.256	43.773	**46.979**

The chi-square test statistic, χ^2, with n – 1 degrees of freedom, is computed as:

$$\chi^2_{n-1} = \frac{(n-1)s^2}{\sigma^2_0}$$

where:

n   =   sample size
s^2 =   sample variance
σ^2_0 =   hypothesized value for the population variance.

Similar to other hypothesis tests, the chi-square test compares the test statistic, χ^2_{n-1}, to a critical chi-square value at a given level of significance and n – 1 degrees of freedom. Note that since the chi-square distribution is bounded below by zero, chi-square values cannot be negative.

Example: Chi-square test for a single population variance

Historically, High-Return Equity Fund has advertised that its monthly returns have a standard deviation equal to 4%. This was based on estimates from the 1990–1998 period. High-Return wants to verify whether this claim still adequately describes the standard deviation of the fund's returns. High-Return collected monthly returns for the 24-month period between 1998 and 2000 and measured a standard deviation of monthly returns of 3.8%. Determine if the more recent standard deviation is different from the advertised standard deviation.

Answer:

State the hypothesis. The null hypothesis is that the standard deviation is equal to 4% and, therefore, the variance of monthly returns for the population is $(0.04)^2 = 0.0016$. Since High-Return simply wants to test whether the standard deviation has changed, up or down, a two-sided test should be used. The hypothesis test structure takes the form:

$$H_0: \sigma^2_0 = 0.0016 \text{ versus } H_a: \sigma^2 \neq 0.0016$$

Select the appropriate test statistic. The appropriate test statistic for tests of variance using the chi-square distribution is computed as follows:

$$\chi^2 = \frac{(n-1)s^2}{\sigma^2_0}$$

Specify the level of significance. Let's use a 5% level of significance, meaning there will be 2.5% probability in each tail of the chi-square distribution.

State the decision rule regarding the hypothesis. With a 24-month sample, there are 23 degrees of freedom. Using the table of chi-square values at the back of this book, for 23 degrees of freedom and probabilities of 0.975 and 0.025, we find two critical values, 11.689 and 38.076. Thus, the decision rule is:

Reject H_0 if $\chi^2 < 11.689$, or $\chi^2 > 38.076$

This decision rule is illustrated in the following figure.

Decision Rule for a Two-Tailed Chi-Square Test of a Single Population Variance

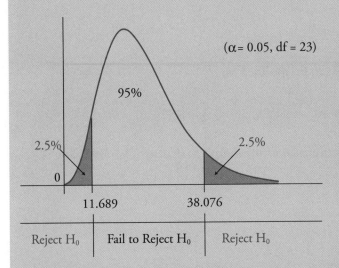

$(\alpha = 0.05, \text{df} = 23)$

95%

2.5%

0

2.5%

11.689   38.076

Reject H_0 Fail to Reject H_0 Reject H_0

Collect the sample and calculate the sample statistics. Using the information provided, the test statistic is computed as:

$$\chi^2 = \frac{(n-1)s^2}{\sigma_0^2} = \frac{(23)(0.001444)}{0.0016} = \frac{0.033212}{0.0016} = 20.7575$$

Make a decision regarding the hypothesis. Since the computed test statistic, χ^2, falls between the two critical values, we fail to reject the null hypothesis that the variance is equal to 0.0016.

Make a decision based on the results of the test. It can be concluded that the recently measured standard deviation is close enough to the advertised standard deviation that we cannot say that it is different from 4%, at a 5% level of significance.

Testing the Equality of the Variances of Two Normally Distributed Populations, Based on Two Independent Random Samples

The hypotheses concerned with the equality of the variances of two populations are tested with an *F*-distributed test statistic. Hypothesis testing using a test statistic that follows an *F*-distribution is referred to as the *F*-test. The *F*-test is used under the assumption that the populations from which samples are drawn are normally distributed and that the samples are independent.

If we let σ_1^2 and σ_2^2 represent the variances of normal Population 1 and Population 2, respectively, the hypotheses for the two-tailed F-test of differences in the variances can be structured as:

$$H_0: \sigma_1^2 = \sigma_2^2 \text{ versus } H_a: \sigma_1^2 \neq \sigma_2^2$$

and the one-sided test structures can be specified as:

$$H_0: \sigma_1^2 \leq \sigma_2^2 \text{ versus } H_a: \sigma_1^2 > \sigma_2^2, \text{ or } H_0: \sigma_1^2 \geq \sigma_2^2 \text{ versus } H_a: \sigma_1^2 < \sigma_2^2$$

The test statistic for the F-test is the ratio of the sample variances. The F-statistic is computed as:

$$F = \frac{s_1^2}{s_2^2}$$

where:

s_1^2 = variance of the sample of n_1 observations drawn from Population 1
s_2^2 = variance of the sample of n_2 observations drawn from Population 2

Note that $n_1 - 1$ and $n_2 - 1$ are the degrees of freedom used to identify the appropriate critical value from the F-table (provided in the Appendix).

 Professor's Note: Always put the larger variance in the numerator (s_1^2). Following this convention means we only have to consider the critical value for the right-hand tail.

An F-distribution is presented in Figure 9. As indicated, the F-distribution is right-skewed and is truncated at zero on the left-hand side. The shape of the F-distribution is determined by *two separate degrees of freedom*, the numerator degrees of freedom, df_1, and the denominator degrees of freedom, df_2. Also shown in Figure 9 is that the *rejection region is in the right-side tail* of the distribution. This will always be the case as long as the F-statistic is computed with the largest sample variance in the numerator. The labeling of 1 and 2 is arbitrary anyway.

Figure 9: *F*-Distribution

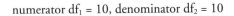
numerator $df_1 = 10$, denominator $df_2 = 10$

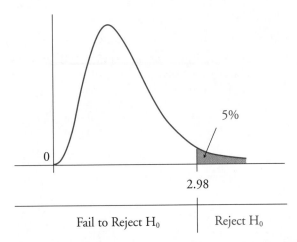

5%

0

2.98

Fail to Reject H_0 | Reject H_0

Example: *F*-test for equal variances

Annie Cower is examining the earnings for two different industries. Cower suspects that the earnings of the textile industry are more divergent than those of the paper industry. To confirm this suspicion, Cower has looked at a sample of 31 textile manufacturers and a sample of 41 paper companies. She measured the sample standard deviation of earnings across the textile industry to be $4.30 and that of the paper industry companies to be $3.80. Determine if the earnings of the textile industry have greater standard deviation than those of the paper industry.

Answer:

State the hypothesis. In this example, we are concerned with whether the variance of the earnings of the textile industry is greater (more divergent) than the variance of the earnings of the paper industry. As such, the test hypotheses can be appropriately structured as:

$$H_0: \sigma_1^2 \leq \sigma_2^2 \text{ versus } H_a: \sigma_1^2 > \sigma_2^2$$

where:

σ_1^2 = variance of earnings for the textile industry

σ_2^2 = variance of earnings for the paper industry

Note: $\sigma_1^2 > \sigma_2^2$

Select the appropriate test statistic. For tests of difference between variances, the appropriate test statistic is:

$$F = \frac{s_1^2}{s_2^2}$$

Specify the level of significance. Let's conduct our hypothesis test at the 5% level of significance.

State the decision rule regarding the hypothesis. Using the sample sizes for the two industries, the critical *F*-value for our test is found to be 1.74. This value is obtained from the table of the *F*-distribution at the 5% level of significance with $df_1 = 30$ and $df_2 = 40$. Thus, if the computed *F*-statistic is greater than the critical value of 1.74, the null hypothesis is rejected. The decision rule, illustrated in the figure below, can be stated as:

Reject H_0 if F > 1.74

Decision Rule for *F*-Test

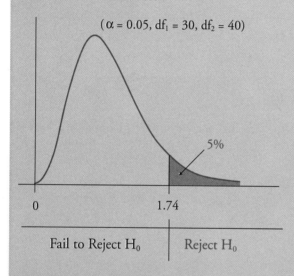

Collect the sample and calculate the sample statistics. Using the information provided, the *F*-statistic can be computed as:

$$F = \frac{s_1^2}{s_2^2} = \frac{\$4.30^2}{\$3.80^2} = \frac{\$18.49}{\$14.44} = 1.2805$$

 Professor's Note: Remember to square the standard deviations to get the variances.

Make a decision regarding the hypothesis. Since the calculated *F*-statistic of 1.2805 is less than the critical *F*-statistic of 1.74, we fail to reject the null hypothesis.

Make a decision based on the results of the test. Based on the results of the hypothesis test, Cower should conclude that the earnings variances of the industries are not statistically significantly different from one another at a 5% level of significance. More pointedly, the earnings of the textile industry are not more divergent than those of the paper industry.

LOS 11.j: Distinguish between parametric and nonparametric tests and describe the situations in which the use of nonparametric tests may be appropriate.

Parametric tests rely on assumptions regarding the distribution of the population and are specific to population parameters. For example, the z-test relies upon a mean and a standard deviation to define the normal distribution. The z-test also requires that either the sample is large, relying on the central limit theorem to assure a normal sampling distribution, or that the population is normally distributed.

Nonparametric tests either do not consider a particular population parameter or have few assumptions about the population that is sampled. Nonparametric tests are used when there is concern about quantities other than the parameters of a distribution or when the assumptions of parametric tests can't be supported. They are also used when the data are not suitable for parametric tests (e.g., ranked observations). Nonparametric tests are often used along with parametric tests. In this way, the nonparametric test is a backup in case the assumptions underlying the parametric test do not hold.

One example of a nonparametric test is a test using data ranks (e.g., largest, second-largest, third-largest, etc.) for two data sets and examining the correlation of ranks between the two sets. We might use this to test the correlation between firm size rank and earnings per share rank for a given set of firms.

Another example is a runs test. If we look at a series of stock price changes (either up or down), a runs test would give us the probability that an observed series of daily price changes (e.g., $+ + - + - - +$) could result, given that each price change is random.

KEY CONCEPTS

LOS 11.a

The hypothesis testing process requires a statement of a null and an alternative hypothesis, the selection of the appropriate test statistic, specification of the significance level, a decision rule, the calculation of a sample statistic, a decision regarding the hypotheses based on the test, and a decision based on the test results.

The null hypothesis is what the researcher wants to reject. The alternative hypothesis is what the researcher wants to prove, and it is accepted when the null hypothesis is rejected.

A two-tailed test results from a two-sided alternative hypothesis (e.g., $H_a: \mu \neq \mu_0$). A one-tailed test results from a one-sided alternative hypothesis (e.g., $H_a: \mu > \mu_0$, or $H_a: \mu < \mu_0$).

LOS 11.b

The test statistic is the value that a decision about a hypothesis will be based on. For a test about the value of the mean of a distribution:

$$\text{test statistic} = \frac{\text{sample mean} - \text{hypothesized mean}}{\text{standard error of sample mean}}$$

A Type I error is the rejection of the null hypothesis when it is actually true, while a Type II error is the failure to reject the null hypothesis when it is actually false.

The significance level can be interpreted as the probability that a test statistic will reject the null hypothesis by chance when it is actually true (i.e., the probability of a Type I error). A significance level must be specified to select the critical values for the test.

LOS 11.c

Hypothesis testing compares a computed test statistic to a critical value at a stated level of significance, which is the decision rule for the test.

The power of a test is the probability of rejecting the null when it is false. The power of a test = 1 – P(Type II error).

A hypothesis about a population parameter is rejected when the sample statistic lies outside a confidence interval around the hypothesized value for the chosen level of significance.

LOS 11.d

Statistical significance does not necessarily imply economic significance. Even though a test statistic is significant statistically, the size of the gains to a strategy to exploit a statistically significant result may be absolutely small or simply not great enough to outweigh transactions costs.

LOS 11.e

The *p*-value for a hypothesis test is the smallest significance level for which the hypothesis would be rejected. For example, a *p*-value of 7% means the hypothesis can be rejected at the 10% significance level but cannot be rejected at the 5% significance level.

LOS 11.f

With unknown population variance, the *t*-statistic is used for tests about the

mean of a normally distributed population: $t_{n-1} = \dfrac{\overline{x} - \mu_0}{s/\sqrt{n}}$. If the population variance is

known, the appropriate test statistic is $z = \dfrac{\overline{x} - \mu_0}{\sigma/\sqrt{n}}$ for tests about the mean of a

population.

LOS 11.g

For two independent samples from two normally distributed populations, the difference in means can be tested with a *t*-statistic. When the two population variances are assumed to be equal, the denominator is based on the variance of the pooled samples, but when sample variances are assumed to be unequal, the denominator is based on a combination of the two samples' variances.

LOS 11.h

A paired comparisons test is concerned with the mean of the differences between the paired observations of two dependent, normally distributed samples. A *t*-statistic

is used: $t = \dfrac{\overline{d} - \mu_{dz}}{s_{\overline{d}}}$, where $s_{\overline{d}} = \dfrac{s_d}{\sqrt{n}}$, and $\overline{d}$ is the average difference of the *n* paired

observations.

LOS 11.i

The test of a hypothesis about the population variance for a normally distributed

population uses a chi-square test statistic: $\chi^2 = \dfrac{(n-1)s^2}{\sigma_0^2}$, where *n* is the sample

size, s^2 is the sample variance, and σ_0^2 is the hypothesized value for the

population variance. Degrees of freedom are n – 1.

The test comparing two variances based on independent samples from two

normally distributed populations uses an F-distributed test statistic: $F = \dfrac{s_1^2}{s_2^2}$, where s_1^2 is

the variance of the first sample and s_2^2 is the (smaller) variance of the second sample.

LOS 11.j

Parametric tests, like the *t*-test, *F*-test, and chi-square tests, make assumptions regarding the distribution of the population from which samples are drawn. Nonparametric tests either do not consider a particular population parameter or have few assumptions about the sampled population. Nonparametric tests are used when the assumptions of parametric tests can't be supported or when the data are not suitable for parametric tests.

CONCEPT CHECKERS

1. Which of the following statements about hypothesis testing is *most accurate*?
   A. A Type II error is rejecting the null when it is actually true.
   B. The significance level equals one minus the probability of a Type I error.
   C. A two-tailed test with a significance level of 5% has z-critical values of ± 1.96.

2. Which of the following statements about hypothesis testing is *least accurate*?
   A. The power of test = $1 - P(\text{Type II error})$.
   B. If the computed z-statistic = -2 and the critical z-value = -1.96, the null hypothesis is rejected.
   C. The calculated z-statistic for a test of a sample mean when the population variance is known is: $z = \dfrac{\overline{X} - \mu_0}{\dfrac{\sigma^2}{\sqrt{n}}}$.

Use the following data to answer Questions 3 through 7.

Austin Roberts believes that the mean price of houses in the area is greater than $145,000. A random sample of 36 houses in the area has a mean price of $149,750. The population standard deviation is $24,000, and Roberts wants to conduct a hypothesis test at a 1% level of significance.

3. The appropriate alternative hypothesis is:
   A. $H_a: \mu < \$145{,}000$.
   B. $H_a: \mu \geq \$145{,}000$.
   C. $H_a: \mu > \$145{,}000$.

4. The value of the calculated test statistic is *closest* to:
   A. 0.67.
   B. 1.19.
   C. 4.00.

5. Which of the following *most accurately* describes the appropriate test structure?
   A. Two-tailed test.
   B. One-tailed test.
   C. Chi-square test.

6. The critical value of the z-statistic is:
   A. ± 1.96.
   B. $+2.33$.
   C. ± 2.33.

7. At a 1% level of significance, Roberts should:
   A. reject the null hypothesis.
   B. fail to reject the null hypothesis.
   C. neither reject nor fail to reject the null hypothesis.

Use the following data to answer Questions 8 through 13.

An analyst is conducting a hypothesis test to determine if the mean time spent on investment research is different from three hours per day. The test is performed at the 5% level of significance and uses a random sample of 64 portfolio managers, where the mean time spent on research is found to be 2.5 hours. The population standard deviation is 1.5 hours.

8.   The appropriate null hypothesis for the described test is:
    A. $H_0: \mu = 3$ hours.
    B. $H_0: \mu \leq 3$ hours.
    C. $H_0: \mu \geq 3$ hours.

9.   This is a:
    A.   one-tailed test.
    B.   two-tailed test.
    C.   paired comparisons test.

10.   The calculated z-statistic is:
    A.   −2.67.
    B.   +0.33.
    C.   +2.67.

11.   The critical z-value(s) of the test statistic is (are):
    A.   −1.96.
    B.   +1.96.
    C.   ±1.96.

12.   The 95% confidence interval for the population mean is:
    A. $\{1.00 < \mu < 3.50\}$.
    B. $\{0.54 < \mu < 4.46\}$.
    C. $\{2.13 < \mu < 2.87\}$.

13.   The analyst should *most appropriately*:
    A.   reject the null hypothesis.
    B.   fail to reject the null hypothesis.
    C.   reach no conclusion because the sample standard deviation was not given.

14.   A study was conducted to determine whether the standard deviation of monthly maintenance costs of a Pepper III aircraft is $300. A sample of 30 Pepper IIIs had a mean monthly maintenance cost of $3,025 and a standard deviation of $325. Using a 5% level of significance, which of the following is the *most appropriate* conclusion regarding the *difference* between the hypothesized value of the population variance and the sample variance?
    A.   The population and sample variances are significantly different.
    B.   The population and sample variances are not significantly different.
    C.   There are no tests that may be used to test variance differences in small samples.

Use the following data to answer Questions 15 through 18.

Two samples were drawn from two normally distributed populations. For the first sample, the mean was $50 and the standard deviation was $5. For the second sample, the mean was $55 and the standard deviation was $6. The first sample consists of 25 observations and the second sample consists of 36 observations. (Note: In the questions below, the subscripts "1" and "2" indicate the first and second sample, respectively.)

15. Consider the hypotheses structured as H_0: μ_1 = $48 versus H_a: $\mu_1 \neq$ $48. At a 1% level of significance, the null hypothesis:
    A. cannot be rejected.
    B. should be rejected.
    C. cannot be tested using this sample information provided.

16. Using a 5% level of significance and a hypothesis test structure of H_0: $\sigma_1^2 \leq 24$ versus H_a: $\sigma_1^2 > 24$, the null hypothesis:
    A. cannot be rejected.
    B. should be rejected.
    C. cannot be tested using this sample information provided.

17. Consider the hypotheses structured as H_0: $\mu_1 \leq$ $48 versus H_a: $\mu_1 >$ $48. At a 5% level of significance, the null hypothesis:
    A. cannot be rejected.
    B. should be rejected.
    C. cannot be tested using the sample information provided.

18. Using a 5% level of significance for a test of the null of H_0: $\sigma_1 = \sigma_2$ versus the alternative of H_a: $\sigma_1 \neq \sigma_2$, the null hypothesis:
    A. cannot be rejected.
    B. should be rejected.
    C. cannot be tested using the sample information provided.

19. If the significance level of a test is 0.05 and the probability of a Type II error is 0.15, what is the power of the test?
    A. 0.850.
    B. 0.950.
    C. 0.975.

20. Which of the following statements about the *F*-distribution and chi-square distribution is *least accurate*? Both distributions:
    A. are asymmetrical.
    B. are bound by zero on the left.
    C. have means that are less than their standard deviations.

21. The appropriate test statistic for a test of the equality of variances for two normally distributed random variables, based on two independent random samples, is the:
    A. *t*-test.
    B. *F*-test.
    C. χ^2 test.

22. The appropriate test statistic to test the hypothesis that the variance of a normally distributed population is equal to 13 is the:
    A. t-test.
    B. F-test.
    C. χ^2 test.

23. William Adams wants to test whether the mean monthly returns over the last five years are the same for two stocks. If he assumes that the returns distributions are normal and have equal variances, the type of test and test statistic are *best* described as:
    A. paired comparisons test, t-statistic.
    B. paired comparisons test, F-statistic.
    C. difference in means test, t-statistic.

24. Which of the following assumptions is *least likely* required for the difference in means test based on two samples?
    A. The two samples are independent.
    B. The two populations are normally distributed.
    C. The two populations have equal variances.

25. For a hypothesis test with a probability of a Type II error of 60% and a probability of a Type I error of 5%, which of the following statements is *most accurate*?
    A. The power of the test is 40%, and there is a 5% probability that the test statistic will exceed the critical value(s).
    B. There is a 95% probability that the test statistic will be between the critical values if this is a two-tailed test.
    C. There is a 5% probability that the null hypothesis will be rejected when actually true, and the probability of rejecting the null when it is false is 40%.

COMPREHENSIVE PROBLEMS

1. Ralph Rollins, a researcher, believes that the stocks of firms that have appeared in a certain financial newspaper with a positive headline and story return more on a risk-adjusted basis. He gathers data on the risk-adjusted returns for these stocks over the six months after they appear on the cover, and data on the risk-adjusted returns for an equal-sized sample of firms with characteristics similar to the cover-story firms matched by time period.

    A.   State the likely null and alternative hypotheses for a test of his belief.

    B.   Is this a one- or two-tailed test?

    C.   Describe the steps in testing a hypothesis such as the null you stated in part A.

2. For each of the following hypotheses, describe the appropriate test, identify the appropriate test statistic, and explain under what conditions the null hypothesis should be rejected.

    A.   A researcher has returns over 52 weeks for an index of natural gas stocks and for an index of oil stocks and wants to know if the weekly returns are equal. Assume that the returns are approximately normally distributed.

    B.   A researcher has two independent samples that are approximately normally distributed. She wishes to test whether the mean values of the two random variables are equal and assumes that the variances of the populations from which the two samples are drawn are equal. As an additional question here, how should the degrees of freedom be calculated?

    C.   A researcher wants to determine whether the population variances of two normally distributed random variables are equal based on two samples of sizes n_1 and n_2. As an additional question here, how should the degrees of freedom be calculated?

    D.   A researcher wants to test whether the variance of a normally distributed population is equal to 0.00165. As an additional question here, how should the degrees of freedom be calculated?

ANSWERS – CONCEPT CHECKERS

1. **C** Rejecting the null when it is actually true is a Type I error. A Type II error is failing to reject the null hypothesis when it is false. The significance level equals the probability of a Type I error.

2. **C** $z = \dfrac{\overline{X} - \mu_0}{\dfrac{\sigma}{\sqrt{n}}}$ (σ^2 is the variance)

3. **C** H_a: $\mu > \$145,000$

4. **B** $z = \dfrac{149,750 - 145,000}{24,000 \ / \sqrt{36}} = 1.1875$

5. **B** The alternative hypothesis, H_a: $\mu > \$145,000$, only allows for values greater than the hypothesized value. Thus, this is a one-sided (one-tailed) test.

6. **B** For a one-tailed z-test at the 1% level of significance, the critical z-value is $z_{0.01} = 2.33$. Since the test is one-tailed on the upper end (i.e., H_a: $\mu > 145,000$), we use a positive z-critical value.

7. **B** The decision rule is to reject H_0 if z-computed > z-critical. Since 1.1875 < 2.33, Roberts will fail to reject the null.

8. **A** H_0: $\mu = 3$ hours

9. **B** This is a two-sided (two-tailed) test. We want to test if the mean "differs from" 3 hours (i.e., H_a: $\mu \neq 3$ hours).

10. **A** The normally distributed test statistic $= z = \dfrac{(2.5 - 3.0)}{1.5 \ / \sqrt{64}} = -2.67$.

11. **C** At $\alpha \ / \ 2 = 0.025$, the critical z-values are: $\pm z_{\alpha \ / \ 2} = \pm z_{0.025} = \pm 1.96$.

12. **C** The 95% confidence interval is $\{2.5 \pm (1.96)(0.1875)\} = \{2.5 \pm 0.3675\} \rightarrow \{2.1325 < \mu < 2.8675\}$.

13. **A** Decision rule: reject H_0 if $z_{computed} < -1.96$ or if $z_{computed} > +1.96$. Since $-2.67 < -1.96$, reject H_0.

14. **B** The wording of the proposition is a little tricky, but the test structure is H_0: $\sigma^2 = 300^2$ versus H_a: $\sigma^2 \neq 300^2$. The appropriate test is a two-tailed chi-square test. The decision rule is to reject H_0 if the test statistic is outside the range defined by the critical chi-square values at $\alpha \ / \ 2 = 0.025$ with df = 29. The test statistic is:

$$\chi^2 = \dfrac{(n-1)s^2}{\sigma_0^2} = \dfrac{(29)(105,625)}{90,000} = 34.035$$

The critical chi-square values are 16.047 on the left and 45.722 on the right. Since the χ^2 falls between these two values, we fail to reject the null hypothesis. This means the population standard deviation is not significantly different than $300.

15. **A** A two-tailed t-test is appropriate. The decision rule is to reject H_0 if the t-statistic is outside the range defined by $\pm t$ at $\alpha = 0.01$ with df = 24. The t-statistic = t_{24}

$$= \frac{\bar{x} - \mu_0}{s / \sqrt{n}} = \frac{50 - 48}{5 / \sqrt{25}} = 2.0 \,. \pm t_{24} \text{ at } \alpha = 0.01 = \pm 2.797; \text{ therefore, } H_0 \text{ cannot be rejected.}$$

16. **A** The chi-square test is used to test hypotheses concerning a single population variance. Since this is a one-tailed test, the decision rule is to reject H_0 if $\chi^2 >$ the critical chi-square value at $\alpha = 0.05$ with df = 24.

$$\chi^2_{n-1} = \frac{(n-1)s^2}{\sigma_0^2} = \frac{(24)(25)}{24} = 25.0 \,. \text{ The right-tail critical chi-square value is } 36.415.$$

Since $\chi^2 = 25 \leq 36.415$, H_0 cannot be rejected.

17. **B** A one-tailed t-test is appropriate. The decision rule is to reject H_0 if the computed t-statistic > t-critical at $\alpha = 0.05$ with df = 24. The computed value of the t-statistic

$$= \frac{\bar{x} - \mu_0}{s / \sqrt{n}} = \frac{50 - 48}{5 / \sqrt{25}} = 2.0 \,, \text{ and } t\text{-critical} = t_{24} = 1.711. \text{ Since } t > t\text{-critical}, H_0 \text{ should}$$

be rejected.

18. **A** The F-test is appropriate to the equality of population variances. The decision rule is to reject H_0 if the computed test statistic, F, exceeds the critical F-value at $\alpha / 2$. For the information provided, $F = s_1^2 \,/\, s_2^2 = 36 \,/\, 25 = 1.44$. At a 0.025 level of significance with $d_1 = 35$ and $d_2 = 24$, F-critical = 2.18. Since F < F-critical (1.44 < 2.18), we fail to reject the null hypothesis.

Professor's Note: Many F*-tables do not contain numerator df of 35. On the exam, CFA Institute will design problems such that the df are contained directly in the tables that you will be given on the exam. If the tables do not contain the exact df you need, interpolate the critical value based on the closest available df values.*

19. **A** The power of a test is 1 – P(Type II error) = 1 – 0.15 = 0.85.

20. **C** There is no consistent relationship between the mean and standard deviation of the chi-square distribution or F-distribution.

21. **B** The F-test is the appropriate test.

22. **C** A test of $\sigma^2 = \sigma_0^2$ is a χ^2 test.

23. **A** Since the observations are likely dependent (both related to market returns), a paired comparisons (mean differences) test is appropriate and is based on a t-statistic.

24. **C** When the variances are assumed to be unequal, we just calculate the denominator (standard error) differently and use both sample variances to calculate the t-statistic.

25. **C** A Type I error is rejecting the null hypothesis when it's true. The probability of rejecting a false null is [1 – Prob Type II] = [1 – 0.60] = 40%, which is called the power of the test. A and B are not necessarily true, since the null may be false and the probability of rejection unknown.

ANSWERS – COMPREHENSIVE PROBLEMS

1. A. The null hypothesis is typically the one the researcher wants to disprove. In this case, that would be that the mean risk-adjusted return on the cover stocks is less than or equal to the mean risk-adjusted return on the control stocks. The alternative is that the mean risk-adjusted returns on the cover stocks is greater than the mean risk-adjusted return on the control stocks. Rejecting the null will offer statistical support for the proposition the researcher wants to "prove" (the alternative).

    B. This would be a one-tailed test since the alternative is "greater than."

    C. The steps in a hypothesis test are as follows:
    *   State the hypothesis.
    *   Select the appropriate test statistic.
    *   Decide on the appropriate level of significance.
    *   Determine the decision rule.
    *   Collect the data.
    *   Calculate the sample statistics.
    *   Make a decision based on the decision rule for the test.
    *   Make decisions or inferences based on the results.

2. A. Since these two returns likely exhibit significant correlation and are, therefore, not independent, a paired comparisons test is appropriate. Differences between the returns on the two indices each week will be used. The standard deviation of the differences is used to construct a t-test of the hypothesis that the mean weekly difference is significantly different from (not equal to) zero. Reject if the t-statistic is greater/less than the positive/negative critical value.

    B. This is a test of a difference in means and is a t-test. The test statistic is the difference in means over a standard deviation calculated from the pooled variances of the two samples. Reject if the t-statistic is greater/less than the positive/negative critical value. When the variances are assumed to be equal for a difference in means test, we can use the variance of the pooled samples, and the degrees of freedom are simply $n_1 + n_2 - 2$ (total number of observations in both samples minus two).

    C. The test statistic is the ratio of the larger sample variance to the smaller sample variance. This statistic follows an F-distribution with $n_1 - 1$ and $n_2 - 1$ degrees of freedom. Reject equality if the test statistic exceeds the upper critical value.

    D. The test of whether the population variance is equal to a particular value is done with a test statistic with $(n - 1)$ times the sample variance in the numerator and the hypothesized variance (0.00165 here) in the denominator $\dfrac{(n-1)s^2}{s_0^2}$.

    The test statistic follows a Chi-square distribution. Reject the null of a population variance equal to 0.00165 if the test statistic is greater than the upper critical value or less than the lower critical value. The degrees of freedom are simply $n - 1$.

The following is a review of the Quantitative Methods: Application principles designed to address the learning outcome statements set forth by CFA Institute®. This topic is also covered in:

TECHNICAL ANALYSIS

EXAM FOCUS

This topic review introduces the "story" that underlies technical analysis, and you should understand how this differs from fundamental analysis. You should learn what the technical indicator names mean. Confusion regarding which indicators are contrarian indicators and which are smart money indicators is normal. I suggest you try to remember which are the smart money indicators because there are only three of them; then you will know that the others are contrarian indicators. The real distinction here is whose actions are driving the indicator. For smart money indicators, the "smart" people driving the indicator values are bond traders (confidence index and TED spread) and investors buying on margin (margin debt).

LOS 12.a: Explain the underlying assumptions of technical analysis.

Underlying all of technical analysis are the following assumptions:

- Values, and thus prices, are determined by supply and demand.
- Supply and demand are driven by both rational and irrational behavior.
- Security prices move in trends that persist for long periods.
- While the causes of changes in supply and demand are difficult to determine, the actual shifts in supply and demand can be observed in market price behavior.

The major challenge to technical analysis is the efficient markets hypothesis (EMH). Followers of the EMH believe that all available information associated with both fundamental and technical analysis is impounded in current security prices. EMH followers argue that technical trading rules require too much subjective interpretation and that decision variables change over time.

Fundamental analysts believe that a security's price is determined by the supply and demand for the underlying security based on its economic fundamentals, such as expected return and risk. Fundamentalists believe they can forecast value changes by analyzing earnings and other publicly available data.

The difference between fundamental analysis and technical analysis is the assumption about the speed at which new information is impounded into prices. Technicians believe the reaction is slow, while fundamentalists believe prices adjust quickly. In addition, efficient market hypothesis analysts feel the price adjustment happens almost instantaneously.

Fundamentalists, through their research, look for changes in the basis of value, which eventually leads to changes in the supply and demand for the stock. Technicians look for evidence of changes in supply and demand through market signals and indicators.

Efficient market followers say all this looking is a hopeless and profitless exercise, since prices will change very rapidly in response to new information.

The difference in the three views is illustrated in Figure 1, where the following interpretations can be made:

- Fundamentalists look for reasons why the valuation band will shift upward. The shift will happen when they find it. Price changes will occur over a period of days or weeks, as analysts determine the situation. The fundamentalists' price-adjustment process is described by the path from Point 1 to Point 2.
- Technicians look for signs that the valuation band has moved. Technicians base their strategies on the premise that price changes will occur over a long period, as indicated by the path from Point 1 to Point 3.
- EMH advocates hold that when the value band shift happens, the price will shift rapidly. This adjustment process is described by the path from Point 1 to Point 4.

Figure 1: Technical, Fundamental, and EMH Price Adjustment Process

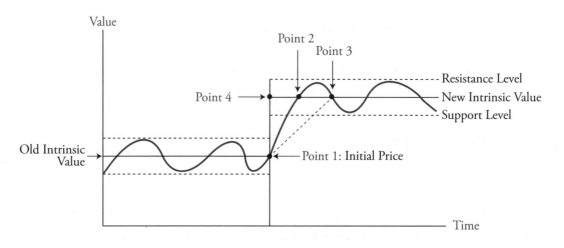

LOS 12.b: Discuss the advantages of and challenges to technical analysis.

Technical analysis offers the following advantages:

- It is quick and easy.
- It does not involve accounting data and analytical adjustments for differences in accounting methods.
- It incorporates psychological, as well as economic, reasons behind price changes.
- It tells *when* to buy (not *why* investors are buying).

The **major challenge to technical analysis** is the *efficient market hypothesis*. Efficient market analysts feel all available information is impounded in the current security price. They argue that technical relationships may not be repeated. Technical analysis is also challenged by the argument that technical rules require too much subjective interpretation and that technical decision variables change over time.

Technical analysis often involves some sort of trading rule. Some of the challenges to technical trading rules are as follows:

- Almost without exception, EMH studies using autocorrelation and runs tests have found no evidence that prices move in trends (i.e., past price patterns may not be repeated in the future). EMH followers say that the market appears to react quickly and completely to the release of new information.
- If technical trading rules worked, the price movements would become a self-fulfilling prophecy. That is, if enough people believe the price is going to rise $5 per share once a specific breakout price is reached, the buying pressure at the breakout price will cause the $5 price increase, although it will likely be temporary.
- If technical trading proved to be successful, others would copy it. As more traders implemented the strategy, its value would be neutralized.
- Interpreting the rules is too subjective, and the decision variables change over time.

LOS 12.c: List and describe examples of each major category of technical trading rules and indicators.

 Professor's Note: The wording of this LOS does not ask you to calculate these measures, only to identify them. Focus your attention on what high and low values of the indicators suggest to an analyst, not on the actual numeric values that are identified as bullish or bearish values.

Technical trading rules and indicators fall into four classes:

- The *contrarian* view. Contrary-opinion technicians (contrarians) argue that the majority is generally wrong, so they recommend doing the opposite of what the majority of investors are doing.
- *Follow the smart money* view. Smart-money technicians feel that smart investors know what they are doing, so they suggest "jumping on the bandwagon" while there is still time.
- *Momentum indicators* are used to make decisions based on the direction of market prices.
- Technical analysts employ a variety of *price- and volume-based indicators*.

Contrary Opinion Rules

Contrary-opinion technicians use the following six technical indicators:

1. **Cash position of mutual funds.** The mutual fund cash position is a function of investor expectations and the institution's view of market expectations. Contrary-opinion technicians feel that mutual fund cash positions are a good indicator of institutional investors' expectations and that they are usually wrong at picking the peaks and troughs of the market cycle.

$$\text{mutual fund ratio} = \frac{\text{mutual fund cash}}{\text{total fund assets}}$$

- If the mutual fund ratio (MFR) is greater than 11%, it implies funds are holding cash and are, therefore, bearish on the market. In this case, contrary-opinion technicians are bullish.
- If the MFR is less than 4%, it implies funds are investing cash and are, therefore, bullish on the market. Contrary-opinion technicians are consequently bearish.

Another way to look at this is that when the mutual fund cash ratio is high, contrarians are bullish because these cash holdings indicate potential future buying power in the market.

2. **Investor credit balances in brokerage accounts.** Credit balances are uninvested cash. Falling credit balances mean "normal" investors are bullish, so contrarians will be bearish and sell. Rising credit balances mean "normal" investors are bearish, so contrarians will be bullish and buy. A technical view of a build-up in credit balances would be that there is an increase in potential future buying power in the market, which is considered to be bullish.

3. **Opinions of investment advisory services.** The bearish sentiments index is used to indicate the level of bearish sentiment among investment advisors. If more than 60% of investment advisory services are bearish, contrarians are bullish. If less than 20% of advisors are bearish, advisors are relatively bullish, so contrarians are bearish and sell.

4. **Over-the-counter vs. NYSE volume.** Over-the-counter (OTC) issues are more speculative than NYSE issues, and speculative trading increases at market peaks. The level of speculative trading is measured using the ratio of OTC volume to NYSE volume. If the volume ratio is increasing, speculation is increasing; therefore, contrarians are bearish. If the ratio is decreasing, investors are bearish, and therefore contrarians are bullish.

5. **CBOE put/call ratio.** Contrarians use the put/call ratio as an indicator of investors' bearishness. As such, contrary-opinion technicians become bullish as the ratio increases. If the put-call ratio is equal to or greater than 0.6, the market is bearish, so contrarians are bullish. If the ratio is less than or equal to 0.4, the market is bullish, so contrarians are bearish.

6. **Stock index futures.** Some contrarians track the relative number of futures traders who are bullish. When 70% or more of index futures speculators are bullish, contrarians become bearish. When 30% or less of speculators are bullish, contrarians become bullish.

Professor's Note: Don't worry about the "trigger points" such as 70% bullish or 20% bearish. These are specific to the individual technical analyst. Do worry about how a high or low measure of these indicators would be viewed by a contrarian.

Smart Money Rules

Smart money technicians use the following three indicators to help them determine what the smart investors are doing.

1. **Confidence index.** The Confidence Index published by *Barron's* measures the ratio of average yields on high-quality corporate bonds to the average yields on a broader set of bonds.

$$CI = \frac{\text{Barron's average yield on 10 top grade corporate bonds}}{\text{Dow Jones Average 40 bonds}} \text{ or } CI = \frac{\text{quality bond yields}}{\text{average bond yields}}$$

   Note: this ratio is always less than one.

   In periods of confidence, investors sell high-quality bonds and buy lower-quality bonds to increase yields. Quality bond prices will fall and their yields rise. Lower-grade bond prices rise and their yields fall. Thus, the confidence index (CI) ratio will increase during periods of confidence (e.g., from 0.07 / 0.10 = 0.7 to 0.08 / 0.09 = 0.89). Note that the CI moves in the opposite direction of yield spreads. In periods of confidence, yield spreads narrow and the CI gets bigger. In periods of pessimism, spreads widen and the CI falls.

2. **T-bill—eurodollar yield spread.** Some technicians believe that spreads will often widen during times of international crisis as money flows to a safe haven in U.S. Treasury bills. An increasing "TED" spread is a bearish indicator.

3. **Debit balances in brokerage accounts (margin debt).** Debit balances in brokerage accounts represent the level of margin trading, which is usually only done by knowledgeable investors and traders.
   - An increase in debit balances would indicate an increase in purchasing by astute buyers. This is a bullish sign for smart money technicians.
   - A decline in debit balances would indicate astute traders are selling stocks. This is a bearish sign for smart money technicians.

Momentum Indicators

Breadth of market. The technician's story in this case is that:

- The indices represent a few large companies, not the whole market.
- The market has many medium and small companies.
- Frequently, the index goes one way while smaller issues go the other. Broad market moves include both large and small companies. How do you gauge the strength of market support (i.e., the breadth of the market)? Compare the advance-decline line with the market index.

The advance-decline line is a running total of the daily advances less the declines on the NYSE. If the advance-decline line and the index move together, the movement is broadly based across the market. A divergence between the trend in the index and the advance-decline line would signal that the market has hit a peak or trough.

Stocks above their 200-day moving average. The market is believed to be overbought—a bearish indicator—when over 80% of the stocks are selling above their

200-day moving averages. Similarly, the market is considered to be oversold—a bullish indicator—if less than 20% of the stocks are selling above their 200-day-moving averages.

Stock Price and Volume Techniques

Dow Theory. The Dow Theory states that stock prices move in trends. There are three types of trends: major trends, intermediate trends, and short-run movements. Technicians look for reversals and recoveries in major market trends.

Importance of volume. Price alone does not tell the story. Technicians attempt to gauge market sentiment, as well as direction, to determine changes in supply and demand. Thus, they look at the volume that accompanies price movements. Price changes on low volume tell us little. Price changes on high volume tell us whether suppliers or demanders are driving the change.

$$\text{upside-downside volume ratio} = \frac{\text{volume of stocks that increased}}{\text{volume of stocks that declined}}$$

If the upside-downside ratio is 1.75 or more, it indicates that the market is overbought. This is a bearish signal. If the ratio is 0.75 or lower, it reflects that the market is oversold. This is a bullish signal.

Support and resistance levels. Most stock prices remain relatively stable and fluctuate up and down from their true value. The lower limit to these fluctuations is called a support level—the price where a stock appears cheap and attracts buyers. The upper limit is called a resistance level—the price where a stock appears expensive and initiates selling.

Moving average lines. Technicians believe stock prices move in trends. However, random fluctuations in prices mask these trends. By using moving averages (10 to 200 days), technicians can eliminate the minor blips from graphs but retain information about any change in longer-term trends in prices.

Relative strength. When prices of an individual stock or industry change, it is difficult to tell if the change is stock-specific or caused by market movements. If the stock price and the market index value are changing at the same rate, the ratio created by dividing one by the other will remain constant. This ratio is called the relative strength ratio:

$$\text{relative strength} = \frac{\text{stock price}}{\text{market index value}}$$

- If the ratio increases over time, the stock is outperforming the market, which is a positive trend.
- If the ratio declines over time, the stock is underperforming the market, which is a negative trend.

Graphs. Some technical analysts are called chartists due to their extensive reliance on charts and graphs to indicate market directions.

- *Bar charts*. Price is plotted against time.
- *Point-and-figure charts*. Price is plotted on the y-axis, but movement along the x-axis is only plotted if a preset price reversal occurs.

Technicians read charts looking for patterns. Why? Technicians feel that history repeats itself, so by looking at past trends, they will be able to identify the beginning of new trends.

KEY CONCEPTS

LOS 12.a

The underlying assumptions of technical analysis are:

- The market price of securities is determined solely by supply and demand.
- Supply and demand are influenced by rational and irrational factors.
- Security prices move in trends that persist for appreciable lengths of time.
- Shifts in supply and demand can be determined by the actions of the market itself.

LOS 12.b

The advantages of technical analysis are:

- It is quick and easy.
- It does not depend heavily on financial statements and is largely unaffected by accounting differences.
- It incorporates psychological, as well as economic, reasons behind price changes.

Challenges to technical trading rules include:

- The efficient market hypothesis says price adjustments happen too quickly to trade on.
- The behavior of past prices and market variables may not be repeated in the future.
- Interpreting technical data requires much subjective judgment by the analyst.
- The indicator values that are thought to be bearish or bullish signals can change over time.

LOS 12.c

Contrarian technical analysts are bullish when most stock market investors are bearish, as indicated by:

- Mutual fund cash positions are larger than normal (greater than 11% of assets).
- Investor credit balances in brokerage accounts are rising.
- Most investment advisory opinions are bearish.
- Over-the-counter stock volume is decreasing relative to NYSE volume.
- The CBOE put/call ratio is high.
- A low percentage of stock-index futures traders are bullish.

Contrarians are bearish when most investors are bullish. (Mutual fund cash positions are less than normal, investor credit balances are falling, few advisors are bearish, OTC volume is increasing relative to NYSE volume, put/call ratio is low, and a high percentage of index futures traders are bullish.)

Smart-money technical analysts are bullish when they believe knowledgeable investors are bullish and bearish when these investors are bearish. Smart-money indicators include:

- *Barron's* confidence index (ratio of high quality bond yields to the yields on average quality bonds) increases when bond investors are bullish and buying lower quality bonds, and decreases when bond investors are bearish and shifting assets into higher quality bonds.
- The T-bill to Eurodollar yield spread (TED spread) widens during periods of crisis.
- Debit balances in brokerage accounts increase when margin buying (which tends to be done by more experienced investors) increases. Debt balances decrease when margin buying decreases.

Technical analysts use momentum indicators to read the direction of the market.
- The advance-decline line (advances less declines daily on the NYSE) indicates the breadth of a market increase or decrease. If the line moves in the same direction as the market, the increase or decrease is broadly based, but a divergence signals a peak or trough.
- If the percentage of stocks selling above their 200-day moving averages is high, this indicates overbought market conditions, a bearish signal. If this percentage is low, the market is oversold, a bullish signal.

Price- and volume-based indicators used by technical analysts include:
- Dow Theory.
- Upside-to-downside volume ratio.
- Support and resistance levels.
- Moving average lines.
- Relative strength ratios.
- Bar charts and point-and-figure charts.

CONCEPT CHECKERS

1. Which of the following statements is *least likely* an advantage of technical analysis?
   A. It tells the analyst when to buy.
   B. It tells the analyst why investors are buying.
   C. It incorporates psychological, as well as economic, reasons for price changes.

2. Which one of the following statements about technical analysis is *most likely* accurate? Technical analysis:
   A. requires very little subjective judgment.
   B. has been shown to outperform fundamental analysis.
   C. is not heavily dependent on financial accounting statements.

3. When the investment advisory "sentiment" index exceeds a 60% negative opinion rating, contrary-opinion technicians will do which of the following?
   A. Sell.
   B. Buy.
   C. Hold.

4. When the relative over-the-counter (OTC) to NYSE volume ratio is increasing, contrary-opinion technicians would do which of the following?
   A. Hold.
   B. Be bearish and sell.
   C. Be bullish and buy.

5. If the *Barron's* confidence index (CI) increases (and the implied yield spread narrows), investors are doing which of the following?
   A. Selling quality bonds.
   B. Buying quality bonds.
   C. Selling common stocks.

6. When investors are pessimistic, the CI will do which of the following?
   A. Increase.
   B. Decrease.
   C. Remain constant.

7. When debit balances (i.e., margin debt) in brokerage accounts increase:
   A. smart money technicians interpret this as a bearish sign.
   B. smart money technicians interpret this as a bullish sign.
   C. contrary-opinion technicians interpret this as a bullish sign.

8. Technicians feel that which of the following statements is *most likely* accurate?
   A. Stock prices move in trends.
   B. History does not tend to repeat itself.
   C. Prices adjust quickly to new information.

9. Which of the following would be a bullish sign to a smart money technician?
    A. The Barron's confidence index increases.
    B. The T-bill Eurodollar yield spread widens.
    C. Debit balances in brokerage accounts decline.

10. If the relative strength ratio (stock price over market price) increases, the market index:
    A. value increase equals the stock price increase.
    B. value percentage increase is less than the stock price percentage increase.
    C. value percentage increase is greater than the stock price percentage increase.

11. Which one of the following is a bearish signal to a smart money technical analyst?
    A. The T-bill Eurodollar yield spread narrows.
    B. The Barron's confidence index increases.
    C. Debit balances in brokerage accounts fall.

12. Which of the following is considered a bullish indicator to a contrarian?
    A. Low/falling credit balances in brokerage accounts.
    B. High OTC volume ratio.
    C. High put/call ratio.

ANSWERS – CONCEPT CHECKERS

1. **B** Technical analysis gives signals when to buy and incorporates psychological and economic reasons for price changes. Technical analysis does not have any explanatory power—it does not give a reason why investors are buying or selling.

2. **C** Technical analysis does require subjective judgment to interpret its rules. It has not been shown to outperform fundamental analysis. Technical analysis relies on price patterns and does not incorporate accounting data.

3. **B** When the majority of people are negative, as the sentiment index indicates, contrary-opinion technicians take the opposite opinion and will be bullish and buy.

4. **B** The OTC market is more speculative than the NYSE market. When people are buying more speculative issues, the majority of people are bullish. Contrary-opinion technicians will take the opposite stance—they will be bearish and sell.

5. **A** In periods of confidence, investors sell higher-quality bonds, and buy lower-quality bonds looking for yield. This happens when the confidence index rises or when spreads narrow.

6. **B** When investors are pessimistic, the confidence index falls.

7. **B** When margin debt balances in brokerage accounts increase, smart money technicians will see this as a bullish sign that investors are buying. Contrary-opinion technicians will take the opposite stance and will be bearish.

8. **A** Technicians believe that stock prices move in trends, that history does tend to repeat itself, and that prices react slowly to new information.

9. **A** A smart money technician will follow the behavior of other investors. Bullish signs would be increases in the confidence index, a narrowing of the T-bill Eurodollar spread, and increases in brokerage account debit balances.

10. **B** If the relative strength ratio (stock price / market index value) increases, the percentage increase in the stock price must be greater than the percentage increase in the market index value.

11. **C** A smart money technician will follow the behavior of other smart investors. Bearish signals would be a wider T-bill Eurodollar spread, a falling Barron's confidence index, and falling debit balances (margin debt) in brokerage accounts.

12. **C** A high put/call ratio indicates investors are bearish, which would be a bullish indicator to a contrarian.

15 Questions: 22.5 Minutes

1. Allan Jabber invested $400 at the beginning of each of the last 12 months in the shares of a mutual fund that paid no dividends. Which method will he correctly choose in order to calculate his average price per share from the monthly share prices?
   A. Arithmetic mean.
   B. Harmonic mean.
   C. Geometric mean.

2. The central limit theorem and Chebyshev's inequality apply to which distributions?

	Central limit theorem	Chebyshev's inequality
A.	Normal only	Normal only
B.	Normal only	Any distribution
C.	Any distribution	Any distribution

3. Colonia has only two political parties, the Wigs and the Wags. If the Wags are elected, there is a 32% probability of a tax increase over the next four years. If the Wigs are elected, there is a 60% probability of a tax increase. Based on the current polls, there is a 20% probability that the Wags will be elected. The sum of the (unconditional) probability of a tax increase and the joint probability that the Wigs will be elected and there will be no tax increase are *closest* to:
   A. 55%.
   B. 70%.
   C. 85%.

4. Analysts at Wellborn Advisors are considering two well-diversified portfolios based on firm forecasts of their expected returns and variance of returns. James argues that Portfolio 1 will be preferred by the client because it has a lower coefficient of variation. Samantha argues that Portfolio 2 would be preferred by the client because it has a higher Sharpe ratio. The client states that he wishes to minimize the probability that his portfolio will produce returns less than the risk-free rate. Based on this information, the client would *most likely* prefer:
   A. 100% in Portfolio 1.
   B. 100% in Portfolio 2.
   C. some combination of Portfolios 1 and 2.

5. Ralph will retire 15 years from today and has saved $121,000 in his investment account for retirement. He believes he will need $37,000 at the beginning of each year for 25 years of retirement, with the first withdrawal on the day he retires. Ralph assumes that his investment account will return 8%. The amount he needs to deposit at the beginning of this year and each of the following 14 years (15 deposits in all) is *closest* to:
   A. $1,350.
   B. $1,450.
   C. $1,550.

6.   The current price of Bosto shares is €50. Over the coming year, there is a 40% probability that share returns will be 10%, a 40% probability that share returns will be 12.5%, and a 20% probability that share returns will be 30%. Bosto's expected return and standard deviation of returns for the coming year are *closest* to:

	Expected return	Standard deviation
A.	15.0%	7.58%
B.	17.5%	5.75%
C.	17.5%	7.58%

7.   Nikki Ali and Donald Ankard borrowed $15,000 to finance their wedding and reception. The fully-amortizing loan at 11% requires equal payments at the end of each of the next seven years. The principal portion of the first payment is *closest* to:
     A. $1,500.
     B. $1,530.
     C. $1,560.

8.   Which of the following statements about probability distributions is *least accurate*?
     A. Continuous uniform distributions have cumulative distribution functions that are straight lines from zero to one.
     B. The probability that a continuously distributed random variable will take on a specific value is always zero.
     C. A normally distributed random variable divided by its standard deviation will follow a standard normal probability distribution.

9.   Market technician Christine Collies uses the Barron's confidence index as a "smart money" indicator and uses the CBOE put-call ratio as a contrarian indicator. Given that both of these indicators have recently risen sharply, her market outlook based on each indicator is *most likely*:

	Confidence index	Put-call ratio
A.	Bullish	Bullish
B.	Bearish	Bullish
C.	Bearish	Bearish

10. Given the following data:
     - There is a 40% probability that the economy will be good next year and a 60% probability that it will be bad.
     - If the economy is good, there is a 50% probability of a bull market, a 30% probability of an average market, and a 20% probability of a bear market.
     - If the economy is bad, there is a 20% probability of a bull market, a 30% probability of an average market, and a 50% probability of a bear market.

     The unconditional probability of a bull market is *closest* to:
     A. 20%.
     B. 32%.
     C. 50%.

11. X, Y, and Z are independently distributed. The probability of X is 30%, the probability of Y is 40%, and the probability of Z is 20%. Which of the following is *closest* to the probability that either X or Y will occur?
    A. 70%.
    B. 58%.
    C. 12%.

12. Which will be *equal* for a 1-year T-bill with 360 days to maturity?
    A. Bank discount yield and money market yield.
    B. Money market yield and holding period yield.
    C. Effective annual yield and bond equivalent yield.

13. The percentage changes in annual earnings for a company are approximately normally distributed with a mean of 5% and a standard deviation of 12%. The probability that the average change in earnings over the next five years will be greater than 15.5% is *closest* to:
    A. 2.5%.
    B. 5.0%.
    C. 10.0%.

14. Which of the following is *least likely* correct concerning a random variable that is lognormally distributed?
    A. It has a symmetric distribution.
    B. The natural logarithms of the random variable are normally distributed.
    C. It is a univariate distribution.

15. A discrete random variable x can take on the values 1, 2, 3, 4, or 5. The probability function is $Prob(x) = x/15$, so the cumulative distribution function is

    $\sum_{n=1}^{x}\left(\dfrac{n}{15}\right)$. The cumulative probability, F(4), and $P(2 < x \le 5)$ are:

	F(4)	$P(2 < x \le 5)$
A.	0.267	0.80
B.	0.267	0.93
C.	0.667	0.80

SELF-TEST ANSWERS: QUANTITATIVE METHODS

1. **B** The harmonic mean of the 12 purchase prices will be his average price paid per share.

2. **C** Both the central limit theorem and Chebyshev's inequality apply to any distribution.

3. **C** The unconditional probability of a tax increase is: $0.2(0.32) + 0.8(0.6) = 54.4\%$.

   The joint probability that the Wigs will be elected and there will be no tax increase is:

   $0.8(0.4) = 32\%$. The sum is: $54.4 + 32 = 86.4\%$.

4. **B** A portfolio that has a higher Sharpe ratio will have a lower probability of generating returns less than the risk-free rate. With a target return equal to the risk-free rate, the safety-first ratio for a portfolio is $(E[R_p] - R_f) / \sigma_p$, which is also the Sharpe ratio. Portfolio 2 will have a lower probability of returns less than the risk-free rate. Since both portfolios are well diversified and Portfolio 1 has a lower Sharpe ratio than Portfolio 2, any allocation to Portfolio 1 would decrease the overall portfolio's Sharpe and safety-first ratios, increasing the probability of returns less than the risk-free rate.

5. **B** Step 1: Calculate the amount needed at retirement at t = 15, with calculator in BGN mode.

   N = 25, FV = 0, I/Y = 8, PMT = 37,000, CPT PV = –426,564

   Step 2: Reduce this by the t = 15 value of current savings.

   $426{,}564 - 121{,}000(1.08)^{15} = 42{,}732$

   Step 3: calculate the required deposits at t = 0,1,....,14 to result in a time 15 value of 42,732, with calculator still in BGN mode.

   PV = 0, N = 15, I/Y = 8, FV = 42,732, CPT PMT = –$1,457.22

   To check, in BGN mode, N = 15, I/Y = 8, PMT = 1,457.22, PV = 121,000,

   CPT FV = –426,564.39.

6. **A** $E[R] = (0.4)(10) + (0.4)(12.5) + (0.2)(30) = 15\%$

   Variance $= (0.4)(10 - 15)^2 + (0.4)(12.5 - 15)^2 + (0.2)(30 - 15)^2 = 57.5$

   Standard deviation $= \sqrt{57.5} = 7.58\%$

7. **B** The interest portion of the first payment is simply principal × interest rate = $(15{,}000 \times 0.11) = 1{,}650$.

   Using a financial calculator: PV = 15,000, FV = 0, I/Y = 11, N=7, CPT PMT= $3,183

   Principal = payment – interest = 3,183 – 1,650 = 1,533

8. **C** A standard normal probability distribution has a mean of zero, so subtracting the mean from a normal random variable before dividing by its standard deviation is necessary to produce a standard normal probability distribution.

9. **A** An increase in the confidence index typically indicates that high-grade bond yields and average bond yields are moving closer together, which is bullish when used as a smart money indicator. An increase in the put-call ratio indicates that options traders are buying more puts than calls, which would be bullish when used as a contrary indicator.

10. **B** Using the total probability rule, the unconditional probability of a bull market is 0.50(0.40) + 0.20(0.60) = 32%.

11. **B** Probability of X or Y is P(X) + P(Y) − P(XY).

    0.3 + 0.4 − (0.3)(0.4) = 58%

12. **B** Since the money market yield is the holding period yield times #days / 360, HPY × 360 / 360 = HPY = MMY.

13. **A** The standard error of a 5-year average of earnings changes is $\frac{12\%}{\sqrt{5}} = 5.366\%$.

    15.5% is $\frac{15.5-5}{5.366} = 1.96$ standard errors above the mean, and the probability of a 5-year average more than 1.96 standard errors above the mean is 2.5% for a normal distribution.

14. **A** A lognormal distribution is skewed to the right (positively skewed).

15. **C** F(4) is the probability that x ≤ 4, which is (1 + 2 + 3 + 4) / 15 = 0.667, or 1 − 5 / 15 = 0.667.

    The probability that 2 < x ≤ 5, which is P(x = 3, 4, or 5), = (3 + 4 + 5) / 15 = 0.80. This is also F(5) − F(2) = (1 + 2 + 3 + 4 + 5) / 15 − (1 + 2) / 15 = 0.80.

FORMULAS

nominal risk-free rate = real risk-free rate + expected inflation rate

required interest rate on a security = nominal risk-free rate
+ default risk premium
+ liquidity premium
+ maturity risk premium

effective annual rate = $(1 + \text{periodic rate})^m - 1$

continuous compounding: $e^r - 1 = \text{EAR}$

$$PV_{\text{perpetuity}} = \frac{PMT}{I/Y}$$

$$FV = PV(1 + I/Y)^N$$

$$NPV = \sum_{t=0}^{N} \frac{CF_t}{(1+r)^t}$$

general formula for the IRR: $0 = CF_0 + \dfrac{CF_1}{1+IRR} + \dfrac{CF_2}{(1+IRR)^2} + \cdots + \dfrac{CF_N}{(1+IRR)^N}$

$$\text{bank discount yield} = \frac{D}{F} \times \frac{360}{t}$$

$$\text{holding period yield} = \frac{P_1 - P_0 + D_1}{P_0} = \frac{P_1 + D_1}{P_0} - 1$$

effective annual yield = $(1 + HPY)^{365/t} - 1$

$$\text{money market yield} = HPY\left(\frac{360}{t}\right)$$

population mean: $\mu = \dfrac{\sum\limits_{i=1}^{N} X_i}{N}$

sample mean: $\overline{X} = \dfrac{\sum\limits_{i=1}^{n} X_i}{n}$

geometric mean return (R_G): $1 + R_G = \sqrt[n]{(1+R_1) \times (1+R_2) \times \ldots \times (1+R_n)}$

harmonic mean: $\overline{X}_H = \dfrac{N}{\sum\limits_{i=1}^{N} \dfrac{1}{x_i}}$

weighted mean: $\overline{X}_W = \sum\limits_{i=1}^{n} w_i X_i$

position of the observation at a given percentile, *y*: $L_y = (n+1)\dfrac{y}{100}$

range = maximum value − minimum value

excess kurtosis = sample kurtosis − 3

$$MAD = \dfrac{\sum\limits_{i=1}^{n}\left|X_i - \overline{X}\right|}{n}$$

population variance $= \sigma^2 = \dfrac{\sum\limits_{i=1}^{N}(X_i - \mu)^2}{N},$

where μ = population mean and N = number of possible outcomes

sample variance $= s^2 = \dfrac{\sum\limits_{i=1}^{n}(X_i - \overline{X})^2}{n-1}$, where $\overline{X}$ = sample mean and n = sample size

coefficient of variation: $CV = \dfrac{s_x}{\overline{X}} = \dfrac{\text{standard deviation of x}}{\text{average value of x}}$

Sharpe ratio $= \dfrac{\overline{r_p} - r_f}{\sigma_p}$

joint probability: $P(AB) = P(A \mid B) \times P(B)$

addition rule: $P(A \text{ or } B) = P(A) + P(B) - P(AB)$

multiplication rule: $P(A \text{ and } B) = P(A) \times P(B)$

total probability rule:
$P(R) = P(R \mid S_1) \times P(S_1) + P(R \mid S_2) \times P(S_2) + \ldots + P(R \mid S_N) \times P(S_N)$

expected value: $E(X) = \Sigma P(x_i)x_i = P(x_1)x_1 + P(x_2)x_2 + \ldots + P(x_n)x_n$

$Cov(R_i, R_j) = E\{[R_i - E(R_i)][R_j - E(R_j)]\}$

$Corr(R_i, R_j) = \dfrac{Cov(R_i, R_j)}{\sigma(R_i)\sigma(R_j)}$

portfolio expected return: $E\left(R_p\right) = \sum_{i=1}^{N} w_i E(R_i) = w_1 E(R_1) + w_2 E(R_2) + \ldots + w_n E(R_n)$

portfolio variance: $Var\left(R_p\right) = \sum_{i=1}^{N} \sum_{j=1}^{N} w_i w_j Cov\left(R_i, R_j\right)$

where $w_i = \dfrac{\text{market value of investment in asset i}}{\text{market value of the portfolio}}$

Bayes' formula:

updated probability $= \dfrac{\text{probability of new information for a given event}}{\text{unconditional probability of new information}} \times \text{prior probability of event}$

combination (binomial) formula: $_nC_r = \dfrac{n!}{(n-r)!r!}$

permutation formula: $_nP_r = \dfrac{n!}{(n-r)!}$

binomial probability: $p\left(x\right) = \dfrac{n!}{(n-x)!x!} p^x \left(1-p\right)^{n-x}$

for a binomial random variable: $E(X) = np$

for a normal variable:

90% confidence interval for X is $\overline{X} - 1.65s$ to $\overline{X} + 1.65s$

95% confidence interval for X is $\overline{X} - 1.96s$ to $\overline{X} + 1.96s$

99% confidence interval for X is $\overline{X} - 2.58s$ to $\overline{X} + 2.58s$

$z = \dfrac{\text{observation} - \text{population mean}}{\text{standard deviation}} = \dfrac{x - \mu}{\sigma}$

SFRatio $= \dfrac{\left[E\left(R_p\right) - R_L\right]}{\sigma_p}$

continuously compounded rate of return: $r_{cc} = \ln\left(\dfrac{S_1}{S_0}\right) = \ln\left(1 + HPR\right)$

for a uniform distribution: $P\left(x_1 \le X \le x_2\right) = \dfrac{\left(x_2 - x_1\right)}{\left(b - a\right)}$

sampling error of the mean = sample mean – population mean = $\overline{x} - \mu$

standard error of the sample mean, known population variance: $\sigma_{\overline{x}} = \dfrac{\sigma}{\sqrt{n}}$

standard error of the sample mean, unknown population variance: $s_{\bar{x}} = \dfrac{s}{\sqrt{n}}$

confidence interval: point estimate ± (reliability factor × standard error)

confidence interval for the population mean: $\bar{x} \pm z_{\alpha/2} \dfrac{\sigma}{\sqrt{n}}$

tests for population mean = μ_0: z-statistic $= \dfrac{\bar{x} - \mu_0}{\sigma / \sqrt{n}}$, t-statistic $= \dfrac{\bar{x} - \mu_0}{s / \sqrt{n}}$

test for equality of variances: $F = \dfrac{s_1^2}{s_2^2}$, where $s_1^2 > s_2^2$

test of mean differences = 0: t-statistic $= \dfrac{\bar{d}}{s_d}$

test for equality of means:

t-statistic $= \dfrac{(\bar{x}_1 - \bar{x}_2) - (\mu_1 - \mu_2)}{\left(\dfrac{s_1^2}{n_1} + \dfrac{s_2^2}{n_2}\right)^{1/2}}$ (sample variances assumed unequal)

t-statistic $= \dfrac{(\bar{x}_1 - \bar{x}_2) - (\mu_1 - \mu_2)}{\left(\dfrac{s_p^2}{n_1} + \dfrac{s_p^2}{n_2}\right)^{1/2}}$ (sample variances assumed equal)

Appendix A:
Areas Under the Normal Curve

Most of the examples in this book have used one version of the *z*-table to find the area under the normal curve. This table provides the cumulative probabilities (or the area under the entire curve to left of the z-value).

Probability Example

Assume that the annual earnings per share (EPS) for a large sample of firms is normally distributed with a mean of $5.00 and a standard deviation of $1.50. What is the approximate probability of an observed EPS value falling between $3.00 and $7.25?

If *EPS* = x = \$7.25, then $z = (x - \mu)/\sigma = (\$7.25 - \$5.00)/\$1.50 = +1.50$

If *EPS* = x = \$3.00, then $z = (x - \mu)/\sigma = (\$3.00 - \$5.00)/\$1.50 = -1.33$

Solving Using The Cumulative *Z*-Table

For z-value of 1.50: Use the row headed 1.5 and the column headed 0 to find the value 0.9332. This represents the area under the curve to the left of the critical value 1.50.

For z-value of –1.33: Use the row headed 1.3 and the column headed 3 to find the value 0.9082. This represents the area under the curve to the left of the critical value +1.33. The area to the left of –1.33 is 1 – 0.9082 = 0.0918.

The area between these critical values is 0.9332 – 0.0918 = 0.8414, or 84.14%.

Hypothesis Testing – One-Tailed Test Example

A sample of a stock's returns on 36 non-consecutive days results in a mean return of 2.0 percent. Assume the population standard deviation is 20.0 percent. Can we say with 95 percent confidence that the mean return is greater than zero percent?

$H_0: \mu \leq 0.0\%$, $H_a: \mu > 0.0\%$. The test statistic = *z*-statistic = $\dfrac{\bar{x} - \mu_0}{\sigma / \sqrt{n}}$ = (2.0 – 0.0) / (20.0 / 6) = 0.60.

The significance level = 1.0 – 0.95 = 0.05, or 5%. Since we are interested in a return greater than 0.0 percent, this is a one-tailed test.

Using The Cumulative *Z*-Table

Since this is a one-tailed test with an alpha of 0.05, we need to find the value 0.95 in the cumulative *z*-table. The closest value is 0.9505, with a corresponding critical *z*-value of 1.65. Since the test statistic is less than the critical value, we fail to reject H_0.

Hypothesis Testing – Two-Tailed Test Example

Using the same assumptions as before, suppose that the analyst now wants to determine if he can say with 99% confidence that the stock's return is not equal to 0.0 percent.

H_0: μ = 0.0%, H_a: $\mu \neq$ 0.0%. The test statistic (z-value) = (2.0 – 0.0) / (20.0 / 6) = 0.60. The significance level = 1.0 – 0.99 = 0.01, or 1%. Since we are interested in whether or not the stock return is nonzero, this is a two-tailed test.

Using The Cumulative Z-Table

Since this is a two-tailed test with an alpha of 0.01, there is a 0.005 rejection region in both tails. Thus, we need to find the value 0.995 (1.0 – 0.005) in the table. The closest value is 0.9951, which corresponds to a critical z-value of 2.58. Since the test statistic is less than the critical value, we fail to reject H_0 and conclude that the stock's return equals 0.0 percent.

Cumulative Z-Table

Standard Normal Distribution
$P(Z \leq z) = N(z)$ for $z \geq 0$

z	0.00	0.01	0.02	0.03	0.04	0.05	0.06	0.07	0.08	0.09
0.0	0.5000	0.5040	0.5080	0.5120	0.5160	0.5199	0.5239	0.5279	0.5319	0.5359
0.1	0.5398	0.5438	0.5478	0.5517	0.5557	0.5596	0.5636	0.5675	0.5714	0.5753
0.2	0.5793	0.5832	0.5871	0.5910	0.5948	0.5987	0.6026	0.6064	0.6103	0.6141
0.3	0.6179	0.6217	0.6255	0.6293	0.6331	0.6368	0.6406	0.6443	0.6480	0.6517
0.4	0.6554	0.6591	0.6628	0.6664	0.6700	0.6736	0.6772	0.6808	0.6844	0.6879
0.5	0.6915	0.6950	0.6985	0.7019	0.7054	0.7088	0.7123	0.7157	0.7190	0.7224
0.6	0.7257	0.7291	0.7324	0.7357	0.7389	0.7422	0.7454	0.7486	0.7517	0.7549
0.7	0.7580	0.7611	0.7642	0.7673	0.7704	0.7734	0.7764	0.7794	0.7823	0.7852
0.8	0.7881	0.7910	0.7939	0.7967	0.7995	0.8023	0.8051	0.8078	0.8106	0.8133
0.9	0.8159	0.8186	0.8212	0.8238	0.8264	0.8289	0.8315	0.8340	0.8365	0.8389
1.0	0.8413	0.8438	0.8461	0.8485	0.8508	0.8531	0.8554	0.8577	0.8599	0.8621
1.1	0.8643	0.8665	0.8686	0.8708	0.8729	0.8749	0.8770	0.8790	0.8810	0.8830
1.2	0.8849	0.8869	0.8888	0.8907	0.8925	0.8944	0.8962	0.8980	0.8997	0.9015
1.3	0.9032	0.9049	0.9066	0.9082	0.9099	0.9115	0.9131	0.9147	0.9162	0.9177
1.4	0.9192	0.9207	0.9222	0.9236	0.9251	0.9265	0.9279	0.9292	0.9306	0.9319
1.5	0.9332	0.9345	0.9357	0.9370	0.9382	0.9394	0.9406	0.9418	0.9429	0.9441
1.6	0.9452	0.9463	0.9474	0.9484	0.9495	0.9505	0.9515	0.9525	0.9535	0.9545
1.7	0.9554	0.9564	0.9573	0.9582	0.9591	0.9599	0.9608	0.9616	0.9625	0.9633
1.8	0.9641	0.9649	0.9656	0.9664	0.9671	0.9678	0.9686	0.9693	0.9699	0.9706
1.9	0.9713	0.9719	0.9726	0.9732	0.9738	0.9744	0.9750	0.9756	0.9761	0.9767
2.0	0.9772	0.9778	0.9783	0.9788	0.9793	0.9798	0.9803	0.9808	0.9812	0.9817
2.1	0.9821	0.9826	0.9830	0.9834	0.9838	0.9842	0.9846	0.9850	0.9854	0.9857
2.2	0.9861	0.9864	0.9868	0.9871	0.9875	0.9878	0.9881	0.9884	0.9887	0.9890
2.3	0.9893	0.9896	0.9898	0.9901	0.9904	0.9906	0.9909	0.9911	0.9913	0.9916
2.4	0.9918	0.9920	0.9922	0.9925	0.9927	0.9929	0.9931	0.9932	0.9934	0.9936
2.5	0.9938	0.9940	0.9941	0.9943	0.9945	0.9946	0.9948	0.9949	0.9951	0.9952
2.6	0.9953	0.9955	0.9956	0.9957	0.9959	0.9960	0.9961	0.9962	0.9963	0.9964
2.7	0.9965	0.9966	0.9967	0.9968	0.9969	0.9970	0.9971	0.9972	0.9973	0.9974
2.8	0.9974	0.9975	0.9976	0.9977	0.9977	0.9978	0.9979	0.9979	0.9980	0.9981
2.9	0.9981	0.9982	0.9982	0.9983	0.9984	0.9984	0.9985	0.9985	0.9986	0.9986
3.0	0.9987	0.9987	0.9987	0.9988	0.9988	0.9989	0.9989	0.9989	0.9990	0.9990

CUMULATIVE Z-TABLE (CONT.)

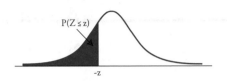

STANDARD NORMAL DISTRIBUTION
$P(Z \leq z) = N(z)$ FOR $z \leq 0$

z	0.00	0.01	0.02	0.03	0.04	0.05	0.06	0.07	0.08	0.09
0.0	0.5000	0.4960	0.4920	0.4880	0.4840	0.4801	0.4761	0.4721	0.4681	0.4641
-0.1	0.4602	0.4562	0.4522	0.4483	0.4443	0.4404	0.4364	0.4325	0.4286	0.4247
-0.2	0.4207	0.4168	0.4129	0.4090	0.4052	0.4013	0.3974	0.3936	0.3897	0.3859
-0.3	0.3821	0.3783	0.3745	0.3707	0.3669	0.3632	0.3594	0.3557	0.3520	0.3483
-0.4	0.3446	0.3409	0.3372	0.3336	0.3300	0.3264	0.3228	0.3192	0.3156	0.3121
-0.5	0.3085	0.3050	0.3015	0.2981	0.2946	0.2912	0.2877	0.2843	0.2810	0.2776
-0.6	0.2743	0.2709	0.2676	0.2643	0.2611	0.2578	0.2546	0.2514	0.2483	0.2451
-0.7	0.2420	0.2389	0.2358	0.2327	0.2297	0.2266	0.2236	0.2207	0.2177	0.2148
-0.8	0.2119	0.2090	0.2061	0.2033	0.2005	0.1977	0.1949	0.1922	0.1894	0.1867
-0.9	0.1841	0.1814	0.1788	0.1762	0.1736	0.1711	0.1685	0.1660	0.1635	0.1611
-1.0	0.1587	0.1562	0.1539	0.1515	0.1492	0.1469	0.1446	0.1423	0.1401	0.1379
-1.1	0.1357	0.1335	0.1314	0.1292	0.1271	0.1251	0.1230	0.1210	0.1190	0.1170
-1.2	0.1151	0.1131	0.1112	0.1093	0.1075	0.1057	0.1038	0.1020	0.1003	0.0985
-1.3	0.0968	0.0951	0.0934	0.0918	0.0901	0.0885	0.0869	0.0853	0.0838	0.0823
-1.4	0.0808	0.0793	0.0778	0.0764	0.0749	0.0735	0.0721	0.0708	0.0694	0.0681
-1.5	0.0668	0.0655	0.0643	0.0630	0.0618	0.0606	0.0594	0.0582	0.0571	0.0559
-1.6	0.0548	0.0537	0.0526	0.0516	0.0505	0.0495	0.0485	0.0475	0.0465	0.0455
-1.7	0.0446	0.0436	0.0427	0.0418	0.0409	0.0401	0.0392	0.0384	0.0375	0.0367
-1.8	0.0359	0.0351	0.0344	0.0336	0.0329	0.0322	0.0314	0.0307	0.0301	0.0294
-1.9	0.0287	0.0281	0.0274	0.0268	0.0262	0.0256	0.0250	0.0244	0.0239	0.0233
-2.0	0.0228	0.0222	0.0217	0.0212	0.0207	0.0202	0.0197	0.0192	0.0188	0.0183
-2.1	0.0179	0.0174	0.0170	0.0166	0.0162	0.0158	0.0154	0.0150	0.0146	0.0143
-2.2	0.0139	0.0136	0.0132	0.0129	0.0125	0.0122	0.0119	0.0116	0.0113	0.0110
-2.3	0.0107	0.0104	0.0102	0.0099	0.0096	0.0094	0.0091	0.0089	0.0087	0.0084
-2.4	0.0082	0.0080	0.0078	0.0076	0.0073	0.0071	0.0069	0.0068	0.0066	0.0064
-2.5	0.0062	0.0060	0.0059	0.0057	0.0055	0.0054	0.0052	0.0051	0.0049	0.0048
-2.6	0.0047	0.0045	0.0044	0.0043	0.0041	0.0040	0.0039	0.0038	0.0037	0.0036
-2.7	0.0035	0.0034	0.0033	0.0032	0.0031	0.0030	0.0029	0.0028	0.0027	0.0026
-2.8	0.0026	0.0025	0.0024	0.0023	0.0023	0.0022	0.0021	0.0021	0.0020	0.0019
-2.9	0.0019	0.0018	0.0018	0.0017	0.0016	0.0016	0.0015	0.0015	0.0014	0.0014
-3.0	0.0014	0.0013	0.0013	0.0012	0.0012	0.0011	0.0011	0.0011	0.0010	0.0010

APPENDIX B:
STUDENT'S *t*-DISTRIBUTION

df	Level of Significance for One-Tailed Test					
	0.100	0.050	0.025	0.01	0.005	0.0005

df	Level of Significance for Two-Tailed Test					
	0.20	0.10	0.05	0.02	0.01	0.001
1	3.078	6.314	12.706	31.821	63.657	636.619
2	1.886	2.920	4.303	6.965	9.925	31.599
3	1.638	2.353	3.182	4.541	5.841	12.294
4	1.533	2.132	2.776	3.747	4.604	8.610
5	1.476	2.015	2.571	3.365	4.032	6.869
6	1.440	1.943	2.447	3.143	3.707	5.959
7	1.415	1.895	2.365	2.998	3.499	5.408
8	1.397	1.860	2.306	2.896	3.355	5.041
9	1.383	1.833	2.262	2.821	3.250	4.781
10	1.372	1.812	2.228	2.764	3.169	4.587
11	1.363	1.796	2.201	2.718	3.106	4.437
12	1.356	1.782	2.179	2.681	3.055	4.318
13	1.350	1.771	2.160	2.650	3.012	4.221
14	1.345	1.761	2.145	2.624	2.977	4.140
15	1.341	1.753	2.131	2.602	2.947	4.073
16	1.337	1.746	2.120	2.583	2.921	4.015
17	1.333	1.740	2.110	2.567	2.898	3.965
18	1.330	1.734	2.101	2.552	2.878	3.922
19	1.328	1.729	2.093	2.539	2.861	3.883
20	1.325	1.725	2.086	2.528	2.845	3.850
21	1.323	1.721	2.080	2.518	2.831	3.819
22	1.321	1.717	2.074	2.508	2.819	3.792
23	1.319	1.714	2.069	2.500	2.807	3.768
24	1.318	1.711	2.064	2.492	2.797	3.745
25	1.316	1.708	2.060	2.485	2.787	3.725
26	1.315	1.706	2.056	2.479	2.779	3.707
27	1.314	1.703	2.052	2.473	2.771	3.690
28	1.313	1.701	2.048	2.467	2.763	3.674
29	1.311	1.699	2.045	2.462	2.756	3.659
30	1.310	1.697	2.042	2.457	2.750	3.646
40	1.303	1.684	2.021	2.423	2.704	3.551
60	1.296	1.671	2.000	2.390	2.660	3.460
120	1.289	1.658	1.980	2.358	2.617	3.373
∞	1.282	1.645	1.960	2.326	2.576	3.291

Appendix C:
F-Table at 5 Percent (Upper Tail)

F-Table, Critical Values, 5 Percent in Upper Tail

Degrees of freedom for the numerator along top row
Degrees of freedom for the denominator along side row

	1	2	3	4	5	6	7	8	9	10	12	15	20	24	30	40
1	161	200	216	225	230	234	237	239	241	242	244	246	248	249	250	251
2	18.5	19.0	19.2	19.2	19.3	19.3	19.4	19.4	19.4	19.4	19.4	19.4	19.4	19.5	19.5	19.5
3	10.1	9.55	9.28	9.12	9.01	8.94	8.89	8.85	8.81	8.79	8.74	8.70	8.66	8.64	8.62	8.59
4	7.71	6.94	6.59	6.39	6.26	6.16	6.09	6.04	6.00	5.96	5.91	5.86	5.80	5.77	5.75	5.72
5	6.61	5.79	5.41	5.19	5.05	4.95	4.88	4.82	4.77	4.74	4.68	4.62	4.56	4.53	4.50	4.46
6	5.99	5.14	4.76	4.53	4.39	4.28	4.21	4.15	4.10	4.06	4.00	3.94	3.87	3.84	3.81	3.77
7	5.59	4.74	4.35	4.12	3.97	3.87	3.79	3.73	3.68	3.64	3.57	3.51	3.44	3.41	3.38	3.34
8	5.32	4.46	4.07	3.84	3.69	3.58	3.50	3.44	3.39	3.35	3.28	3.22	3.15	3.12	3.08	3.04
9	5.12	4.26	3.86	3.63	3.48	3.37	3.29	3.23	3.18	3.14	3.07	6.01	2.94	2.90	2.86	2.83
10	4.96	4.10	3.71	3.48	3.33	3.22	3.14	3.07	3.02	2.98	2.91	2.85	2.77	2.74	2.70	2.66
11	4.84	3.98	3.59	3.36	3.20	3.09	3.01	2.95	2.90	2.85	2.79	2.72	2.65	2.61	2.57	2.53
12	4.75	3.89	3.49	3.26	3.11	3.00	2.91	2.85	2.80	2.75	2.69	2.62	2.54	2.51	2.47	2.43
13	4.67	3.81	3.41	3.18	3.03	2.92	2.83	2.77	2.71	2.67	2.60	2.53	2.46	2.42	2.38	2.34
14	4.60	3.74	3.34	3.11	2.96	2.85	2.76	2.70	2.65	2.60	2.53	2.46	2.39	2.35	2.31	2.27
15	4.54	3.68	3.29	3.06	2.90	2.79	2.71	2.64	2.59	2.54	2.48	2.40	2.33	2.29	2.25	2.20
16	4.49	3.63	3.24	3.01	2.85	2.74	2.66	2.59	2.54	2.49	2.42	2.35	2.28	2.24	2.19	2.15
17	4.45	3.59	3.20	2.96	2.81	2.70	2.61	2.55	2.49	2.45	2.38	2.31	2.23	2.19	2.15	2.10
18	4.41	3.55	3.16	2.93	2.77	2.66	2.58	2.51	2.46	2.41	2.34	2.27	2.19	2.15	2.11	2.06
19	4.38	3.52	3.13	2.90	2.74	2.63	2.54	2.48	2.42	2.38	2.31	2.23	2.16	2.11	2.07	2.03
20	4.35	3.49	3.10	2.87	2.71	2.60	2.51	2.45	2.39	2.35	2.28	2.20	2.12	2.08	2.04	1.99
21	4.32	3.47	3.07	2.84	2.68	2.57	2.49	2.42	2.37	2.32	2.25	2.18	2.10	2.05	2.01	1.96
22	4.30	3.44	3.05	2.82	2.66	2.55	2.46	2.40	2.34	2.30	2.23	2.15	2.07	2.03	1.98	1.94
23	4.28	3.42	3.03	2.80	2.64	2.53	2.44	2.37	2.32	2.27	2.20	2.13	2.05	2.01	1.96	1.91
24	4.26	3.40	3.01	2.78	2.62	2.51	2.42	2.36	2.30	2.25	2.18	2.11	2.03	1.98	1.94	1.89
25	4.24	3.39	2.99	2.76	2.60	2.49	2.40	2.34	2.28	2.24	2.16	2.09	2.01	1.96	1.92	1.87
30	4.17	3.32	2.92	2.69	2.53	2.42	2.33	2.27	2.21	2.16	2.09	2.01	1.93	1.89	1.84	1.79
40	4.08	3.23	2.84	2.61	2.45	2.34	2.25	2.18	2.12	2.08	2.00	1.92	1.84	1.79	1.74	1.69
60	4.00	3.15	2.76	2.53	2.37	2.25	2.17	2.10	2.04	1.99	1.92	1.84	1.75	1.70	1.65	1.59
120	3.92	3.07	2.68	2.45	2.29	2.18	2.09	2.02	1.96	1.91	1.83	1.75	1.66	1.61	1.55	1.50
∞	3.84	3.00	2.60	2.37	2.21	2.10	2.01	1.94	1.88	1.83	1.75	1.67	1.57	1.52	1.46	1.39

Appendix D:
F-Table at 2.5 Percent (Upper Tail)

F-Table, Critical Values, 2.5 Percent in Upper Tails

Degrees of freedom for the numerator along top row
Degrees of freedom for the denominator along side row

	1	2	3	4	5	6	7	8	9	10	12	15	20	24	30	40
1	648	799	864	900	922	937	948	957	963	969	977	985	993	997	1001	1006
2	38.51	39.00	39.17	39.25	39.30	39.33	39.36	39.37	39.39	39.40	39.41	39.43	39.45	39.46	39.46	39.47
3	17.44	16.04	15.44	15.10	14.88	14.73	14.62	14.54	14.47	14.42	14.34	14.25	14.17	14.12	14.08	14.04
4	12.22	10.65	9.98	9.60	9.36	9.20	9.07	8.98	8.90	8.84	8.75	8.66	8.56	8.51	8.46	8.41
5	10.01	8.43	7.76	7.39	7.15	6.98	6.85	6.76	6.68	6.62	6.52	6.43	6.33	6.28	6.23	6.18
6	8.81	7.26	6.60	6.23	5.99	5.82	5.70	5.60	5.52	5.46	5.37	5.27	5.17	5.12	5.07	5.01
7	8.07	6.54	5.89	5.52	5.29	5.12	4.99	4.90	4.82	4.76	4.67	4.57	4.47	4.41	4.36	4.31
8	7.57	6.06	5.42	5.05	4.82	4.65	4.53	4.43	4.36	4.30	4.20	4.10	4.00	3.95	3.89	3.84
9	7.21	5.71	5.08	4.72	4.48	4.32	4.20	4.10	4.03	3.96	3.87	3.77	3.67	3.61	3.56	3.51
10	6.94	5.46	4.83	4.47	4.24	4.07	3.95	3.85	3.78	3.72	3.62	3.52	3.42	3.37	3.31	3.26
11	6.72	5.26	4.63	4.28	4.04	3.88	3.76	3.66	3.59	3.53	3.43	3.33	3.23	3.17	3.12	3.06
12	6.55	5.10	4.47	4.12	3.89	3.73	3.61	3.51	3.44	3.37	3.28	3.18	3.07	3.02	2.96	2.91
13	6.41	4.97	4.35	4.00	3.77	3.60	3.48	3.39	3.31	3.25	3.15	3.05	2.95	2.89	2.84	2.78
14	6.30	4.86	4.24	3.89	3.66	3.50	3.38	3.29	3.21	3.15	3.05	2.95	2.84	2.79	2.73	2.67
15	6.20	4.77	4.15	3.80	3.58	3.41	3.29	3.20	3.12	3.06	2.96	2.86	2.76	2.70	2.64	2.59
16	6.12	4.69	4.08	3.73	3.50	3.34	3.22	3.12	3.05	2.99	2.89	2.79	2.68	2.63	2.57	2.51
17	6.04	4.62	4.01	3.66	3.44	3.28	3.16	3.06	2.98	2.92	2.82	2.72	2.62	2.56	2.50	2.44
18	5.98	4.56	3.95	3.61	3.38	3.22	3.10	3.01	2.93	2.87	2.77	2.67	2.56	2.50	2.44	2.38
19	5.92	4.51	3.90	3.56	3.33	3.17	3.05	2.96	2.88	2.82	2.72	2.62	2.51	2.45	2.39	2.33
20	5.87	4.46	3.86	3.51	3.29	3.13	3.01	2.91	2.84	2.77	2.68	2.57	2.46	2.41	2.35	2.29
21	5.83	4.42	3.82	3.48	3.25	3.09	2.97	2.87	2.80	2.73	2.64	2.53	2.42	2.37	2.31	2.25
22	5.79	4.38	3.78	3.44	3.22	3.05	2.93	2.84	2.76	2.70	2.60	2.50	2.39	2.33	2.27	2.21
23	5.75	4.35	3.75	3.41	3.18	3.02	2.90	2.81	2.73	2.67	2.57	2.47	2.36	2.30	2.24	2.18
24	5.72	4.32	3.72	3.38	3.15	2.99	2.87	2.78	2.70	2.64	2.54	2.44	2.33	2.27	2.21	2.15
25	5.69	4.29	3.69	3.35	3.13	2.97	2.85	2.75	2.68	2.61	2.51	2.41	2.30	2.24	2.18	2.12
30	5.57	4.18	3.59	3.25	3.03	2.87	2.75	2.65	2.57	2.51	2.41	2.31	2.20	2.14	2.07	2.01
40	5.42	4.05	3.46	3.13	2.90	2.74	2.62	2.53	2.45	2.39	2.29	2.18	2.07	2.01	1.94	1.88
60	5.29	3.93	3.34	3.01	2.79	2.63	2.51	2.41	2.33	2.27	2.17	2.06	1.94	1.88	1.82	1.74
120	5.15	3.80	3.23	2.89	2.67	2.52	2.39	2.30	2.22	2.16	2.05	1.94	1.82	1.76	1.69	1.61
∞	5.02	3.69	3.12	2.79	2.57	2.41	2.29	2.19	2.11	2.05	1.94	1.83	1.71	1.64	1.57	1.48

APPENDIX E:
CHI-SQUARED TABLE

Values of χ^2 (Degrees of Freedom, Level of Significance)
Probability in Right Tail

Degrees of Freedom	0.99	0.975	0.95	0.9	0.1	0.05	0.025	0.01	0.005
1	0.000157	0.000982	0.003932	0.0158	2.706	3.841	5.024	6.635	7.879
2	0.020100	0.050636	0.102586	0.2107	4.605	5.991	7.378	9.210	10.597
3	0.1148	0.2158	0.3518	0.5844	6.251	7.815	9.348	11.345	12.838
4	0.297	0.484	0.711	1.064	7.779	9.488	11.143	13.277	14.860
5	0.554	0.831	1.145	1.610	9.236	11.070	12.832	15.086	16.750
6	0.872	1.237	1.635	2.204	10.645	12.592	14.449	16.812	18.548
7	1.239	1.690	2.167	2.833	12.017	14.067	16.013	18.475	20.278
8	1.647	2.180	2.733	3.490	13.362	15.507	17.535	20.090	21.955
9	2.088	2.700	3.325	4.168	14.684	16.919	19.023	21.666	23.589
10	2.558	3.247	3.940	4.865	15.987	18.307	20.483	23.209	25.188
11	3.053	3.816	4.575	5.578	17.275	19.675	21.920	24.725	26.757
12	3.571	4.404	5.226	6.304	18.549	21.026	23.337	26.217	28.300
13	4.107	5.009	5.892	7.041	19.812	22.362	24.736	27.688	29.819
14	4.660	5.629	6.571	7.790	21.064	23.685	26.119	29.141	31.319
15	5.229	6.262	7.261	8.547	22.307	24.996	27.488	30.578	32.801
16	5.812	6.908	7.962	9.312	23.542	26.296	28.845	32.000	34.267
17	6.408	7.564	8.672	10.085	24.769	27.587	30.191	33.409	35.718
18	7.015	8.231	9.390	10.865	25.989	28.869	31.526	34.805	37.156
19	7.633	8.907	10.117	11.651	27.204	30.144	32.852	36.191	38.582
20	8.260	9.591	10.851	12.443	28.412	31.410	34.170	37.566	39.997
21	8.897	10.283	11.591	13.240	29.615	32.671	35.479	38.932	41.401
22	9.542	10.982	12.338	14.041	30.813	33.924	36.781	40.289	42.796
23	10.196	11.689	13.091	14.848	32.007	35.172	38.076	41.638	44.181
24	10.856	12.401	13.848	15.659	33.196	36.415	39.364	42.980	45.558
25	11.524	13.120	14.611	16.473	34.382	37.652	40.646	44.314	46.928
26	12.198	13.844	15.379	17.292	35.563	38.885	41.923	45.642	48.290
27	12.878	14.573	16.151	18.114	36.741	40.113	43.195	46.963	49.645
28	13.565	15.308	16.928	18.939	37.916	41.337	44.461	48.278	50.994
29	14.256	16.047	17.708	19.768	39.087	42.557	45.722	49.588	52.335
30	14.953	16.791	18.493	20.599	40.256	43.773	46.979	50.892	53.672
50	29.707	32.357	34.764	37.689	63.167	67.505	71.420	76.154	79.490
60	37.485	40.482	43.188	46.459	74.397	79.082	83.298	88.379	91.952
80	53.540	57.153	60.391	64.278	96.578	101.879	106.629	112.329	116.321
100	70.065	74.222	77.929	82.358	118.498	124.342	129.561	135.807	140.170

INDEX

Notes

Notes

Notes

Notes

Notes

Notes

Notes

Notes

Notes

Notes